Who's
Your
Fave
Rave?

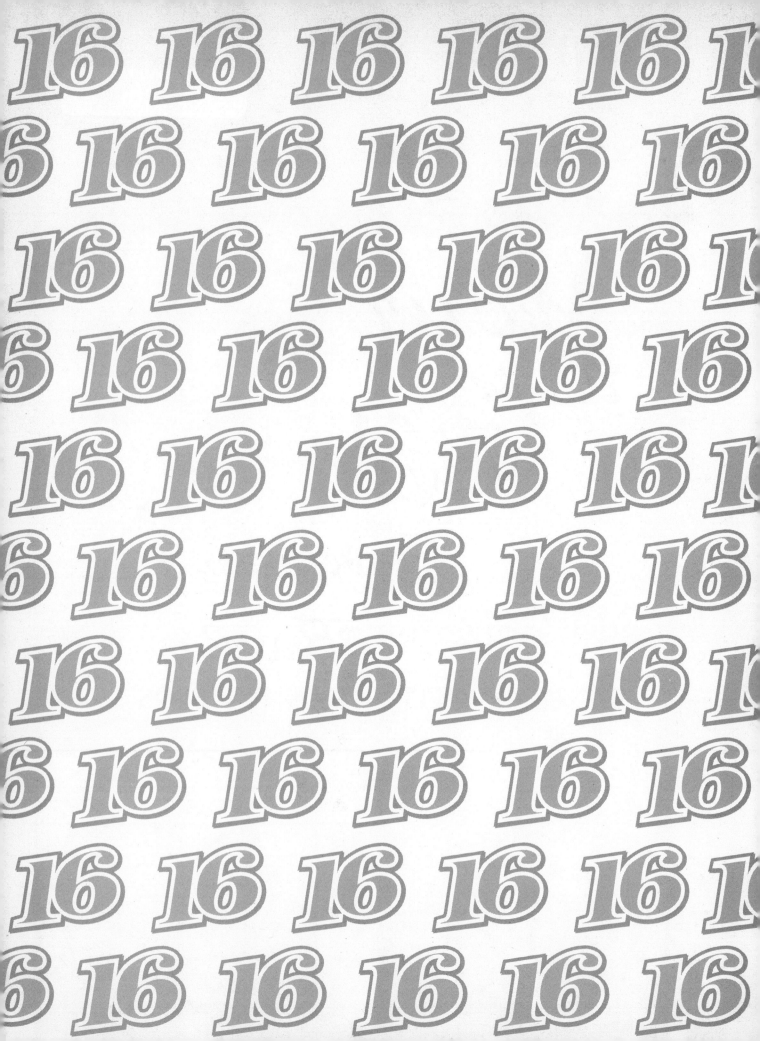

Who's Your Fave Rave?

RANDI REISFELD AND DANNY FIELDS

BOULEVARD BOOKS, NEW YORK

WHO'S YOUR FAVE RAVE?

A Boulevard Book / published by arrangement with
the authors.

PRINTING HISTORY
Boulevard edition / August 1997

The *16 Magazine* trademark, logo, and articles,
photographs and designs are used
courtesy of Sterling/MacFadden.
Lyrics for "I Wanna Be Your Dog"
reprinted by permission of Art Collins.

The Putnam Berkley World Wide Web site address is
http://www.berkley.com

ISBN: 1-57297-253-X

BOULEVARD
Boulevard Books are published by The Berkley Publishing Group,
200 Madison Avenue, New York, New York 10016,
a member of Penguin Putnam Inc.
BOULEVARD and its logo are trademarks
belonging to Berkley Publishing Corporation.

PRINTED IN THE UNITED STATES OF AMERICA

10 9 8 7 6 5 4 3 2 1

Contents

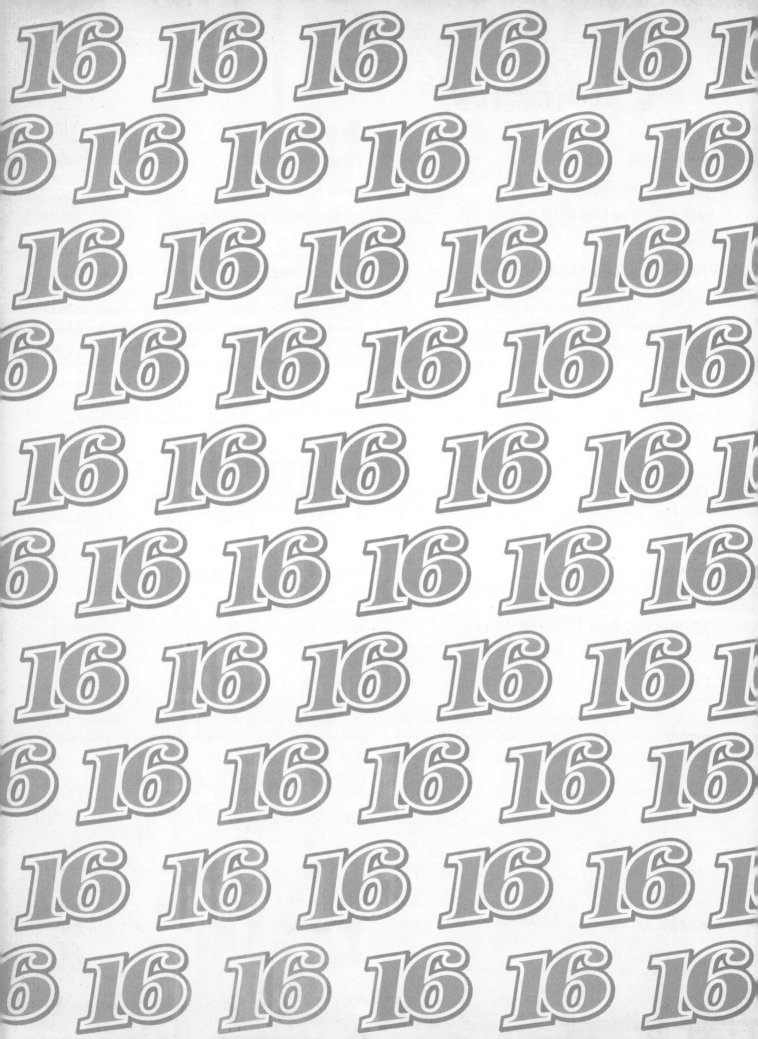

Introduction

16 Magazine began as "The Magazine for Girls," but it wasn't about self-help. It didn't give make-up tips, tell you how to lose weight or where to find fashionable clothes. It wasn't about trends or fads, didn't preach, and didn't offer much in the way of realistic advice. Its only product was fantasy. It was (and remains) a magazine for girls who idolized boys—boys on celluloid, boys on vinyl; pretty boys whose 8 x 10 glossy faces could be pinned up on the bedroom wall—and who, from any angle, were always looking back at you. *16* was the magazine for *you*. And if you were a teenage girl in the '50s, '60s, '70s, or '80s, chances are it was part of your life.

The history of *16* is the history of pop culture; more specifically, a history of the teen idols every era produced, from Rudolf Valentino to Frank Sinatra to Elvis, the Beatles, the Bobbys, Bradys, Bay City Rollers, and New Kids on the Block. They were our "fave raves," the performers we idolized from afar, whose records we bought, movies we lined up for; whose television shows we made unshakable appointments with; whose fan clubs we joined—and who we got to "know" through the pages of *16.* It was a magazine written for us: whose editorial style mirrored our language; whose editors were careful to never come between us and our stars. *16* didn't talk down to us and intrinsically understood *why* we had to know Paul's favorite color; what David ate for breakfast; if Bobby would like us.

Yes, it was often dismissed as just as much fluff by the "legitimate" press, but *16 Magazine* was written for us before *we* were "legitimate"—or as Gloria Stavers, its founding editor used to fondly explain, "*16* is for the girl who is too old for daddy's knee, but too young for the boy next door." It filled a need during that slice of our lives; a time just as precious and powerful as any time before or to come.

As renowned celebrity photographer Lynn Goldsmith wrote in her book, *Photo Diary* (Rizzoli), "Teen idols were a good thing, especially for us girls. They gave us our own set of heroes, our own magazines to buy, our own styles, our own identities as teenagers. It was part of growing up. Some of us loved the greats like Elvis and the Beatles, but our feelings were no different from the feelings of those who loved Fabian, David Cassidy or New Kids on the Block. Bless them all. The beauty of loving someone at that age is the likelihood you'll love them forever."

16 was the first magazine to capture that fantastical celebrity magic for a very specific teenage audience: since its inception in 1957 (with Elvis as the first cover boy), an entire genre has blossomed. Today, teen magazines are newsstand staples, poured over just as voraciously by young girls as they ever were. Though many copied the formula, no other publication has ever successfully captured the magic that was *16* in it's heyday. Back then, millions of little girls understood—now that they're big girls, they still do.

This book, then, is for them. And for us. Authors Randi Reisfeld and Danny Fields, as editors and consultants, have been part of the *16* family for much of its forty-year history. Inside these pages are our own memories juxtaposed with the memories of the millions of (now baby-boomer) readers whose hands a copy of the magazine once passed through—as well as the memories of the stars we wrote about. As with the magazine itself, the real power of this book is in its photos; every picture told a story and the stories in *Who's Your Fave Rave?* will take the reader back—and backstage, too.

We may not have been ready for reality back then; but we are now.

BEGINNINGS

The genesis of *16* is as simple and straightforward as the "hey, kids, let's put on a play" mentality, prevalent in the '40s and '50s. A French-born literary agent, Jacques Chambrun, (whose claim to fame was that he once represented Somerset Maugham) wanted to be a magazine publisher and in 1956, he saw an opportunity. Elvis Presley was a cash cow—and Chambrun wanted to milk it any way he could. He bought a batch of previously published Presley stories and photos from a newspaper editor in Memphis, and handed the material over to Desmond Hall, a former actor, former editor (one of the founding editors of the fashion magazine *Mademoiselle*), and at that time, an agent in Chambrun's New York office. Hall in turn passed it all on to his client, New York-based editor/writer George Waller, who fashioned the material into a one-shot "All About Elvis" magazine. Unsurprisingly, sales were excellent, and early in 1957, Waller, who had written all the text and chosen all the photos, suggested to Chambrun that he publish a magazine for young girls, featuring young male rock and roll singers, and young male rock and roll groups.

"*Seventeen* was very popular at the time," Waller recalls, "and Des Hall proposed that the new magazine be called *16*, the idea being that it would appeal to girls up to the age of 16."

So "*16*, the magazine for girls," was in fact started by three middle-aged men, looking to fill what they perceived as a publishing niche—and looking to make a buck. Or several.

Although Waller was recruited as the nascent magazine's sole editor/writer/photo editor, none of the founding trio thought a male name on the masthead was a particularly savvy move, so they simply invented a female name. "Georgia was suggested by my own first name," Waller explains. "Winters was Des Hall's middle name." Thus, *16* got its first "Editor-in-Chief," Georgia Winters.

The first issue of *16 Magazine* is dated May, 1957. Its cover price: 15 cents. For the next year, the magazine only came out quarterly. While Waller filled its pages with such young "hot" performers as Elvis, Pat Boone, even James Dean—though dead, he could still sell magazines—he did not personally interview any of the subjects, but worked from press releases, previously published material, and some stories commissioned specifically for *16*. Photos were supplied gratis by press agents and if absolutely necessary, purchased from photo agencies. If it was cheaper to commission an artist to do a pencil rendering of a star, that was acceptable and was often used to bolster the amount of coverage a celebrity got.

From the get-go, *16* was done on the cheap. Waller, its only staffer, worked from home. And while some funds were spent on photos and stories, Chambrun's ironclad rule was always "get it for as little as you can." That went not only for the editorial content, but for the quality of the paper it was printed on: newsprint was the norm, and in the beginning, aside from the covers, there were no color pin-ups. There were also no outside advertisements: it was Chambrun's theory that to invite advertisers was to invite editorial interference, and the mercurial Frenchman would have none of that. The magazine did not accept outside ads for twenty years.

Despite its bare-bones presentation, *16* enjoyed a slow but steady climb in newsstand sales. No snazzy studio sessions with the celebrities, no ritzy graphics, no scandalous revelations, no matter. What sold *16 Magazine* was the stars, and the young girls who loved them. That, and no competition. Fans were quick to realize that *16 Magazine* was the only place they could go to find information (such as it was) and photos. It was a fan book for them, a *Photoplay* or *Life* magazine, filled with the young stars they cared about.

Such was *16 Magazine* when Gloria Stavers entered in 1958.

Gloria Stavers

16 was conceived by Messrs. Chambrun, Hall, and Waller, but Gloria Stavers gave it life. She was the heart and soul of *16 Magazine.* Although she left in 1975 and the publication has undergone changes in ownership and editorship, her spirit remains at its core. Gloria never owned the publication in a legal sense (upon Chambrun's death in 1976, Desmond Hall inherited it; later it was sold to the Sterling/MacFadden Partnership), but she owned it morally, emotionally, and creatively. Everything *16* ever was, it was because of her.

Born in Wilmington, North Carolina, in October 1926, Gloria Gurganus grew up in the nearby town of Goldsboro. She was a gawky little girl who was a complex combination of insecurities coupled with brazenness; she had a boldness fueled by big dreams.

After high school, she married a man named Frank Staveridis, primarily to get away from Goldsboro, and lived with him first in Washington, D.C. and then in Ithaca, New York. Bored with marriage, Frank and domesticity, she packed up one day and moved to New York City, with her name minus an "idi," and only her beauty and brains to rely on. They served her well.

As a runway and photographer's model on the fringes of the New York jet set in the '50s, Gloria hung out at El Morocco, where she rubbed sequined gowns and sleek elbows with Marilyn Monroe and Mickey Mantle (with whom, it is rumored, she had an affair). Gloria was a star in a nightlife world of beautiful girls, celebrities, and immensely rich, older (often European) men.

By the late '50s, the health problems that would plague her all her life (a childhood bout with rheumatic fever and a bad back) began interfering with her modeling career. Gloria needed a different job. At a party in 1958, she met Jacques Chambrun. His magazine, *16*, had grown to the point where it needed another staffer, not on the editorial side, but as clerical help to deal with the huge volume of reader mail that was starting to pour in. Gloria was hired to open up reader mail and collect the dollar bills sent in for subscriptions. She was paid 50 cents an hour, quite a comedown from her modeling fees.

It was a job well below Gloria's intellect or interests, but she needed the money. She studied the publication itself, of course. She also began to read the letters that were in the envelopes she'd been assigned to open. Most were full of breathless declarations of adoration for the idols of the day. All were full of questions, but not about the process that goes into making a recording or how much money a star was raking in. The new stars (mostly boys) were young—the readers (mostly girls) were young. The readers cared about the things they could relate to: how old was the performer, did he have a girlfriend, what did he eat for breakfast, what was his favorite TV show, or subject in school, what music did he listen to.

Those questions reminded Gloria of what she cared most deeply about when she was 14—the color of *his* eyes, the color of *his* hair—what adults would call "dumb little things." (Nothing could be dumber than the quintessential *16* question "What's your favorite color?" But yes there was something dumber: the teen idol who *didn't understand* the question—however, as Gloria would say, that's getting ahead of our story.)

Gloria collected a list of the most commonly asked fan questions and went forth bravely, knocking on the doors of the young stars of the day in a series of appointments set up by their press agents. That first list of questions, compiled from the letters Gloria had been reading, eventually became the *16* staple, 40 Intimate Questions. Through the years, every teen idol in the pages of *16* has answered some variation of that original list.

Gloria's approach was instantly successful. She began to make a name for herself in the entertainment industry, and in the process, she gave the magazine an identity and very impressive sales. Late in 1958, Chambrun appointed her editor-in-chief of *16 Magazine.*

Gloria had no real journalistic training, and *16* never was "journalistically correct," not in terms of balance, anyway. There were no "reviews" except glowing reviews. Gloria never printed anything negative about a performer; if the performer him- or herself ever confessed something—or negative news came out that could not be ignored—Gloria put a positive spin on it, eliciting sympathy from the readers (e.g., a star's drinking problem was attributed to a "dread disease"). She understood implicitly that the readers would never be angry at their "fave," they'd be angry at the magazine. She was also careful to present the performer without grown-up vices. "Except for the Beatles, I never printed a picture of someone with a cigarette or a drink," Gloria once declared.

If *16* under Gloria was light on deep conflict and/or celebrity exposés, it was heavy on familiarity and "firsts," as in first-person stories "written" by stars with whom readers were on a first-name basis. It was understood that the reader knew who Paul was—no last name or other attribution was needed. Same with Davy, Herman, Mark, or Leif. The reader and the star, after all, were friends. Fantasy is what the magazine was built on—not lies, please, but a rosy version of some parts of the truth.

Every story in *16* was an "intimate" story—and any teen idol worth his top banner space on the front cover was sure to turn up in certain benchmark articles. Beyond 40 Intimate Questions were the private 'n' personal Hates & Loves, Life in Pix, Baby Pix, Life Stories, and At Home With. There was heavy drama ("The Plot to Destroy David!") and sometimes terror ("The Secret Curse that Hangs over the Beatles!"). There was pathos ("The Night I Cried/Almost Died/The Tears I Tried to Hide") and accounts of battles either invented or real ("Monkees-Saj Fight!"). All the stories ended with the contention that what you heard was just another one of those rotten rumors forever being inflicted on our beloved idols (rumors sometimes invented by *16*'s editors only to be subsequently debunked); or that whatever was "wrong" in a star's life could be fixed—would be made better—because of you. You were the missing ingredient; your love, support, and letters would see your beloved through the crisis *du jour*. (And by the time you said "Yeah, right," you were ready to move on to other magazines.)

Sex was also taboo, but it sure was hinted at. Of course "Our Perfect Night Together" turned out not to include a bedroom scene, nor did "What I Do after Dark," "Meet Me in the Dark," or "What He Does When the Lights Go Out." The readers of *16*, it was never forgotten, were presexual, both in behavior and imagination, and it was not considered the magazine's mission to walk young girls into womanhood. That would best be left to natural forces.

Side by side with the drama, innuendo, and fantasy was the fun. Whatever else *16* was, it was always fun, often irreverent, sometimes just plain silly. For its first twenty years, the front covers featured drawings of animals with "floating" heads of the stars. The prose inside was some amalgamation of slang and "Gloria-isms."

She made up and borrowed currently used abbreviations: *issue* was *ish*; *because* became *cos*; *favorite*, of course, was *fave* or sometimes *fav*. And, with a tip of the tam to the Brit Invasion, *love* became *luv*.

She made up phrases. *Closerthanthis* did a good job of describing itself. A *fave rave* is of course more than a mere rave. Information and photos became *fax & pix* (this, of course, predated the facsimile machine). Gloria is even credited in some circles (though there is no documentation for this) with dubbing the Beatles "the Fab Four."

And she pushed the practice of ending every sentence— or just about—with an exclamation point! Or two!!

That said, however, Gloria was relentless in her belief— and in her teachings to her staff—that *16* had to "get it right, godammit!" Names had to be spelled correctly; "facts," such as they applied to a record, television show, movie, or performer, had to be right. Gloria's staff cowered, but learned— quickly. Working for her was a crash course in professionalism, organization, and on-the-job skills.

Publicists and artists' representatives were often the target of Gloria's rage. "Do I have to do your fucking job for you, *man*?" was not an uncommon threat, shouted at the top of her lungs to many a record company, TV network, or film company press agent. People who didn't do their jobs as thoroughly as Gloria thought they should were often put through the verbal shredder.

To the performers themselves, however, Gloria was something else: an advisor, a friend, a person who believed in you when it seemed nobody else did, even a lover—although fewer times than gossip would have one believe. The *16* superstars from 1958 to 1975 knew that Gloria would never hurt them or their careers in any way. They believed she could make them; they felt sure she would never break them. The trust wasn't misplaced. And it made her very powerful.

TV producers begged Gloria to get letter-writing campaigns underway that would keep a sagging show on the air. Gloria advised stars on which recordings to release. She changed what they said in interviews to make them more "reader friendly." She consulted with them on which film and TV roles to take—her opinion was often solicited by captains of industry. The *Saturday Evening Post* wrote in 1967, "Gloria

Stavers's power today is truly awesome. The teenagers she influences pour about nine billion dollars a year into the economy and record companies, cosmetics manufacturers and clothing firms are all scrambling eagerly for a share of the loot. Talent agencies count the number of pages in *16* devoted to their clients as an indication of the act's popularity. Record companies seek Gloria's approval before launching publicity campaigns for their artists."

Of course, it was always a two-way street, and God help the performer who didn't do as Gloria asked. When her cause was just, Gloria was a pit bull, as Mark Lindsay will testify later in this book.

During the '60s and early '70s rumor had it that a performer had to have sex with Gloria to get into *16*, but that is totally untrue. Not that Gloria didn't have affairs with a few of the faves, but, as is recounted by the stars themselves later in this book, the impetus was generally love. Or lust. Not a one copped to sleeping with her for business purposes.

To be introduced in *16*, a performer did need Gloria's stamp of approval; to stay in *16*, readers had to respond via their letters, postcards, phone calls. Coverage ended as one's popularity waned.

Gloria knew a picture was worth a thousand words and, even printed on *16*'s cheesy paper, launched a thousand dreams. Partly because there was no budget for a photographer, and partly because she believed no one else could do it right, she took her own photos. She'd learned how from being on the other side of the camera, as a model. She used an old Rolleiflex, and she was scrupulous about the photos, the sharpness of focus, the way each was cropped. She knew that the fantasy of the readers depended on those photos, and that the reader would very likely strip them out of the magazine and pin them up on her wall. Her idol, her fave rave, was the face she wanted staring at her when she woke up in the morning, and the last face she wanted to see when she went to bed at night. She might even, if the pose were right, practice kissing him on that pinup. Gloria shot and printed the photos the readers wanted. And all editorial staff members had to learn the Gloria technique for photographing a fave; it is a style instantly recognizable to this day to photography agents all over the world.

No matter what, and above everything else, Gloria cared about her readers. It went beyond their financial support of the magazine; it went beyond even her own identification with them. Throughout her tenure as editor, she continued to read their letters—every last one that came in. And when a reader tearfully confessed that she couldn't sleep at night because her love for Bobby Sherman was that strong, Gloria understood. Many a reader, over the years, knew Gloria knew the pain of being "unloved, unpopular, and overweight." Their parents didn't understand them, or thought them silly, but Gloria said through the pages of *16*, "I understand; I know what you're going through; it hurts." And she tried to help. Of course, she was laughed at in the (male-dominated) legitimate press, even called "the Mother Superior of the Inferior," by people who ridiculed girls and women and what was meaningful to them.

But Gloria knew the truth. "Girls from 10 to 15 are in a period of development more intense than any other period in their lives" she once said. "They are hungrier than they'll ever be, so they eat more. They see something they want, a skirt or a pair of boots, and they want it more than they'll ever want anything in their lives. By the time a girl actually reaches 16, she's ready to leave the dreamworld; and *16* is way behind her."

By the mid-'70s, Gloria, too, was looking to put *16* behind her. Other pursuits, mostly spiritual, engaged her, (although she had planned on writing a book about Jim Morrison) and she was anxious to explore them.

She left the magazine in 1975 and did pursue other interests. She wrote freelance articles and a column for a rock magazine; she moved here and there in the New York rock 'n' roll world; and she became ever more involved in her search for the "path," as she called her pursuit of enlightenment.

In the fall of 1982, Gloria was diagnosed with lung cancer, though she'd been a two-cigarettes-a-day person all her adult life. The disease spread during that winter, not responding to therapy. On April 1, l983, Gloria died at New York Hospital.

All the people whose lives she touched will never forget her: the stars, her staff, her colleagues, her friends, and, of course, the readers. This book, dedicated to Gloria's memory, is her legacy, along with dreams counted in the millions.

Preface by Dave Marsh

*Dave Marsh grew up reading **16**, before being corrupted by the MC5 in his native Detroit, and going on to lead a life of degradation as a rock critic, editor, and author of more than two dozen books.*

When you tell people that Gloria Stavers and *16 Magazine* basically invented rock and pop culture journalism as we know it today, they think you're just talking about the fact that Gloria was close to Jim Morrison of the Doors, or that she ran an early story that helped keep *Rolling Stone* afloat, or that she was the first person to take good photographs of teen stars, or that you're being charitable because Gloria had the courage to run a *16* obituary for her great friend Lenny Bruce.

Nope. Gloria was the first real pop journalist, no qualification necessary. An explanation may help, however. The reasons for Gloria's stature don't have anything to do with the most prominent incidents of her career; they have to do with the way that she used *16* every issue, month after month from 1958 to 1975, to express her absolute loyalty to a specific vision of teen culture. *16* became groundbreaking and inspiring because, in that sense, it had absolute integrity. That integrity didn't come from Gloria's loyalty to Shaun Cassidy or Bobby Sherman or Elvis or the Beatles or any other star. It didn't emerge because she adored Win a Dream Date contests and "What's your favorite color?" interviews. It flowed out of the only thing that a good magazine can possibly base itself upon, which is a commitment to the needs, desires, hopes, and aspirations of the people who read it—and *16*'s audience was purely kids.

When I was a kid who read it, which was in the first half of the '60s, *16* was different from any of the other teen magazines because its editor refused to condescend to us and our dreams. That set the standard good pop journalism has to live up to, and I know that I'm not the only one who felt that way. I have heard writers who grew up far from newsstands, in small towns in the south and the Midwest, talk about traveling miles to get each new issue of *16* as it appeared, and always—always—the reason was that they felt that in it, they would find a voice they could trust. Such a voice was rare then; it is rare now, too.

What would we have made of it, if we had learned that the woman who put our favorite magazine together was a tall, beautiful former model who had marvelous Southern manners, imperious ways, a legion of famous and handsome boyfriends, and an interest in religious spirituality as intense as any you'll ever encounter? That she was a Manhattan sophisticate who knew seemingly everyone who was anyone and who was so acute about music that Albert Grossman used to play test pressings of new Dylan albums for her before anyone else had heard them?

Actually, the kids who read her probably would have figured it all made sense, because it would take somebody that complex and perceptive to come up with something as boisterous and intense as *16*. It's only now, when we have adopted pretenses about maturity and art and other stuffed-shirt nonsense, and "outgrown" (that is, lost all sense of) our desire to win the Dream Date, that we'd have trouble figuring out why such an extraordinary human devoted most of her waking hours to turning out a teen 'zine.

More than anything else, *16* was about the teenage crush—whether that meant a crush on Paul McCartney, Donny Osmond, Rick Nelson, or the guy with the flaming tongue in Kiss. Or, for that matter, Bob Dylan or Lenny Bruce or Jim Morrison. Pick your fantasy—it was all O.K. with Gloria Stavers, whether you preferred the Osmonds, Paul Revere and the Raiders, Bobby Darin, or Alice Cooper. Gloria discovered several of the people in that list; she played a crucial role in the careers of every one of them. Without her understanding and commitment, it would have been impossible for the Jackson 5 to have become the first black teen idols (so without her, no Michael Jackson? perhaps even that) or for an act as weird and controversial as Cooper's to reach true mass success.

Gloria Stavers knew how to do this, what chances to take, how to present something off-the-wall to young *16* readers, because she trusted us. And that came about because, as her friend the journalist Lisa Robinson put it, "she was what she wrote about." Certainly, however much she grew, Gloria was exactly that when she left her hometown of Goldsboro, North Carolina, in the early '50s. In *16*, this vivacious, flirtatious, surprisingly wide-eyed and innocent woman created her perfect world, where all faces were blemish-free and each cute boy was looking for someone like…you. Her advice column, which may have been the magazine's most important feature and was certainly its most amazing one, provided a lifeline for kids who were stuck in places like Goldsboro, with hormones and imaginations aflame. Danny Fields told me years ago that she could be brusque with stars but she was invariably polite and considerate with her readers; and when it came time for my own daughters to become *16* readers, that was how it went in our apartment, too. Gloria lived not far away on the East Side, and she could quickly lose herself in that pubescent world where the cute boy was life's only really important goal.

Yet the stars also loved her. I can remember doing a story on Shaun Cassidy for which my most important credential did not seem to be that it was going to run in *Rolling Stone* but that Gloria said I was all right. Most of the other stars from the period, from Dion to Mitch Ryder to Gene Simmons of Kiss, felt the same way.

Gloria's colleagues venerated her. Danny, one of my early mentors in the music world, learned his craft from being her competitor at *Datebook*, which he began editing in 1966: "Do what they do," his boss told him, and he did so—whether editing *Datebook*, managing Iggy and the Stooges, or eventually succeeding Gloria at *16*. That *16* story about *Rolling Stone* not only put the new San Francisco rock mag on the map with rock lovers all over the country; it also generated enough quarters (for sample copies) to keep Jann Wenner and his staff eating for a few crucial weeks. Personally, I felt that rock writers had permission to do any damn thing they wanted to do—as long as they did it honestly and with respect for their audience. This was a lesson that could best be learned from *16*, which could be shameless in its exploitation of star-lust but never, never patronized or lectured or talked down.

Gloria Stavers was one of the most beautiful people I have ever known. Her skin was the most beautiful I have ever seen, her jet black hair could mesmerize almost as much as her piercing eyes, and her leggy elegance never wavered. She read voraciously and widely, but she didn't dwell on book learning; she was shrewd as well, and perhaps a little prescient—at least, she always seemed to know what was going to come next, and if she didn't, she never let herself show the least bit of surprise. When you are that sharp, that insightful, that beautiful, you don't have to worry about being hip—your existence defines it. So you can spend your time, instead, lifting up those around you, and this Gloria did, in the magazine and in her myriad friendships. The silly movie *The Idolmaker* made her out to be an opportunist exploiter and that is what she never was. Bobby Darin might call from the West Coast trying to figure out what shirt to wear, and Gloria might figure it out for him, but she didn't need a commission—she did that because she loved Bobby, because he was smart enough, talented enough, beautiful enough to merit her interest. She taught only by example—it would have been beneath her to explain. She knew, and if you had a brain in your head you could know a lot too simply by picking up on her radar instincts.

Gloria did not live into old age (she died in 1983), which untracked us a bit; today's rock world could use her example on how to handle that transition past youth with greater dignity and grace. Death from cancer is not a pretty thing, and yet I can remember seeing Gloria in the hospital, right before the end, and she remained glorious, like something Tennessee Williams might have invented in a good mood, in command even as she waned. As you will discover in this book, there has never been anyone like her, or anything quite like the *16* she invented. Out of such things comes the future—a different future than we could have possessed (or even dreamed of dating) without such a creature. Do such people ever die? As well to ask if we ever did stop loving them, or missing them. Certainly not. Their glow remains forever near, their effect too intense, for that to be possible.

Introduction by Dick Clark

Someone who knew Gloria well, and knew her power, was a man wielding not inconsiderable power of his own in the world of pop culture. Dick Clark, "the perennial teenager," is now a major producer of television series, specials, and awards shows. In the late '50s and early '60s he was the master of ceremonies of TV's *American Bandstand* and could, like Gloria, make or break a performer's career. Dick, who used to consult *16*—"because I read everything the kids read"—remembers Gloria well, as a business associate and as a friend.

ALWAYS AHEAD OF THE GAME

Gloria was very glamorous, very attractive. She had her finger on the pulse of what kids were thinking about, which impressed me. We both, as adults, could "think young," and see what was interesting and ascertain what the future would bring in the next few months. We didn't have a crystal ball, but we could, with a little information, figure out what was going to happen before it happened. We would trade notes about performers and we were very giving to one another. Whatever we found out, we shared. It was good for our businesses.

Gloria was a very driven person; she worked very hard, all hours of the day and night: she'd go to the ends of the earth to get her work done. I liked her because she was so imaginative and hard-working. She was just a dynamic go-getter, a real doer. Others assigned work out, but she did the dirty work herself.

Gloria helped *American Bandstand*, and the show helped *16*. It was a two-way street. We kept track of the kids and who was popular. She would publish stories about them; we would have them on as guests. It was a snowball effect, one augmented the other. The show grew, and so did the magazine.

She might call and tout me on a talent, or ask me about someone new she'd heard about. It was always an indication that she was ahead of the game. She knew what she'd have to be writing about in the next several months. She created the precursor, the forerunner of *Rolling Stone*, and *Spin*, and *Vibe* and all that followed. She was just doing it early, before they were.

SHE CREATED THE PICTURES YOU REMEMBER FOREVER

She would give the reader the inside story—the "real, untold story" of whatever. But it was very innocent and naïve, as was the world we lived in. Of course, we did have drinking, there was a smattering of drugs, there must have been groupies—since the beginning of time, I think. She probably knew more [about backstage goings–on] than I did. But she'd never think of writing about that in the magazine.

Gloria expanded on the truth and made it into the mold of what she thought her audience wanted to see and read about. She created the images. There was a formula of what young girls were interested in: he's available, he's the All-American boy, wholesome and clean and all that stuff. That was the '50s image. Whether or not it was true didn't matter. Your assignment was to create an image. Even if a scandal occurred that was the opposite of one's image, no one would have written about it. It would have been bad for the magazine, bad for the talent, and the talent was the source, the lifeblood of the magazine. And Gloria worked hard at personal relationships with the talent—she was smart enough not to jeopardize that.

And I'm sure she helped make some careers, and added years to the careers of others. Some performers have an audience today because of the memories created for them by Gloria and *16*. Those childhood impressions last a lifetime. And she created the pictures that you remember forever.

Acknowledgments

Without these people, this book would not have happened. Thanks to:

FRAN LEBOWITZ of Writers House who helped conceive and nurture this from outline to manuscript.

ELIZABETH BEIER, who fearlessly took a shot with a complicated project.

NOLA LEONE, who gets our kissable, pin-up-able gratitude. Nola embodies the good-hearted, diligent spirit of *16 Magazine* and helped us contact so many of the artists interviewed for the book.

Former editors EILEEN BRADLEY, STEVE DENAUT, and SANDY NEWMARK for their memories and contacts.

MRS. LOUISE GAINEY, Gloria's mother—finally, the book we promised is a reality!

CHRIS DINAPOLI, ABE DULBERG, YVONNE ELLIMAN, DANNY GOLDBERG, STEVE HARRIS, JACKIE JAROSZ, JANET MACOSKA, DAVE MARSH, MIMI MENENDEZ, JON REA, JOAN SCOTT, MORTEN TULLER, GEORGE WALLER, SUE WEINER, and KAREN WILLIAMS, for their very special contributions.

Every artist who contributed his or her memories, and every artist's representative who facilitated the interviews.

Randi Reisfeld wishes to mention mostly, and always with love, Marvin, Scott, Stefanie, and Peabo. Danny Fields wants to remember his mother, always so impatient to see the finished product.

The 60s:

TAKE ONE

1960–1963

THE SIXTIES *16* MAGAZINE 1960–1963

Remember the famous song "Good Timin'"? According to the lyrics, you had to have "a-ticka, ticka, ticka good timin'"—if you did, everything good would come your way. *16 Magazine* had it, in spades. For it began and took off, right alongside the burgeoning world of rock 'n' roll. Although its first cover date was May 1957—with Elvis, of course, as its first cover boy (along with crooners Jimmie Rodgers, Pat Boone, and Paul Anka)—the magazine found its wings in the '60s. With Gloria Stavers at the controls, it flew to dizzying heights.

In *16*-land, the '60s is actually two periods. During the first half, teenagers were rockin' to the homegrown beat of American singers. Dick Clark's *American Bandstand* ruled. If you were a teenager in the late '50s and early '60s, you wanted to dance on *American Bandstand*. Reflecting that, many of *16*'s earliest issues covered the "*Bandstand* regulars," teens from Philadelphia who appeared daily on the show.

If you were a young performer, you wanted to be a teenage idol and perform on *American Bandstand*. It meant fame, fortune, and adoring fans; it didn't mean you were a talentless pretty face: there were no negative connotations at the time.

Most of the idols of the early '60s were singing sensations: *16*, after all, was founded specifically to be about the rock and rollers. But some TV idols did make the cut—many of them added singing to their repertoire (whether they had talent or not). And some rockers did expand into movies and television. Music, in one form or another, was at the heart of the early issues.

In this part of the decade *16* had no editorial staff other than Gloria. Which is why most of the artists interviewed for this book talk about her and the magazine as if they were one entity. They were.

COVER PRICE: 25 cents

COLOR PINUPS: Only the covers were printed on glossy pages, and they were not always in color. There were no posters, no centerfolds; a pinup meant a full-page black & white or, later, cheesy tricolor.

SALES: 275,000 monthly (averaged out, from inception to end of 1963).

Elvis Answers 40 Intimate Questions

16 proudly presents the boy Young America loves—revealed for the first time in his own words!

HE WAS OBVIOUSLY EXHAUSTED. His dark hair fell boyishly over his forehead as he flopped into a soft, yielding couch. He let out a long, audible sigh. From anybody else it would have been just a sigh, but it sounded different from him. There was a lot of the male animal in it. It was a sigh that had helped make him pretty famous, along with a lot of other male animal characteristics.

Elvis Presley was about to be interviewed. He had worked all day. He took off his jacket, rolled up his shirt sleeves, and threw his legs over the arm of the couch. He was ready to begin.

These are the questions he was asked and his word-for-word answers—just as he spoke them. They reveal the *true* and *actual* Elvis Presley, *exclusively* for the readers of "16."

DID YOU EVER HAVE A PET?
I've had quite a few dogs. I love them.

DO YOU HAVE ANY DOGS NOW?
I have a monkey and his name is Jimbo, cute devil. I have two dogs. One is Dook and one is Sweet Pea. I have a lot of fun naming animals. I had dogs named Muppy-Dee and one called Salpin and another was named Whidland.

OF ALL THE SONGS YOU'VE SUNG, WHICH DO YOU LIKE THE BEST?
"Treat Me Nice." I think that song is wonderful. I picked it out after hearing it on tape in my hotel room. It's a great number.

WHEN YOU WERE A LITTLE BOY, WHAT WAS YOUR AMBITION IN LIFE?
All I wanted to be was a truck driver.

HOW OLD DO YOU WANT TO BE BEFORE YOU GET MARRIED?
I will get married any time I find the right girl. I haven't found her yet.

HOW MANY CHILDREN DO YOU WANT?
I want as many children as I possibly can have.

WHY DID YOU AND NATALIE WOOD STOP DATING?
Natalie and I were never more than good friends. I took her to my home because she had never been in the South. Despite the fact that she travelled under a different name, the papers got it and made a circus out of it. She got a lot of bad publicity because they said she went with me just to get her name in the papers. She's a sweet girl and a good friend.

Even El answered 40 Intimate Questions: this article appeared in the November 1960 issue of 16.

ELVIS

Years of *16* Popularity: 1957–1963

Arguably the century's greatest star, Elvis Presley was *16*'s *raison d'être* in May of 1957. At the start, the editors had no personal connection, nor access, to the King of Rock and Roll, just a desire and the know-how to capitalize on the phenomenon. From the first one-shot issue onward, the publisher relied on stories purchased from a Memphis newspaper editor, which were then converted stylistically to fit the nascent fanzine formula. Stock photos were added. The lack of direct access did not negatively affect the new publication's sales—as anything related to Elvis did, it made money.

Alas for *16*, Elvis went into the army in 1958, and during his 2-year stint in the service, with no recordings and no appearances, interest in him and access to material flagged considerably. Still, something about him appeared in every issue, and upon his return to his public, his coverage in *16* grew accordingly. *16* positioned itself as the Elvis magazine of record, and attempted to remain so.

By the time of Elvis's discharge from the army, Gloria Stavers was in place as editor, and she pursued him for exclusive *16* interviews and photos. He was not, of course, the easiest guy in the world to get access to, but Gloria was relentless, and finally did get her one-on-ones, after which a stream of Elvis articles and information kept flowing until the mid-'60s when young girls turned their interest elsewhere.

Gloria Stavers and Elvis Presley on the set of Kid Gallahad *in 1962.*

The cover of the January 1959 issue featured a cartoon of an army-bound Elvis who nevertheless remembered Mom.

Paul Anka

Years of *16* Popularity: 1957–1963

Well before he did it his way, or anyone was havin' his baby, 17-year-old Paul Anka was one of the first *16 Magazine* teenage idols. He not only looked as young and fresh-faced as the readers, he wrote and sang songs they could relate to. "Diana," his first hit, was about a crush on an older baby-sitter; while "Puppy Love" railed against adults who scoffed at teenage love. And in 1959, every teenage girl in North America wanted to put her head on his shoulder.

Significantly, Paul was the very first teen idol to do an actual interview for the magazine. Before that, stories were written from other sources or from publicity handouts. Gloria Stavers, in an interview, recounted the day she anxiously knocked on the teen crooner's hotel door. "I was dressed chicly, and I opened the door and there was Paul, in this sports shirt with those baggy pants, wearing a nervous smile on his face. We both started to laugh and it turned out that he was as nervous as I was, because this was his first interview, too."

Paul Anka actually preceded Elvis as the first person Gloria Stavers tried out her 40 Intimate Questions on. That encounter was written up like this:

One hundred and forty pounds of dark, handsome dynamite leaned back in his dressing room chair and smiled. "Forty intimate questions?" he asked. "Boy! That means I have to tell all my secrets!"

Today, Paul Anka, like *16*, celebrates 40 years in entertainment. He is an international superstar who continues to write and release new music. He has performed all over the world, sold many millions of records, and amassed a fortune along the way. Who says you can't get there from the pages of *16*?

Though we didn't prevail upon Paul to divulge all his secrets today, we did ask for his memories, which he gladly shared.

PAUL ANKA LOOKS BACK

"*16* BELIEVED IN ROCK 'N' ROLL"

"With respect to rock 'n' roll, back in those days, we were a very small community. We all kind of clung together knowing that this was something much bigger than we first realized. We all knew there was a lot of resentment and a lot of hurdles to overcome, because the music was not yet an established form. Remember, no one other than teenagers had yet embraced this music. In order to be accepted into society, we had to first make it over the hurdle.

"Within the core of this very small community, we had few allies, but they were powerful. We had Gloria Stavers and *16 Magazine,* Dick Clark, and a few disc jockeys who were plugged into this incredible roller coaster. Outside of that, it was quite difficult to get supporters. Motion pictures were using music by established composers. Madison Avenue had not adapted. So back then you had supporters—a group of people that believed in us—and Gloria was the key person in the media."

"ALWAYS PRIVY TO WHAT I WAS DOING"

"The energy back then was very much that of a small community. Everybody's personality was at the forefront—as was each person's character. We had more time then. There was caring there that doesn't prevail today because of the enormity of the business. Consequently, I had the kind of relationship to Gloria where she was always privy to what I was doing, and she knew it.

"She was one of the pioneers. We would stop by *16*'s office, or she would phone us to discuss any news or problems she heard about—whether it concerned me, Annette, Frankie Avalon, whomever. She kept in constant contact with all of us."

"YOU SEE DICK CLARK, YOU TALK TO *16*"

"So the routine was, you release a record, you talk to Gloria, you see Dick Clark. They had the power to get your records out there. That was the little network of people—the essential program. If you had any kind of integrity, when you were releasing a record, you had to talk to Gloria to let the world know what you were doing—to let the kids in the

Paul Anka

States know. [Paul is Canadian.] Today, it's different, you don't have that communication with one person in the media.

"Gloria also acted as a link between the few of us who were teen stars in those days. She'd phone and say something like, 'Hi, Paul. What are you doing? I just spoke to Frankie, he's coming in. And Bobby said he's going to do this record. I know Annette's doing a picture, I just spoke to her.' Talking to Gloria was like talking to a relative. That was the atmosphere back then. Everybody liked each other. Everybody knew each other. It was a real camaraderie."

"WHAT SHE WROTE WAS TRUE"

"Because Gloria really did know us, and because we really were close in those days, whatever she wrote about me—whether it was in first or third person—was accurate. Frankie Avalon and I really were good friends. I really did know Arlene Sullivan from *American Bandstand*. Once, *16* wrote that I'd known the girl I would marry the first time I saw her—obviously, that turned out to be true!" [Paul married Anne, a former model and mother of his 4 daughters.]

"You can't compare the scene back then with the one today. It's like apples and oranges. Back then, being in *16* was all positive. You had a record out and kids bought the record and they bought *16 Magazine* at the same time, with the same dollar. So it was very positive, very important, and you were very much a part of a family. It *was* your family! Part of the cog in the wheel."

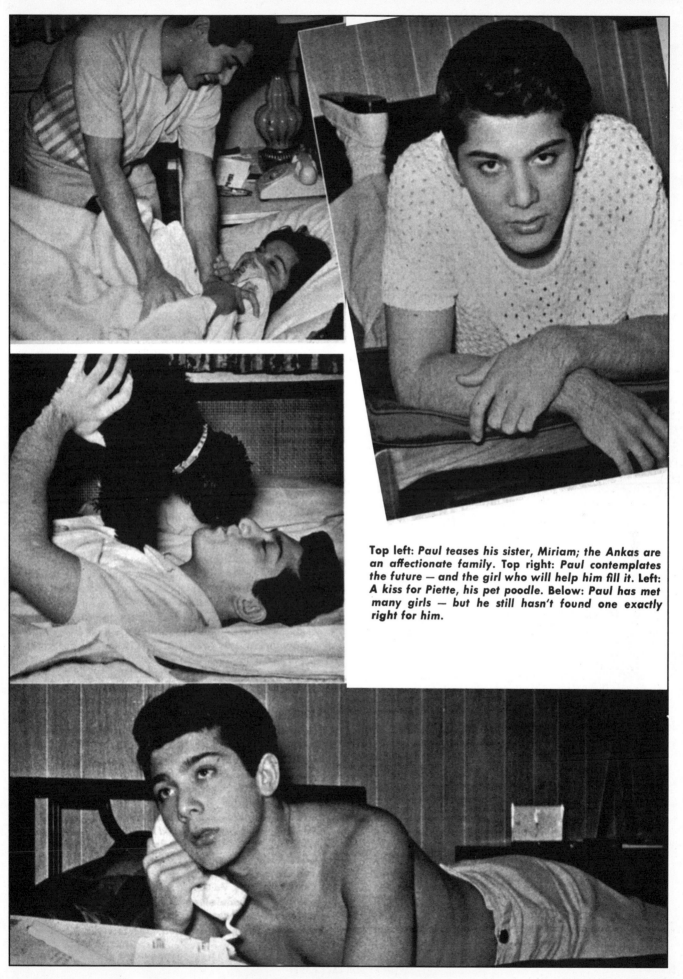

Top left: Paul teases his sister, Miriam; the Ankas are an affectionate family. Top right: Paul contemplates the future — and the girl who will help him fill it. Left: A kiss for Piette, his pet poodle. Below: Paul has met many girls — but he still hasn't found one exactly right for him.

Although Paul was revered as a singer, 16 didn't discuss his records or his sales figures. It presented—as always—the personal side, as interpreted by Gloria. These pictures appeared in the March 1961 issue of 16.

Frankie Avalon

Years of *16* Popularity: 1959–1963

Frankie Avalon, best remembered for his teen hits "De De Dinah," "Venus," and "When a Girl Changes from Bobby Sox to Stockings" and his beach movies (including *Beach Blanket Bingo* with Annette) was the first, and ultimately most successful, of the South Philadelphia fleet of teen idols, which included Fabian and Bobby Rydell. That was significant for two reasons: his original manager, Philadelphian Bob Marcucci, a powerful player in early rock 'n' roll who headed up his own Chancellor Records label, lives on in legend as the original "idol maker," and, of course, that city was home to Dick Clark and *American Bandstand*. "We all started out together," Frankie remembers, "and we all helped each other become successful."

Though the entertainment press has tended to dismiss Frankie as little more than a "former teen idol," in fact he really was a talented singer, musician (he played trumpet), and entertainer. Today, he tours year-round in the fabulously successful, if nostalgia-tinged, *Golden Boys of Bandstand* revue, along with Fabian and Bobby Rydell. It was backstage at a Las Vegas gig that we caught up with him. "Those early teen idol years were a very productive time for me," Frankie said. "I was in the recording studio, traveling around the world, making movies, doing TV appearances and interviews. It was so hectic—how much can you remember?"

A lot, as it turns out.

Frankie Avalon Looks Back

IT WAS THE KIDS ASKING THE QUESTIONS THEMSELVES

"*16 Magazine* was a very important part of my life, for many, many reasons. Back in the late '50s and early '60s, I was just starting to get recognition and *16 Magazine* was just coming on the scene. So we were both novices at the time.

"At the time I hit, I was doing interviews for all sorts of publications, like *Photoplay* and *Movie Land* and others. They were very professional articles that were done with sophistication. *16*'s interviews were anything but! They were down-to-earth, geared specifically for a young reader's heart and mind. They were the kinds of articles with questions and answers that kids could relate to—that's what *16* was about.

"It was always written up as intimate, one-on-one. The interviews that we did, the articles that were done on me, they were as if a kid who was my fan sat in a room with me, one on one, and wanted to know about me. That was Gloria's talent. She had her finger on the pulse of what young people wanted to know, and how they wanted to know it. A lot of time, talent, and dedication went into it. *16* had its own style. The kids related to it, and at the same time, it opened the door for a lot of entertainers."

MY HATES & LOVES— THEY'RE THE SAME TODAY!

"Did the articles accurately portray me? Absolutely! Every quote, all the articles were very accurate. I just looked back at an old article called 'The Things I Hate & The Things I Love.' It is as accurate today as it was back then! I haven't changed. I didn't write it, but yes, those were things I did say. Gloria knew me. Out of our professional friendship came a personal friendship—because we did go to dinners, we did do things together, we had fun together.

"As a matter of fact, it was me who gave her the nickname GeeGee. Sonny Troy, who was my best friend at the time (and is still a dear friend), and I had developed a sort of pig Latin language and we turned Georgia into GeeGee. And she took that as a sort of pen name for her gossip column."

Frankie Avalon

I READ THE FAN MAIL & ANSWERED IT

"In those early days, I got a lot of fan mail. I saw it all. I was very much a part of it, especially when I first started. I would go to the house of my fan club president, where thousands of letters a week would arrive. I would sit there and read some, and answer as much as I could. And a lot of times, I'd be en route somewhere, on a train, a plane, a bus, or whatever and sit down with postcards and write a lot of the kids who were buying my records and thank them. It was important.

"I don't think there were any negatives about being in *16*—it was all positive. In those days, being a teen idol was a good thing. It was a tremendous help to my career, because it was a way that kids could relate to someone like me, who was selling records. It was their way of getting to know me. Those were the days when kids really wanted to be a part of it all and *16* was the originator, the first to let them share in our lives.

"Maybe the best part, after all, of being a *16 Magazine* icon is the loyalty and dedication of that audience. They were there for me then, and they're here for me now. What more could any performer ask?"

Gloria Stavers presents Frankie Avalon with a Gold Pretzel, in the First National Annual Twist Awards, at the Concord Hotel in South Fallsberg, N.Y., in January 1962.

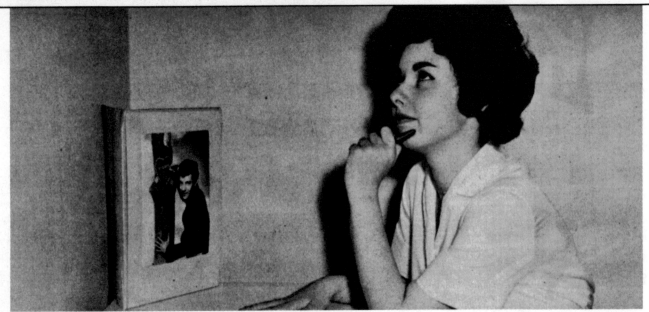

Alice Klein ponders the best way to express all the things she wants to pour out to Frankie.

FRANKIE, PLEASE DON'T LEAVE ME!

by Alice Klein

The heartfelt plea of a teenage fan who sees the boy of a million dreams growing up — and growing away from her.

Dear Frankie:

As I sat in the dim, crowded club watching you, handsome and elegant, take your fifth bow after singing your third encore — I felt tears well up in my eyes. I blinded them back and wondered what was wrong with me. I had just watched my most favorite boy in the world give a superb performance — so why should I be sad?

As the lights went up and the final strains of your theme, Avalon, faded away, I heard my mom saying, "Why, Alice, he's marvelous! He's wonderful! You never told me how good he is!"

"No, Mom," I replied sarcastically. "Only a million times."

"Alice," Dad said, "I'm glad you made us come here. This boy is going to be a big star one day. You mark my word."

"O.K., Pop," I replied, "I'll take it from you."

When my family and I left the club, I turned and re-read the huge lettering on the sign out front: ONE WEEK'S EXCLUSIVE ENGAGEMENT! FRANKIE AVALON—AMERICA'S NEW PRINCE CHARMING—EVENING SHOWS 8:30 AND 11 P.M.

"America's new prince charming," I thought. "Yes, that's what is wrong! That was it! America's — the world's. I remember when he used to be mine. Just mine."

Frankie, please forgive me — but, well, I don't understand what's going on. It was just a few short years ago that you emerged with a fantastic impact onto the 'teen scene. You swept us all up with your magic. You made me fall in love with you. You knew that. There was nothing that could stop it.

Now that you have wooed and won me — and millions of other girls just like me — you are leaving. You're becoming a big star, you're making movies, doing all the TV shows — and now you're singing in night clubs. Frankie, all I can see in the futures is YOU going away from ME — from all of us romantic, adoring teenagers. We have our good points and we have our bad — but, boy! we really love you.

And Frankie, I especially love you. What could be more important than that? What could mean more? You don't have to go away from us. With us, you're tops. The first. Number one. Out there, in the adult world, you're more or less a beginner. You have to prove yourself. You'll be working and slaving every day and night proving yourself, again and again.

Frankie, you don't have to do that for us. We know how great you are. We know how great your talent is and what a fine artist you are. So why not just stay with us — where you belong?

Frankie, please read this. Weigh each word. Try to understand what I am saying to you. Try — and Frankie, please don't leave me!

This quintessential fan's lament, and Frankie's personal response, appeared in September 1960.

I'll never ever leave YOU! by Frankie Avalon

A reassuring reply—and a promise to all teenagers that they will always be first in their idol's thoughts.

DEAR ALICE:

I have read your letter fifty times. I've almost memorized it. I don't know just where to begin. You see, your letter to me is probably one of the finest tributes I've ever been paid.

Ever since I was five years old, I've wanted to be an entertainer. I wanted to go into show business and I dreamed of being a star. *And* ever since I was five years old, I have worked with that goal in mind.

Now, Alice, I am 19. I've grown up. I'm a man. Step by step, my career has grown with me. Slowly but surely, I have managed to achieve each separate step upward. You know — better than anyone — that you, and those like you, have made this possible for me. It is you who have placed me on the threshold of stardom.

You tell me what your family said when they saw me in a night club. Alice, don't you realize that when they enjoyed my performance, another door was opened to me? Do you realize that by bringing them to the club, you opened that door for me? I had always dreamed of playing clubs — places where the family could come to enjoy a good dinner and see a show. Well, it's happened — thanks to you.

Now, I'll tell you something else. In my effort to expand, to reach stardom, I have learned that I must not, I *cannot*, ever stand still. I *have* to grow. But I don't want to do it alone — I want to do it with you. I want you to grow with me. I want to know that you wish not only to hear my records, or see me doing a rock and roll show — I want you to want to see and enjoy my movies, my TV appearances, and, yes, my club dates.

You see, I need you, *really need you*. And I need you more than you need me. I want to know that no matter where I am, or what my performance is, you are out there looking and listening and approving.

And please remember this — no matter what I do anywhere, I will always put you first. Yes, first and foremost — I will be with the people who understand me best — *the young and vibrant teenagers of America* — the ones who decide who tomorrow's stars will be.

In September 1959, 16's banner trumpeted, "The Fantabulous Fabian!"

Fabian

Years of *16* Popularity: 1959–1962

To cynics of a certain age, singer Fabian is synonymous with everything negative about being a teen idol. In fact, the adjective, *manufactured* often precedes the designation. Pop history dismisses him as someone with little talent, specifically recruited to make the little girls scream and sell lots of records, whose run at the top was fleeting, and whose strings were manipulated by an all-powerful manager. To a large degree, that's true. To an even larger degree, that's a shame.

As the legend goes, 14-year-old Fabian Forte of South Philadelphia had no performing aspirations or training before being "discovered" sitting on a stoop outside his home. The person doing the discovering was Bob Marcucci, a big name in nascent rock and roll, who was having sweeping success with Frankie Avalon. Bob understood the importance of a "look"—and one look at young Fabian was all it took to convince him that this kid, who resembled a young Elvis or Ricky Nelson, could be a star; *would* be a star. And he was: before his 18th birthday, he'd recorded "Tiger," "I'm a Man," and "Turn Me Loose."

That the teenager was desperately shy and lacked confidence was beside the point. To Fabian himself, it *was* the point. He'd only taken Bob up on his "I can make you a star" offer because his father had been felled by a heart attack—that was the reason he'd been sitting outside on the stoop that fateful night—and he needed the money. He ended up spending most of his teen idol years in emotional agony, very much stung by the criticism. As it turned out, Fabian's teen idol fame really was fleeting; within three years, he'd disappeared from the charts and the pages of *16 Magazine*.

Today, Fabian remains active and onstage once again, as part of *The Golden Boys* of *Bandstand* revue. When we knocked on Fabian's dressing room door backstage in Las Vegas, he tried to remember those years as a *16 Magazine* teen idol. Fabe's fame may have been fleeting; his memories are sharp and distinct.

Fabian Looks Back

"YOU'RE MEETING SOMEONE IMPORTANT— BE NICE"

"It was a major big deal to be in *16 Magazine*. Even though I wasn't cognizant of the magazine before, because I never thought of show business as my destiny, I rapidly found out that *16* was powerful, sort of like *People* magazine is today. So I knew it was a big, big deal.

"In those days, of course, I was under such major control of my management. I did whatever they told me. They'd say, 'You're going to New York to meet somebody important—so be nice.' Basically, I didn't have to be any different with Gloria. I was nice! I just wasn't perfect. I was normal, doing the normal things kids did in those days. Back then we were all presented as squeaky clean. You couldn't say certain things. You couldn't smoke. They would whitewash whatever you were doing personally—I knew that, so I would never tell the whole truth, you know what I mean?"

"I WAS SHY"

"Two things I hated most were the set-up dates and the actual interviews. Of course, I participated in them without question. I was very uncomfortable being interviewed because I was basically a very shy person. Gloria saw that and helped me out a lot. I remember that fondly. Gloria was a sweetheart, more helpful than anything else. She knew that I wasn't comfortable being interviewed. You know, I'm still not!"

BOBBY RYDELL

Years of *16* Popularity 1960–1962

Like Frankie and Fabian immediately before him, Bobby Rydell, whose most famous songs were "Volare," "Wild One," and "Swingin' School," fit neatly into the great tradition of early '60s teen idols. He emerged from that hotbed of teen singers at the time—South Philadelphia; he could really sing; he wore his hair in a pompadour; and he really was a skinny teenager of 17 when he had his first hit record, "Kissing Time."

Bobby was the prototypical nice guy and presented as such in *16*. He wanted stardom badly and considered the magazine crucial to his success.

Bobby first appeared in *16* in the March 1960 edition.

Bobby remains today in Philadelphia. "I will never leave the East Coast until the Eagles win the Super Bowl—so I think I'm gonna be here for a long, long time," he says. He tours, along with Frankie and Fabian, in the year-round *Golden Boys of Bandstand* revue. On a hot Las Vegas night, backstage at the Desert Inn, Bobby leaned back and reminisced.

BOBBY RYDELL LOOKS BACK

16: "NO BAD STUFF, NO BULL"

"I first met Gloria Stavers in either very late 1959 or early 1960. She was absolutely a wonderful lady. There were a lot of magazines out there at the time that were always trying to find some kind of hook or something, like 'Bobby Rydell Is on His Deathbed' or something else totally false. And then they'd write some bull, cock-eyed story. But Gloria's direction was always more like, 'What's this guy really like?' Or she'd print some interesting fact, like 'Bobby likes to do imitations.' Then to illustrate that, we'd do a shoot where I would impersonate Red Skelton, James Cagney, and Frank Fontaine. But all along she was just a very nice person, not only to me but to two very dear friends of mine, Frankie Avalon and Fabian."

Bobby Rydell and his friend "Scout."

"WHAT IMAGE? IT WAS ME!"

"Gloria always represented me as being a nice guy. Everything she wrote was pure, clean, and funny stuff. I don't think there was ever an article about a 'bad side' of Bobby Rydell. But that's because there really wasn't any. It's funny because I remember my publicity agent at the time, Connie DeNave, used to say jokingly to my manager, 'We have to get Bobby involved in something—he's too nice! We should make up a paternity suit, or something else controversial.' But Frankie Day, my manager, would say, 'No, that's not Bobby's image, that's not who he is.' In those days, of course, something like that would have destroyed my career. Besides, I really was—and still am—a nice guy. They say nice guys finish last. That's fine. That's all well and good with me.

"About the only 'controversial' articles *16* ever did were the ones pitting the current superstar against up-and-comers. Like, who's the new guy on the block? Who's going to be the next Elvis Presley? Who's going to fill Ricky Nelson's shoes? But that was about as controversial as it got."

"DID I HAVE A GIRLFRIEND? ACTUALLY, YES"

"Of course, the big question was, Who was I dating? Did I have a girlfriend? And, especially, Were there marriage plans? That's where Gloria blurred the line a little. She knew I was dating someone. In fact, I met this girl when I was 15, and I had my first hit record at 17. So we were together, and quite seriously, all the time I was a teen idol. Her name is Camille, and we've now been married 28 wonderful years and have been blessed with two great children and a grandson.

"But back then, the fans didn't want to know that I was, in fact, unavailable. It would have been detrimental to my career and I wanted to be a star. I knew *16* could help and I trusted Gloria to be very, very discreet, which she always was. My memories are all happy. Back then, it didn't take a lot to make us happy. It was wonderful. It really was a wonderful world."

Do you believe in 'teen marriages?

No, not at all. The 'teen years are the formative years. If it's real love, it can wait.

How long do you think a boy and girl should go together before they marry?

My mom and dad went together for six years before they tied the knot. I won't need that much time. I think a year would be long enough.

Can you name one girl whom you admired?

Dodie Stevens. She is a happy, warm, and wonderful person.

What kind of clothes do you like to wear?

I'm a clothes bug from 'way back. I like all kinds, but prefer casual things—like a big, bulky sweater with Continental slacks.

On a vacation, where in the world would you like to go?

I've always had a desire to visit our fiftieth state—Hawaii.

Is there anything about yourself physically that you would like to change?

Well, I'd like to gain some weight. I eat like a horse, but I must work it all off.

Do you still live at home?

Yes, I do. I have no desire to have an apartment of my own. I love my folks, and one of my greatest thrills is when I get to spend time with my family and friends.

What do you look for in friends?

I like people whom I can confide in and trust. I want someone near me who can share everything with me. I also like a friend to have a good sense of humor.

What kind of music do you enjoy most? Who are your favorite singers?

I love all music. Right now, I'm on a "cool" jazz kick. My favorite singer is Frank Sinatra, but I like many others, too.

Have you ever thought of going into movies?

I'll say I have. It is one of my greatest ambitions, but I want to be very sure that I am ready before I make the plunge.

Do you have anything to say to ambitious young people?

Yes, I do. No matter what your dream is, don't try to attain success the "easy" way. There is no easy way. Work, training, education, and the help and advice of a wiser person—all these are necessary for success.

Bobby with his Dad and Mom. He lives at home and has no desire for an apartment of his own.

This is from a spread titled "Bobby Rydell Answers 40 Intimate Questions," April 1960.

Annette

Years of *16* Popularity: 1959–1963

Annette was one of the first important female idols in *16*, in an era when female stars ran neck and neck in popularity with the boys. Her celebrity, of course, predated the existence of the magazine, since she had become one of 24 Mouseketeers on TV's *The Mickey Mouse Club* in 1955, at the age of 12, and eventually the most popular of them all by far. Viewers saw her go from girl to buxom woman before their very eyes, but in *16 Magazine*, she was always presented as a nonthreatening intimate friend, the girl next door, a kind of adoring older sister. In other words, you never had to worry that she might "steal" Frankie Avalon from you, dear reader.

Annette went on to appear regularly in Dick Clark's TV dance shows and, through her role in that genre, became best friends (or so it was presented in *16*) with the other "girl regulars" on the show and with teen actress Shelley Fabares. As a recording artist, she had five Top 40 singles, including "Tall Paul" in 1959.

In the early '60s, not yet 20, she became one of the first teen movie stars of the era, appearing with Frankie Avalon in a series of highly successful "beach party" films. Now suffering from multiple sclerosis, she is retired from show business. Her excellent autobiography, *A Dream Is a Wish Your Heart Makes: My Story*, was published in 1994.

Annette added her own memories of her *16* days in a faxed reply to our questions.

Annette Reminisces

What do you remember about your days in *16*?

I knew Gloria as GeeGee, and we became very close. *16* was always very kind to me. I got many covers and even my own column, with questions from fans, which I answered. The magazine helped me with my career to always be in the focus, and it always covered your current crushes!

You were presented in *16* as someone who could be "best friends" with the readers. In reality, do you think you had anything in common with these young girls?

Yes, since we were the same age, the readers and myself had the same crushes and were most likely interested in the same men!

How did *16*'s readers react to your relationship with Paul Anka?

The readers were both excited and fascinated with my involvement with Paul Anka.

Frankie Avalon, Paul Anka, and many superstars of the early rock era have emphasized the strong bond you all had. Did you also feel this sense of community spirit?

Absolutely, the bond still exists today between us. In fact, I spoke with Frankie today. They accepted me and took great care of me.

Gloria got her Annette stories via in-person one-on-one interviews: they really were friends.

WOULD YOU LIKE TO BE FRIENDS WITH ANNETTE?

THEN READ THIS PAGE!

By GEORGIA WINTERS

DID YOU read Annette's wonderful article starting on Page 10, *My Friend, Arlene?* If you didn't, please do. You'll discover what a wonderful and precious thing true friendship is (if you *did* read the article, of course, you already *know*).

No one can have enough friends. And if you've very few, you will certainly be anxious to make more. Which brings me to the point of this piece: *Would YOU like to be friends with Annette?*

If you would, here's the way to bring it about: enter now 16's fabulous, brand-new contest, **WHY I WANT ANNETTE FOR MY FRIEND**, and write a one-page letter telling why.

Uh-huh, that's all there is to it. Just take a single sheet of writing paper, write at the top of it *Why I Want Annette For My Friend*, and then write your reasons (describe the qualities Annette has that you admire and that make you wish she could be your buddy). *Be sure to write on one sheet only — and only on one side of the sheet!*

When you've completed your letter, fill in the coupon on this page, cut it out, clip it to your letter, and mail them to 16 Magazine. *Your contest entry will NOT be accepted unless it is accompanied by the contest coupon!*

To the writer of the best letter, 16 will award a *complete* "Annette" outfit — chosen especially for her by Annette herself! In addition, the winner will receive a personal letter from Annette — a friendly, intimate letter in her own hand!

There'll be prizes awarded to the Runners-Up, too — among them, Annette's wonderful LP's for Buena Vista Records.

So come on! Enter the contest *now!* And be sure to read the Contest Rules before you write your letter!

PLEASE NOTE! YOU CANNOT ENTER THE "WHY I WANT ANNETTE FOR MY FRIEND" CONTEST UNLESS YOU MAIL COUPON WITH YOUR ENTRY! FILL IT IN, CUT IT OUT, AND ATTACH IT NOW!

CONTEST RULES

1. You must write and submit a short letter, on one sheet only (*no writing on the back, please!*) telling why you want Annette to be your friend.

2. You must submit at least one clear photograph of yourself taken fairly recently. You may send as many photos as you like — but NO photos will be returned to you. On the back of your photo, write your age, height, weight, color of hair and eyes, and complexion.

3. You must attach to your letter and photos the entry coupon printed at the bottom of this page. You will not be eligible to enter the contest unless you mail the coupon with your entry.

4. One contest winner only will be selected. The winner's award will be a complete "Annette" outfit, chosen by Annette herself, plus a personal letter from Annette. Runners-up will receive awards which will include Annette's LP's for Buena Vista Records.

5. Pictures of the winner and the text of her award-winner letter will be published when the contest results are announced in a future issue of 16 Magazine. (*Note:* When you sign the entry coupon, you give 16 Magazine permission to publish your pictures and letter.)

6. Judges for the contest are the Publisher and Editor of 16 Magazine. All entries will be judged on the basis of merit.

7. Closing date for the contest is midnight of July 21, 1960. No entries postmarked after that date will be accepted.

This astonishing invitation, to become "friends" with Annette, turns out to be a bit of a ruse; the winner gets, perhaps, a bit less than the headline suggests.

Annette

16 **made it appear as if you were best friends with Shelley Fabares—was that accurate?**

Shelley and I have been "soul mates" since age 11. She is still my very best friend today. We live close and speak all the time. She is very supportive of me and my M.S.

How did you get along with contemporaries like Hayley Mills, Connie Francis, Sandra Dee, and Patty Duke?

I always tried to get along with everyone. Of all of them I was probably closest to Connie Francis and Hayley Mills because we were singers. Hayley and I worked together on some of the same shows at Disney!

Some child stars are bitter and believe they were cheated out of a "normal" childhood. How do you feel your fame affected you? Would you encourage your children to pursue a career in show business?

My years growing up in the business were some of the happiest times of my life, and having a boss like Walt Disney was a dream come true. He was a second father to me. My children had a taste of showbiz when they were younger. My daughter, Gina (29), studied acting for a while, but settled for a position behind the scenes in entertainment marketing. My middle son, Jack (25), is currently producing several TV shows and movies. And my youngest, Jason (21), is a drummer in a rock and roll band and just got signed to Disney's Hollywood Records division.

What are your happiest memories of being a *16 Magazine* superstar? What are the worst?

Having a friend like Gloria was a giant plus and a wonderful memory. There were no negatives!

DION

Years of *16* Popularity: 1960–1961

If most of the idols in *16* so far were presented as pretty close to who they really were, Dion DiMucci was a different story altogether. He was the first among the "squeaky clean" singers of the early '60s who was anything but. Through most of the early '60s, as he has since acknowledged, Dion was a heroin addict.

As a member of Dion and the Belmonts, he had two huge hits in 1959 and 1960, "Teenager in Love," and "I Wonder Why." As a soloist, starting in 1960, he recorded a string of Top 10 records that included "Runaround Sue" and "The Wanderer." He was inducted into the Rock and Roll Hall of Fame in 1989.

With his street-guy Bronx image, Dion was a *16 Magazine* superstar in 1960 and 1961—and, most notably, the first of perhaps a half dozen idols with whom Gloria Stavers was romantically involved. Indeed, Gloria's affair with this sexy, successful star 13 years her junior is likely to have contributed to her much undeserved reputation for rapaciousness. She simply adored Dion, and the feeling was mutual.

Because she was intimately involved with Dion, Gloria knew about his drug problem. She also knew it would spell disaster (for him and the readers who loved him) to even hint at it in the magazine. Nevertheless, she did try to give her Dion stories a bit of a streetwise edge, separating him from some of the slicker idols of the day.

Dion's memories are sharp and sweet. He spoke to us from his home in Florida in July of 1996.

DION LOOKS BACK

"WHAT I COULDN'T SAY"

"I loved Gloria, she was wild. I was from the Bronx, and she was a whole different breed of woman. I got a kick out of the way she was so different. I was 19 and she was 32, and we both discovered Lenny Bruce together.

"She was interviewing me for the magazine, and she told me that I couldn't tell people I was taking drugs, or about any serious problems I had. She told me to smile, put down the cigarette, and don't threaten anyone. She knew the minds of teenagers so well. I recorded 'Wish Upon a Star' after a conversation with her. I wrote a song about Gloria called 'The Road I'm On.' Some of my real thoughts are on that."

BETWEEN THE COVERS

"Did I become her lover to get into *16*? Definitely not, not at all. That's not my thing. I was naïve, and I thought I was really special. I was kind of defiant and arrogant, and it was a time, the early days of rock and roll, of rebellion and revolution, breaking the showbiz traditions. And the magazine was kind of *in* that showbiz tradition, yet the stars were a lot of the new rebels. I couldn't control what was written in the magazine, so the rebellious side was only hinted at, and Gloria and I understood that's the way it had to be.

"But she was so different from anyone I'd ever known, as if she were from another planet. I kind of, maybe, approached her, and she responded, and we had an affair for almost three years. I used to pour my heart out to that woman. She would come to Baltimore, Philly, Boston, where I was playing, and we would sit in my hotel room and I would just brainstorm, run things by her, visions and dreams, to get her reaction, to learn from her. At that time, all I knew was my neighborhood in the Bronx, nothing too much beyond that. It baffled me. At 19, I had a lot more questions than answers, and it was those kinds of things I could talk to her about.

"Knowing her was part of my inner life, my real life, and the stuff in the magazine was cool, it made you feel good seeing your face on the cover or having a story written about you, but that was an ego thing, different from my real life."

"GOING OUR SEPARATE WAYS"

"Then I started developing a love for the girl that I've now been married to for 33 years, a girl from my neighborhood who just stole my heart. [Sue Butterfield, aka "Runaround Sue"]. So I started drifting away. And I heard stories that Gloria was going with different people, and she was open with me, she would tell me. There was Mickey Mantle, and then Lenny Bruce—you know I don't have to tell you that she was very selective. And I came to realize that Gloria was looking for something different than I was looking for. But even as it

DION'S PRIVATE PHOTO ALBUM

"Here I am at 5 months. Kinda fat, huh?"

"At age one I met a horse. Boy, I look scared!"

The most intimate pictures from his personal scrapbook — selected by Dion himself!

YES — here they are! The most intimate pictures from Dion's personal scrapbook, selected by Dion himself. And he wrote the captions himself, too.

It's all here — the picture story of his life so far! It's another 16 Magazine bonanza — an exciting, original feature, exclusive with us . . . and with a surprise on every page!

"Second from left is my sis, Joanie. I'm sitting on my dad's shoulders."

"At 12 I began to make appearances for real. I sang 'Jambalaya' and played the guitar."

"I was 10 when I took my first Holy Communion."

"The finalists at my music school recital. That's me with the shaved head at left."

In November, 1960, Dion shared his Private Photo Album with 16's readers.

"With one of my dearest friends, WINS deejay Bruce Morrow."

"See, I can be serious at times!"

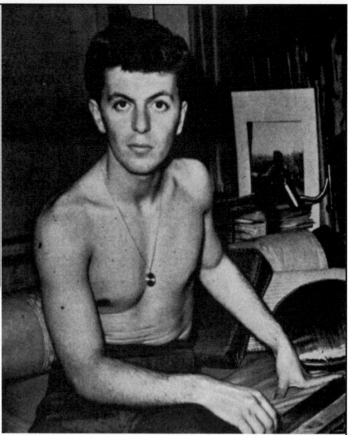

"This is when I'm happiest — playing and singing!"

AND FINALLY, 16'S OWN PIN-UP POR-
TRAIT OF DION — TAKEN ESPECIALLY
FOR 16 MAGAZINE BY BRUNO OF HOLLY-
WOOD! ▶

Dion

*Artists' renderings were often used in lieu of black & white glossies. This one was done by Josh King for **16** Magazine.*

was ending, we were compassionate toward each other, tolerant, and really understanding. All the same, there was a secret part of her life that I couldn't crack, there were areas where she was very guarded, like a closet that you couldn't go into.

"There's so much great stuff about her I'll never forget—how we both hated vibrato singing and that fucking woo-woo tuxedo shit. We were gung-ho against a lot of that. We loved Bo Diddley and Little Richard, that was exciting for us. Until then, there was no such thing as teenagers, we had no identity. You sat down at the table at 13 and you were told to

shut up, and at 19 you became an adult. So now we had our music. And the things Gloria and I would talk about were real. Lenny Bruce—this guy was talking from his gut, he was saying some stuff that was reaching me, that was connecting. Problems or solutions, at least he was real. That's the stuff Gloria and I would talk about.

"**16** was Disney World; she knew it, I knew it. The reality was underneath it all. I thought she was one of the most terrific people I've ever known, a really important part of my younger years."

WHO'S YOUR FAVE RAVE?

The Bobbys: Darin, Vinton, Vee

Back in the beginning, it sometimes seemed that you had to be named "Bobby" to be a teen idol, or at least that it certainly didn't hurt your chances. In fact, besides Bobby Rydell, there were only three major early Bobbys—Vinton, Vee, and Darin, all singers reaching the height of popularity in and around the years 1960 and 1961. Have trouble knowing which was which? Hope this helps:

Bobby Darin

Bronx-born Bobby Darin (né Walden Robert Cassotto) was probably the most musically gifted (certainly the most prolific) of the three. He began as a rocker with "Splish Splash" in 1958, moved into middle-of-the-road recordings, and "went Vegas" in the early '60s. His amazing but short life (he died in 1973 at the age of 37) included marriage to his Hollywood leading lady, Sandra Dee, and a bout with hippy-mysticism toward the end. His last major hit was "If I Were a Carpenter" in 1966.

Darin was a very good friend of Gloria Stavers (she appeared to have a weakness for Bronx boys with a swagger), and indeed became dependent on her advice vis-à-vis his career and personal life as well. The romance and marriage of Bobby Darin and Sandra Dee was big news everywhere, and played up as a tender example of true love among the rich and famous in the pages of *16*.

Bobby Vinton

Bobby Vinton, whose real full name was Stanley Robert Vinton, came on the scene in the early '60s with two huge ballads, "Roses Are Red" and "Blue Velvet." The earnest and swoony nature of the songs did much to define Vinton's image, especially in *16*, where his coverage was rather straightforward and predicated on his talents as a recording star.

Gloria Stavers became close with his family and got hold of his "baby" pictures, and virtually everything to do with his career. Like many others of his era, he remains more popular in Great Britain (than in the U.S.A.), where audiences tend to be loyal and sentimental. His last U.S. record to chart was "My Melody of Love," in 1974. There was a revival of interest in him in 1986 when his recording of "Blue Velvet" was used in David Lynch's movie of the same name.

'In Defense of Bobby Darin

by Georgia Winters

You've read what his critics have said about him. Now read what his friends, who really know him, say about Bobby.

WHEN ROBERT CASSOTTO was a little boy he learned the hard way that some people have to fight, and fight very hard, for every single good thing they get in this life. He learned about poverty, death, disease, and heartbreak. He learned to fend for himself in a cold, bleak world that had no place for the weak. That Robert Cassotto was not destroyed by his society or turned into a criminal is a small miracle.

But then Robert — who grew up to be a man named Bobby Darin — is a sort of a miracle anyway. With all the strikes against him, he has emerged as an educated, kind-hearted, brightly alert and extremely talented singer-performer-actor. He has made a marriage of the heart and soon will be a father. He has taken ugliness, fear, and evil and turned them into beauty, courage, and goodness. Bobby Darin's battle has not been an easy one. He has *had* to be tough at times, to push and fight. He's had to act rough in a rough world.

When that army of people who thrive on being super-critical (and this includes an entire battalion of newspaper and magazine writers) recently took the ax to Bobby, they found that picking his bones wasn't so easy. Bobby Darin wouldn't take it lying down.

Bobby Darin's arrogance was not made up by any journalists; it was a notorious component of his reputation, and inspired this story from the September 1961 issue of 16.

going UP

BOBBY VINTON is Zooming toward the Stars.

BOBBY VINTON is a lot of talent. He began as a band leader, and became the top young band leader in the U.S. But big as he was, he became a lot bigger as a singer — and with his handling of *Roses are Red* on the Epic label, a number one hit backed by a sale of millions of copies, Bobby hit his peak.

But Bobby hasn't turned his back on his band. His father was a bandleader and, while growing up in Canonsburg, Pa., Bobby absorbed the sounds and traditions of the great name bands.

"I always wanted a big band with a young sound for young people," Bobby says. "I was sure that kids of my generation wanted a full swinging group which would play even rock and roll with a solid beat and rich voicing."

Bobby organized his first band in high school, played proms and parties. For students at nearby Duquesne University he later formed a second group, which was soon a favorite at teenage dances in Pittsburgh's ballrooms. Bobby began singing a few numbers with the orchestra and his vocals soon became the band's most popular feature.

He continued working closely with arrangers to crystallize his musical ideas. By late 1960 he had achieved "the Vinton sound," recorded it and sent tapes to Epic. The label quickly signed the talented and personable young bandleader.

Guy Lombardo first discovered Bobby at a hop outside Pittsburgh and promptly introduced him on Sam Levinson's "Celebrity Talent Scout," a television show where famous artists debut their talented finds.

In November 1960 Bobby's outfit was featured as Band of the Month on NBC's Saturday Prom and played with a succession of stars including Bobby Vee, Sam Cooke and Jimmy Clanton. Bobby then made a nationwide tour with the "Fall Edition of the Biggest Show of Stars for '60," a big, barnstorming teenage troupe starring Fabian, Chubby Checker, Brenda Lee and others for whom he provided musical accompaniment and with whom he often shared the vocal mike.

In December, the Vinton orchestra mounted the bandstand for the Brooklyn Paramount's famous Christmas show. The annual teenage spectacular smashed all existing attendance records and catapulted Bobby to national prominence.

Bobby was born on September 3, 1940. His favorite foods are hot dogs and spaghetti, his favorite singers are Ray Charles, Anita Bryant and Doris Day. In sports, he enjoys baseball and basketball, and his pet hobby is collecting shirts (he has over a hundred of them). His big weakness is buying *anything* that is on sale. He digs movies and going for long walks — and he likes girls who give all their attention to him and don't flirt with other guys. When he likes a girl, he phones her two or three times a day. He is the home-type; he loves to visit a girl's home and meet her folks.

You can write to Bobby Vinton at 171 Smith Street, Canonsburg, Pa.

In October 1962, 16 predicted the stardom of Bobby Vinton.

A LOVE LETTER TO YOU FROM BOBBY VEE

Dearest,

I'm so glad to have this chance to write a letter to someone who cares enough about me to write me and follow my career. Since I don't get enough time to personally answer all of the letters I get this is one letter to you to make for all the ones I didn't write!

I had a ball in England in November, but it was good to get back home. After some one-nighters on the Coast I went home for a wonderful Christmas with my folks. Early this year I returned to Hollywood to cut some records.

Speaking of records, I cut an LP in Italy — and you should have heard me singing "Run To Him" in Italian!

Before I close let me tell you that I have a little secret right now — and if things work out well you may be seeing me in a movie! But no matter what — I'll see you in my dreams!

As Ever ___

Bobby Vee

This Love Letter from Bobby Vee (from the March 1963 issue) was only partly "written" by the singer. "It's my handwriting," Bobby acknowledges, "and most of what's here, I would have said—except I never would have written 'Dearest,' and I never would have ended with the words, 'I'll see you in my dreams.' I strongly suspect Gloria dictated that part!"

Bobby Vee Looks Back

Bobby Vee's first break came when he and his band substituted for Buddy Holly at a show in the Midwest shortly after Holly's death in a plane crash. Vee (real full name: Robert Thomas Velline) was 16 at the time, and soon landed a recording contract with his group, the Shadows. His big hits included "Devil or Angel" and "Take Good Care of My Baby," which went to #1.

Bobby Vee in *16* was depicted as open, innocent, and genuinely delighted with his success and his fans. That was not far from the truth, as he recently told us in this interview.

"I WAS SORT OF UNCONSCIOUS AT FIRST"

"I wasn't aware of *16 Magazine* before I was in it. I was too caught up in the excitement of rock 'n' roll to be aware of the promotional side. I was 16 and completely unconscious about the self-promotion part of the business. It never entered my mind that there was marketing involved. To me, the excitement involved making a record and performing it on *American Bandstand*.

"The first time I recall hearing about *16*, I was working at the Brooklyn Paramount Theater. I'd had a hit with 'Susie Baby,' and was coming out with 'What Do You Want?' That's when I met Georgia—Gloria, of course—and did my first interview. It was all fine, but *16* was sort of a minor distraction at first. Then I saw the excitement of my manager, my record company, and realized that coverage in it meant a lot to them. That's how I came to understand the importance of the magazine."

"MY IMAGE: NICE GUY WHO DIDN'T GET THE GIRL"

"My image, I think, was created by the songs I sang, not the stories in *16*. I was the nice guy who never got the girl. Think of the words in 'Take Good Care of My Baby,' and 'Run to Him.' When I look at the articles, that's what was reflected. What a nice guy I was! That sort of created the image. I didn't write those songs (Carole King/Gerry Goffin did) but I chose to sing them.

"To a large degree, the songs and the image really were me. I'm a Midwestern guy with Midwestern values. The only big difference between the image and the reality was that I always *had* a girlfriend. When I was 16, I started dating Karen, the girl who eventually became my wife. So, as opposed to the image, I did get the girl—and the girl got me. In December 1996, we celebrated our 33rd wedding anniversary. I still feel the same about her now as I did back then. I thought she was the most beautiful girl in the world.

"Of course, my real-life relationship was not mentioned in *16*. But I never looked at it as hiding anything. It just never came up. Gloria never even asked about that kind of stuff. So I was presented as being available, even though I never really was. It didn't bother me, I wasn't much into the image thing. I do remember there was an article entitled, 'I've Never Been in Love,' which did bother Karen. She was a little uncomfortable about that.

"But other than the girlfriend thing, I don't remember *16* protecting me, or needing to protect me. I didn't smoke, do drugs, or have any other real vices. Some had, of course. I used to share a dressing room with Dion and Del Shannon and we became fast friends. Del was always dieting, or giving up cigarettes or booze, or something. That was never reported in *16*. Nor was Dion's heroin addiction; I was aware of that, but not his affair with Gloria.

"Gloria respected her readers by not reporting those details. She cared about her readers, and tried to show them, this is the way life should be."

WHAT A WIMP!

"Gloria wrote all those first-person stories on me. She'd take some of what I said in our interviews and then embellish it. Luckily, I never took it too seriously back then, because when I look at them now, boy, do I look like a wimp! She portrayed me as being very shy, and even used the word 'meek' in one article. I was shy, but never meek.

"I eventually realized that the magazine, the fantasy, had a life of its own and a purpose of its own and that I was a vehicle for the purpose. The articles reflected the music of the time. It was from the heart, simple, relationship stuff, uncomplicated, all about feelings. And that was something every teenager—including me—could relate to, feeling shy, lonely, looking for a friend, looking for love. In that sense, the readers did 'know' me through the articles.

The Bobbys: Darin, Vinton, Vee

"Being in *16* never hurt my career; if anything, it helped. There were so few vehicles in those days for the fans to get to know the performers. *16* was like MTV with the sound turned down, a way for people to get to know about someone they cared about. *16* was like the print version of *American Bandstand*."

DELIVER DE-LETTER:
THE FAN MAIL

"I read the mail to the extent that I could. I had a secretary in Fargo who got all the fan mail. She showed me a lot of it; we'd sit down and go over it. I did answer what I could.

"The truth is, the most poignant fan letter I ever got was sent just recently. A woman wrote that she was a fan back in the early '60s, she'd bought all the records and read all the magazine articles. She was from an abusive home. And she used to hide in the cellar and play my records over and over. And that's how she survived those years. So whenever I'm tempted to think that the articles, or the songs, were just so fluffy, I remember that. In fact, if I had to pick one song to be remembered by it would be the simple, but sincere, 'More than I Can Say,' which captures the essence of the music at that time. It was music from the heart."

NOW: "A FAMILY AFFAIR"

"I still record, I still tour—I do about 100 dates a year. I perform a lot of different material, including the songs that weren't such big hits, but I do requests, of course. My current shows are designed for my diehard fans, who have become like members of the family. I love going out and performing for them, and for the new fans. I'm based in Minnesota, where I run my own recording studio. I have a daughter, who is not in the business, and three sons, Jeff, Tom, and Robby, who have their own band. They do rockabilly, with a stand-up bass, and sometimes they accompany me on the road. It's a family affair now and I couldn't be happier."

Rick Nelson

Years of *16* Popularity: 1958–1963

Ricky Nelson, born in 1940, had an incredible career. Handsome, talented, and rich, he was the son of bandleader Ozzie Nelson and singer Harriet Hilliard Nelson, and a star (playing himself) from the age of 9 (along with his older brother David) on his parents' weekly radio show, *The Adventures of Ozzie and Harriet.* In the early '50s the show became a successful TV series, with mischievous Ricky the star and hero. "I don't mess around, boy," Ricky's attitudinal comment on all his little ventures, became a favorite motto of his own generation.

When he started singing on the show, in 1957, he became a bona fide teen idol. This combination of TV and hit records proved to be a potent key to teen superstardom for him and other performers in later years. If there were a shortlist of the Great Fave Raves of all time, Ricky Nelson would certainly be on it. He had nearly 20 Top 10 hits, including "Travelin' Man" and "Hello, Mary Lou," before the string broke, although he came back with the gold single, "Garden Party" in 1972.

In his teen idol days, he was very cooperative with *16.* Befitting his massive popularity, his presentation was extensive; it appeared as if *16* was everywhere Ricky was, that the writers knew his every thought. The March 1959 issue featured an astonishing 47 photos chronicling Ricky on tour. Ricky was never a close personal friend of Gloria Stavers. But he was such a big star that their personal relationship, or lack of it, hardly mattered. It was people of Ricky Nelson's stature—and there were certainly not that many of them—who made teen fan magazines, with *16* as the flagship of the fleet, such a publishing success.

Rick Nelson died in a plane crash in 1985 and was inducted into the Rock and Roll Hall of Fame in 1987. His brilliance as a teen idol had overshadowed—though not for the many musicians who continue to pay him tribute—his vast talents as a singer and songwriter.

Ricky or Rick? The usage changed, often referring to the teen idol as Ricky, and the musician as Rick. In *16,* however, he was always referred to as Rick. His real full name was Eric Hilliard Nelson.

THE THINGS I

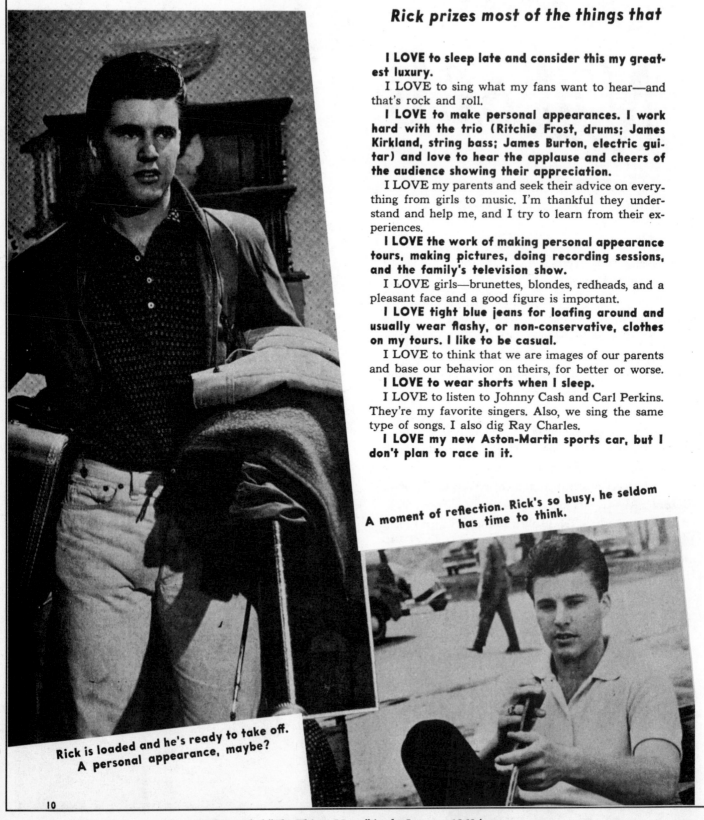

Rick prizes most of the things that

I LOVE to sleep late and consider this my greatest luxury.

I LOVE to sing what my fans want to hear—and that's rock and roll.

I LOVE to make personal appearances. I work hard with the trio (Ritchie Frost, drums; James Kirkland, string bass; James Burton, electric guitar) and love to hear the applause and cheers of the audience showing their appreciation.

I LOVE my parents and seek their advice on everything from girls to music. I'm thankful they understand and help me, and I try to learn from their experiences.

I LOVE the work of making personal appearance tours, making pictures, doing recording sessions, and the family's television show.

I LOVE girls—brunettes, blondes, redheads, and a pleasant face and a good figure is important.

I LOVE tight blue jeans for loafing around and usually wear flashy, or non-conservative, clothes on my tours. I like to be casual.

I LOVE to think that we are images of our parents and base our behavior on theirs, for better or worse.

I LOVE to wear shorts when I sleep.

I LOVE to listen to Johnny Cash and Carl Perkins. They're my favorite singers. Also, we sing the same type of songs. I also dig Ray Charles.

I LOVE my new Aston-Martin sports car, but I don't plan to race in it.

A moment of reflection. Rick's so busy, he seldom has time to think.

Rick is loaded and he's ready to take off. A personal appearance, maybe?

10

Rick revealed "The Things I Love" in the January 1960 issue.

LOVE

make up his life. To name a few . . .

I LOVE living home now, but I may get an apartment in two years—when I'm 21.

I LOVE a girl who accepts a date because she wants to go out with ME, not because she wants to be seen with a celebrity.

I LOVE to hear from my fans, and get as many as 10,000 letters a week from them.

I LOVE to kiss a girl on our first date if I think it's all right with her—and I can usually tell.

I LOVE children and hope to have at least three when I marry.

I LOVE to play the drums and the piano as well as the guitar.

I LOVE to collect sports shirts and sweaters.

I LOVE the outdoors, and enjoy plain food like roast beef, steak, potatoes, and gravy.

I LOVE people around me who are calm and not excitable. People who rush around usually have no place to go and nothing to do when they arrive.

I LOVE to exercise end enjoy all sports in season.

I LOVE a snack between meals—mainly ice cream and cokes.

I LOVE singing rock and roll because it's music I understand and it is a form of self-expression.

I LOVE music and enjoy my lessons with Vincente Gomez on classical guitar.

Well, that's it—and don't ask me to do an encore. It's time to head for the studio to rehearse with the rest of the Nelson family, and I LOVE that.

Rick sings with a concentration that focuses all of his feelings in the words of the song.

On the TV set. It's a rehearsal for a Nelson family episode—and Rick is great.

That's Rick in a period costume for a TV drama. He's an accomplished actor in many roles.

PAUL PETERSEN

Years of *16* Popularity: 1962–1965

There was a time when Paul Petersen was as big as Elvis. Not in the real world, silly, but most certainly in *16*-land. A representative cover, from September 1964, actually poses the burning question, "Elvis Out? Petersen In?" And bizarrely enough, he did have at least one thing over the King—a weekly TV show (he was Jeff Stone on *The Donna Reed Show*) in addition to a recording career ("My Dad" was a Top 10 hit in 1962, but—admit it—what we all remember is "She Can't Find Her Keys"). Don't laugh; in the niche world of teen idols, it doesn't come any more surefire than that. Rick Nelson, of course, had pioneered the phenomenon. Paul Petersen—and after him, Bobby Sherman, the Partridge Family, Donny & Marie, and the Bradys—reaped the benefits, willingly and gratefully.

Of his years as a top teen idol, Paul Petersen today says, "I was a full and willing participant in it all. If I was portrayed in *16* as clean-cut, straightforward, opinionated—I *was* that guy. Isn't that something? And what's the proof? The proof is that today I am 51 years old and I am a conservative Republican who gets his hands dirty doing what I hope are worthwhile things to make this world a better place. I'm cleanin' up this little corner of the world that I know intimately. And isn't that what Jeff Stone should have grown up to be?"

Indeed, in a very real sense, Paul never left those years behind him. He is the president and founder of a watchdog organization called A Minor Consideration, which, through the clout of the Young Performers' Division of the Screen Actors' Guild and government agencies, looks out for the emotional, financial, and legal well-being of showbiz kids today.

PAUL PETERSEN, 1997

"I WAS CHASIN' IT"

"It wasn't an accident what happened to me. I won a competition over 5,000 kids to be one of the original Mouseketeers because I could sing and dance better than most anybody. I continued to get jobs in big things, like *Playhouse 90* playing Cary Grant's son, because I could perform. I had a talent to amuse—that old wonderful Noël Coward line. Moreover, when I did the work, I was on top of my game.

"I had a television and a musical career, a couple of gold records along the way. I had a great time. I was visible. In my day, you could understand the lyrics to popular songs and sex couldn't kill you. Ricky Nelson invented this television bubblegum star—they called us bubblegum stars—and it had to do absolutely with exposure.

"I remember being in *16*. Gloria was like a great pal. Every time I came through New York I'd see her, or whenever she was in L.A., we'd get together. Did I want to be in *16*? Are you kidding? I was chasin' it. I felt like it was a competition: me vs. Johnny Crawford, Don Grady, Bobby Sherman, and all the rest. I actually did know Elvis and he used to call me little brother. I mean, he was Elvis, for God's sake; I was a little pale imitation. We both drove fast cars, both took advantage of our celebrity. The difference was, he was surrounded by a bunch of idiots and I was out there on my own, learning lessons. It has not passed my attention that I have now outlived him by a significant number of years."

"WAS I THAT GUY? YOU BET I WAS"

"Many of the articles on me in *16* were first person— I didn't write them exactly, but I cooperated fully. Articles like, 'Paul Petersen Warns Girls, "Get Out of That Rut,"' I did say those things. However tepid or shallow they appear now, at the time, that was what I did. And I did care about looking right when I went out of the house and the way girls behaved around me. I did like the color blue! I did tell girls they wore too much makeup, and if you remember the era, they did! All that hair spray and the bouffant hairdos.

"I *was* that guy and I trusted Gloria and *16* to portray me accurately. Look, we both knew we were playin' the game, but, for instance, when *16* had a contest, 'Have a Party with Paul Petersen,' I was a willing participant, and enjoyed it. My attitude was, what's wrong with being rich and famous? Nothing!

"Besides, those were fun days. It was kind of fun to know that Paul Petersen loved Cobras and fast cars and faster women…not that *16* quite put it that way. I was the president and founder of the Cobra owners club. I still love cars. *16* used to write that I thought my sisters were the most beautiful girls in the world. I did think that then, and they're still the apples of my eye. Of course, according to them, they're both younger than me now (one used to be older!).

"Was I really as 'perfect' as I was portrayed? I was responsible, let's put it that way. Did I smoke? Did I drink? You bet I did, and so did most of my contemporaries—but for the most part, that was later on. And then, I was honest about it. I never hid it from anybody."

"I COULDN'T STAND THE SMELL"

"I'm not sure *16*'s readers had any big misconceptions about me. But I'll tell you what I didn't like. I didn't like the craziness, the screaming, and the plucking at my clothes, the general craziness that attended being a celebrity. Showing up at events where kids would tear apart a store, and the screaming and the rocking the limousine and the grabbing cufflinks, that happened to me, and to the others. It's like sexual harassment—you want to talk about being an image, some sexual object…that's what a teen idol is. In fact, for a long time I stopped performing because I found that I couldn't stand the smell…of excited 14-year-old girls. And it is an odor. And I didn't care for it.

"I was raised by people and by circumstance where the content of your character was important. I would see the opposite when I went out on the road [to perform]. All I had to do was step onto a stage and the girls would start screaming. They wouldn't stop and listen to the songs or to hear what I had to say. Now, looking back, I see that for them, it wasn't about that. But at the time it was bothersome to me."

"GUYS RESENTED ME— AND WOULDN'T HIRE ME LATER ON"

"Being a *16 Magazine* teen idol didn't embarrass me so much as get me into a lot of fights! You gotta understand, when you're 15, 16, 17 years old, and girls your age are swooning, all that does is piss off their boyfriends. And for that period of time, that meant fisticuffs. Now it means gunfire.

"The worst part of that was that it made the transition [into adult actor] more difficult. Because many of the young men who resented me at age 16 ended up having positions of authority in this industry later on. They took it out on me, as well as other male former teen idols. They didn't take it out on the young women who were teen idols, because they are objects of their lust still. It's true. You can quote me on that."

"THE DATES WERE REAL"

"Speaking of girls, what I remember most in *16* were all those 'Win a Date with Paul' contests. Of course I did them. In most cases, they were very pleasant. I always enjoyed being with people and knew how to bring out the shy girls, make them talk about themselves.

"As for actual girlfriends? I went out with a lot of people. Yes, there were publicity dates with Hayley Mills and Donna Lauren; those were real too. I didn't marry a fan, though; I married an actress." [Paul's first wife was Brenda Benet, who subsequently married Bill Bixby and later killed herself. He is currently wed to Rana Platz-Petersen, a former actress who is now a registered nurse; they have two college-age children.]

"I ANSWERED THE FAN MAIL"

"In spite of playing the game willingly, I also took the craft of acting, of performing, seriously. I wanted to be good, and I worked with quality people. My God, look at the people on *The Donna Reed Show*. Donna Reed, two-time Emmy winner. Carl Betz, Emmy winner. Shelley Fabares, two-time nominee—and then there's Paul Petersen. Chopped liver. To these people, excellence was important. I learned from that.

"What I took most seriously was another lesson I learned from them—the responsibility of being a celebrity. We had a willingness to sign autographs, to be kind to people, to answer fan letters, to take seriously a pledge to stay drug-free, to show up on time. Those are important things.

"My mother, Wilma, God bless her, under the name Renee Adler, was my fan club president. And we put aside one Saturday every month to deal with it. I signed every autograph, every picture, I read representative samples of all the fan mail. We did those things. I took it as important. Even when it was overwhelming, when they delivered the stuff in sacks. Even when I got to a certain point of fame that if someone simply addressed their letter, 'Paul Petersen, U.S.A.,' the post office knew to deliver it to my home. That always amazed me. You're talking letters in the thousands. But I took

"THE NIGHT I CRIED" by PAUL PETERSEN

58

"The Night I Cried," by Paul Petersen, from the May '64 issue, is a tale of one bummer of a night:
at the end, the reader—you, girl—just wanted to hug him. Which of course, was the point. Always.

It was a night in which nothing went right. And there was no one to talk to and tell how he felt...lost and lonely and sadder than he had ever felt before in his life.

IT STARTED OUT to be a hop just like any other one — except that it was a very big one. I flew into town and that's when the very first bad thing happened. No one was waiting to meet me at the airport. I checked my bags out and took a seat to wait for the radio station representative. I didn't know where I was supposed to go or what I was supposed to do — so all I could do was wait. I didn't want to call the station because I felt sure the guy was on his way. He probably got caught in heavy traffic or something.

Some teenage girls who knew I was coming into town were at the airport. They rushed over to me and started talking and asking for autographs. At first, that was fine, but somehow the group seemed to be getting larger and larger. Word was out, I guess. Believe me, I am always happy to meet new people and answer questions and sign autographs, but somehow this day I just knew things were going to get out of hand.

And, sure enough, they did! As the crowd got bigger, it got wilder. At one point I looked at my watch and realized I had been in the airport for almost two hours. If a responsible adult didn't come to my rescue soon, I felt the group of girls there might get out of control — and then anything could happen. I had had my jacket and shirt torn off before. I had had my cufflinks whipped off and my buttons snipped off. But I had always had police protection and managed to hurry through the throng to safety. Now, I was stranded. There was no one to help or protect me. I was quietly counting on the good taste and judgment of the girls gathered there to keep order.

Just when the unchecked bomb of enthusiasm was about to explode, some cat with a cigar dangling from his mouth pushed his way through the crowd and announced that he was the station representative who had come to pick me up.

"You're late, you know," I said.

He didn't even bother to acknowledge this or to apologize. I was steaming all the way back to town. We went straight to where the hop was to be. When I saw my name spelled wrong on the big marquee outside the arena, I realized that this was not going to be my night! But I made up my mind to make the very best of everything.

Inside, I inquired about rehearsal time. Another disinterested station rep looked at me as though I had just sprouted horns and said, "We don't have time for you to rehearse, sonny."

It was really a blow. By this time I knew that the only people who really cared for me were the kids out in the audience. I cared for them too, and I didn't want to disappoint them with a second-rate performance.

The show turned out to be great. I felt happy as I stood there and heard the yells and clapping of the fans who'd gone to the trouble to come out to see me. I did three encores (in spite of the bad band), and then the bubble burst.

After the show I was exhausted and famished. The deejays and a station group took me to a restaurant for dinner. I picked up the menu and began to feel better. I decided that I'd have a steak, French fries and salad. When I said this to the waiter, one of the station people turned my way and said in a loud voice, "*We* are all just having hamburgers!"

That's when I snapped, or came as close to it as I ever have. Very slowly, without speaking, I got up from the large table where we were sitting and moved to a smaller one. I sat so that my back was to all those people. I was tired and hungry. I knew that the only sensible thing for me to do was get away and eat before I did something I might later regret. I ordered my meal and ate it alone. Not one of the fellows from the other table came over to speak to me or ask what was wrong.

When the meal was over, I was told that we were all *supposed* to go to some party. I wanted to go home, but if it was something involving record people I felt I had to go for business reasons. Well, I might have gone on home for all it was worth. It wasn't a business party, so I decided to let my hair down and have a ball. Most of the people were older than me, but there was one girl in my age group there. I asked her to dance and we tore the place apart for a while. Just as I was getting to know her conversationwise in a quiet corner, one of the station deejays came over and horned in — to put it mildly. He started pouring on the charm and maneuvered it so that his back was to me and I couldn't even see the girl!

Suddenly, I said to myself — "*Paul, what are you doing here? What's going on, anyway? This isn't your way of life and these aren't your kind of people.*"

I got up, bid a polite goodnight to everyone in the room, thanked the host and hostess, hailed a cab and went to my motel.

When I first walked into the room, I felt relieved. I turned on the radio, took off my shoes and lay back on the bed. All at once I felt sadder than I ever have in my entire life. It was such a lost and lonely feeling! I wanted so desperately to have someone there — a girl who understood — to talk to.

I realized that you can go through anything and put up with anything if you have someone who knows you and cares for you nearby to share the situation with — someone you merely glance at and she knows what you're thinking.

When you're alone and get hurt by something, you feel like you could explode. But when someone else is there to turn to, it takes the edge off it. When you have a girl to face things with — well, then you can face anything.

After you've worked so hard all day, it is wonderful to have a girl to discuss things with. You can ask her how you were on the stage and she can either tell you, "Great!" — or give constructive criticism. She'll sit up and yak with you till your tension is eased. Funny, but in a way you could almost say you need someone to *complain to*.

If you don't have that "someone" there — or in your life somewhere — it's like talking to yourself or talking to a mirror. Nothing comes back to you. You're all alone.

I cried that night — and I'll never forget it. I may cry again some day. But that doesn't mean that I'll never find what I'm looking for. She may be right around a corner, right now, or she may be far away in my future. But I know she is there waiting for me, and I know deep in my heart that one day I will find her. And when I do, I'll never have to cry again.

Paul Petersen

it seriously. I really believed then and I believe now, those are the people that made it all possible. They still do.

"The people out there have a reservoir of affection that is so deep that it moves me to tears sometimes. I still meet plenty of people my age, when I travel around the country, who say, 'My children's names are Jeff and Paul.' And I know exactly what they're saying. God bless 'em."

THE DOWNSIDE: "WE GOT NO CREDIT"

"Was there a downside to being a *16* teen idol? Of course there was. Lots of them—and not only for me. Early success brings its own special, significant problems. It did for me, and for thousands of others, and it continues to do so today.

"We did 39 *Donna Reed* episodes a year for eight years and I never missed a day, I was never late. I knew my lines. In all those years, I missed maybe one interview. I did the work. What pissed me off, 10 years later, is that I was given no credit for being that person. How sad that our culture changed so brutally that young performers, teen idols, were suddenly considered objects of ridicule. Teenagers in showbiz are not given credit for their success until long after the fact—25 years after is a good timeline. That's devastating.

"Adolescents aren't always in the correct place to matriculate into an adult career, and they make it tough on you. For example, Don Grady, 12 years on *My Three Sons*, was in fact hugely skilled musically. That's where his true talents and his interests were, and yet his TV success mitigated against him entering the music business. Eventually, he did the music for Michael Crawford's show in Las Vegas and people finally recognized that's where his true talents were. Same for [*Leave It to Beaver*'s] Tony Dow. It took Tony Dow 12 years to get into the Directors' Guild. How absurd."

"MY EDUCATION WAS COMPROMISED"

"Of course, my education was compromised. I couldn't continue it. When you are tagged as the archetypal All-American boy in a world where protest and long hair and drugs and antisocial is the norm, you're asking for trouble. You can't walk across a college campus and be accepted; it doesn't work that way. It is so hard. Celebrity follows you, and it is really difficult when you represent a certain kind of culture, and the real world has half a million troops in Vietnam. Not to mention just the aftereffects of celebrity. It gets very painful, to have to overcome that.

"It took me 9 years after high school to get to college. It wasn't only the problems of being a teen star and my image.

It was also the upsets of gettin' into the drug culture. That'll slow anybody down. But when I finally did get there, college changed my life. I went to Yale, in Connecticut—I got out of Hollywood."

"PICK YOUR PARENTS WITH CARE"

"I work with a lot of stage parents now, and of course I had stage parents. The whole subject is still hard for me… I still reduce my mom to tears when I get on this subject. Though she admits she enjoyed my success more than I did, and suffered my failures more than I. She still doesn't understand that to this day, when I go to the supermarket, I still get recognized. She doesn't.

"When *The Donna Reed Show* took off, and when the records began to happen, we were no longer in control of our lives. We were part of the star-making machine. We were willing participants. We played the game. But we didn't understand the consequences.

"We didn't understand that fame was a drug. That's the poison. And this is not just about being the best athlete in a small town. You're talking about the kind of notoriety that extends to every corner of the earth now and doesn't go away. This is the unique feature of modern celebrity. You think that when you're finished with your series, you're gonna lay this kid behind you. But as Adam Rich is finding out now, with his current troubles with the Nicholas Bradford character he portrayed on *Eight Is Enough*, you can't. The fact is, you can't kill this person. This entity continues to exist, thanks to reruns, Nickelodeon, and nostalgia shows.

"This is something showbiz parents can't understand, and how could they? They are naïve and inexperienced when they begin and there has been a conspiracy of silence in this industry to keep this knowledge quiet. This is no mystery to me, or others—nor is parents squandering their kids' money. That's been going on for 80 years.

"Of all the teen stars of my era, it was only Ron Howard's parents who completely understood, because they were veterans of the industry. They knew that you need to keep your feet on the ground at all times. Rance and Jean Howard were able to maintain their home, they lived within *their* income—not the kids' income. They were never swayed by Ron and Clint's success. They are rare.

"As a dearly departed friend once said to me, 'In this business, you gotta pick your parents with care.'"

Paul Petersen

"WHAT DID IT ALL MEAN?"

"At the time, me and the other young stars were engaged in a friendly competition. But we never shared the real secrets and truth about our lives, because at the time you didn't do that. If we'd only known to turn to each other…about our parents, about our school problems, what it was like to be singled out and identified when you're trying to have a quiet dinner and people want your autograph and your training says 'do that.'

"I would ask the ex-fans reading this book to reflect on what it all meant? And are we helping our children to choose worthwhile and substantial pop idols?

CLIFF RICHARD

Years of *16* Popularity: 1958–1963

Cliff Richard was in many ways the Elvis Presley of England. Born Harry Webb in India to British parents in 1940, he moved to England seven years later, and it was there he became Great Britain's biggest solo star, with over 100 (!) Top 40 singles starting in 1958, and 13 #1 hits. He was also a movie star, playing a manipulated teen idol in 1960's classic *Expresso Bongo.*

Although he had but a few big hit singles in the U.S., Cliff Richard was the spearhead of the British musical invasion of America. His fame in America was really a spillover of his enormous success in the U.K. and on the Continent. In spite of that, it was his brooding, innocent good looks that helped him into the pages of *16.*

There, among the Bobbys, the Pauls, and the *Bandstand* regulars, he was certainly the only non-American teen idol until the Beatles came along four years later. In fact, it could be maintained that his stardom in *16* was wishful thinking on the part of Gloria Stavers, since he was never as immensely popular in the U.S. as he was abroad; many of the stories about him carry the theme "Let's bring Cliff here!"

He continues to be a performing and recording star of household-word status in Britain, though a virtually forgotten quantity on this side of the ocean.

WHO'S YOUR FAVE RAVE?

FACT SHEET ON Cliff Richard

Real name: *Harry Rodger Webb.*

Height: *5′ 11″.*

Weight: *159 lbs.*

Coloring: *Dark brown hair and dark brown eyes.*

Born: *Lucknow, India, October 14, 1940.*

Home and family information: *Presently lives in North London with his mother and three sisters.*

Favorites—Singers: *Elvis Presley and Peggy Lee.*

Actors: *John Wayne and Liz Taylor.*

Food: *Indian curry with rice.*

Hobby: *Showing motion pictures.*

Sports: *Swimming, archery and badminton.*

Dating status: *Single and no steady girl. Likes to double-date either to a movie or an amusement park.*

What looked for in a date: *Looks don't matter, but cheerfulness and friendliness do.*

What looked for in a friend: *His closest friends are the boys he works and travels with. They are all sincere and loyal boys with a good sense of humor.*

Ultimate ambition: *To become a good actor.*

Pet peeve: *Smokey rooms.*

Secret Longing: *To own a tropical island.*

Addresses—Record Co.: *Epic Records, 799 Seventh Ave., New York, N. Y.*

Fan Club: *Geri Casper, 65-61 Saunders St., Forest Hills 74, N. Y.*

Cliff's fact sheet was presented in the November 1963 issue.

The 60s: TAKE TWO

1964– 1969

THE SIXTIES *16* MAGAZINE 1964–1969

Remember that song "Glory Days"? Partly because of, again, timing, but mostly because of Gloria Days—and nights—*16* was at its peak in the second half of the decade: sales-wise and also as a power. It was boom time, fueled at first by what the music world still calls The British Invasion.

Early in 1964, JohnPaulGeorge&Ringo—one word, as we at *16* knew them to be—descended and brought with them a tidal wave of British talent, all young, all very happening, and all very much embraced, lock, stock, and *Billboard* charts, by a huge demographic of teenage American baby boomers. Oooh-eee baby, *this* was something new, this scruffy long-haired look was something even quasi-hip parents could *not* relate to: this was *ours*.

Teenagers gave a collective boot-out-the-back-Jack to the scrubbed-clean teen idols their older sisters worshipped: adios, Elvis, farewell, Frankie, Fabe, Ricky, and, uh, "buh-bye" to the Bobbys. The one 'n' only Paul with it *all* was a hooded-eyed mop-top named McCartney.

It was only natural that *16* would jump on the Brit band-wagon; Gloria certainly knew how to go with the flow, if not keep several paces ahead of it. In 1964, a different-looking *16* hit the stands. Well, not that different. Floating heads still bobbed on the cover, but the faces came from "across the sea," and new phrases replaced the groovy, ginchy early '60s slang. Hep cats became mop-tops; girls became birds; and when you fell, you were in *L-U-V!*

Other changes were not so hip. Girl stars were only interesting if they were "related" to a boy. Instead of the independent Hayley, Connie, and Annette, we got Beatle-birds Jane, Pattie, and Maureen. No Mamas without Papas; even Cher did not stand alone.

By 1966, Americans launched a counterattack of music stars. Soon Paul Revere & the Raiders; the Cowsills; Dino, Desi & Billy; and, mostly, the Monkees swiped back the loyalty of *16* readers. And there was for the first time a "dark side," sexier, scarier, but that much more exciting: the Doors on the charts, *Dark Shadows* on the tube.

The second half of the '60s saw something else for the first time—actual newsstand competition. Spurred by the Beatles, new magazines suddenly appeared on the scene. The main competitor was *Tiger Beat*. No two words drew Gloria's ire more: she considered *Tiger Beat* to be a mortal enemy and woe to the celebrity who gave "them" an exclusive.

By that time, however, *16* had a great advantage: *16* had simply been doing it longer, better, and more thoroughly than any latecomers to the game.

How powerful was *16* in making or breaking a career? The perception—Gloria was best at that, of course—was huge. Bluntly, "Everyone catered to our ass," according to Gloria's second-in-command in the mid-to-late '60s, Steve DeNaut. "At the time, we were the world's largest-selling celebrity magazine. *16* made stars: if we plugged 'em, most of America's teens read about them. The stars knew it, and for the most part agreed to anything we asked, no matter how silly they might have felt about it. A push from Gloria would keep them at the top of the heap, which of course translated into money and continued acting jobs and recording contracts. The networks knew it and got us whatever we asked for. If they didn't have it—say, new photos of *Dark Shadows*—they had them taken just for us. Whatever we asked for, we got. They jumped through hoops for us."

Most of the stars of that era remember it all as fondly as the fans still do, as the following section of this book attests.

COVER PRICE:
16 remained a 25-cent bargain until 1970, when it leapt to 35 cents!

COLOR PINUPS: It wasn't until the January 1969 issue that *16* got glossy color pinups—and only two besides the cover, at that. The dearth of decent-quality paper did not adversely affect sales.

SALES: *16* had its highest sales ever in that part of the decade. In 1967, it sold (on the newsstands) just under 1,000,000 copies per month. Magazines of its genre usually sell between 200,000 and 300,000 copies. No cheesy-paper teen fanzine had ever come close to that figure, nor has one since.

And that 1,000,000 sales figure didn't take into account the ever-popular "pass-along readership" factor, in other words, how many other readers the person who bought the magazine shared it with or passed it along to. Conventional wisdom inflated the figure 4-fold and the magazine brazenly bragged on its masthead, "*16* Is the Top Favorite of over Seven Million Readers."

MEET ENGLAND'S

TOP STARS!

THE BEATLES ARE COMING would be more like it. In fact, they are here. You already know (and love) Cliff Richard, England's top rock-and-roll star. Now let him introduce you to the fabulous Beatles — and the rest of England's top record stars.

Meet George, Ringo, John and Paul—the four dynamic young men who are known all over the world as The Beatles. Beatle-mania started in Liverpool and has come all the way to The Ed Sullivan Show in America. Capitol Records is negotiating for the boys and they are doing a movie for United Artists.

The Beatles first appeared in 16 in the issue dated March 1964, which in retrospect makes it seem as if it was late covering them. However, it was actually on the stands in January of that year, and had in fact gone to press in November 1963.

THE BEATLES

Years of *16* Popularity: 1964-1966

The Beatles were...the Beatles. There has been nothing like them in the history of popular music, or as musical teen idols. By the time they arrived in America in the winter of 1964, they were a page one news story everywhere. Within months, they had the top five songs on the *Billboard* charts in one week, a feat not likely ever to be repeated. They were adorable, irreverent, British, they had revolutionary hairstyles, and there were four of them to love.

Everyone in the media wanted the Beatles, and being the #1 teen fan magazine didn't count for all that much when *Time* and *Life* and Ed Sullivan and hundreds of thousands of fans (bear in mind that the streets around their hotels in midtown New York had to be closed off when the Beatles were in residence) were fighting for a piece of the action.

But Gloria Stavers was not discouraged by the struggle to get to them; she wanted to make *16 the* Beatles magazine of record, and it certainly had the best American coverage of them in their mop-top years. Through her friend Nat Weiss, who was a business associate of Brian Epstein's, she made contact with the group's road managers, Neil Aspinall and Malcolm Evans, and contracted them to write a series of articles on the group. She also got stories from Johnny Hamp, a TV producer in London. This was one of the few times when Gloria had to be truly aggressive to get material on a popular phenomenon, and she welcomed the challenge.

She eventually did get access to each Beatle. In an article in *Career Girl* magazine (circa 1967) Gloria breathlessly described her initial encounter with the Fab Four. "I burst through the door [presumably, of their hotel room] and said, 'Hi! I'm from *16*!' They all jumped up and shook my hand and said, 'You don't look sixteen—you look much younger!'" According to Gloria, from that moment, a lasting friendship

developed. How deep that "friendship" ever was, or really went, is debatable, but it is true that she was one of the few photographers invited to cover the shooting of the movie *Help!* in the West Indies at a time when few journalists could get near them.

"*16* WAS CUTESVILLE ON ICE" —PAUL M.

Naturally, thousands of journalists and photographers came and went through the revolving door that was the Beatles phenomenon and it's safe to say that Paul, George, and Ringo remember few, if any, of them.

However, when we contacted Paul McCartney about his memories of *16* and Gloria Stavers, he did recall her and the publication. "We were aware of *16 Magazine* even before we came to America. We knew it was America's greatest teen magazine. We knew we needed to be in it, although we thought of it as 'cutesville on ice.' I remember Gloria as being very dignified, very professional, totally businesslike. She inspired respect from all of us."

By 1966, however, the Beatles were getting a bit "hippy" and "druggy" for *16*'s young audience and were growing facial hair—ugh! Besides, younger, cuddlier, and more malleable groups such as Herman's Hermits and the Monkees had been spawned in the wake of the Beatles. Amazing but true, Beatles coverage in *16* slowed down and, except for an occasional update, had completely stopped well before the group broke up in 1969.

*The Beatles were shot by famous photogs the world over: this was taken by **16**'s own Gloria Stavers, in the West Indies during the filming of **Help!** Some were published in **16**, others have never been in print before now.*

JOHN LENNON

answers 40 intimate questions

What is your full real name?
John Winston Lennon.
Where and when were you born?
I was born on October 9, 1940, in Liverpool, England.
What is your height, weight and coloring?
I have medium brown hair and brown eyes, and am just under six feet tall. I weigh 159 pounds.
How did you first get interested in music?
My mother (who passed away when I was 13) used to sing and play the banjo for me. My dad sang too.
Who looked after you after your mother passed away?
My Aunt Mimi. She's a wonderful lady and is terribly "knocked out" by the way I got to the top.
Did your father remarry?
Yes, and I have two stepsisters, Julia and Jacqueline, whom I'm quite fond of.
Why do you prefer not to talk about your marriage?
For only one reason: that sort of thing is terribly personal. It's really private business.
But what if your fans want to know?
For the record, here are the facts: I met Cynthia in Art School and I flipped for her. Soon, we were married. We now have one eight-months-old son, John.
Where do you live?
For the time being, we stay with Aunt Mimi or Cynthia's mum when we're not traveling. I try to take Cynthia everywhere I go.
Is it true that she has never seen The Beatles work on stage?
More or less. She is the quiet type and won't come around when there are screaming crowds—and such has been the case for the past year.
What do you dislike about your work?
Having to get up at 5 A.M. to make a booking in some faraway city. It's murder!
What kind of clothes do you like to wear?
Neat lines in dark shades. I love suede, leather and cord.
What kind of clothes do you dislike?
Baggy things or anything in a bright color.
Is it true that you and Paul wrote *She Loves You* the day before it was recorded?
It was a few hours more than 24.
What is your hobby?
Painting. I was a serious art student in college.

How was high school?
Dreadful. I was so bad in math and science that I almost failed.
What subjects did you like most?
Writing, athletics and art.
Who does the falsetto effects and harmonica on The Beatles' records?
Me, John Lennon.
What kind of music do you like?
Real rhythm and blues and gospel.
Who are your favorite singers?
The Shirelles, Little Richard, Ben E. King and Chuck Berry —to name a few.
Who are your favorites for acting?
Brando and Brigitte Bardot.
What are your favorite foods?
Curry, jelly and tea.
Do you have a pet fear?
Yes, growing old. I hate the thought of that. Who'd want to hear a croaking Beatle of 80?
Who in the group said you Beatles are "crummy" musicians?
We don't profess to be brilliant musicians. I'd be the first to say that our success is all out of proportion to our musical talent.
What do you dislike about yourself?
The fact that I'm so short-sighted. Off stage, I have to wear very thick glasses. On stage, I can't see the crowd, but I know they are there by their screams. The boys have a lot of fun telling me the *wrong* door to go through, and I often end up in a cupboard!
Do you think the group will ever split up?
We all know that one Beatle is no good. I tried singing on my own once, and I never felt so soft (out of it) in my life.
What is your ambition?
The first one is to write a musical with a lot of humor in it.
What is the other one?
To make a lot of money; to be a real millionaire.
Do you have a secret longing?
Yes, to buy a house that is on its own grounds, surrounded by high shrubbery and very private.
What kind of people do you dislike?
Stupid people. I can't stand to be around slow-witted dumb-heads.
What is your pet hate?
Driving cars.
What do you plan to invest your money in?
I'd like to invest in a string of high-class clothes shops.
Why did The Beatles cancel all one-nighters throughout England?
Because of the riots. Now, when we play any town, we visit *three* nights. This way everyone who wants to see us gets a chance.
Who deserves most credit for helping The Beatles to get where they are today?
Brian Epstein, without a doubt. We used to hang around his record shop, playing discs but not buying them. Little did any of us dream we were destined to work together one day.
What was the very first name of the group?
The Quarrymen. We had many names later, until The Silver Beatles finally was just nipped to The Beatles.
How did you decide on your "puddin-basin" haircuts?
Well, our hair was just growing most of the time. One of us got dunked in a pool once and the hair dried in that "position." All the rest dug it — so that was that.
Are you going to publish a book of poetry?
I'm thinking of it, but it may be too Liverpudlian for Americans.
What was your first professional booking?
In Hamburg, Germany, in August of 1960. We filled in for a group called Cass And The Casanovas, who couldn't make it.
When did you first play Liverpool professionally?
At the end of '60, when we got back from Germany. Because the public didn't know who we were, we were billed as being "Direct From Hamburg!"
What are the best addresses to write to the Beatles?
Our office is at Sutherland House, 5th floor, 5-6 Argyll Street, London, W.1., England; for fan Club information write to Beatles, U.S.A., Box 305, Radio City Station, New York City 10019.

John answered these customized questions for the June 1964 issue.

PAUL McCARTNEY'S BIGGEST SECRET

JEALOUSY is a green-eyed, vicious thing. It did its best to destroy Paul's love for Jane Asher — and forced him to live a lie. This is the story of his SECRET nightmare.

PAUL McCARTNEY stood listening on the phone. Slowly his sparkling, impish eyes clouded over and soon his look was one of dread and great concern. His pink cheeks turned white and he looked for all this world like a man who had just seen death.

"Put on a disguise," he finally whispered into the mouthpiece. "I'll send the driver over and he'll bring you to the usual place."

As a second thought, he added, "Don't worry, Jennie. We'll straighten it out."

Paul hung up the phone and moved across the room like a man in a nightmare. He spoke calmly to the driver, who departed immediately, but Paul McCartney really *was* living a nightmare. The most important thing in his life was being slowly and viciously taken from him. The girl he loved was being cruelly and systematically destroyed by those who *claimed* to love Paul. The end was in sight and there was no way out.

It all began when Paul met Jane Asher on a British TV show. She was only a consultant, but Paul managed to get to her, introduce himself and ask her for a date. The Beatles were not so famous then and were considered by some to be beneath a society girl like Jane. But Jane didn't give a fig for that wash. She happily accepted Paul's invitation and that's the way the big love in Paul's life began. It was inevitable that the public would learn about the sweethearts. They were both getting too well known to go unrecognized and, in fact, they did not try to hide their romance.

Then the trouble began. At first, it was only a couple of nasty letters and crank phone calls, and Jane and Paul brushed them aside, but as time went by the hate campaign conducted by a group of girls who "loved" Paul took on giant and frightening overtones. Jane would get calls from girls who would not identify themselves, but would mutter menacing threats and hang up. Some of the letters were detailed descriptions of what the "under-*un*-signed" were going to do to Jane to ruin her forever. Jane was threatened daily by such things as having acid thrown in her face ("... so that you will be so ugly that Paul will hate you," the writer claimed), being crippled ("... you will be a burden and he will despire you"), being burned ("... your hair will fall out and you will be scarred for life"), and finally — on that dreadful day of the phone call to Paul — that she would be *murdered!*

Living in fear of these threats day after day took its toll on Jane's nerves, and when she received a note that someone was planning to kill her, it was just too much to bear. In her despair she turned to Paul for help.

After a long discussion, Paul and Jane decided that their only alternative was to keep their love-life "top secret." They stopped going out in public together. When they went to a private party or a film they traveled in disguise and in separate cars. When Paul visited Jane at her home, he was sneaked inside the house in milk trucks and the like. To all the world it seemed as though their famous romance had "cooled." Paul denied that he went steady with Jane and claimed that he dated many other girls.

As the rumors died down, so did the evil fervor of the girls who claimed that they would see Jane ruined or *dead* before they would let her "take Paul from us." The letters grew infrequent and the phone calls ceased. The ordeal of pretending not to care for one another was almost as hard on Paul and Jane as the "hate seizure" had been, but they remained calm and courageous through it all.

Then a wonderful thing happened. It started slowly and the two young lovers were afraid it was too good to be true at first. The mail that came to Jane's house changed its tone completely. Instead of "hate" letters, Jane began to get "love" letters from Paul's fans. Not a few of these mentioned the stories in *16,* which explained to Paul's fans what a fine, lovely person Jane really is. Many of Paul's fans became ardent Jane Asher fans. They saw her movie (*Masque Of The Red Death*) and flipped for her. They read about the nice things she does for their hero and began to feel kindly toward her. They learned that Jane didn't want Paul all to herself, that she understood how the fans felt and wanted to be their friend and share Paul with them — and they felt love and admiration for her. In fact, the tide has turned so completely that if Paul and Jane *don't* get married eventually, many of their fans will be heartbroken!

As the mail poured in, Jane and Paul realized that they would no longer be forced to keep their love a secret. They could go out together again, be seen together, say what they pleased to the press — and best of all, to their loving fans who had stood up for them and seen Paul through this terrible ordeal.

Paul and his "Jennie."

Paul, of course, was the most popular Beatle. The picture accompanying the revelation of his "biggest secret" indicates why. This is from the February 1965 issue.

The Fab Four were goaded to explode by nasty lies about them, according to the cover of the October 1966 issue.

The Rolling Stones

Years of *16* Popularity: 1964–1966

The Stones were the "anti-Beatles," basing their music on American r&b roots rather than the softer English music hall style that influenced the Beatles' sound. Rebellious, good-looking, stylish, and sexy, they were the bad boys of the first British Invasion, and wildly popular in America. Their signature song, "Satisfaction," reached #1 on the American charts in 1965, and there was no stopping the Stones from that moment on. Along with the Beatles, they have certainly been the most influential band in the history of rock music; what's more, although it's nearly 30 years since the Beatles broke up, the Rolling Stones continue as a recording and performing entity.

The Stones were by no means "cuddly," therefore providing the touch of spice that *16* always liked in the mix. In the August 1964 issue, in a story headlined "Has England Gone Too Far?", they were described as "sloppy, pallid, unkempt, and weird-looking," prophetically complimentary adjectives when applied to teenagers of later decades.

MISSED THE BOAT?

That the Stones were not essential in *16*'s world of Beatles, Hermits, and DC5, is illustrated by this anecdote: In the spring of '66, I (co-author Danny Fields) was the editor of *Datebook* magazine, a weak rival of *16*'s. The Rolling Stones held a floating press conference on a boat that embarked from New York's 79th Street pier, but the inept photographer assigned by my publisher to accompany me arrived with no film, and the time it took to stock him up caused us to get to the dock as the Stones' boat was pulling away. I was heartbroken.

A black limousine pulled up next to me, and Gloria Stavers got out. I had met her once before in my life, and she had not been very cordial. At this moment, a little man with a motorboat approached us and said he could take us out to the Stones' yacht for $20. It was not an amount I could come up with myself, so I said to Gloria, "Would you like to split it, and catch the boat?"

"Fuck it," she said, "the Rolling Stones aren't worth ten dollars." She got back into her car and was driven away. In retrospect, I don't think the pulling power of the Stones in *16* was the only factor at work; when Gloria was clearly to be only one of many photographers in a situation, she lost interest. For her, it was a *16* exclusive, or nothing at all.

(l. to r.) Bill, Keith, Charlie, Brian, Mick—The Rolling Stones, circa 1965.

THE ROLLING Has England Gone

Write and tell us what YOU think!

THE DADS are yelling and the Mums are pulling their hair out — but their sons and daughters just couldn't care less. The Rolling Stones may be sloppy, pallid, unkempt and weird-looking, but the teenagers of England have gone absolutely bananas over these five fantastic young men.

The Stones (that's the *only* hip thing to call them) are a thing unto themselves. No other group can touch them, either musically (a combination of hard-rock and down-home true rhythm 'n' blues) or for looks (let the pictures speak for themselves).

So here they are, one at a time, for you to meet and greet on their first trip to America!

MICK JAGGER

Mick plays the harmonica and is lead singer. He was born in Hampstead, London, England, on July 26, 1944. He is tall and dark, and when he starts to move in front of the mike, the girls go wild. His favorite dance is his own interpretation of the Twist. He went to school at the London School of Economics and used to be considered an "egghead."

KEITH RICHARD

Keith, who vaguely resembles a brunet English sheep dog, plays the guitar with The Stones. He also was born in Hampstead, his birthday being December 18. He is 20 years old. Keith has a dry (oh, very dry, sense of humor), and insists that his previous occupation was a "layabout." His hobby is sleeping and his dislikes include "the fuzz." His likes include guitars, boats and gardening of a sort. He insists that the first film he ever starred in was *The Sheik* with Rudolph Valentino!

BRIAN JONES

Brian divides his first love equally between the guitar and the harmonica. Born in London on February 28, 1944, he lists his favorite composers as Lennon-McCartney — followed by Johannes Sebastian Bach! Because *gear* is one of his favorite words, he uses it to describe the kind of clothes he likes to wear. Brian, whose warm smile draws screams of delight from his avid fans (when he finally decides to turn it on), had various jobs before tying up with The Stones. His biggest concern in life right now is how to stop smoking.

Keith and Mick.

Bill Wyman.

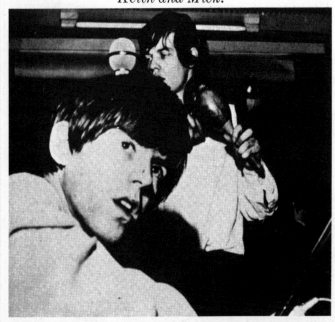

*The Rolling Stones' first appearance in **16** was the August 1964 issue setting them up for future use, if need be, as (our very own) juvenile delinquents.*

STONES– Too Far?

BILL WYMAN

Bill, who looks like a young, handsome Abraham Lincoln, plays bass guitar with the group. He makes his home in Beckenham, Kent, England. He was born on October 24, 1941. Chuck Berry and Jimmy Reed have greatly influenced his musical thinking. He used to be an engineer, and likes cashew nuts and astronomy. Dislikes: arguments, marmalade and traveling.

CHARLIE WATTS

The last "nutty head" in this row of Stones is drummer Charlie Watts. Charlie makes his home in Wembley, Middlesex, where he was born on June 2, 1941. He digs the soul and "roots" music of Muddy Waters and Bo Diddley. For singing, he chooses Sammy Davis, Jr., and Mick Jagger. An art lover, he goes for Picasso. Charlie used to be a graphic designer (a hip one, of course), and he lists his hobbies as GIRLS!

Bill, Charlie, Brian and Mick in Ready Steady Go.

Rolling Stones—Mick Jagger, Keith Richard, Brian Jones, Bill Wyman and Charlie Watts.

WATCH OUT, WORLD—HERE COME THE ROLLING STONES!

Bill, Keith and Brian on Thank Your Lucky Stars.

Dave Clark 5

Years of *16* Popularity: 1964–1967

Somewhere between the adora-Beatles and the raucous Rolling Stones stood Dave Clark and his perfectly polished band: Mike Smith, Rick Huxley, Lenny Davidson, and Denis Payton—the DC5, as they were quickly tagged. A popular London-based beat group who'd enjoyed success on their home turf, they were poised to launch worldwide when their single, "Glad All Over" knocked the Beatles' "I Want to Hold Your Hand" out of the #1 spot on Britain's charts in January 1964.

Armed with that ditty, plus the follow-up, "Bits & Pieces," they landed, as *16* would put it, "on these shores" during that first wave of the British invasion. According to Dave himself, in fact, for a good 18 months (during '64 and '65) the British Invasion *was* those three supergroups. "What a lot of people forget is that we had a couple of years of a clear run."

That was serendipitous for *16*, since getting quotes, pix, and cooperation from the DC5 was a snap compared to getting anything exclusive from JohnPaulGeorge&Ringo and far more important than chasing mischievous Mick and his lot. That said, however, it also should be noted that *16* never attempted to portray the DC5 as more popular than the Beatles. The DC5 almost never got the top banner, and sometimes they weren't mentioned on the cover at all. Still, a great relationship between magazine and musicians did form. It was during the DC5's first appearance on *The Ed Sullivan Show* in March 1964 that Gloria Stavers turned up, pen in hand, 1,000-watt charm turned on.

DAVE DISHES!

"It's only now that you realize what an amazing time it was. It was a whole cultural revolution in music, fashion, the arts. It was exciting, and we didn't have the horrific things that we have today, like heavy drugs, AIDS. Instead, we just had a lot of freedom.

"We started as a band in 1962, and prior to late 1963, we hadn't even heard of *16 Magazine*; it wasn't sold in England. We hadn't heard of *The Ed Sullivan Show*, either. So when we started making music, we had no great ambition to be involved with either one. In fact, we didn't even go professional really until after our second hit single. But, of course, everything changed from that moment on.

"It was after that first *Sullivan* appearance that *16* came on the scene. That's when we got the full import of how powerful the magazine was, and of course, were happy to be in it. Part of that had to do with Gloria Stavers, its editor-in-chief and pretty much the only person we dealt with at first. We met for the first time in New York at the Warwick Hotel— it was the only hotel to stay at in those days because they tolerated the screaming mobs outside.

"Gloria was not only classy, but very lovely. And she didn't look like a journalist. She looked like a model, tall, slim, elegantly dressed, like she'd just walked off the catwalk. We didn't expect her to pull out a pad and pen and start interviewing us. We may have reacted to her more as a beautiful woman than a journalist, but over the years, we realized how brilliant she was. She knew what the kids wanted. She helped them to fulfill their dreams. When it got into what they would like, or what they hoped for, she obviously knew and had great taste."

FAIR ALL OVER

"*16*'s interviews were always done with the entire band, not just the lead singer or 'the cute one,' or the band member the group was named for. I was pleased that the boys got their justified recognition, which they should have. Often, the press just hones in on one or two people. But we were the DC5, not just Dave Clark. It was a unit and it didn't matter who contributed what, and as a unit it worked. So I liked what *16* did, they actually got to delve into the individual guys and I thought that was important. This was *the* magazine

name DAVE'S NEW DOG and WIN a treasure chest from DAVE and the DC 5!

HI!

It's me, Dave Clark—and my brand-new friend, an 18-month-old Great Dane named (of all things!) "The Honorable Lanes Turn The Executives." Now, anyone plainly knows that you simply can't run around calling a dog like so, "Here, 'The Honorable Lanes Turn The Executives'—here!" Why, he'd have eaten up half the garden before you could get all that out!

So you see what my problem is: I *have* to have a simple, straight-to-the-point (but super-groovey) nick for this noble chap. "T.H.L.T.T.E." was a surprise gift from one of my American booking agents, and is a very special kind of Great Dane that you can't get in England. My Boxer "Spike" and myself are are having quite a rave-up with our new friend, but — like I said — we need a name to call him by.

Now, that's where you come in: could you help me out? There is a coupon on this page for any of you *16* readers to mail in with your suggested name for my new dog. When all the suggestions are in, I'm going to read them and pick out the one name I think is most suitable for my Great Dane. And your work won't be in vain. The originator of the name I choose is going to get a surprise English *DC5 Treasure Chest* from myself and the rest of the guys.

Here is a small sample of what will be in your *DC5 Treasure Chest*:

A lovely leather handbag from England's famous Carnaby Street (I'll pick it out myself).

A large, personally autographed black and white picture of the Dave Clark 5.
A set of English crest cuff links.

A bottle of my favorite English cologne.

The sound track of *Catch Us If You Can*, plus a copy of a taped interview we did for the movie.

A sterling silver identification bracelet, with your name on one side and mine on the other.

A personal, handwritten "thank you" note from me, and a picture of my Great Dane and me for you to keep and pin up on your wall—

A portable hairdryer from Mike Smith.

A gold and opal pin from Denis Payton.

A teardrop pearl pendant on a gold chain from Rick Huxley.

A pink perfume atomizer from Lenny Davidson.

All this plus a free one-year subscription to 16 Magazine!

Now, all of that is a pretty pleasing bundle for any girl to find on her doorstep—so get busy and fill in the coupon and mail it off to *16*! Who knows, you may be the lucky one who'll pick just the right name for my dog—and who will be the lucky winner of this one-of-a-kind *Dave Clark 5 Treasure Chest!*

The Name Dave's Dog contest appeared in the May 1966 issue. It looked like a come-on, but it wasn't.

STRANDED on a DESERT ISLAND
with ^ONE OF THE DAVE CLARK FIVE!

Imagine YOU all alone on a tropical isle with your choice of one of the Dave Clark Five! But which one will it be? Test yourself and see!

YOU are stranded on a desert island — a very lovely one, granted — but you are all alone! Ah, what's this? Here comes your guardian angel and she is going to let you have one of five things to relieve your loneliness!

Read what those dolls, the Dave Clark Five, choose, then write your own personal choice in the blank space left for you — and find out which one of the boys would make the ideal companion for you!

YOU MAY CHOOSE ONE LONG-PLAYING RECORD ALBUM TO LISTEN TO. WHICH DO YOU PICK?

Dave: Anything by the Beach Boys.
Mike: Buddy Greco Singing Sweet And Tender.
Denis: Any Stan Getz recording.
Rick: Django Reindhart — any LP by him.
Lenny: Make Way For Dionne Warwick.
YOU: . . . .

YOU MAY CHOOSE ONE SWEETHEART TO BE WITH YOU. WHOM DO YOU CHOOSE?

Dave: One who can cook!
Mike: A sweet and very feminine girl.
Denis: A fishing rod.
Rick: Gladys Bloggs.
Lenny: Natalie Wood.
YOU: . . . .

And then, of course, there were the silly articles, like the one from the February 1965 issue. The fans loved it;
Dave and the band had no problems with it.

YOU MAY CHOOSE ONE FAVORITE FOOD. WHAT DO YOU PICK?

Dave: Steak.
Mike: Roast beef and Yorkshire pudding.
Denis: Chinese food.
Rick: Any Chinese dish.
Lenny: Curried chicken.
YOU: . . . .

YOU MAY CHOOSE A BEST FRIEND TO KEEP YOU COMPANY. WHOM DO YOU PICK?

Dave: Spike, my Boxer dog.
Mike: The girl in the second question.
Denis: Sid Bloggs.
Rick: Fred Bloggs.
Lenny: John Henry.
YOU: . : . . . .

YOU MAY SELECT ONE TV SHOW TO WATCH. WHAT DO YOU PICK?

Dave: Ready, Steady, Go — our best pop music show.
Mike: Ready, Steady, Go.
Denis: Steptoe And Son.
Rick: Steptoe And Son.
Lenny: The Flintstones.
YOU: . . . .

YOU MAY SELECT ONE MOVIE STAR WHOSE FILMS WILL BE SHOWN TO YOU. WHOM DO YOU CHOOSE?

Dave: Paul Newman.
Mike: Steve McQueen.
Denis: Humphrey Bogart.
Rick: Kim Novak.
Lenny: Kirk Douglas.
YOU: . . . .

Dave Clark 5

that catered to what the kids wanted to know—what each individual one of the guys was about, what their likes and dislikes were.

"And I can honestly say we never had any big fallout. There were no jealousies; we pretty much felt similarly on group matters. We agreed to not go professional until we had our second #1 record because we didn't want to be a flash in the pan. We agreed to stop when we had our last million-seller, to go out a success. So we started and ended and there was never any animosity or whatever. I realize now how lucky we were, because we never had one dispute. That is fact. It's a bit like a football team, because there's one captain and somebody's got to make the decision—whether it's the right or the wrong one, you don't know until later—but if you get four or five 'generals' that's going to be a problem.

"Did the actual articles reflect who we really were? There was some artistic freedom taken, the odd inaccuracy, sometimes what would come out in the magazine might be the wrong 'favorite color' or whatever, but we were asked, we did do the interviews. I think we were presented pretty much as we were. But without any embellishments added, we might have been boring!

"I wouldn't have done this many articles for *16* if I didn't like what had been written. We obviously liked it and that's the reason we were always happy to do interviews, always cooperative. In those days, everybody was after us to do things, but we always gave *16* quite a bit of our time."

CONTESTS! GIVEAWAYS! YOU CAN WIN!

"What I remember most about *16* is all the contests. Obviously Gloria decided what the prizes would be, and then she'd ask us for pictures, albums, or some personal item of clothes or whatever. Whatever she picked was what kids wanted. So the prizes might not have been our idea, as the magazine wrote it up, but fair enough. We felt *16* knew what people wanted—besides, we wouldn't have had the time to do it ourselves anyway.

"There was one contest that might've seemed farfetched, but was actually quite real. I had received a dog as a gift, and Gloria ran a contest where *16*'s readers could give the pup a name. And that really happened. The dog was a champion Great Dane that was unavailable in England. It was a gift from my American agents, and had pedigree papers with the name, 'The Honorable Lanes Turn the Executives.' Naturally, you can't really call a dog that; it was too much of a mouthful.

"So it was Gloria who came up with the idea to have *16*'s readers get involved. 'Why not let us name the dog?' she asked me. That was fine. I still remember the winning entry: Rocky. And that was long before the Stallone movies."

"THE NIGHT I ALMOST DIED!"

"Of course there were always stories that were glossed up, embellished. But in our case, not as often as one might think. When the headline, 'The Day They Almost Died' ran, it wasn't a come-on. The article recounted a true story that happened to us, about the time we thought we were going to die in a plane crash. We'd missed our flight out of Hong Kong and had to get somewhere for a TV gig, and the only seats available were on an Air India flight. Midway through the flight, the aircraft got hit by lightning and dove down at a sharp angle. As the plane was hurtling downward, I remember thinking, 'Screw it, I'm not going to get a chance to drive my new car!' The stupid things you think of. Anyway, when the story came out in *16*, there was a lot of truth to it. Of course, it was embellished somewhat, some artistic freedom was taken, but that, again, was okay."

"HAS THE JIVE FIVE CRUSHED THE BEATLES BEAT?"

"Then again, there were other types of articles that had very little truth in them. Most of the press, *16* included, jumped on the 'rivalry' bandwagon, which was something completely created by them. It was us against the Beatles, us against the Stones, they'd pit each of the guys in one group against members of the others. That was a big thing in all the magazines, and totally false. But no one got angry. We laughed about it with John and Paul, because there was no rivalry, just healthy competition. And one that obviously sold magazines: people who were Beatles fans bought it for that; people that were DC5 fans bought it too.

"Still, the perception lives on. Tom Hanks said it on a talk show when he was promoting his movie, *That Thing You Do*—he discussed the rivalry between the DC5 and the Beatles as if it were fact. He was a DC5 fan and asked to meet me while he was making his movie."

"WHAT WE HAD TO HIDE"

"Did *16* cover up behavior that might have been unacceptable to its readers? Let me put it this way. It was a different time. It wasn't just *16*; we had this rapport with the

Dave Clark 5

English press as well. Certainly Gloria was one of those people who would come right out and ask, 'Is this true?' And you could say, 'Yes, but I'd rather you not print it,' and that was respected. I always felt you should be truthful, because if you're not, it gets exaggerated out of proportion and in the end, it would have been better to just say yes, we did do this, or we didn't do this.

"Were we fooling around? Of course, we're human, but all the guys had serious girlfriends. We didn't have groupies lined up outside the door—I mean, we did, but not lined up for feasting. Girls in the room, you get that, but that's all been printed.

"But (that said) there were no dark things in a closet. We were what we were—warts and all. Sometimes people think, oh, that's an image, and when they close the door, they're completely different. But it was quite accurately printed, what we were really like. The English groups as a whole, I think, were fairly open. The Beatles were, and even the Stones, who went out of their way to be controversial. They felt that's how they had to be to make it in America.

"As for us, the image had its advantages and disadvantages. We wore these white collars in our first appearance; people thought we were whiter than white. But that's life, you know."

WHAT MADE IT ALL HAPPEN

"Those first two years were the most exciting. We went from earning about $30 a week to, after being on *The Ed Sullivan Show*, having our own plane! And playing to 30,000 people. The whole thing changed overnight, and it all happened because of the unique combination of radio, the Sullivan show, and *16 Magazine*. Radio stations made your records, but they couldn't project the faces behind the performance. So you needed the Sullivan show for that: it took you into every American home. *16 Magazine* was the icing on the cake, because it actually got into who the guys in the group were, what you liked, what you didn't like, which couldn't be portrayed on radio and television. So it was a combination of the three coming together; one without the other wouldn't have worked. *16* was an enormously powerful magazine; it gave us our audience."

"DID I GET YOUR LETTER?"

"We actually read a lot of our fan mail. We spent so many hours in the plane—we had our own DC5 (!)—we actually did read it, 'cause it's a long jump between New York and L.A. or whatever. It would be wrong to say we read each one, because there were hundreds on each trip. But the way it worked was, somebody from our fan club would go through them all and pull out the ones we should read. We'd go through it, and if they had requests that could be fulfilled, we did it, if there were photos to sign, we would, whatever.

"The truth is, if a fan sent a letter to us through *16*, the chances we read it were even better. Because Gloria sent us stacks of mail and all that stuff, we actually did read it. I think you owe that to your fans. Without them, you're not going to sell any records or whatever. There comes a stage where you have to have two sides of you, the private side and the public side. You should switch off from one to the other. But reading the mail is how you stay in touch with the fans.

"We took that as important, but we had a pretty good attitude about the fame aspect. Here's something I did say in *16* that was true and I still believe it: You're only as good as your next record. If the bubble bursts tomorrow we've achieved more than we ever dreamed of achieving; we were never under any false illusions. It's great, if you take that attitude, you enjoy it. You're not on a tightrope where you feel that if the next record doesn't succeed it's the end of the world."

THE SONG THAT MEANS THE MOST

"If I had to choose one song to be remembered by, it would be 'Because.' It was a special song. They made a mistake with it in England and put it on the B side. The record company felt a ballad wouldn't sell after having four or five big hits and up-tempo songs. I knew that was wrong, but I thought, well, I wrote it, maybe I'm just too close to it. So I allowed myself to be swayed. But by the time we were ready to release it in America, I felt more strongly about it. So when the president of the record company in America also refused to release it as an A side, I said, fine, if you don't, then I'm not going to release another record.

"He responded with a cable that said, 'This will ruin your career. You've got 48 hours to change your mind, or your career will be ruined!' I sent a cable back saying, 'I'm sorry, we are releasing it.' And, of course, it went on to be one of our biggest selling singles.

"The moral of the story is, you have to go with your gut feeling. You'll never know if you were right or wrong until later. That's life. But if I had the chance to do it all over again, I'm sure I'd do all the same things."

DAVE CLARK 5 THE DAY THEY ALMOST DIED!

THEIR plane was zipping down the runway when suddenly there was the sound of ripping fabric and scraping metal—!

ON FRIDAY, November 20th last, Dave Clark, Mike Smith, Denis Payton, Rick Huxley and Lenny Davidson piled aboard their chartered twin-engine Martin 404 for the fast hop from San Francisco to Las Vegas.

"We fastened our safety belts," Dave recalls, "and the captain taxied to the end of the runway and made a final check of all the instruments. It is a beautiful plane and we really enjoyed the flights in it between dates. The seats convert into beds and there is a galley that can serve anything from fish and chips to caviar.

"Just before take-off I looked around the cabin, casually. Lenny, who is our lead guitarist, was slumped in his seat with his eyes shut. He couldn't wait to catch up on his beauty sleep. The rest of the fellows were chatting or glancing at the magazines we had just purchased. I wasn't thinking of anything in particular as the plane edged forward and then, with a sudden thrust of power, was zipping down the runway. All at once there was a loud, shattering noise — the sound of ripping fabric and scraping metal — and the plane rocked violently from side to side. I turned all around trying to figure out what had happened, but from where I was sitting I could not see that our plane wing had tangled with the wing of a big DC6."

News Bulletin! **The Dave Clark Five narrowly escaped disaster when their chartered plane was involved in a crash with another plane in take-off from the San Francisco Airport. The boys were badly shaken up. Both planes were damaged, and fire engines and ambulances were rushed to the scene. . . .**

This startling announcement broke through the music on radio stations all across the country — and millions of teeners (and avid DC5 fans) clamored into their phones, demanding to know what had happened. When the smoke had died down (both literally and figuratively), Dave and the boys were able to set the record straight from their point of view.

Dave: "I'm a fatalist. I mean, I think if your time has come, nothing can stop it. I know that air collisions — whether they are on the ground or in the sky — can be very serious, but I have complete confidence in our personal pilot. It must be well-founded, for he saved us in this one."

Denis: "It all happened before I knew it. I'm glad of that. Anticipation is the best or worst of anything. If I'm going to die, I want to go without knowing it. As we rocked to a standstill, our stewardess told us to get out

THE DAVE CLARK 5

the door at the back as fast as we could. I suppose we were all thinking of the danger of leaking petrol and fire, so we bundled out pretty quickly."

Lenny: "I new least of all what had happened. I had my eyes closed when the two planes collided — and I was nodding away happily. I woke with a start as I felt the impact, and asked the boys, 'What happened?' They told me we had been in a collision. 'What — in the air?' — I gasped. 'No, you clot, we're still on the ground,' they said — and I nearly fainted from relief."

Mike: "We bundled out of the plane and people came running toward us looking far more alarmed than we felt. We were escorted back to the airport lounge and someone brought coffee to steady our nerves. It had just happened — *wham!* — like that, and we were out of the plane before we had any idea what a narrow escape we'd had. The two pilots had a time wrenching their craft apart, then both planes were grounded for repairs."

Rick: "We'd had a near miss, sure, but it wasn't that that scared me so much as the news and rumors I *knew*

Articles like this—from the April 1965 issue—were not simply sensationalistic come-ons: the group almost did perish in an air crash, and more than once!

DAVE

DENIS

LENNY

RICK
MIKE

were about to cross the Atlantic. I didn't want my wife to hear anything bad and get upset. Later, I learned that one report said we'd crashed in the air over the airport! And there we were, all the while safe and sound, drinking coffee, when the calls started coming through. First of all, Epic Records rang up and nearly had kittens until we got on the line and assured them we were all right and could continue the tour when we got another plane."

A final word from Dave: "It was an alarming experience, without my actually sensing the physical shock of fear. There was none of this business of last thoughts and frantic prayers. It was only later that we realized that it could have been a much closer call — even a disaster — so let's once again thank our great pilot, Capt. Hollingdale, for his expert handling of his craft in a tight spot.

"And don't worry, this won't stop us from flying. It hasn't even made us jittery about planes. What happened was a chance in a million, and it won't occur again. So we'll soon be back — flying all over those lovely United States!"

Dave Clark 5

BITS 'N' PIECES

- The Dave Clark 5 appeared on *The Ed Sullivan Show* more than any other group: 18 times in 3 years.
- The Beatles were not the only ones to make a movie based on a song title: "Catch Us if You Can," made in 1965, can be caught on video.
- They had 17 *Billboard* Top 40 hits, but only one that reached the top spot: "Over & Over."
- Today Dave lives, quite well, in London. He has stayed musically active, but only gets involved in projects that, as he puts it, "fire me up." One of those projects was producing the stage musical *Time*, with Cliff Richard, which was an enormous success in London. Other artists Dave has produced include Stevie Wonder and the late Freddie Mercury.
- It is true that Dave Clark owns all the rights to the music of the DC5, but untrue that he set up the deal because he knew it would make him extremely rich

(though it has). "I own all my own publishing and masters, always have, from the start. It was a matter of artistic control, not because I knew what a clever move that was. Back in those days, I had no money. I worked as a stuntman in the movies, used whatever income I had to finance the records. That's how important it was for me to retain musical freedom. So I made a great deal, I took no money up front, but I owned the masters, and all the rights reverted back to me. I just said, I have to have total creative freedom. If it bombs, I haven't got anybody to blame but myself, and if it hits, great. This is how I always felt, and still do. If you're true to yourself and it doesn't succeed, that's life. But if it succeeds, it's a great satisfaction. But I've always felt if you do things right, you reap the rewards. If not, at least you haven't sold yourself. And that's the way I've always treated life. I just believed in having the artistic freedom of choice, the greatest reward you can get."

The Dave Clark 5 in action—one of the most appealing Bundles From Britain to drop on our shores!

Peter Noone
aka Herman of Herman's Hermits

Years of *16* Popularity: 1965–1967

Whether they called him Herman or by his real name, America's teenage girls fell for Peter Noone, bouffants over bell-bottoms, especially after getting to know him in *16*. Swept in on the tidal wave of the British Invasion, Manchester's Herman's Hermits were collectively younger, cuddlier, and more lovable than the Beatles, the Stones, the Dave Clark 5. Significantly, they were also *way* more accessible, as were their cutesy pop-tinged songs, "Mrs. Brown, You've Got a Lovely Daughter," "(I'm Into) Something Good," "Wonderful World," "Henry the Eighth." Judged solely by the coverage in *16*, it would appear that Herman and his Hermits were second only to the Beatles in overall Brit-group popularity. They were by far the most photographed, most extensively interviewed, the most willing participants. Thanks to *16*, readers practically lived with them; we saw them waking up in the morning, traveling, backstage, onstage, hanging out. Where they went, we went.

Peter Noone, the youngest and cheekiest of the bunch, was easily elected as the squeal-eliciting teen idol. He was especially available to *16* because of his instant—and as it turned out—lasting friendship with Gloria Stavers. Right from the start, she practically maneuvered herself into the band.

As she'd done with the careers of several stars before him, and as she'd do with many after, Gloria helped shepherd Peter's career and shape his image. But their friendship turned out to be based on more than a professional alliance. Peter, along with his wife, Mireille, steadfastly attended to Gloria in the months leading up to her death. They brought her food, newspapers, companionship, love. Gloria's personal friends were on hand, of course, but Peter Noone was the only celebrity who came to see her in the hospital where she spent her final weeks.

Peter Noone's Secret Confessions

"WHICH ONE ARE YOU? SIT THERE!"

"I will never forget the first I'd heard of *16 Magazine*—it was the day I first met Gloria Stavers. It was also the day we first touched down at Kennedy Airport in early 1965. We'd already broken in England and actually had a record on the charts in the U.S.A. We didn't even know it, but apparently *16* had already done some sort of introductory piece on us.

"So we got off the plane and there she was—camera in tow. We were shepherded into these vans, and Gloria hopped in with us and immediately started taking our pictures and giving orders. She didn't bother introducing herself, just pointed the camera and demanded, 'Which one are you?' 'You, move over there, sit next to him!' 'You, over there.' She was pushy, she wasn't friendly, she wasn't Miss Personality, just very aggressive. And, you know, we'd never met any women like that before. But with all that, she wasn't off-putting. There was something about her that we liked right away.

"Even though we didn't know who she was at first, clearly she was someone important. Everybody else there, the record company guys, the bookers—even Neil Bogart [who'd later go on to run Casablanca Records and become one of the most legendary music industry icons of the '70s] was at the airport that day—they all seemed to know who she was, and want her to be with us at all times. It was strange to me, because it seemed *they* were the more important people, but everyone gave her the most respect. She became a part of the band from then on."

WAKE-UP CALL

"I was only 16 myself at the time, very naïve. Gloria paid the most attention to me right from the start. And that was fine with me and with the others in the band, because we all liked her.

"That's how it started, and for several years it didn't let up. Gloria would show up in my hotel room at 8 in the morning because she wanted a picture of me getting up. And wherever we went in the States, she'd come with us, in the car, on the plane, always taking pictures, millions of pictures. If we were in California, she'd show up in California. Once we rented Cary Grant's house to make a movie and she stayed with us. She was always photographing us. I think she took like 6,000,000 pictures.

PETER (HERMAN) NOONE begs

"Please Be MY Bird"

Somewhere a girl is waiting — and someday Peter/Herman will find her. That girl might very well be YOU.

SOMEWHERE in this wide, wide world there is a girl waiting just for me. I believe this with all my heart — because, you see, I too am waiting . . . waiting for her.

So far, I haven't even laid eyes on her, but I know exactly what she looks like. And I know exactly what she *is* like — because this is the girl I love; this is *my* bird.

May I tell you about her? I want to very much, because deep down inside of me a small voice keeps whispering, "Maybe she's out there among *16*'s millions of teen readers! Maybe she's reading these words, right now! And maybe she'll write to you and tell you all about herself — and you'll know, you'll just *know,* the two of you, that you were meant for each other."

This, then, is written to *you* — with the hope that *you* are the one. And just so you'll know what I mean by the *one,* I will tell exactly how I feel about the girl I dream about . . . what she looks like and what she *is* like.

She is blonde, and she is brunette. Her eyes are blue, and brown, and turquoise — oh, many colors. She is tall (but no taller than I am), and medium, perhaps even a trifle short. She is pretty, and not really pretty — physically — at all.

Are you confused? You needn't be. What I am saying is that it is completely unimportant to me whether her hair is black, brown, red or golden; whether her eyes are every color of the rainbow; whether she stands five feet six inches or five feet three inches; whether she is radiantly beautiful or somewhat plain. What I see in my dreams — and what I look for wherever I go — is that special face that glows with honesty, integrity, grace and dignity . . . a natural face, unmarked with heavy make-up, but with just a touch of cosmetics to emphasize the natural loveliness of her *inner* beauty. For inner beauty is lasting beauty — and that is the quality of beauty I seek in the girl I want to be my bird.

I *do* want a beautiful girl, you see; but beautiful beneath the skin — good and generous and intelligent and articulate — because these are the qualities that transform a girl whatever she may lack in physical beauty. They leap to the eye and enchant the ear and leave a lingering impression that surface beauty alone can never match.

Naturalness is the key, of course. Only a natural human being is a lovely human being; a girl who deliberately imagines that she is someone else — a popular star, perhaps — and copies the other's personality and mannerisms is hurting herself much more than she knows, for whatever she says and does is *affected*. And no man (myself included) wants a carbon copy; he wants the real thing.

The girl I want for my very own is lovely from the inside. She is sensitive — and she is understanding. Let me repeat that: she is *understanding*. To someone in show business, like me, an understanding girl is a very precious person. Show business is a demanding, hectic and unpredictable mistress — and every entertainer needs an enormously understanding mate who is not jealous of the time he (or she) spends away from home in pursuit of a successful career and does not complain about it or make an issue of it.

The girl I want to be my bird will be in love with *me,* Peter Noone — as well as with Herman, up there on the stage. Because there is a great difference between Peter Noone and Herman (although I hope you're fond of them both!). In my private life, away from the stage lights and the music and the crowds, I do not carry on in the way I perform when I want to please my (and the Hermits') fans. My personality is quite different — and I need someone who appreciates the difference, and who loves both Peter *and* Herman. Since Herman spends so much time in the glittering world of show business, Peter is fond of getting away from it in the company of a few close friends with whom he can talk about many things, and listen to records, and enjoy a casual snack at home or in an out-of-the-way cafe. The girl I want for my own must take *naturally* to this private part of my life — and enjoy it fully as much as she enjoys seeing me perform in public.

Last, but by no means least, the girl who is waiting for me is *trusting*. She would know, instinctively, that I loved her and needed her even if my work took me to the other side of the world. Trust and understanding are the only weapons a married couple have to combat the separations and gossip of show business. But if two people have them, and a strong love to weld them together, nothing can ever come between them.

If *you* are that special someone waiting somewhere, *please* be my bird. Tell me who you are and where you are — for I too am waiting . . . waiting for *you.*

In March 1967, Peter "begged" (!) for you to be his "bird."

Peter Noone *aka Herman of* **Herman's Hermits**

Portrait of a young Herman taken by Gloria Stavers.

"And it was always very clear that it was all business, all for the magazine, not a sexual thing. It was obvious that she wasn't sexually attracted to me. Later, of course, I'd heard rumors about her, but I never saw any of that; I obviously wasn't one of the people she was attracted to."

HANGING OUT

"After hours, I never hung out with the band; I much preferred hanging out with Gloria, 'cause she knew where to go: clubs in Soho where the band would never go, folksy places like the Bitter End, Max's Kansas City. She introduced me to Phil Ochs. She was sophisticated, she knew everybody in showbiz and in the fashion industry. All that was much more attractive to me than the sort of 13-year-old girls who were running around after us, so I liked to hang out with her. She was hip. She introduced me to people like [the artist] Peter Max, people I was never going to meet hanging out with the Hermits. If I'd hung out with them, all I'd have met was some Mutual of Omaha salesman at the bar at the Hilton.

"The relationship Gloria and I developed became very much a mentor-student one. She widened my horizons remarkably. I would ask her serious questions about the music, about our direction: 'What do you think?' 'Is this going to work?' 'Should we be touring America so much?' She was like our consultant and we certainly benefited from the coverage. People who were big in those days were the people whose pictures were in *16 Magazine.* Of course, the music was important, and we might have sold records and achieved success without it, but *16* made us much bigger. It was the only way kids could find out what they wanted to know—who Paul McCartney and Herman loved—most mainstream publications were not dealing with that aspect."

A SHIT FIT

"Of course there were other teen magazines around at the time—*Tiger Beat* is the one I remember—and Gloria was fiercely competitive. We always gave *16* the first shot at everything, mostly out of loyalty, but partly because we feared her reaction if we didn't. She would get furious with me if I did something for *Tiger Beat*, I mean physically furious. She'd throw a big shit fit, she'd scream, 'How could you do this to me?' She was just furious one time because a girl from *Tiger Beat* had been to the house in California and sort of beat her to the punch, got pictures of us in the pool, stuff like that. And we were all kind of embarrassed because this girl had just shown up—kind of like Gloria had that first day at the airport—and started taking pictures. She did a kind of photo essay, 'A Day in the Life of Herman's Hermits.' Perhaps that had been Gloria's idea as well, because when she found out, she was so furious I almost felt she might hit me. She was so wound up, like a spring ready to pop.

"I was more embarrassed than afraid. I was just embarrassed that we'd done this thing for *Tiger Beat*, because we really were loyal to *16*. Gloria was our one, the first person we met when we got off the plane. Besides, *16* seemed classier than any others. It didn't have any advertisements in it."

"YOU BELONG TO EVERY GIRL"

"We showed up in *16* in all sorts of intimate photos, but never with girlfriends, or groupies that were hanging around. Gloria wouldn't take that kind of picture because she believed that every girl, every reader, 'owned' me. That girl, that *16* reader, was somebody to be protected. You couldn't hurt her,

Peter Noone *aka Herman of* Herman's Hermits

Portrait of a young Herman (left), with the Hermits, taken by Gloria Stavers.

you mustn't say 'shit' onstage or that sort of thing, that's what Gloria taught us. She was the protectress of this little flock of children.

"There was never any sex in *16*. Not only that, we never discussed it. The word never came up between us. Yes, of course there were groupies on the road and after the shows; our band, like other bands, did what bands do with them. Not only did Gloria not cover that sort of thing, she didn't bother being around for it. She didn't hang out at the hotel with us.

"She also didn't photograph, or report on, other silly things we did on the road. We had this thing, we'd get naked and run up and down the lobbies of hotels. But that never appeared in *16*. The readers wouldn't have wanted to know or see it. Of course Gloria knew about all of it, but we implicitly trusted her. We never questioned that she would do the right thing.

"We also fully believed that *16* built this audience for us; *16* built us from being an anonymous record act to being an act, personalities that everyone knew. And as much as she focused on me, she always included the other guys in the band, too. No publication in England was doing that. In England, no one knew the other guys in the band, we just didn't have a publication like that. But thanks to *16*, the girls

in America knew 'Lek's Favorite Hobbies,' stuff like that. Each member got his little page of coverage."

"THE NICEST SIDE OF ME"

"*16*'s stories about me were often written in first person, but I didn't write them. And it wasn't even a situation where I'd sit down and do an interview. Gloria didn't do interviews. Rather, she directed the story she wanted. There weren't often 'stories' anyway, it was more 'Herman's Loves' and all that. A lot of which, I can say now, she made up. She would always change what you really said so it wouldn't offend people. I'd say 'shit,' she'd change it and make it all fluffy.

"We used to fill out these 'fact sheets,' not just for *16*, but for other magazines too. And we always used to write crap. We'd write silly things. If it asked, 'What's your favorite food?' we'd write, 'Afghanistan steak.' And that's how it would show up in the other magazines; it never did in *16*. Gloria always fixed it. Once, she changed it to egg yolks, chips, and steak!

"All that said, still I really *was* the character in the magazine. That's really how I was, quite a nice character. I didn't really want to hurt anybody's feelings and Gloria knew that. I actually did, as *16* said, want to get married and have children. I *was* sort of a romantic guy. Although I wasn't

Peter Noone *aka Herman of* Herman's Hermits

perfect, the guy that *16*'s readers got to know really was me—at least the decent part of me. Gloria ignored anything that could be construed as negative and simply chose the side of me that was the nicest and put that forth in *16*."

"*16* GOT 'BUMS IN THE SEATS'"

"Other musicians felt that being in *16* trivialized the music, and I probably should have been concerned about that. But I never was. Herman's Hermits really *was* bubblegum music. It could have evolved into something more, but we never got the opportunity to get to the next stage, maybe change the name or something. When you're called 'Herman' it's really tough to move along. The big detriment to being in *16* is that now we're remembered not for our music, but more a creation of *16* and magazines like it.

"But let me tell you something. In those days, we were very happy to be a creation of *16 Magazine*. It got 'bums [as in derrieres] in the seats,' as we used to say—people sitting down at the concerts who paid the money and bought the records. Fifty percent of what Herman's Hermits did was tour, and we made much more money from touring than we did from record sales, 'cause the record deals were awful in those days. Touring was where you made the money.

"In retrospect, perhaps we'll never be respected for our music. But *16* always respected the fans, and so did I. I really did."

"IT'S OVER, PETER"

"There was never any bullshit. Gloria was very straightforward with us. When we first started, she told us that when we become 'important' our name would be on the cover, in *16*'s top left-hand corner. And for several years, it was.

"Then, everything changed, the music changed, the climate changed. I knew how big I *wasn't* when I picked up the magazine one day and it was Monkees, Monkees and Davy. And down at the bottom, in a tiny little circle, was Herman, at the bottom of a tree or something. Someone else had replaced me in the top left-hand corner.

"I'll never forget the day Gloria said, quite seriously, 'It's over, Peter. It's gone.' I thought, 'Really great, I just arrived for a 50-day tour and you tell me my music's over. It's gonna be the Doors and Grateful Dead and Big Brother. My kind of stuff isn't gonna be around.'

"But I knew she was right. I knew that Jimmy Page wasn't gonna be playing on Herman's Hermits records. There

was Hendrix and the whole San Francisco thing. There was no way we could compete, unless we got busted for acid or something. The passing thought, 'We'll all get busted for acid and then they'll accept us,' was there. But of course we never did that.

"Gloria was the first person to pick up on Jim Morrison—but she did it because he was photogenic, not because he made good records. He couldn't sing, couldn't dance, couldn't write poetry, but looked good, right?

"Knowing all that, there's still a part of me that believes that the day I got married was the day I stopped being in *16*. It was like I cheated Gloria, or whoever it was Gloria was writing for. When she ran pictures of the wedding, it was like an obituary for the Herman thing. After that, every now and then I'd show up in the Where Are They Now? section. But I knew that was coming. I didn't want it to go on forever. The whole Herman thing was kind of sinister in a way."

WHERE'D EVERYBODY GO?

"Still, I remained friends with her. For Gloria had become a friend, and I'm not the type of person who gives up on friends. So in the ensuing years, when we certainly weren't discussing Herman's Hermits anymore, whenever I was in New York, I'd call her. We'd go to dinner, whatever. And when my wife and I had an apartment on Park Avenue, Gloria would come over and take pictures of us, just for us.

"When she got sick, we spent time with her, ferried her back and forth to the hospital. We'd run interference with the nurses, who she just terrorized. She was kicking ass all over the hospital, and I was making excuses for her—'You have to excuse her, she's very sick.' And I'd try to explain to Gloria, 'You just told this woman she's a complete imbecile who'd be better off dead, and then you said, "Can I get some lightly buttered toast?"' So Mireille and I would go bring her stuff…decent food.

"What still astounds me is that aside from her personal friends, we were the only ones around. When she most needed people, she had all these people she'd done amazing things for…where were they? Had they all just used her, all the rock people?

"Her lasting legacy, I think, can be summed up like this: Every gig I do now, somebody comes up to me with an old copy of *16*—a photo of me holding a doll or something. Strange thing, isn't it? The power *16* still has."

Luke Halpin

Luke Remembers

Years of *16* Popularity: 1964-1966

As Sandy Ricks on the TV series *Flipper*, which ran from 1964 to 1968, N.Y.C.-born and -raised Luke Halpin was one of the most engaging "boy next door" types to make it big in *16*. Educated in schools for child-professionals, he was in several Broadway shows before landing the child star part in the two original *Flipper* movies in the early '60s. Too old to play young "Bud Ricks" by the time *Flipper* went on the air, he got the part of the newly invented older brother, "Sandy." He was the only star, human or animal, to make the transition from *Flipper* movies to *Flipper* television.

Luke's status as a pinup boy was never hurt by the fact that his TV wardrobe always had him in shorts, scuba gear, or something equally minimal, nor by his blond hair, freckles, and the wonderful way he bonded with Suzy, which was the TV dolphin's name in real life.

Luke Halpin now lives outside Orlando with his second wife and 6-year-old son. He also has two children from a previous marriage. He no longer acts, but works as a boat pilot and marine technician in film and TV production. His latest credit is *Speed II*, and we spoke to him from the Key West set of that movie.

"I remember reading those articles in the teen magazines. I didn't answer a lot of those questions. They never got me in any trouble, but that was a weird period in my life. Dating was difficult when I was working on the show, because the girls I would've liked to go out with, wanted to go out with Sandy, not with me. Sometimes I'd read things about myself and think, I didn't really say that and I don't really feel that way but, well, you know…not all of it was accurate. One of the things that stands out in my mind was someone—not *16*—wrote that I didn't like the Rolling Stones. Which wasn't true. I *loved* the Rolling Stones. And I thought, wait a minute, what's the story here? But I was too busy working to make some kind of statement about it.

"I never knew how famous I was until the show was over. I saw enormous amounts of fan mail, but I didn't relate to what it was. I wasn't really aware that girls all over the world had pictures of me on their walls. It was amazing to me to find out what an international hit we were; I think in some places like Japan, *Flipper* is still running.

"The whole experience was a lot of fun, but what people don't really understand is that this is really a lot of hard work. When it's 7 A.M. in the winter in Florida, and it happens to be a 35- or 40-degree day with the wind blowing, and you've gotta get in the water, well, that's not fun. So there was hard work that went into this."

"ALL ABOUT ME!" by LUKE HALPIN

Read the questions you asked in your letters to Luke — and his frank and full answers!

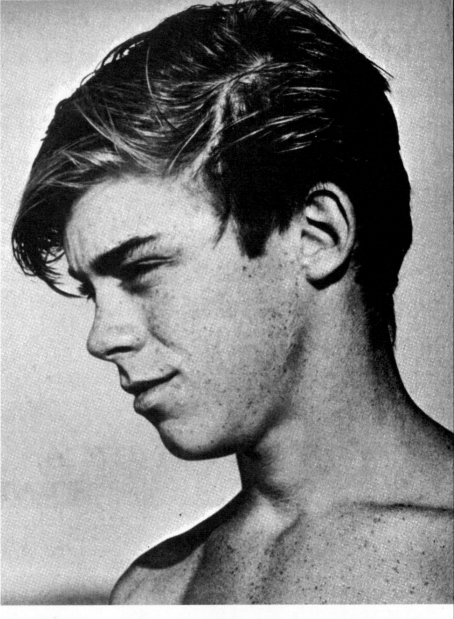

WOW, do I get letters! And letters and letters and letters and, oh well — you know what I mean! And I *love* each and every one of them. But guess what? Right now it is just impossible for me to sit down and personally answer each one — as much as I *want* to.

Since I find that a lot of questions are repeated often in my mail, I have decided to accept *16*'s kind invitation to tell all about myself and, at the same time, let you friends of mine out there in on the real facts about yours truly, Luke Halpin. Here goes:

"Do you live with your parents?"

Definitely. I'm not one of those cats who prefer a bachelor pad. My mom, dad and I live in a modern house in northeast Miami, with a big swimming pool out back. My dog "Whiskey" took an unexpected dip last week when he stepped into the water to grab one of his toys that had fallen in. He really didn't know from water, and you should have seen his look of shock when he bobbed up. I had to go in and get him out. Well, he's no *Flipper*, that's for sure. Recently, a local newspaper printed my home address and phone number. I had *some* time for a while, what with the cars driving by with folks staring in and the boats (there's a channel next to our house) motoring slowly by with more of same. I felt as though I was in a goldfish bowl, but eventually the traffic subsided and everything is back to normal.

"What kind of car do you have?"

Am I *glad* you all asked that! I used to want a Corvette, but finally I decided on a GTO. I am 17 and you can drive in Florida at that age. I use the car on dates and use it to drive to work. A company car used to pick me up, but it's loads more fun to go tooling in at the wheel of my own GTO!

"Have you ever met Patty Duke?"

Surely. I've known Patty for years. We were friends when we studied at *Quintano's School For Professional Children*. We lived in the same Long Island neighborhood, and used to take the Astoria subway into town together. I really like her. She is a lovely, nice person. I never miss her show.

"Is the porpoise on Flipper real?"

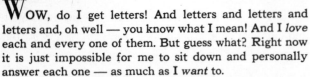

Luke at his adolescent sexiest, in a spread from March 1965.

I'll say. I don't know where some of you got the idea that the porpoises are made of rubber. There are four differents ones used on the show. Their names are Patty, Cathy, Suzie and Scotty. I named them. They are all girls. It seems girl porpies are brighter than boys!

"Do you do your own underwater work?"

Yes. There are no stunt men or stand-ins on *Flipper*. Going underwater is the most interesting part of my work. You have no idea how beautiful it is down there. Once I brought mom a lovely piece of coral. When it dried, it looked like a small black Japanese tree. She keeps it on the mantelpiece.

"Do you wear any jewelry?"

I have two rings that I usually wear. One is a gold "Boy On A Dolphin" ring made from the original antique coin. I understand that there are only four such coins in existence. The producer of the show, Mr. Tors, gifted me with it. I have a diamond and gold ring that my folks gave me about a year ago. I also have a cross on a chain, but I can't wear it on the show because it gets tangled with the equipment I have to use underwater. I wear an underwater wristwatch that is owned by MGM.

"Did you ever make a record?"

Yes. I made an MGM LP called *Flipper's New Adventure*. I narrate the whole story and there is a musical background. On it you can actually hear the sounds porpoises make. If you can't get it at your record store, tell them to order it for you from MGM Records, 1540 Broadway, New York City.

"Would you ever make a singing record?"

As my mom says, "All boys sing!" I sang in the Broadway shows, *Take Me Along* and *Annie Get Your Gun*. If I'm approached, I'd surely like to try it.

"How do you spend your spare time?"

Listening to records. I like all the current hits and I enjoy mom's collection of TV and movie themes. I love listening to the sound track of *West Side History*.

"How did you get started in movies?"

Mr. Tors came to New York for general interviews for someone to play in the original *Flipper* movie. I got an appointment. He asked me if I could swim and I told him yes. He then asked me if I would swim with a *dolphin* — and I said yes. I was a good swimmer (I'd learned in the rough ocean off Long Island). I was just turning 14. He watched me swim in a hotel pool and liked me. Later, he took me to Nassau and introduced me to my first porpoise. I was hesitant to jump in with her. One of the owners, Mrs. Santini, got in with her and showed me how easy it was. The next day I dove right in. I'm still friends with "Mitzi," that first dolphin. Two weeks ago I went to see her where she lives in Key West. I feel sure she recognized me. Porpoises are very sensitive and we have to keep our nails cut low to keep from hurting them.

"Do you have a pet expression that you use a lot?"

You'd better believe it! That's the expression.

"How can we write to you and be sure to get an answer?"

If you write to me personally at 12100 N.E. 16th Ave., Miami, Fla., (send a self-addressed, stamped envelope) I'll personally answer as soon as I can, but I am 'way behind on my mail! For a faster reply, send a self-addressed, stamped envelope to my fan club, in care of Gregg Simpson, 611 South Mashta Drive, Key Biscayne, Miami, Fla.

The Mamas & The Papas

Years of *16* Popularity: 1965–1967

The Mamas & the Papas had a dozen hit singles in their heyday, their vocal harmonies and songs were fabulous, and their aura virtually shouted "Summer of Love, L.A. style." They could, and did, have publicity anywhere and everywhere, but why were they regulars in *16*? They were older, kookier, definitely tinged with a psychedelic aroma, and in no way squeaky clean or cute. There's little question Gloria was enamored of their talent. She told the *Saturday Evening Post* that Denny Doherty was her favorite singer; moreover, "I once saw him sing the birds off the trees. You think I'm kidding. They came down and sat on the ground to listen." Of course, there was more: Gloria and Papa Denny were lovers, and this was no secret in the music industry.

Were the Mamas & the Papas out of place in *16*? Yes, and no way—they were presented as being eccentric enough to be colorful and interesting, and besides, everyone in America was singing their songs.

Papa Denny and Mama Michelle agreed to share their memories.

Papa Denny Remembers

Denny Doherty spoke to us in August of 1996 from Toronto, where he is active in TV and theater. "I met Gloria in the Virgin Islands. The whole group was down there, hanging out. We had mutual friends; Gloria had just come from Nassau where she was photographing the Beatles making *Help!* We had just recorded, and she, having her finger on the pulse of everything, knew who we were. We were both in the same place at the same time, and had an incredible first meeting and romance. My first impression was, right off the bat: foxy lady. Good looking, independent woman. She had an agenda, was taking care of business, but liked to play. Didn't give her heart away often, only here and there. She took care of whatever her personal needs might be, but there was no permanent commitment. No time for that. She had a magazine to run. I was this laid-back guy in the islands, and here came this whirlwind. It lasted on and off, back in New York, and in Los Angeles, but not for long. But it was very intense.

"It became apparent that it wasn't going to be a forever thing when she came to Los Angeles for a photo shoot. I got the feeling from her that if I wasn't going to stick around and be there when she wanted, then she didn't want anything. She didn't want someone who was going to be in California while she was in New York as her lover. She was saying something like, 'If you love me, you'll stay with me,' and I was like, 'Come on, Glo, let's try.' But she said, 'No, if we can't have it all the way, then it's been nice.' She had given me a medallion, and then she took it back.

"She was never aggressive. She could set up a mood and a situation, but she would never make the first move. She would set it up, and make it very easy. I think she knew that I wasn't going to be around for a long time. I wrote a nice song about her, called 'Gloria.'

"As for being in *16*, well, we did get the GeeGee Award. I know we were a little off-center for *16*, and I know our relationship had something to do with it, but she wasn't stupid—we were a very, very popular group. She was very tough, very professional, wouldn't take any shit. You could hear her on the phone back at the office cracking the whip. When I stayed at her apartment in New York, she'd stay out and boogie till dawn, but when the office opened, she'd be there. She was a homebody too, liked to stay curled up at home.

The Mamas & The Papas

"The way I remember her best was sitting on a boat called the *Hotai*; she'd come through the Panama Canal, and we chartered the *Hotai* and took it out for the night. Gloria just loved sitting on the trampoline between the hulls, skipping over the ocean like a stone, with the sun setting behind her, and her hair blowing in the wind. That was the islands for us, and everything that was good about it. When she took the medallion back, that was her way of saying thank you. She said, 'If we're together, you have the medal, if we're apart…no.' And she said it was time to give it back."

Mama Michelle Recalls the 1960s

Michelle Phillips, now an actress and a force in Hollywood A-list social circles, spoke to us from Los Angeles: "I attributed appearing in *16* to Denny's relationship with Gloria. I thought that liaison didn't hurt us. I remember Gloria being with us a lot—we were so crazy at that period, we were dropping acid all the time. But I remember her being with us a lot in the Virgin Islands. She was a lot of fun to be with, and she just adored Denny, they were having a great, great time. It was a mad island romance, and I think there was never much beyond that.

"It's coming back to me—we won a GeeGee Award in *16*, and we were so amazed at all the coverage we were getting. We were on the cover of the *Saturday Evening Post*, and *Life* magazine did a 6-page spread, we were in *Time* and *Newsweek*. It was really a rags-to-riches story; it happened so quickly that we were just astonished that it was happening at all. We hadn't been on stage together until we had a #1 album, and there we were at the Hollywood Bowl. It was meteoric. We were all shocked.

"Cass and I really had no role models, white women singers who were at the top of the charts. There'd been Connie Francis, but she was pop—I guess we were folk rock—and there were the black singers, and the world was segregated then. It's amazing to think that when Otis Redding appeared at Monterey, it was the first time he was ever on a stage with white people.

"And I think in the world out there, it was expected that women would be docile and obedient. I remember I was doing a cover shoot for *Teen* magazine, and I guess they usually put models on the cover who got paid by the day or hour. And the stylist asked me to wear this green beret she had with her, as in Green Berets, Vietnam superkillers, you know. I said, 'You must be joking!' And she was stunned; you could tell that no one had ever argued with her; she was, after all, the stylist. I walked out, and I told them if they wanted someone to wear a green beret, they'd have to get themselves another girl. And in the next issue, they had an article called 'Mama Was a Heavyweight,' and it wasn't about Cass, it was about me, I was Captain Bringdown. They wrote about me walking out, and how I was unpatriotic. Now nothing like this ever, ever came up with Gloria Stavers, and I cannot imagine that it would have.

"I agree with Diana Vreeland of *Vogue*, who said, 'There were only two decades, darling, the '20s and the '60s.' Well, I agree with her about the '60s in any case. There was a total revolution of music, politics, fashion. It was an explosion of self-expression, and it happened in every level of society. You want to know something really scary, I have been waking up every morning—and I don't know how to stop this because it's virtually self-propelled—but I've been waking up singing 'I'm Henry the Eighth I Am.' I've been trying to think of another song, but nothing helps."

SPIN OUT with the MAMAS & the PAPAS!

Or Pull the Plug and Let's All Go Down the Drain Together!

NOW THAT the M & Ps have established bathtubs as the latest status symbol (I trust you saw their *old* one on the cover of their outasite Dunhill LP, *If You Can Believe Your Eyes And Your Ears*)—let's hop right in with John, Michelle, Denny and Cass and see how the water is. (It's cray-see, that's how it *is*, mon.)

I suppose YOU are all wondering why WE asked you here today...

An intentionally goofy way of doing a "nonstory," which nevertheless iconized a particular artist or group. Denny is the goateed Papa. This is from the August 1966 issue.

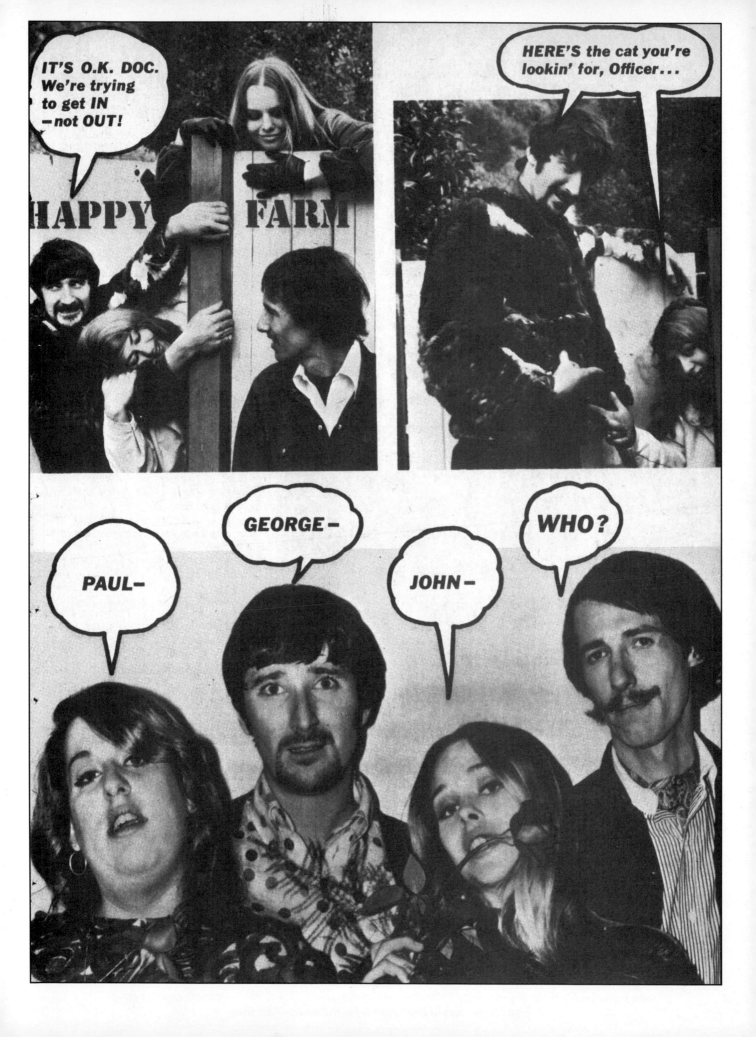

10 FAX ON KURT RUSSELL

Kurt Russell was born on March 17, 1951, in Springfield, Massachusetts. (He was born on St. Patrick's Day!)

Kurt is five feet and eleven inches tall, weighs 165 pounds and has blond hair and blue eyes.

Kurt is quite a baseball player and hopes someday to play professional baseball.

He has guest-starred on many top TV shows including *Twilight Zone, The Fugitive, The Man From U.N.C.L.E., Daniel Boone, The Virginian,* an episode of *The Wonderful World of Walt Disney* called *Willie and the Yank, Love American Style* and *Then Came Bronson.*

He loves to go dancing and visits the California discos every chance he gets.

Kurt is now attending Moorpark Junior College and is currently living with three of his college chums in Agoura, California.

He's quite a cook! Kurt can whip up a tasty pot roast and salads are his "specialty"!

His favorite actor is Marlon Brando, his favorite group is Creedence Clearwater Revival and his favorite color is blue.

Kurt is the star of a brand new Walt Disney motion picture, The Computer Wore Tennis Shoes. **Don't you dare miss it!**

You can write to Kurt Russell at Walt Disney Productions, 500 S. Buena Vista, Burbank, California 91505. (Be sure to put "I am A *16* Reader" on the outside of your envelope!)

10 Fax on Kurt Russell came out in the March 1970 issue.

Kurt Russell

It wasn't so much lack of cooperation, as Kurt clearly did whatever was asked; it was simply a collective shrug on the part of the readers. Kurt Russell did not generate excitement. Whether that was due to being the wrong age at the wrong time (too young in the beginning and by the time he got hunky, we had the Monkees), or because of the nerdy Disney tag, is a tough call. Whatever the "it" factor is that makes a teenage idol, Kurt Russell didn't have it back then. We're sure it pains him to this day....*Not*!

Years of *16* Popularity: 1967–1970

Today, he rakes in $12 million per picture as a big-screen action hero; once upon a time, Kurt Russell served as a *16 Magazine* staple. (Tell us again how you can't get there from here....)

Gosh-darn wholesome, blond, and dimply-cute, the teenage Kurt was very much of the demographic—*and* he was always working. He signed his first movie deal in 1962 at the age of 10, and seems to have filmed a picture a year for the next decade. They include such Disney TV and movie "classics" as *Follow Me Boys, Something's Happened to Dexter, The Horse in the Gray Flannel Suit,* and *The Computer Wore Tennis Shoes.* Before all those, even, he starred in a short-lived ABC series, *The Travels of Jamie McPheeters*—which marks the first occasion *16* had to write about him. It was the February 1964 issue. Alas, by the August issue of that year, the program—Trivia alert: it costarred the (pre–*Andy Williams Show* and pre–Donny) Osmond Brothers!!—had been canceled.

Still, because of all the flicks, there was never a dearth of Kurt info, as well as always new Disney-supplied photos to run. Kurt was a bona fide fave, all right, but in spite of his age, cuddle-quotient, and ubiquity, he was never a rave. Never did his photo make the cover; rarely was his name even mentioned there. He didn't front a column, and there were few "personal" stories about him—never a "Night I Cried/Died/Tears I Tried to Hide" confection. Instead, there was simple, straightforward coverage: announcements for each of his new movies, Fact Files, and, once, "My Life in Pix."

Why the less-than-personal touch at a time, after all, when to be in *16* meant celebrity and reader were closerthanthis?

We continued covering Kurt, right on through the '70s—he was our SuperDream in '77. He escaped the teen dream stigma to star in such blockbuster movies as Escape from New York.

Dino, Desi & Billy

Billy, Desi & Dino, circa 1965: "We did countless photo sessions for 16," Desi remembers: this is one.

Years of *16* Popularity: 1965–1970

Even consummate trivia-mavens get flummoxed over the "fave rave" status of this trio. What exactly were they again? TV actors? Movie stars? A rock group? Yet even without being able to pinpoint a specific spot on the showbiz map, most pop-culture-heads over the age of 30 would agree that "DD & B," in a *16 Magazine* sense (as opposed, say, to an advertising firm sense) does have a familiar ring. Herewith, a refresher:

All three were privileged Beverly Hills kids—two with showbiz pedigrees—and together they were a musical trio who recorded and performed from 1965 to 1970. The group released four albums; their two biggest singles were "I'm a Fool" and "Tell Someone You Love Them."

The Dino in question was Dean Martin, Jr.; and Desi was the son of Lucille Ball and Desi Arnaz, Sr., whose 1953 birth was the most anticipated event of the *I Love Lucy*–lovin' world, and whose first baby portrait made the cover of *TV Guide*. Billy Hinsche was the son of a Beverly Hills real estate agent to the stars. Dino and Billy, both born in 1951, met in kindergarten and as legend goes, started rockin' together by the end of elementary school. Drummer Desi completed the trio, which officially formed in 1965.

"We weren't looking for a career when it started; we were just a garage band," Desi said recently, noting, "Of course, we had a pretty nice garage!" File under: it pays to have friends in high places. DD & B had some pretty powerful sets of ears pressed to that "garage" wall: none other than Dino's dad's ratpack comrade, Frank Sinatra, who did the boys a biggie—got 'em signed to his own Reprise Records label. And so a teen idol troika was born.

With the release of their first album and a summertime tour, *16* got busy, ingratiating itself with DD & B and the powers behind them: parents, agents, managers, whatever it took to get these babes in the mag. The boys and their minions were willing participants in it all. "My mom kept a scrapbook of all my *16 Magazine* clippings," Desi revealed. (One can only imagine Lucille Ball, cigarette in one hand, vigilantly clipping articles like "Dino, Desi & Billy Tell On Each Other.") That, and other remembrances, were graciously shared by Desi—who now lives in Las Vegas with his dance-studio owner wife, Amy, and their daughter, Haley—in a recent phone interview.

DESI TELLS ALL

"I was 12 when it all started; 13 when 'I'm a Fool' came out. We were together for five years, during which time all our voices changed—so our music changed dramatically too over that period. And though it was never perceived that way, the music was what it was all about for us. In those days, we were kids. We didn't aspire to a career per se. We just wanted to make good music, and were having a great time doing it. We

Dino, Desi & Billy

really could play, too. Billy had been playing piano since the age of 3: he was a prodigy. Dino always had a guitar in his hand. My dad gave me conga lessons; I'd been playing drums since I was 3 years old. I'd been in 2 bands before Dino, Desi & Billy, including a Dixieland band with the kid who played Little Ricky on *I Love Lucy*.

"When the publicity started, that seemed natural—being in magazines, being in the public eye, wasn't exactly foreign to us (!!). This was normal, it was our reality, so it never overwhelmed us. But being in *16* wasn't something we ever dreamed about, because again, forming the trio wasn't a career move: it was three kids making music, which at the time was every teenage boy's dream.

"But when it all took off, we willingly participated in the teen press. Back then, it was *16 Magazine*, with Gloria Stavers being the one who interviewed us, and *Tiger Beat*, who also had one editor in charge. We thought of both those women as our aunts. The joke was that we did so many photo sessions and interviews for 'Aunt' Gloria that we practically lived with her. We never minded; everyone was very nice to us.

"It was really like a family back then, a much more personal touch. Our first manager, Matt Grey, was Dean Sr.'s road manager. Our second manager, Bill Howard, was also our Little League coach: he's Dorothy Lamour's son. We got signed to Reprise Records right away—it was owned by people we knew! If *16* wanted something—information, specific photos—Gloria, or later, editor Nola Leone, would just call us up and ask. We'd do whatever they wanted. We filled out countless sets of 'fact sheets.' That was an in-joke among us: 'Okay, time to go up to *16* and fill out another fact sheet.' It was like school! Some of them were long, like an SAT test, and took hours to complete—Gloria was like the school principal, sitting there, making sure we answered every question. And we did! Everything that was printed in *16* came directly from what we wrote. Oh, sure, sometimes the editors might embellish here or there, but they never twisted anything, or printed anything we wouldn't have said—never anything negative or that would have hurt us. Those were our answers; those were the things we said. Sometimes, in fact, they printed *exactly* what we said, exactly as we said it, whether it made grammatical sense or not!

"Yes, *16* liked to 'create' personalities, and we understood that. If we hadn't had the music—if we were just some packaged, put-together group, we would have bristled—but we were always making music. And as long as it stayed about

that, everything else was okay. And we were really good musically—people don't understand that, they were jealous because we were doing what so many others wanted to do, and so they made fun of us—but we were good. The whole period, the Dino, Desi & Billy mania, was just fun for us. We did not take ourselves as celebrities seriously. We did take the music seriously, though. I can't stress enough that we were not some packaged product: we did care about learning the music and making good music.

"What we loved best was touring, but because we were so young, we only went out on the road during the summers and school holidays. Still, we opened for the biggest groups of the time, everyone from Paul Revere & the Raiders to the Beach Boys, the Mamas & the Papas, Herman's Hermits, the Byrds. We all knew each other; it was a very small world back then."

"OF COURSE I GOT TEASED: SO WHAT ELSE IS NEW?"

"Did we get teased for being in *16*? Of course we did, especially in school. But, you know [being the kids of stars], we just got teased anyway—if it wasn't for being in a group and in teen magazines, it was for being Lucille Ball's son. If it wasn't one thing, it was another! [This was said good-humoredly.] It was our lives in general.

"It forced me to tackle, at a really young age, the great mystery of life: who people think you are versus who you really are. You're not your family; you're not your name; you're not your successes or your failures. It has to do with learning who you are, and by circumstance, I was forced to learn that young. It also helped that me, Dino, and Billy were all going through it together. And we did have a real friendship.

"*16* always portrayed us as being a tight trio; that's exactly what we were. There were never any articles that pitted us one against the other. There were articles where we poked fun at each other, 'told on' each other, but it was all good clean fun, and written up in the spirit that we intended. There really were not any jealousies behind the scenes. Of course we were aware that the girls out there each had her 'favorite,' but if anything we were always supportive of one another. If we had any jealousies, it was about stuff that had nothing to do with showbiz—like over a girl we all liked or something like that.

"The funny thing is, I never considered myself good-looking, so when girls would write and say 'you're so cute,' it just felt odd, kind of embarrassing. I mean, I went through serious mutation at that time: within two years I grew, like,

THE SECRET CONFESSIONS OF
DINO, DESI & BILLY

Hollywood's Terrific Trio record their private thoughts and dreams for 16's readers!

DINO MARTIN, JR.

I REMEMBER when Billy and I used to sit on the floor of my den and struggle with songs and sounds that were number one; I remember the first time we recorded—it was much more *work* than I expected, but I enjoyed every minute of it; I remember the first time I heard our song on the radio—I was riding in the car and I nearly went right out through the roof!

I FEEL SAD when a friend of mine (or anyone, for that matter) has a serious problem and there is nothing I can do to help—I try and I usually end sadder, because I only just help mess things up even more; I feel sad (and

10

In October 1965 Dino, Desi & Billy confessed all. "This is what we really said," confirms Desi.

a bit mad) when people make un-funny remarks about my hair—I like it long, and that is *that*!; I feel sad when I have to keep my mouth shut about certain things (that I know are *true*), because I am considered "too young to know."

I FEEL HAPPY when I am with my good friends—they know how I think and feel, and I don't have to explain everything to them (I think anyone is happy with people whom they feel *really* understand them); I feel happy when I walk down the street and hear someone say, "Hey, thats Dino!" (not, "Hey, he's got a Beatle hair-do"); I feel happy when we do a show and the audience likes us—in fact, I feel happy when *anyone* likes us; I feel happy that I've got three older sisters and they are all *divine*—I don't think I'd know as much as I do about life and everything if it weren't for my sisters; I feel happy when I meet a girl with a sense of humor—they are hard to find, but with a sense of humor you can get through anything.

I FEEL ROMANTIC when I'm standing beside a girl and the wind blows her hair across my face (you can tell I've got a "thing" about long hair!); I feel romantic when I meet a girl who doesn't think that just because I'm only thirteen I don't know anything about anything—in other words, girls who treat me like a guy, and not a kid, make me feel romantic.

I AM LOOKING FORWARD TO making more records, doing more public appearances and eventually writing some of our own material; I am looking forward to Bob Dylan's next concert in Los Angeles, more Mae West-W.C. Fields films on the late movies, and the Byrds' next record session—well, I'd better stop, 'cause I could go

Dino

on forever looking forward to things. One important thing, however: we all look forward to getting your letters and answering them, so write to us at *Reprise Records, Warner Brothers Studios, Burbank, Calif.*

DESI ARNAZ IV

I REMEMBER *when I fell off my surfboard last year and had to have 26 stitches taken in my head (who could ever forget that!);I remember having my first ride in an outrigger, which broke into several pieces when it hit a coral reef in Hawaii—and I didn't know how to swim!; I remember learning how to swim directly after that (I was about three and half years old); I remember when I got my first puppy dog of my very own; I remember my first go-cart race—I came in last; I remember the first time I ever appeared on a show—it was* Art Linkletter's House Party, *and I was three.*

I FEEL SAD *when there is nothing to do on a rainy day—I just mope about the house; I feel very sad when I come home with a bad report card; I feel sad when I have a disagreement with any of my few best friends.*

I FEEL HAPPY *when we have a good rehearsal with the group and don't goof around; I feel happy when I win a go-cart race; I feel happy when I hit a home run in baseball; I feel happy when I get wonderful news—like hearing that we would do an appearance at the Hollywood Bowl and that our record was climbing up the charts; I feel happy when I ride a great wave on my surf board; I feel happy when I go for a long stroll down the beach with my dog.*

I FEEL ROMANTIC *when I see a sentimental movie (but please don't tell!); I feel romantic when I sit with a girl by a campfire on the beach; I feel romantic when I see my "steady" at school, or when I am dancing with her.*

I AM LOOKING FORWARD TO *a tour (with the Beach Boys) in Hawaii; I am looking forward to being in Jan Dean's movie, being on Dean Martin's TV show and appearing on Sammy Davis' Thanksgiving Special; I am looking forward to getting my first motorcycle and my first car; I am looking forward to growing up.*

Desi

Dino, Desi & Billy

In their days as "columnists,"
Lucie and Desi looked over everything.

5 inches, got taller and thinner, so what I looked like when **16** first started covering us, and later, was completely different.

"The truth is, there really was nothing to cover up, nothing going on behind the scenes that we could keep secret anyway. Everything about my life was printed, from day one! It was all public. That was my childhood; that was my reality. It was only later on, after DD & B, that I got into some serious trouble. I'd had some tremendous success outwardly, but something was missing inwardly. So between the ages of 15 and 25, I did some serious soul searching. I eventually studied spiritual inner development based on author Vernon Howard's principles. What did I learn? That life isn't a race to win, but a school for your higher education; and that everything in life is temporary—time defeats it all. And most of all, that success doesn't come from outward validation; it's not out there, it's inside."

"MY OLD FRIEND"

"Dino, Desi and Billy pretty much ended in a natural way. I got into acting, starting with my mom's sitcom *Here's Lucy.* I was on that for two and half seasons, then left to do the movie *Red Sky at Morning.* The group had just recorded our last two singles, 'Lady Love' and 'A Certain Sound.' Dino and Billy were in college and Dino at the time wanted to go to medical school. We thought maybe we'd just record and not tour, but that didn't work—after all, there was no MTV back then. We did some solo projects; Billy became part of the Beach Boys tour group; Dino and I hooked up with Terry Melcher (Doris Day's son, who wrote—among other things—'Kokomo' for the Beach Boys) and had a group.

"But eventually we went our separate ways. I stayed in acting—I did more movies, theater, and a TV series called *Automan,* which actually has kind of a cult following now. Billy stayed in the music world, writing, singing, performing, producing. As for Dino, the one thing that probably wasn't in **16** was his passion for flying. He always had it and was actually flying at the age of 15, though during our years as a trio, he didn't have his pilot's license. [Authors' note: Dino joined the Air Force and was killed in a 1987 crash.)

"Two years ago, I wrote a song for him called 'My Old Friend,' which we may actually release—'we' being myself, Billy, and Dino's brother, Ricci Martin."

DEAR DESI...

"If **16** wrote about me more than the other two, it's because of *Here's Lucy,* my mom's sitcom that my sister Lucie and I co-starred on. With that show, my acting career began, and so **16** had more to say about me. In fact, that was the time—1968–1970—that the Dear Lucie, Dear Desi column started appearing. My sister and I ostensibly answered reader mail and gave advice. I say ostensibly because honestly, I don't remember writing the column. However, I will say that I'm sure it was done with our approval: by the time of the column, I'd known Gloria and Nola so long, they would have known what I'd say in that column."

[Author's note: In fact, Nola Leone wrote the Dear Lucie, Dear Desi column, and not, as Desi accurately recalls, without their permission or participation. Lucie was involved—to the degree that she'd be consulted for her take on the letters. Their mother, Lucille Ball, was also involved at the outset.

"When we first sat down to discuss the column, it was at the Plaza Hotel in New York," Nola remembers. "Lucille had just broken her leg in a skiing accident, and had a cast on. She insisted on knowing what was going to be in the column, and asked a lot of questions." The world's most famous TV redhead gave her stamp of approval to the project and, as Desi related, proudly kept a scrapbook of her kids' clippings and accomplishments, like any other doting mom. "Mom wanted to see what it was all about," Desi recalls. "She was very much interested in our lives. She kept on top of the little things, the details; she knew the big stuff would take care of itself."]

The COWSILLS

Seemingly cuddly and corn-fed, the Cowsills came together in 16's offices for many an exclusive photo session like this one.

Years of *16* Popularity: 1968–1970

The first of the big family singing groups to be featured in **16**, the Cowsills—six singing siblings, their performing mom, and manager dad—were the inspiration for TV's *The Partridge Family*. They were also, in fact, precursors to such musical dynasties as the Osmonds and the Jacksons, who were poised to hit the pop scene just a year later.

Between 1967 and 1971, the Cowsills released four albums; they are best remembered for the soft-rock, harmony-laced hits, "The Rain, the Park & Other Things" and a cover version of the title song from the play, *Hair*.

Friendly, freckled, fresh-faced, and open as the Iowa cornfields, the Cowsills were hardly the country bumpkins they appeared to be. They came from Newport, Rhode Island, and were adept merchandisers and self-promoters. They were also more than willing to cooperate with the magazine, offering up baby pictures, "intimate interviews," and posing for exclusive photo sessions. While the magazine credited everyone in the band, no attempt at equal coverage was made. Reacting to the fan mail, most of the stories centered on the two youngest boys, John and Barry—13 and 15 at the height of their popularity—with an occasional article on next-oldest Paul, 16. John and Barry got the full monthly dose of **16**-type features: lots of "tell-all" confessionals, a sprinkling of romantic fantasy stories ("We're Not Too Young to Love," or "We're Girl Crazy"), and, always, the 40 Intimate Questions format.

The Cowsills also came with a kid sister and she got plenty of **16** ink as well. Cute-as-a-button Susie Cowsill served a 2-fold purpose: she was close with the boys without being a "romantic rival" to the readers, and she could be counted on to "squeal" on her brothers. In that sense, Susie was very much a precursor to Marie Osmond and La Toya Jackson. But Susie was also someone the readers identified with: at 10 years old, she was close to their own age, and

herself a fan of the pop idols of the day. Of course, she was a fan who got to live out the readers' fantasies: in one article she told about getting "My First Kiss"—from Davy Jones of the Monkees. Later on, she wrote **16** a message that could have come from any of its readers: "I like Mark Lester now, because Davy Jones got married."

Susie is now 37, and plays in a roots rock band, the Continental Drifters. She is married to musician Peter Holsapple and lives in New Orleans, as does Barry. He and Paul, who's in Mexico, no longer perform. John lives in California and remains on the fringes of the music business as an occasional session player.

The Cowsills were presented to **16**'s readers as their happy-shiny-people image indicated. If we at the magazine had suspicions otherwise—that the parents were tyrants; that there were interfamily jealousies—we didn't pursue them. We could see that dad Bud Cowsill, a former military man, clearly ruled the roost and that the kids were mega-obedient—they did as they were told. We heard the rumors of course—that the reason the Cowsills themselves didn't go on to TV fame as the Partridge Family was because Bud could not come to an agreement with the show's producers; that even among the generally pushy lot of stage parents, he was known as a troublemaker.

None of that was ever hinted about in **16**. For one thing, we were not in business to uncover any "dark side"; for another, the fans would not have wanted to hear about it. Whatever the truth really was, time seems to have mellowed at least one member of the clan. Looking back on it all, Susie recently told the magazine *Entertainment Weekly*, "It was a gas, and sure beat going to school."

COWSILLS CONFESS—

"We're Girl Crazy!"

GIRLS are usually the first to admit that they are boy crazy. In fact, they love talking about boys and once they start — it's difficult to get them to stop! On the other hand, boys are very often hush-hush regarding their thoughts about girls. Not so, however, with three of your fav guys — Barry, John and Paul Cowsill! They love to talk about girls — it's their favorite subject!! Since these three beautiful boys are willing to tell you—listen closely right now as Barry, John and Paul unblushingly confess why they are girl crazy!!

BARRY

I love girls—and I'm not the least bit embarrassed to admit it! Personally, I think girls are the greatest thing since —well, since boys! I mean, after all— they go together, don't they? What's a boy without a girl? Pretty unhappy— that's what!!

Of course, I haven't reached the point in my life where I feel that I could settle down to going steady with one girl. Right now, I'm having too much fun dating and getting to know many *different* girls. I often wonder if I'll ever be able to choose just *one* girl, cos there's something so special about each and every one of you! *Every* girl has a certain charm all her own. I guess that's why I'm so girl crazy, cos I have to confess — I actually love *all* of you lovely, feminine, female creatures!

Now, don't you blame us guys for being so fickle and falling for almost every girl we meet! We really can't help it. It's *you girls* who are really to blame! If you all weren't so appealing —we guys wouldn't have such a rough time deciding which is the girl for us! But then again—it really isn't so bad being surrounded by such lovely creatures—*so don't you dare change!* We boys wouldn't know what to do without you!!

JOHN

One of my all-time favorite pastimes is girl-watching! That's because I love pretty things—and I can't think of anything better-looking than a girl! Sometimes I'll see a girl who has long blonde hair and big blue eyes, and I'll think to myself, "Wow — she's my dream girl!". Then, a few minutes later, another girl may pass by. This time, the girl may have short dark hair and sparkling brown eyes, and again I'll think, "There's the perfect girl for me!".

I suppose you've already guessed it by now, but you know—the same thing happens when a redhead walks by! And every time I meet a girl, no matter what kind of personality she has, I always find something about the way she acts that makes me think, "She's really groovy—I'd like to get to know her better!".

At first, this attraction to every girl kind of confused me, but I think I understand it now. The truth is—*I'm girl crazy!* This may sound silly—but I'm *glad* that I am! The way I figure it is that by being girl crazy, I'll get to know and date many different girls. That way, when I really *do* find my dream girl (for *real* this time)—I'll know for *sure* she's the one for me!!

PAUL

There's absolutely nothing wrong with being girl crazy. In fact, I think it's a very natural stage all boys go through. At least, I know all of us Cowsill guys experienced it!

It seems that as soon as a boy reaches the magic age of 13—he suddenly discovers the opposite sex. Girls become extra-special to him, and it's just about this time in his life that he begins dating. And for the rest of his teenage years, he continues to be completely fascinated by girls, getting crush after crush on girl after girl!

Although we guys might seem fickle when we're going through this girl-crazy stage—it's really just a natural part of growing up. This "fickleness" lasts until a guy meets "the girl" who will stop his heart from wandering. To my way of thinking, it's good for a guy to be girl crazy. That's what dating is all about, anyway—meeting and getting to know many girls before deciding to settle down with just one girl.

Another thing I feel it's important to bring up—and in all fairness to us guys—don't you honestly agree with me that most teenage girls are boy crazy?!

44

In December 1970, Barry, John, and Paul Cowsill confessed their romantic fantasies.

DARK SHADOWS

Years of *16* Popularity: 1968–1970

IDOLS:
JONATHAN FRID, DAVID HENESY, DAVID SELBY

Up until *Dark Shadows*, the conventional wisdom had been that *16*'s young readers didn't follow afternoon TV; they were in school during the hours of broadcast. And with the exception of specific after-school programming geared to them, like *American Bandstand* (and later, *Soul Train*), they pretty much didn't. The magazine received little if any mail on the soap stars of the era.

All that changed with *Dark Shadows*. The ABC-TV occult-accented serial, populated with vampires, monsters, mad doctors, and witches, grabbed America's teens by the imagination and bit down hard. It was helped along, starting in 1968 (though the show had been airing since 1966), by *16*.

The show's producer, Dan Curtis, was well aware of *16*'s influence and still treasures the '68, '69, and '70 GeeGee/Gold Star Awards bestowed on the serial by *16* in the Most Popular TV Show category. In a recent interview for this book he said, "The enthusiastic support of editor Gloria Stavers and her *16 Magazine* staff gave *Dark Shadows* a tremendous boost with teenage viewers. The coverage in a publication such as *16* was never anticipated, but soon it became apparent that housewives weren't the only ones watching."

Writing about *Dark Shadows* was something altogether new for Gloria Stavers and her young staff. For the show had few actors who fell into the teen idol mold. At the time, the magazine's "meat and potatoes" were the made-for-mania Monkees, cuddly Cowsills, and perennially hunky Bobby Sherman. None of the Dark Shadows actors, with the exception of David Henesy, was particularly young, cute, or about to strap a guitar on.

But once Gloria began to get mail on *Dark Shadows*, she embraced the show and made it *16*'s own. Gloria formed a liaison with producer Curtis and ABC: whatever *16* wanted—to get the scoop introducing new characters, or to have certain photos taken—it got. The result was that *Dark Shadows* became "all access" territory for *16*'s readers—many of whom were fanatic. They bombarded the magazine with mail pointing out the slightest error in recounting a story line, a bit of dialogue, a heaven-forbid miscaptioned photo. Although most fans were captivated by the characters inhabiting the intriguing world of *Dark Shadows*, they soon, courtesy of *16*, became just as familiar with at least three of the actors in the lead roles, and were soon feeling very much a part of what *16* jauntily termed, "the DS Gang."

Dark Shadows had only one authentic teenager in the cast, David Henesy, who played David Collins. He was between 13 and 15 during the show's heyday. Although *16* dutifully covered young David, it was clear that fans were more riveted by the vampire of the "gang," embodied in the fanged persona of Barnabas Collins. What to do? *16* had little choice but to go ahead and make the very cultured, very stodgy—and, at 40ish, very old by *16*'s standards!—Jonathan Frid into a teen idol anyway. In fact, it was he, in his caped Barnabas guise, that *16* focused on first, making him a monthly "cover boy" next to Bobby, Davy, et al. Talk about frightening!

While Frid, as the magazine flippantly called him, would later grouse that "*16* made it all up," there's overwhelming, first-person evidence to the contrary provided by the editor who covered him, Steve DeNaut. "Jonathan Frid was extremely cooperative, a willing participant in the frenzy. He was amazed at his popularity among young readers; more flattered than anything else." He judiciously filled out *16*'s "all-star fact sheets" in his own handwriting, willingly posed for photos (taken by Steve) in his New York City apartment, and gladly shared baby and growing-up pix with *16*'s readers. "Come on the set, any time" was the standing invite, and *16* took him up on the offer.

A comparison of what Frid wrote on his fact sheets and said in his interviews with the resultant coverage in the

"An Evening With Me" by
David Selby

IF YOU SPEND an evening with me, David Lynn Selby, you'll find it *very* different from the kind of night you'd spend with "Quentin" — for in real life, I'm *quite* a different fellow!

To begin with, I love to dress casually. By that, I mean that I don't like suits and ties (unless they're an absolute "must", of course). On a relaxed evening out, if you were with me you would probably find yourself going for a walk in one of New York's more offbeat, colorful neighborhoods — like the lower East Side. There's a fantastic old Italian section there that really turns me on. The people are very simple. There's always some kind of street festival going on and it's great fun to stroll along listening to a street band and watching the people.

My favorite Italian restaurant is on Mulberry Street. You probably won't be impressed when we walk inside. It's small and simple — and it doesn't even have tablecloths! In fact, the atmosphere is more like that of a home than of a restaurant — which is fine with me, because I'm basically a homebody. Just to be different, I would order my favorite Italian dishes for *you* — and you would order your favorites for *me!* After a long and leisurely dinner, we would sit and talk over our cups of capuccino.

To me, the most important relationship two people can have is *communicating* their thoughts and feelings to one another. I have an insatiable curiosity about what goes on in other people's minds and hearts — especially if that other person is a girl. Maybe I think this way because I want to make up for lost time. You see, when I was younger — like when I was in high school — I was bashful. In those days it was difficult for me to talk with a girl. I guess you could say that I never was a wolf (or even a *were*wolf, come to think of it). Actually, I never could understand guys who took a girl out on a date and spent the whole time dancing to loud music and running from one place to another. When a guy like that gets a girl back to her doorstep at the end of the evening, he is taking a total stranger home. What I mean is — he hasn't taken the *time* to sit down, and talk and listen, and really get to know her.

So if you are set to spend an evening with me, dress casually, prepare to have a relaxed, pleasant time, and be ready to answer my questions and *talk,* because what I really want to know is — all about *you!*

26

"An Evening with Me," by David Selby, was printed in September 1969.

magazine is practically identical. Of course, there *were* some sensationalistic headlines, like the December 1968 banner, shouting "Frid Is Missing!" But by and large, the coverage was accurate, if spirited.

The focus shifted off Frid a bit in the May 1969 issue with the introduction of David "Quentin" Selby, who'd joined the cast earlier that year. It was partly the quirky, villainous, ghostlike character he portrayed, but mostly David's own eerie soulfulness, that Gloria and *16*'s readers latched on to immediately. Full and intense coverage followed—much to the surprise of the stage-trained actor himself. Like Jonathan Frid, David Selby was older than the usual *16* teen idol and somewhat unfamiliar with television work. He was also married—a small fact that, while not unacknowledged, was certainly not dwelled upon in *16*'s coverage. Fantasy, after all, is what *16* has always been about.

David Selby's experiences on *Dark Shadows* and with *16* remain vivid and overwhelmingly positive in his memory. He was eager to relive those days and did so in a recent conversation.

QUENTIN (DAVID SELBY) SPEAKS!

"I had not heard of *16 Magazine*, nor of *Dark Shadows*, before I was *in* both of them! Prior to 1969, I'd done off-Broadway and regional theater. So the whole experience was new to me. I wasn't on the show for very long when Gloria Stavers discovered me and sat me down for my first *16* interview. And when I tell you that she literally dragged me by the hand and said, 'Come on, we're gonna do this,' I am not exaggerating. She hated taking no for an answer. She just told me what it was all about, whereupon I did it willingly.

"I was never much for publicity, but I instinctively trusted Gloria. She was good at coaxing things out of me, at not letting my shyness get in the way of getting me in the magazine.

"She was not only very supportive of the show, she had a lot of confidence in me personally. She'd say, 'You're gonna have a great career, this is only the beginning.' She was so optimistic about me that it made me feel good.

"She also had a certain savvy for what I'd look good in. She'd come to my apartment to take pictures and bring this Errol Flynn pirate shirt—it was white with ruffles—and say, 'You're gonna look terrific in this.' And even if it was something I'd never dream of wearing, when it came out in the magazine, she was invariably right. She had a real fashion sense."

"WAS THAT GUY ME?"

"*16* was largely responsible for whatever kind of image I had. I always came off better than I really was—nicer, a little more romantic. We would do interviews, and from those, Gloria would extract bits and pieces to make up articles. For instance, I remember one about 'Would You Spend the Night with Me?' Which sounds suggestive, but once you got past the title, it was really about what it might be like to spend a (chaste) evening with me. Needless to say, it didn't mention my wife at all! Instead, it gave tips like, 'dress casually,' and 'be prepared to have a relaxed and pleasant time,' and something like, 'be prepared to answer all my questions and talk, because what I really want to know about is you,' meaning, the reader.

"Now, I know I never said exactly that, but that was okay. That's what the reader would have wanted to hear. And that's what made me want to work with *16*, though other magazines came calling. Gloria had this relationship with all of these kids across the country. She was their guiding force. They wrote to her; they talked to her. Besides, no matter what would turn up in *16* about me, I knew that Gloria wasn't going to do me wrong, no matter what. And she never did.

"Career-wise, the exposure was probably a good thing for me. She picked Quentin out and started featuring him in the magazine, and that made a big difference in my career. I honestly believe that was one of the factors that went into more story lines shifting toward me. Because of *16*, my face was out there. There really was a time when *Dark Shadows* and *16* were one."

THOSE SARA LEE BANANA CAKES!

"I was amazed at the power of *16*. I used to get so many fan letters, thousands a week. At first I answered them, but then it got to the point where that was physically impossible. What crystalizes it for me is this one little comment I made in the magazine, about how I liked Sara Lee banana cake. Let me tell you, the minute the article came out with that one offhand statement, our offices were filled with Sara Lee banana cakes! Thousands of gifts would come in.

"After a while, the fame was isolating—I couldn't go anywhere without being recognized. I wouldn't say I was ever resentful of it, but I will tell you that it took me a while to get happy about it. I mean, the power of TV and the power of the media were just overwhelming. But the power of the press was different then. We were so innocent. It's not that

Dark Shadows

*"Frid" watering his rooftop garden as **16**'s reporter/photographer clicked away.*

way now—PR people are everywhere. Now, you have to be careful; now the press comes after you!"

"THE FANS HAVE FOLLOWED ME"

"Those fans who were kids back then, they grew up and have kids of their own now and they are still with me. They've followed my career. They've come to the plays; they've come to the films. I know they were readers of *16*, because they'll be outside the theater with old articles; or they send me letters with old articles—I get letters saying people named their kids Quentin, after me! To all those people I'd like to go back and say thank you! Everyone was so nice to me; the magazine was nice to me. And it all meant a lot to me."

DARK SHADOWS TODAY...

The show has been off the air for 25 years, but for its devotees, the phenomenon remains powerful. There are annual *Dark Shadows* conventions, reunions for fans and cast members, as well as memorabilia on sale, including videos, books, *Dark Shadows* calendars, a full catalogue of merchandise. For more information—including Where Are They Now? updates—contact the *Dark Shadows* Official Fan Club, P.O. Box 92, Maplewood, N.J. 07040

Sajid Khan

Years of *16* Popularity: 1967–1969

Prayerful and polite and a whole lot more spiritual than he really was: 16's image was created through photos like this one.

If you were among the millions who devoured *16* in the latter half of the '60s, you may remember Sajid Khan, or "Saj" as the magazine jauntily referred to him. Chances are, as he faded fast into the deep, dark obscurity from which he came, you haven't thought of him since. Until now.

In the November 1967 issue, *16*'s readers were introduced to "the young Hindu actor" Sajid Khan, who was making his American TV debut costarring with (*Dennis the Menace*'s) Jay North in the NBC series *Maya*. The series had sprung from a feature film of the same name; both were filmed on location in Bombay, India, and chronicled the jungle adventures of a wily pachyderm and the boys who loved her. The show, alas, lumbered along for only a season before it met with extinction; its exotic teenage star, however, met with a more agreeable fate. Thanks largely to *16*, Sajid's American career outpaced *Maya*'s by several years.

That was only partly due to reader demand. Interest existed, to be sure, but hardly to the degree reflected in *16*. It was once again Gloria Stavers who perpetuated the perception of Sajid's popularity long after it had begun to flag. From the start, *16* had focused on him, pretty much ignoring his equally young, equally good-looking costar Jay North. Sajid did outdraw Jay in the mail (possibly because readers still thought of Jay as *Dennis the Menace*), and Saj also cooperated more fully than Jay, never a favorite with the editors, ever did.

But there was another reason for the focus on the soulful-looking Saj. It had to do with Gloria's real interest in presenting young celebrities who were unique: simply because of his Indian heritage, Sajid fit the bill. And because

of his prominence in *16*—in an era when it was being read by 4,000,000 teenagers a month—there was a real chance for him to parlay his teen idol status into more acting work. The young actor had been a successful child star in Indian films; after TV's *Maya* and *16*, he decided to move permanently to Hollywood and capitalize on his budding success. He moved in with a wealthy family in Beverly Hills and enrolled, for a while, in Beverly Hills High School.

During this time, Sajid became duly westernized, but you'd never know it reading *16*. The magazine played the foreign card to the max: even the typeface used in article titles was quasi-exotic-looking (picture a menu in an Indian restaurant). There were photos of him "praying," or meditating, and lots of articles, while always bearing the romantic *16* stamp, in which he articulated the cultural differences between India and America ("In my country, a date is a very serious matter"). And instead of the typical "Be My Girl" entreaty, Sajid's pleas were invariably, "Be My Princess."

That was Gloria's doing; it gave her an opportunity to "teach" the readers about matters worldly and spiritual—which, it just so happened, *she* was getting into herself. Sajid, according to Associate Editor Steve DeNaut, was "not really spiritual at all."

Still, the young Hindu star was a more than willing participant in it all. He remained grateful and extremely cooperative, even humble. The accolades did not go to his head.

SAJID
– KISS HIS TEARS AWAY

WHEN A BOY AND A GIRL SHARE A SPECIAL KISS, IT WILL TURN THE SADDEST

FROWN UPSIDE DOWN—AND MAKE IT INTO A VERY SPECIAL SMILE. TRY IT

AND SEE THE MAGIC OF... A SPECIAL KISS.

IN THE SECRET HEART of Sajid Khan there is a tiny corner with the word SORROW written on it. This is a private place he keeps very much apart from his public life. It's a place of sadness and no sunlight—it is Sajid's vale of tears.

Basically, Sajid Khan is a serious but happy-go-lucky type of guy. If he is sad or worried or unhappy, he doesn't tell anybody or let on a bit—but his sensitive countenance more often than not reveals the occasional secret sorrow he tries so hard to hide. If you love Sajid and would like to truly help kiss his tears away, listen while he tells you about the things you can do to make him happier.

"Being happy depends a lot on the mood I'm in. For instance, if I'm worried about my work—like maybe I feel as though I didn't do a particular scene very well—then I like to have someone around who can give me an objective analysis of my performance. If you were on the set with me and saw me in a sad state later, then maybe *you* could sit down and tell me what you thought I did *well* and what you thought I did *poorly*. I'm sure that would be most helpful. And I *know* it would send my sadness away.

"Sometimes I'm unhappy because of *inner* conflicts. I worry about myself. I seem to be a "split personality" at times, and it really troubles me and makes me miserable! If you were were my friend and cared enough, I'm sure you could cheer me up just by being there to hold my hand or reassure me when I am buried in self-doubt. I love girls who are direct and open, and your directness and openness would be like a bright light shining into the dark areas of my heart.

"Sometimes, like everybody else, I'm just plain 'in a bad mood'. That's when it is especially hard to cheer me up. The only solution to my bad moods is to literally *drag* me out of the house and make me go somewhere! When I'm down, I'll just sit around and mope unless someone is there to arouse my interest in the outside world—like going to a club to watch a performer or to dance in a disco. I'm really wild about dancing. I love romantic, slow dances and fast, energy-consuming dances—and if there are any new steps, I'm a fiend to learn them. By the way, if you are not a very good dancer—don't worry—I'm an excellent *teacher!*

"This story speaks of kissing my tears away. Don't laugh, but the *surest* way in the world to make me smile is to kiss me. I don't mean just rush up and grab me. What I mean is—well, it's kind of like the greatest thrill in the world for a boy and girl to share a special kiss. And we all know that certain, *special* kiss can turn the saddest frown upside down, making it into a great big smile."

You can write to Sajid at 10202 Washington Blvd., Culver City, Calif.

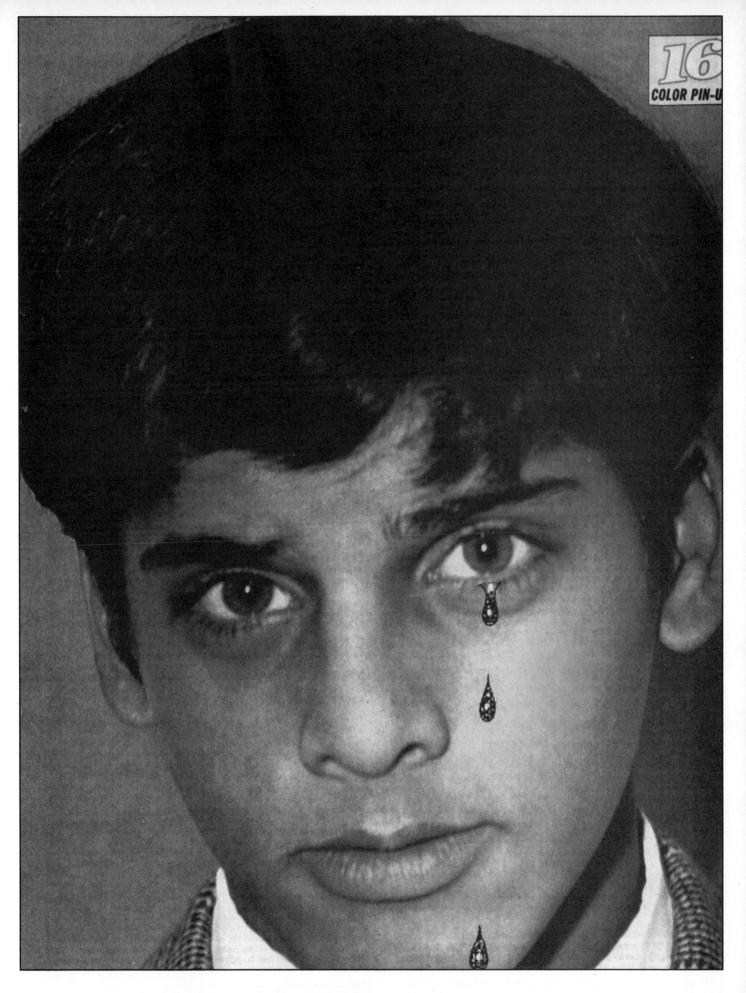

The Sajid 16's readers got to know through pieces like this—and, which spoke about his "secret heart" and his "veil of tears"—inspired them to want to cuddle him and, yes, kiss his tears away!

Sajid Khan

During the years he had no regular TV series or movie, *16*'s coverage never flagged. Photographers and reporters were routinely dispatched to cover Saj, who was presented in exclusive photos at home and in school in Beverly Hills, on a promotional trip to San Francisco, or doing the town in New York. He even "wrote" a column, which began each month with the Indian word *namaste*, or "warmest greetings."

The image created for him by *16* was of a talented young man with a deeply serious and spiritual side, yet someone who could share a laugh, longed for acceptance, and, of course, hoped to meet the "right" girl….In *16* that meant *you, girl*. That image, contrived as it was, in many ways was not far from the truth. Based on the recollections of the various editors who were there, including Nola Leone, Steve DeNaut, and Mimi Menendez, Sajid Khan was extremely sweet, generous (he'd bring gifts to the editors), serious, somewhat lonely, and loyal to his Indian heritage—if not quite to the degree reflected in *16*. If he didn't (like most of the celebrities of the day), actually write the column—Steve DeNaut did—or dictate those first-person stories (that would have been Gloria), he did contribute to all of them. Gloria would pump him for information based on a story idea she had, but he willingly gave interviews, and apparently had no problems with the printed results.

The coverage paid off: Sajid, not known for any musical ability, even won a recording contract—an offshoot, at that time, of teen idol fame—and released a pair of albums on the Colgems label. Gloria actually wrote the liner notes for the first one. Okay, so you probably would have trouble dredging up a memory of any—does "A Closed Heart Gathers No Love" ring a bell?…thought not. Still, his popularity was intense enough for Grosset & Dunlap to sign him to write a book. *Sajid Khan: This Is My Story* came out in 1969.

By the end of 1970, Sajid had all but disappeared from the pages of *16*. Why? At the end of the day, no amount of coverage, no matter how intense, no media-created image, no matter how accurate and appealing, can sustain stardom with a young audience unless the performer continues to have a career. Sajid's early fans grew up and grew away. Because he had no vehicle, no TV show, movie, or hit record, to attract new ones, he, too, grew up and returned to India, where he lives now.

PAUL REVERE & THE RAIDERS

Years of *16* Popularity: 1965–1968

Alongside the British Invasion came an upsurge of home-grown teen idol groups, none more popular during the middle of the '60s than Paul Revere & the Raiders. The group had going for it the unbeatable combination of television and music, first gaining fame as the house band on a variety show (successor to *Your Hit Parade* and precursor to MTV) called *Where the Action Is*. They performed current Top 10 hits, as well as their own songs.

As fan mail started pouring in to (*Action* producer) Dick Clark's office, Gloria was tipped off and *16 Magazine* jumped in. The coverage was all-inclusive and mostly exclusive. Soon, legions of fans understood that the band wasn't named for its cute lead singer after all: the guy at the microphone was Mark Lindsay. Paul Revere himself played keyboards, while the other members of the original lineup were Phil "Fang" Volk on bass, drummer Michael "Smitty" Smith, and Drake Levin, guitarist. By December 1965, "Mark & Raiders" were sharing cover space with the hottest bands of the hour: the Beatles, Herman's Hermits, and another homegrown group, Dino, Desi & Billy. The Raiders bridged the gap between the end of the Beatles' teen idol years and the explosion of the Monkees—and the darker, kinkier days of the Doors that lay just ahead.

Mark Lindsay developed a very personal relationship with Gloria. She was part mentor, part image-maker, part friend. Because of that relationship, the magazine had a phenomenal impact on his career and on his life. To an extent, it still does. "There isn't a day that goes by," explains the still-touring performer, "that someone doesn't come up to me with an old photo and article right out of *16 Magazine*."

Unsurprisingly, Mark has sharp and revelatory memories of his years as a *16 Magazine* teen idol; so when we posed "Our Intimate Questions" to him today, he was eager to participate and set the record straight.

MARK LINDSAY GETS REAL!

Did *16* shape your image in any way?

Not just shape it, Gloria was very instrumental in *developing* my image. She did that from one of our earliest conversations. I'd told her that I was from a small town in Idaho—that I was really a backwoods kid who got thrust into the spotlight overnight. And Gloria related to that. She told me she understood me and was going to help me. Gloria had clothes made for me specifically for the photo shoots. We agreed that the image we were looking for was like a modern-day Errol Flynn, a swashbuckler. But they were outfits you could wear on the street and not get arrested for! It wasn't that different from what Paul Revere & the Raiders were wearing: the tight pants, blousy shirts, that kind of thing. It was Gloria's idea that I wear high boots offstage as well as on.

How did *16*'s emphasis on you affect inter-band relationships?

The problem wasn't so much with the entire band, as with Paul. From the beginning, there was animosity between Paul and Gloria, because he approached her right off, demanding the same amount of coverage she was giving me. She told him basically, if he wasn't getting the fan mail, all the coverage in the world wouldn't do him any good. Besides, Paul was married and the readers knew it—so that spoiled the fantasy right there. Simply, Paul wasn't going to help sell magazines. Even though I was the one getting all the publicity, in the end, it helped sell records for him. But he had an ego, as everyone does, and frankly, he hated that I was getting all the press.

at home with
Mark Lindsay

HIGH UP in the Hollywood Hills, secluded, hidden from the rest of the world, is a beautiful, luxurious, rambling ten-room house that Raider Mark Lindsay calls home. Very few people have had the honor of being Mark's guest there—but now *you* become an exception to all the rules and join Mark as he takes you on a private, personally conducted tour of his new home.

"Hi! It's me, Mark — waiting for you on my swinging electric gate — which is seldom open . . ."

". . . But it's open to you, so come and join me."

"This is a special trip just for you — my **16**-friend."

"Come on in!"

48

In December 1966, 16 took readers "high up in the Hollywood Hills," and through the electronic gate, for a tour of Mark Lindsay's home.

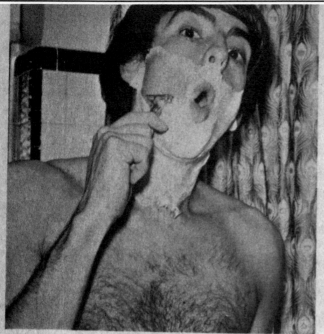

"Time to clean up! Sing in the shower? Sure, and while shaving, too. Doesn't everybody?"

"If you don't mind (and I'm sure you won't), I'll get serious for a few moments and answer a bit of mail."

"Whew! Writer's cramp already. Guess I'll do what I always do — make a few personal calls to my **other 16** friends out there."

"Now, come over here, sit down beside me and listen — I am going to sing a song just for you."

If you think Mark doesn't mean what he says — well, you're zero wrong, little pussycats. Just read the next page, but be sure you're sitting down when you do — cos you might faint dead away!

Paul Revere & The Raiders

Mark and his fashion mentor—Gloria.
(Photo courtesy of Mark Lindsay.)

Any other career advice Gloria gave you?

At the height of our success, she suggested I leave the group. The movie *Wild in the Streets* was being cast, and Gloria thought I'd be perfect for it. And I did audition, and I might have gotten it, but I went to Paul and told him, look, I've got this great opportunity here. Paul got on his knees and went, "How could you leave after all we've meant to each other? How could you do this to me?" He got very maudlin. So I went back to Gloria and said, "Look, I can't in all good conscience leave the group, even though it's probably the best career move. I feel a responsibility to stay with the group."

What was Gloria's reaction?

Gloria had a heart of gold, she really did—but she did not like to be crossed, and she did not like it when you didn't follow through on her ideas. She wasn't above veiled threats and she kind of intimated that if I wanted to commit slow career suicide by staying with the group, she could help hasten the process by taking me out of the magazine. Of course, she never did that, but she was angry at me. In retrospect, of course, she was probably right, the timing was perfect for me to have moved on.

Any other instances of her threatening you or a member of the group, using *16*'s power?

Twice that I can remember, both times involving Paul. Once, Paul was angry about something and told her she wasn't getting any more exclusives. So she retaliated by putting an item in one of her gossip columns intimating that maybe Paul "dated" when he was on the road. Well, of course Paul was married, and at the time, dating others, which Gloria knew all about. So in a sense, she was saying, "Paul, you better not cross me because I know what you're doing." The magazine was quite powerful in those days; a lot of people read it and believed everything they read and saw.

The second instance was actually very poignant. *16* ran a contest, "Win A Day with Mark Lindsay." For the most part, these contests were on the up and up. But this time, Gloria called me and said, "This is not the way I usually do things, and later, we'll do another contest allowing an actual randomly chosen reader to win, but I know of this girl who is dying of cancer, and would you spend the day with her instead?" Well, of course I said yes. I get all choked up when I think about it. I remember riding through Central Park with this little girl, knowing that in six months she wouldn't be here. When she died, Gloria asked us to participate in a benefit honoring this girl—and Paul absolutely refused to do it. I threatened to leave the group, but I think it was Gloria's threat—to publish his real name, which was Paul Revere Dick—that finally swayed him. Like I said, *16* was read by millions and that made it very powerful.

Was there a sexual relationship between you and Gloria?

Contrary to popular belief, no, there wasn't. I mean, I considered Gloria a good friend, and maybe she had eyes for me, but nothing was really overt. Yes, there were times when I thought a more intimate relationship could have developed, but I think we both really wanted to keep it on a business level. I can testify in court that there was nothing of a sexual nature to our relationship.

Paul Revere & The Raiders

_16_'s stories on you were often written in first person. How much of what's written is your actual words?

More than you might think, maybe 70 percent of it. We would do interviews and I would talk at length. Maybe Gloria would amplify it a little, but mostly what you read was what I said. At that point in time, well, I really did think of myself as a white knight. I thought I was going to do some good in this world. I was quite introspective. She portrayed me as this perfect, close-enough-to-touch yet somehow ethereally unattainable guy.

In what ways were you not, in fact, the guy _16_ portrayed you as?

Well, it was the era of free love, and I was quite promiscuous on the road. That was certainly something _16_ never wrote about. But on the whole the Raiders were pretty much clean, on and offstage. Our image wasn't of all-night partyers because we weren't.

Was there ever a time that you wanted your music to be taken more seriously, but felt being in _16_ held you back from that?

Yes and no. I absolutely wanted the Raiders to progress, but it wasn't _16_ that held us back, it was Paul. He said, "fuck the kids, they don't care, just give 'em what they want, which is to hear the same hits over and over again." That was Paul's philosophy and, frankly, one of the reasons I finally did leave the group. All he wanted to do was make money. If he said it once, he said it a thousand times, "take the money and run."

Why do you think your popularity ended when it did?

The part of the '60s when I was popular was still all about innocence. In about '68 the innocence of music died and things became real serious. That was the end of good time rock 'n' roll, because suddenly there was Vietnam, and we didn't win. The music was changing, and Gloria saw that. It was [Jim] Morrison and the Doors. I do remember seeing a layout with Morrison and Gloria and thinking, "gee, I wish that could be me," but I realized we weren't making that kind of music. The Doors were advancing and the Raiders were kind of sailing along doing the same old stuff. A part of me wanted to be doing what Jim was doing, but let's face it, there we were, dancing in our little Revolutionary garb, our tight pants and boots and three-cornered hats. As long as we stuck with that, we'd never be taken seriously. We had one last shot with "Indian Reservation," which was taking a chance for us. Of course, it ended up being our biggest hit ever.

Any final thoughts?

The mid-'60s was a transitional time, from the age of innocence to uh-oh, here we are in reality. And _16_, by giving the stars positive images, gave a lot of kids something to believe in that wasn't harmful. It was Gloria's way of making modern day fairy tales at a time when they just weren't being written anymore. She was like a modern day Mother Goose giving adolescents something to believe in, to make the transition into adulthood a little easier, a little harmless fantasy.

JIM MORRISON

Years of *16* Popularity: 1968–1969

Jim Morrison was *16*'s own dark angel for two years, and Gloria Stavers's as well. It was an historic, metaphoric alliance between Morrison, Stavers, and the readers of *16*.

Initiating the process was Steve Harris, the charming, energetic head of promotion at Elektra Records, for whom the Doors recorded, and a great friend of Gloria's since the days when Harris worked for Bobby Vee and Bobby Rydell. In early 1967, just after the release of the Doors' first album, Harris was trying to get Gloria interested in featuring Jim Morrison as a teen idol; but Gloria resisted—Jim was too sinister for her girls—and Harris persisted, sending Gloria by messenger a never-ending cascade of Jim Morrison photographs, each delivery accompanied by a bouquet of long-stem roses.

The landscape shifted one day toward the end of the winter. Gloria had received an excited call from Dino, Desi, and Billy (it's not certain which of them, if indeed not all three, got on the phone with her) telling her that their hearts' desire was to have the Doors be their opening act "forever." That intriguing lineup never graced a stage, but DD & B, with their greasepaint-filled veins and their own instincts for generating teen hysteria, were reliable barometers of the winds of pubescent tastes. And with her ears all over the place, Gloria was hearing about heat growing in other places where young women talk about fantasy, lust, and rock and roll singers.

Many of the same people who were putting Jim's case to Gloria were doing a similar number to him about her. Bear in mind that he fancied himself above all else a very serious poet and did not want to see his image compromised by proximity to the Monkees and Paul Revere & the Raiders, much as those

two groups have since acquired a certain amount of retro-hipness. "She can make you a *big star*," he was told, and the appeal of that promise was not lost on him, intense poet though he was.

Gloria meanwhile had decided to give it a shot. "Light My Fire," the second single from the Doors, was leaping up the charts, giving the group mass-market credibility, so Gloria told the executives at Elektra to "have Jim give me a call." She intended to put herself, from the outset, in the driver's seat of this relationship.

Jim Morrison wearing Gloria's own coat, in a photo taken in her apartment.

Jim Morrison

Author Danny Fields, a free-lance press agent for the Doors in the fall of 1966, and by late spring of '67 running the Elektra Records publicity department, flew from New York to Los Angeles to oversee the first telephone communication between Gloria and Jim. Fields and Morrison, whose relationship then and always was one of extreme wariness, arrived at Elektra's Hollywood office at about the same time on a June afternoon. Fields phoned Gloria on schedule and handed the phone over to Jim. A few affirmative grunts on Morrison's side ended the conversation, and he handed the phone back to Fields, who was assured by Gloria that her message to Jim had seemed to have gotten across, and vice versa.

Steve Harris arranged the first meeting between Gloria and the group—everyone had to pretend that she wanted to meet all of them, which indeed she did to some extent, but the extraneous members of the band were to be dispensed with when Gloria decided the time was right. Harris and the four Doors came to Gloria's apartment, went out to dinner in the neighborhood, and returned to apartment 12K right after dessert.

"Come with me into the bathroom," Gloria commanded Jim, soon after they all got back to her house. Harris, Robby, Ray, and John went pale with astonishment that anyone would talk to this terrifying person in that manner; they were even more incredulous when he obeyed. Gloria could out-terrify Jim Morrison, because she knew all about how these things worked, and he'd been flying on instinct. Though imaginations in the living room were running wild, no one could have guessed what was happening in Gloria's immaculate lavatory, because when Jim and Gloria emerged, his hair had been brushed straight back off his face. "My girls like to see what boys look like," Gloria explained to her awe-stricken guests, who soon got the idea that they were more or less *de trop*. High above East 63rd Street, Gloria Stavers and Jim Morrison were alone at last.

"So, how was it?" Steve Harris asked Gloria first thing the next morning. Gloria beat about no bushes in her life, and neither did her friends when talking to her. "He was wonderful!" she said, with a teenage enthusiasm her gushiest readers would find hard to match. "You know how he does 'The End,' building and building before that final scream? Well, that's how he made love to me. Very good. Very good." The legendary affair had begun.

It was to be the last great romance of Gloria's life, and it was very intense. When Gloria translated her knowledge of Morrison into the pages of *16*, she of course revealed only a tiny fraction of what she really knew about him, and sweetened and de-fanged the image at the same time.

MONSTROUS!

That Morrison was capable of monstrous behavior was well known to Gloria. Once, when she hadn't seen Jim in several months, she got a call from him saying he was in New York, and staying at the Chelsea Hotel. "Why don't you come right over?" he said, giving her his room number.

She took a taxi to the Chelsea and went up to his room. The door was ajar, as if he'd been expecting her but couldn't be there to let her in. Maybe he was in the shower, Gloria thought, and was being considerate. It was a wishful concept.

Gloria went in—it was a single room—and said "Jim? Are you here?" He was not to be seen, but the bathroom door was closed, and she knocked on that. "Jim?" No answer, and no light to be seen coming from under the door either. She knocked harder, then slowly started to open the bathroom door, as if to give him time and warning. The bathroom was empty. With a creepy feeling, she went through the same routine with the door to the room's one closet. Still no Jim. No note anywhere, not a word, not a sign of him. "Fuck this!" she said, slammed the door to the room behind her, and stormed out of the hotel. When she got back to her apartment, the phone was ringing.

"Hi," said Jim. "I thought we'd be together by now."

"Where the fuck are you?" she demanded. He was using the most romantic and boyish tone of voice in his repertoire; she was using the most pissed-off in hers.

"At the Chelsea. In my room. Where I said I'd be."

"Bullshit! I was just there. I looked everywhere. You were not in that room. What the hell is going on? I even looked in the bathroom and the goddamn closet!"

"But not under the bed," he giggled. Not amused, Gloria hung up on him. It was by no means the end of their relationship, and if she felt humiliated by his treatment of her, it didn't show when she told the story, with great gusto, to her close friends.

It was an odd mix of things that came out of the *16*-Gloria-Morrison affair. Gloria's photographs of him are among the best and most widely seen ever taken, and *16* delivered to the Doors a vast new audience of young girls, who started buying concert tickets and albums just as the group's original fan-base was looking elsewhere for excitement. Morrison's death at the age of 27 has given him a mythic status that he probably never would have achieved if he'd just

JIM MORRISON & "THE MYSTERY GIRL"

Sometimes strange things happen — they are so vivid and so real. But later you find yourself wondering…Did they really happen — or was it all a dream? Do you know?

THE JETLINER gently touched the ground and taxied into the arrival area, its red tail light and wing lights blinking hypnotically. The first-class passenger door opened and the travelers began to file into the area. A tall, lean young man with a long, shimmering mane of light brown hair slowly ambled through the archway. He was wearing a black leather outfit and he blinked briefly at the sudden bright lights in the airport waiting room. He turned and waved back at the two pretty stewardesses who stood by the plane's exit door.

"See you again soon," he called, and though his voice was very soft you could clearly hear each word he spoke.

As he walked toward the baggage area, people turned and stared. They looked first at his hair, and then at his clothes and, finally, at his high black boots. The young man seemed impervious to all this—not coldly indifferent, not embarrassed—just not concerned. It was as though he had endured these same stares a million times and they had ceased to have any meaning for him. So, while the middle-age, middle-class, slightly pompous passersby registered their shock at the sight of him, he glided swiftly in and out of their vision—beautiful, confusing and unforgettable.

He stepped outside, and away from the airport building, and a liveried chauffeur moved toward him. The chauffeur spoke briefly and the young man nodded. A car door swung open and he bent to enter the car, then paused and threw his head back and looked up at the sky. It was late afternoon and the sun was beginning to steal its warmth away. He smiled up at the sun and stepped into the car.

As it rolled along, the young man looked at the sights passing by. He tried to remember where he was, but for the life of him he couldn't.

I never thought this would happen to me. He heard the words in his mind. *But I suppose it had to—sooner or later. Too many towns too close together, too many nights in a row and I get so tired. What a shame, when each one is different and lovely—like a girl I ought to get to know better.*

Snap! He shut his mind off.

Suddenly, he saw a high school, or maybe it was junior high. A crowd of kids were leaving late. *They must have been practicing or cheerleading or something. I remember that. It seems so long ago—but it wasn't.*

All at once he saw a girl standing at a window on the second floor of the building. She seemed to be looking straight into his face; she had an eraser in one hand and the other hand was poised in mid-air, as though she were about to wave. He leaned forward and lifted his hand and smiled. Then the scene was gone.

Next, he saw an enormous sign. From a field yellow large black letters leaped out:

THE
DOORS
TO NITE

Huh. My coat of arms. That's it. Yeah. I'll make a new family crest and sew it on my sleeve one day!

The desk at the motel was grey formica. The desk clerk glared at him. "Yes?" he asked superciliously.

"My name is Jim Morrison. I think I have a reservation."

"Ah, yes, Mr. Morrison." The tone changed to one of friendly reception. "The others are already here. Here is your key. Bellhop, show Mr. Morrison to his room."

The young man closed the door of the room behind him and looked around. One chair; one table; one lamp on the

24

Jim Morrison inspired some of Gloria's best fantasy writing; the "mystery girl" is, of course, Gloria herself.
The issue is January 1968.

table; one bureau; one bed; one TV set. *They* do *all look alike.*

He took off his jacket and put it on a chair, switched on the TV set, turned the blinds down, looked at himself in the mirror for a brief moment, and then stretched out on the bed. The news was on—all bad. Another channel—commercials—another—a cartoon. Finally, a test pattern. He grinned diabolically.

That's it. I'll look at the test pattern.

But sleep—restless and dream-filled—took him away.

He was awakened by a knock on the door.

"Yeah?"

"It's time. Everything O.K.?"

"Yeah, yeah. Everything's fine. I'll be right down."

Young girls were standing outside the motel entrance. He paused and signed some autographs, photographing each face with his mind's camera. Another crowd, slightly larger, was waiting outside the stagedoor, but the road manager hurried him inside explaining to the kids, "No time now. Come back later."

He turned and smiled apologetically just before they closed the door behind him. He hoped they understood.

At first, the dressing room was empty. One bright light bulb illuminated the dirty cracked walls, the dusty mirror, the broken chairs. Empty coat-hangers hung askew on a rack in a corner. The walls were covered with fond memories of another day. "Billy And The Bombers Were Here!" And there were some memories that belonged to today. He wondered where he would be a year from now.

The room began to fill. Musicians came in one by one, booking agents, promo men, photographers, reporters and the blank but anxious faces of hangers-on who somehow always seemed to get through and be there. After a polite length of time, he started for the door.

"Hey," the road manager called, "don't be long. You go on right after intermission."

He nodded yes and walked away. He found himself climbing the backstage stairs. There were several levels and the higher he got, the darker it became. When it was almost black, he saw a little light at the end of a hall. He walked toward it. Inside a little room, he found something that looked like a porthole. He lifted the glass and looked down. He could see the empty stage and security guards. He could see boys and girls milling around in the empty aisles. The first rows of the house were filled with girls who didn't leave their seats—who waited eagerly and sat clutching their handbags, poised and leaning slightly forward. Some of them looked around and he saw their faces. Their eyes were aglow and their lips were slightly parted—delicate and electric.

Suddenly, he was aware of the presence of someone behind him. He turned quickly and found himself looking straight into the eyes of a teenage girl!

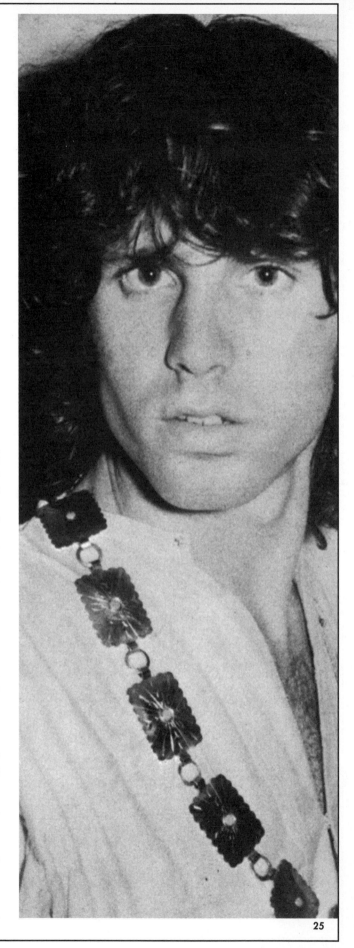

TO BE CONTINUED
Who is she? **Was it** you? **Find out in the February issue of 16! It goes on sale at your newsstand December 21!**

Jim Morrison

Gloria took this picture of a pensive Morrison at a party at the Delmonico Hotel in New York celebrating the success of "Light My Fire." Later that night, he jumped out of a limo (inside of which waited Andy Warhol, Gloria, and others), vomited in the lobby of Elektra Records' president Jac Holzman's apartment house, returned to the car, and asked to be dropped off alone at his hotel. Everyone was glad to be rid of him.

slid into chubby middle age. People are even making a fuss over his very pedestrian poetry, and his grave is the most visited at the Père-Lachaise Cemetery in Paris, where Piaf, Proust, and Oscar Wilde are also interred.

Gloria remained intrigued by Morrison until the end of her life, and was in fact planning to write a book about him, for which she had assembled copious notes, clippings, and, no doubt, memories that will never be known.

WHO'S YOUR FAVE RAVE?

THE MONKEES

Years of *16* Popularity: 1966-1968

Of course the Monkees were invented for television, but they hit the mark, and at their peak they drove the circulation of *16* higher than it ever was before or since. The 1967 "ownership statement" declares monthly sales of a million copies, which of course didn't count pass-along readership; in all, about four million people a month were reading *16* in the Monkees era. A weekly series about a rock band, using many of the cinematic tricks invented for *A Hard Day's Night*, starring 4 boys selected from over 500 who auditioned, and accompanied by a string of genuine hit singles, could hardly fail to enchant teenagers, and indeed it did. With the debut of their show, the Monkees took the top spot on the cover and held it through the end of 1967.

Because the Monkees were considered characters in a TV show and not real people (a distinction some other TV characters had difficulty in comprehending, to their never-ending dismay), *16* had to pay a license fee for each story about them. What's more, story ideas had to be submitted to Screen Gems for their approval, but this process was largely legal ceremony; Gloria was not about to wound the goose that was laying such a very golden egg,

and Screen Gems in turn was in awe of Gloria, and terrified of getting into a fracas with her.

It was quite lovey-dovey, and the actors who played the Monkees cooperated more or less willingly, fully realizing how lucky they were to have landed such a plum series. They were known to display a certain mild contempt for the very naïve questions put to them by *16*'s editors; even actors playing the Monkees had to assert their creative selves every once in a while. Peter Tork was the most cooperative (encouraging his grandmother to help *16*'s editors), Dolenz and Jones would do whatever they were told, and Mike Nesmith was the least cooperative, striving mightily to convey that he cared little about the whole thing. In fact, it was Nesmith (rich in his own right—his mother invented Liquid Paper correction fluid) who shocked the crowd at a 1967 press conference by complaining that as individuals the Monkees were being misrepresented. (Oh?)

Hey, hey, they're the Monkees.

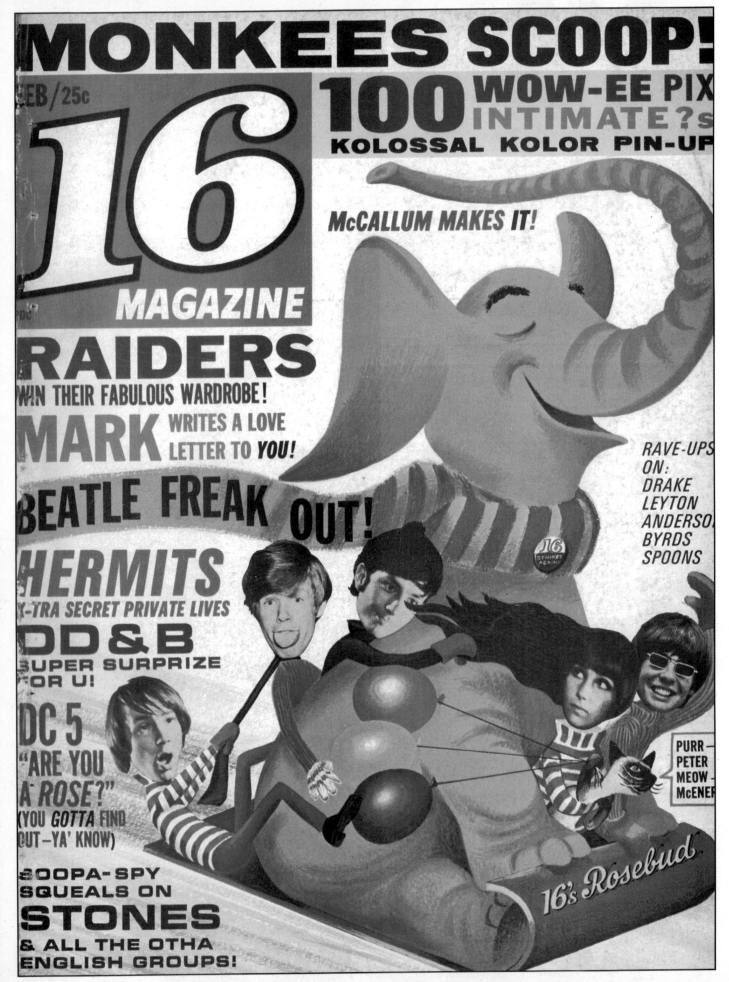

MONKEES SCOOP!

FEB/25c

16
MAGAZINE

100 WOW-EE PIX
INTIMATE ?s
KOLOSSAL KOLOR PIN-UP

McCALLUM MAKES IT!

RAIDERS
WIN THEIR FABULOUS WARDROBE!

MARK
WRITES A LOVE LETTER TO *YOU!*

BEATLE FREAK OUT!

HERMITS
X-TRA SECRET PRIVATE LIVES

DD & B
SUPER SURPRIZE FOR U!

DC 5
"ARE YOU A ROSE?"
(YOU *GOTTA* FIND OUT—YA' KNOW)

SOOPA-SPY SQUEALS ON
STONES
& ALL THE OTHA ENGLISH GROUPS!

RAVE-UPS ON:
DRAKE
LEYTON
ANDERSON
BYRDS
SPOONS

PURR—PETER MEOW—McENER

16's Rosebud

A Monkees-dominated cover, typical of all the covers in 1967.

"40 SECRETS WE NEVER TOLD"

BY THE MONKEES

NBC-TV's ZANY NEW STARS DROP SOME WAY-DOWN SECRETS IN YOUR EARS WHILE THEY DRIVE YOU UP THE WALL!

DAVY JONES

My middle name is Thomas — but please don't tell.

My nick, of course, is Davy — but my secret nick is "Frito."

I am five feet and five inches tall.

I used to hate being short, but I don't mind it anymore.

My dad's name is Harry Thomas.

I have three older sisters: Hazel, Beryl and Lynda — all in their twenties.

The family still lives in a small but very nice house in Manchester, England (where I was born).

I live in a beautiful home in the Hollywood Hills, with a bay window overlooking a spectacular view.

When do I plan to get married? Well, let's see — how about 1974?

I have a secret **crush on Barbara Streisand!**

MICKY DOLENZ

My real name (ha-ha!) is Havershap Spleenblaum, but you can call me Micky — with no e.

I am the world's biggest teaser (wait and see!).

I was born in the middle of Big Bear Lake, in the mountains of California.

I am only seven and one-half inches tall.

I have red eyes and fuschia hair.

I don't think I'll ever get married.

Among my many accomplishments is my ability to play comb and wax paper — and artichoke.

My favorite color is invisible.

I don't like girls who like okra.

I do like girls with long hair or short hair — no matter what, I like to get in their hair.

Four full pages were devoted to the new phenomenon in the January 1967 issue.
Hardly "secrets," these were the basic facts you needed to know to get your Monkee-mania off and running.

The Monkees

In fact, the career of the Monkees is as full of irony as an anthology of O. Henry stories. At the time, "serious musicians" mocked (and perhaps envied) their success, and especially hated the fact that the Monkees had hit records (since others played the instruments on the Monkees' early recordings). Now many years later, genuinely "serious musicians" of our own time, like Michael Stipe of R.E.M., believe that the Monkees should be inducted into the Rock and Roll Hall of Fame, on the grounds that for millions of viewers too young to go to live concerts, the Monkees *were* rock and roll, and inspired thousands of their fans to start rock bands, so they too could have as much fun as Davy, Micky, Mike, and Peter. We leave the argument to aestheticians and social historians; from *16*'s point of view, the Monkees were made in heaven, er…Hollywood, er…heaven, er… what's the difference?

Peter   Micky

RANDI & DANNY ANSWER 24 INTIMATE QUESTIONS!

Through the years, the same questions have come up time and again relative to this magazine, and the entire teen idol phenomenon. Here, once and for all, we take you up-close 'n' personal into the real world of *16*. In no particular order, these are the answers to the questions we've been asked the most often.

WHAT DOES IT TAKE TO BE A TEEN IDOL?

There's no magic formula; however, there are certain defining characteristics—and exceptions to every rule. There is no magic cut-off age where one's chances are forever dashed. But if you're older than 25, you should play a younger character on TV.

Speaking of character: the most popular teen-idol TV characters were smart-aleck rebels with a vulnerable heart of gold.

Speaking of TV, visibility is crucial; a weekly TV show is a big plus. For rockers, a concert tour and MTVisibility.

Looks: boyish rather than mannish is always the rule. If a potential idol looks too much like a fan's father, the fantasy is just not going to work.

IS TEEN IDOLDOM A SUREFIRE CAREER DEATH SENTENCE?

The people more qualified to answer that than we are: John Travolta, Michael Jackson, Kurt Russell, Tom Cruise, Jodie Foster, Cher, Matt Dillon. Also see: Paul Anka, Paul McCartney, Elton John, Mick Jagger. More recently: Michael J. Fox, Patrick Swayze. Talent will out.

OKAY, BUT WHO ELSE, REALLY?

It's a matter of perception: what is success? Talk to Frankie, Fabian, pick-a-Bobby-any-Bobby; even Donny, Davy, or Herman. They all still feel successful. They are still making a living—and really decent money—doing what they love.

DID YOU HAVE TO BE NAMED BOBBY TO BE A TEEN IDOL?

No, but in the early '60s and '70s, it helped. See Darin, Rydell, Vee, Vinton, and most significantly, Sherman.

WHO WAS THE SINGLE MOST POPULAR TEEN IDOL EVER?

In terms of who was on top when the publication sold the most copies, it was that shaggy-haired fab foursome—nope, guess again—the Monkees. In terms of length of stay on the top banner and on the cover, it would be a toss-up between Donny Osmond and Bobby Sherman, with David Cassidy very close behind.

WAS *16* THE FIRST TEEN MAGAZINE?

Yes.

IS IT STILL AROUND TODAY?

Of course! In May 1997, it celebrated 40 years.

DID YOU EVER GET SUED FOR SOMETHING YOU WROTE?

Once. In the November 1973 issue, we had some fun with photos of two stars who couldn't have been more different. In an article entitled "Alice—I Want to Be Like Donny" and its companion piece, "Donny—I Want to Be Like Alice," art director Chris DiNapoli, without computer graphics, actually "switched" heads on the two stars. We superimposed Donny Osmond's head and hat on Alice Cooper's snake-hugging naked body (!!) and did the same with Alice's unkempt head on Donny's completely clothed bod. So thrilled were we with our creation, we even made it the top banner line on the cover. Alice thought it was a hoot. What Donny thought, we never found out: mom Olive Osmond was not amused, as her lawyer soon advised us.

CAN A TEEN IDOL BE "CREATED"?

Not in our experience. Although the term *manufactured* is used by many a cynic to describe any teen idol, we believe

DONNY-"I WANT TO BE LIKE ALICE!"

Could It Really Be True That In His Most Secret Fantasies, Darlin' Donny Osmond Wants To Be Like Alice Cooper?! In His Own Words, Here He Tells Why!

"I recently had this nightmare, in which I was dreaming about doing a concert before 100,000 people. Suddenly the curtains parted, and I stood there on the stage alone. In place of the usual screams of "Donny" and "I love you!", the audience wasn't cheering at all. In fact, they were laughing!

"I was so embarrassed that instead of singing *Too Young*, I ran off the stage to look into the nearest available mirror. And there I saw, to my horror, that I no longer looked like the Donny Osmond everybody knew—but my hair was shoulder length and my face had grotesque make-up on it! In fact, I looked just like Alice Cooper! Just at that moment of realization, I woke up from the dream and ran to the mirror in my bedroom. I was reassured to see that I looked like Donny again, but still I couldn't help wondering what would have happened if I had returned to the stage (in my dream) and performed Alice's act instead of mine!

"The weird fascination that audiences have for Alice intrigues me. They mob his concerts and buy his records and cheer him on—but they don't seem to be "in love" with Alice the way my fans are with me. He's not exactly the kind of guy a girl brings home to Mother!

"It would be fun to be Alice for other reasons, too. He doesn't specialize in love songs, like I do—but his songs have themes like *School's Out* and *Elected.* I'd like to try some songs like that! He and his band write a lot of their own material, and someday I'd like to write songs, too. (Of course my brothers Alan, Wayne and Merrill already write lots of Osmond songs.)

"Alice uses animals in his act, I understand, (Especially snakes!) While I'm not attracted to reptiles, it might be fun to add some dogs and cats to our act! (Jimmy and Jay would especially like that!)

"The use of make-up is a growing phenomenon among rock singers. How do you think I'd look in mascara, rouge, false eyelashes and a wig? I could get all my make-up at a discount from sister Marie's "make-up mart," the mail-order business she sponsors.

"It's funny—in a way, Alice and I are exact opposites. While he lets go and lives out all his wild fantasies *on* stage, he is very quiet and "Fred MacMurray-ish" offstage. His friends know him as a thoughtful and personable fellow. He wouldn't dream of going to the excesses that he does on-stage when he's with friends—he even wears pretty straight clothes when he's not performing!

"But I do somewhat the opposite. My brothers and I are pretty straight *on* stage, but when we get home, we go wild! We have pillow fights and water fights and food fights and we wrestle and practice karate on each other. If we ever tried to express our off-stage feelings during a performance, the show might turn out looking just like Alice Cooper's! And Jimmy would be sure to add peanut butter somewhere in the act.

"Finally, I'd love to wear some of the crazy costumes Alice has adopted. Ripped pants and tops. outfits with spangles—they're all great! I'm getting a little bit tired of our white jumpsuits.

"Both Alice and I want to make a movie—maybe we'll make one together! Wouldn't *that* be the wildest, most way-out thing you've ever seen?

"As you can see, it might not be so preposterous after all for me to become like Alice Cooper. Most important of all, Alice and I both love our fans more than anything—and that gives us a lot in common!"

6

The one Olive Osmond did not like—and probably still doesn't—"I Want to Be Like…"came out in November 1973.

ALICE— "I WANT TO BE LIKE DONNY!"

The Fearsome Fiend Of Freak-Rock Strikes Again With His Most Shocking Revelation Ever—*He* Wants To Be Like *Donny Osmond*!

Alice Cooper and Donny Osmond—the two names hardly fit in the same breath, so different are these two fabulously famous favs. And yet—though it would seem unlikely that either of them is even *aware* of the other—Alice and Donny have taken an intense interest in each other's careers. What's more, they *admire* and *envy* each other! What *is* this world coming to?!

Now that you've heard (on the facing page) why darlin' Donny digs outrageous Alice, here's the other side of the story—now you can learn what wicked, wily Alice thinks about adorable Donny 'Adonis' Osmond! If you've got any gasps-of-surprise left in you, save 'em for *these* confidential confessions—you'll need 'em!

ALICE ON DONNY

"I'd rather see the Osmonds than most rock groups," says rocker Alice Cooper about a group that's as different from Alice's group as different can be. Tho he's only seen the Osmonds on TV, Alice is one of the biggest fans of that singin', swingin' family. He likes the way they do things, their professionalism, their tight show, and the excitement they cause wherever they go.

Years ago, when Alice Cooper and his band were first "getting it all together," they were very conscious of the values of professionalism and putting on a good show. In fact, it was Alice's show, and his eagerness to really entertain his audiences, which made *his* band stand out from the rest. And Alice—more than ever—has tremendous respect for performers who try extra hard to put on a show and give the people something really special to remember.

"I'd like to meet Donny," Alice says. "I think we wouldn't find ourselves too far apart. In a way, we receive the same kind of admiration, Donny and I. It's just that our styles are so different. But I think Donny is great, he's terrific. And the Osmonds make great singles. I especially liked *Down By The Lazy River* and the one that goes, "Yummy, yummy, yummy, I got love in my tummy."

Alice claims that his and Donny's similar backgrounds (Alice comes from a line of fundamentalist ministers, and Donny is a strict Mormon) have been responsible for the tightness, dedication and discipline with which both his group and the Osmonds approach their work. "I've never felt as if I *rebelled* against my strict upbringing," Alice says. "It's more accurate to say that I was very influenced by it, and I've adapted it to my own needs and aims. And when I see the Osmonds work, I know how much *their* background has contributed to making them what they are, and I feel as if I understand what makes them go."

Would Alice really like to be *like* Donny? "Sure!" he exclaims. "In the sense that I like to cause excitement, and to reach the younger kids. *They* really know where it's at, and I would love them to dig what we do. I know that of course they respond differently to me than they do to him, but it's the *fact* that they respond that counts. You know what I'd *really* like to do—I'd like to trade places with Donny for a week. I bet we'd both find out a lot!"

As Alice sums it up, "Entertainment is entertainment, and entertainers gotta do the best they can. Donny does his best, and I hope I do mine."

So, you see, though Alice and Donny are very far apart in many ways, they are very close in others. You'll never have any trouble telling the differences between them, but now that you know what they think of each other, you may want to start thinking about how similar Donny Osmond and Alice Cooper really are!

Randi & Danny Answer 24 Intimate Questions!

that no publication can shove a celebrity down the public's throat and say, "Here, worship him." *16* has always showed the utmost respect for its readers: although it has presented many an unknown, it has not continued coverage without fan support. From the get-go, the readers have always told the editors who they want to read about. Yes, there have been "Editor's Pets" through the years—Lenny Bruce, Al Pacino, Iggy Pop, Barry Manilow, and, currently, Dean Cain come to mind—but none has taken space from a legitimate reader-based fave. All that said, it needs to be noted that Charles Laufer, who used to own *Tiger Beat*, did in fact "create" the DiFranco Family and they did have a hit record. Needless to say, the DiFrancos were idols *non grata* in *16*. We refused to acknowledge their existence and eventually they did go away.

WHY DOESN'T THIS RETROSPECTIVE INCLUDE '80s TEEN IDOL ICONS, LIKE KISS, OR THE COREYS? AND WHERE'S DURAN DURAN?

We ran out of room. Wait for volume 2.

WHO WAS THE MOST TALENTED TEEN IDOL YOU EVER SAW?

RANDI: Michael Jackson. At the ages of 12 and 14, he blew me away.

DANNY: Leif Garrett.

WHY ARE THE ISSUES DATED SO MANY MONTHS AHEAD—WHY DOES THE MAY ISSUE COME OUT IN MARCH?

It isn't done to confound anyone. That practice was started years ago to perpetuate the perception of always being fresh and new, not stale.

WHY SO MANY EXCLAMATION POINTS??!!

It's the enthusiasm, stupid! And the breathless, passionate way the reader feels about every item of ultimate importance about her idols!!

IF A CELEBRITY SAID SOMETHING OBNOXIOUS IN AN INTERVIEW, DID YOU CHANGE IT TO SOMETHING MORE SYMPATHETIC IN THE MAGAZINE?

In spite of *16*'s earnest attempts to (as Gloria pounded into us) "get it right," still, the magazine never pretended to be

journalism. The readers were always the main concern and we tried to protect them. Why protect them from quotes that may have been chauvinistic, selfish, or just plain stupid? Pre-teen girls were our readers and, on the whole, notoriously insecure about their body image. In the '60s and '70s they were too easily led into feeling they had to change themselves to "get" a boy. The irony doesn't escape us that in a publication whose sales depend on the concept of girls idolizing boys, *16*'s editors, whether it was Gloria or any of her successors, tried mightily to infuse whatever self-esteem we could in those readers. "Every girl needs to feel she is worthy, desirable, and has a shot at the object of her affections," Gloria would tell us. She believed that and, to an editor, so did we.

There was another, more pragmatic reason as well. The depth of feeling the readers had for their fave raves knew no parameters: love was blind and it was fierce. If the fave rave *du jour* did, or said, something truly horrendous, and *16* reported it—without some kind of sympathetic spin—invariably, the readers turned on us. "You lied about [name your fave]! He would never have said/done/thought that!" And, most chillingly, "I will never buy *16* again."

YEAH, BUT WE'RE ALL GROWN UP NOW: GIVE US SOME SPECIFICS

There are many in the preceding and succeeding chapters, but as a general rule, if we had a dime for every rock star who answered the question "What Do You Look For in a Girl?" with "big boobs" (which we morphed into "a sense of humor"), we wouldn't be waiting for royalties on this book to retire on. For more examples, keep reading!

WHAT IS THE AVERAGE LENGTH OF A TEEN IDOL'S REIGN AT THE TOP?

The same as an average reader's years with the magazine—about three. At that point, she is ready for real boys and her younger sister wants idols of her own. There are, again, exceptions to every rule. If a performer keeps on working, keeps on having hit records or a hot TV show, the popularity will last.

HOW DO YOU DETERMINE WHO GOES ON THE COVER?

Unsolicited reader mail. From *16*'s inception, the practice of reading, counting, tallying, scoring every letter, on a weekly

Randi & Danny Answer 24 Intimate Questions!

basis, has never been abandoned. The fans tell you who they care about—it is never the other way around.

WHO WAS THE STUPIDEST TEEN IDOL EVER?

We'd have to go with the Bay City Roller who didn't understand the question "What's Your Favorite Color." His answer? "I am not a racialist." True story.

WHO WAS THE SMARTEST?

DANNY: Paul McCartney.

RANDI: I'm still thinking; give me time.

WHO CONSISTENTLY REFUSED TO COOPERATE?

We had no trouble in the '60s, but within the confines of the '70s—you'll have to wait for volume 2 for the '80s—it would be Randolph Mantooth, with *Starsky & Hutch*'s Paul Michael Glaser as runner-up.

'FESS UP: WERE THOSE "WIN A DATE" CONTESTS REAL?

Every one. If we said you were going to win a date with a star, we had the star's full cooperation and we made it happen. If we said you'd win a phone call from a star, we made it happen. Except once: Lorenzo Lamas agreed to a Win a Phone Call contest. We picked a winner; he then refused to make the call. Luckily, the winner was satisfied with a call from Paul McCartney. Only kidding…we don't remember how we made it up to the kid, but we did.

DO KIDS WHO READ THESE KINDS OF MAGAZINES GROW UP TO BE CELEBRITY STALKERS?

No, they grow up to be rich and famous editors and authors. Like us. Really, reading *16* is not harmful to your health. For most balanced individuals, it is a stage in one's life. Girls "try out" the idea of a boyfriend before they're actually ready to have one—and if you're fantasizing, why not put Donny Osmond's picture, or David Cassidy's poster, on the wall? And as long as we live in a society that glorifies the young, the

pretty, the cellulite-free, there will be idols. Do men not idolize/fantasize about Pamela Lee? Cindy Crawford? Elle/Noami/Claudia/Kate? Do grown women not go gaga over Mel? Or Denzel? Most folks then go home to their houses/spouses/car pools/jobs. Fans are consumers; stalkers are just plain nuts—oops, forgot our *16* manners. Not nuts, they have a dread disease.

WHAT'S YOUR FAVORITE COLOR?

DANNY: Morning Glory Heavenly Blue.

RANDI: Green.

WHO WERE YOUR PERSONAL FAVE RAVES?

RANDI: As a fan, Ricky Nelson, Michael Landon, and George Maharis. Then, the Beatles, big time. I knew every word of every song (still do); my best girlfriend and I can still recite the entire script to *A Hard Day's Night*. She used to fantasize that Paul McCartney's car would break down on our street and he'd knock on her door for help (what he'd actually be doing on 68th Drive we never quite fathomed). We stood outside the Delmonico Hotel and screamed; we went to Forest Hills Tennis Stadium and Shea Stadium. We couldn't hear a word, but we remember it all, especially Paul's soaked-with-sweat curly ringlets. We played at "being" the Beatles—they always made me be Ringo. (It was Paul I lusted after.) And in the throes of teen angst, I locked myself in my room and played "She's Leaving Home," over and over again. And even though you didn't ask—yes, I read *16*, lived and breathed it. When I grew up to be an editor, I met and interviewed hundreds of celebrities. Of those, Henry Winkler takes fave rave honors. He was the classiest, the most compassionate and real actual human being I ever covered. And no, I never did meet Paul McCartney, nor do I want to: what if it spoiled the fantasy? It would be gone forever.

DANNY: As a fan, Edith Piaf and Joey Ramone. As an editor, David and Andy Williams.

TOP STAR RECIPE PAGE

THIS MONTH STEVEN TYLER OF AEROSMITH GIVES US HIS FAVORITE RECIPE

This Won't Be Any Fish Story! Oops—That's Just What It Is! Cos It Turns Out That Steven Tyler's Fave Food Is Seafood—And There's Nothing He Likes Better To Eat On The Road Or At Home Than A Delicious Piece Of Buttery Fish! Maybe That's How He Keeps His Lean And Luscious Body Lean And Luscious! But Anyhow, Steven's Very Favorite Fish—The One He Even Cooks Himself At Home And Gets His Girlfriend To Cook For Him Too Whenever He Can—Is Brook Trout! And Here, Steven Shares His Special Delicious Way Of Preparing It!

Hi! This is Steven Tyler! This dish is easy to make, believe me—I'm not really a master chef and I like to take the easy way in cooking! But the result is great—and you're really going to love it! Oh, I guess I'd better tell you one more thing before I give you the recipe. When you're ready to eat this masterpiece—watch out for the bones! This will serve two—I'll be over at eight!

BROOK TROUT MEUNIERE

2 Brook Trout
About a half-cup of flour seasoned with salt and pepper
1/3 cup melted butter
1/4 cup chopped parsley
Lemon wedges

Wash trout and drain leaving head and tail on. Dip fish into flour. Saute trout in half the butter until trout is firm, and brown. Put trout on serving platter and cover with chopped parsley. Add remaining butter to pan drippings. Cook, over medium heat until butter becomes golden brown. Spoon butter over fish. Serve with lemon wedges.

Eat up!

---

16 Curiosities

Lest you think *16* was exclusively about "40 Intimate Love Secrets You Never Knew" and the like, here are some vintage articles that fall outside the standard story formulas. What do you make of the following?

I WANNA BE YOUR DOG
(As recorded by the Stooges on Elektra Records. Lead sung by Iggy.)

So messed up—I want you here.
In my room, I want you here.
Now we're gonna be face to face,
And I'll lay right down in my favorite place.

Now I wanna be your dog.
Now I wanna be your dog.
Now I wanna be your dog.
Well, c'mon.

Now I'm ready to close my eyes.
Now I'm ready to close my mind.
Now I'm ready to feel your hand—
And lose my heart on the burning sand.

Now I wanna be your dog.
Now I wanna be your dog.
Now I wanna be your dog.
Well, c'mon.

LEFT: Aerosmith's randy lead singer Steven Tyler was as handy in the kitchen as he was with a microphone. This fish story appeared in the July 1976 issue.

ABOVE: The lyrics to punk anthem "I Wanna Be Your Dog" appeared in the May 1969 issue for your "Sing Along" pleasure.

THE REAL NIMOY!

LEONARD

SPOCK

DO YOU KNOW THIS MAN? Every Thursday evening at 8:30, EST, he jets into your home on your NBC-TV channel in a show named Star Trek. *All of you who watch the show know him as Spock, and know that he comes from outer space.*

But there's a lot more to Spock than meets the eye — as most of you suspect, judging from the host of letters you've written asking what Spock is really like. To give you the full and true facts, 16 invites you aboard its exclusive flying missile, and — hold on! — here we go to the stratosphere to get answers from none other than Spock himself!

"My full real name is Leonard Nimoy. I've never had a nickname except Spock, the name I use on *Star Trek*.

"I was born on March 26 in Boston, Massachusetts, and I still have a trace of a New England accent in my speech. I came into the world with brown hair and hazel eyes, and I still have them; I also grew to my present six feet and 165 pounds. My mother's name was (and is) Dora, my dad's Max, and I have a brother named Melvin.

"I went to Boston College which, since it is in my home city, kept me close to the family while it also improved my education. Then, in 1954, I married a lovely girl named Sandi. Today we have two children: Julie, 11, and Adam, 10 — and we live in an attractive and extremely comfortable Mediterranean-type house in Fox Hills, California.

62

"When I'm not deeply involved in my role of Spock on *Star Trek*, I enjoy playing the guitar, listening to recordings — I like all kinds of music, prefer the Beatles and the Monkees among the groups and Frank Sinatra and Ray Charles among the individual singers — and catching the newest films; Anthony Quinn is my favorite actor and the actress I admire most is Anne Bancroft. I enjoy TV too, naturally, but I work so late into the evening on *Star Trek* that I rarely have time to watch other shows, and so I have no favorite program.

"The colors I am most partial to are green and blue, and I go for tasty food of every description. Woodworking takes a good deal of my free time (it gives me a kick to work with my hands around the house), and tropical fish and photography are two of my other hobbies. I enjoy fishing and haul out my hook-and-line whenever the mood seizes me.

"My ambition: I want to be the best actor I can possibly become, and I am working very hard to perfect my talents. Eventually, I would like to act in good feature films — in roles which have bite and say something about life.

"If you would like to write to me, I would be delighted to hear from you. Address your letters to: Leonard Nimoy, 1933 Comstock Avenue, Los Angeles 25, California. I will answer every letter I possibly can."

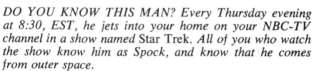

Going forth boldly where no teen mag had ever gone before, we dared to present Spock as a teen idol! This is from the April 1967 issue.

WOULD YOU LIKE TO MARRY TONY PERKINS?

Third in a series of horoscopes foretelling your fate if you mate a star

WHAT DO THE STARS SAY about the boy you're most likely to be attracted to, the kind of date you should bait, the man who's most apt to make you happy? As every student of astrology knows, your fate is written in the heavens—for each of us is one of twelve types of individuals corresponding to one of the twelve signs of the Zodiac. To decide if you are well-mated, simply match his birth-sign with yours and let the stars tell you if your individual qualities mesh!

IS TONY PERKINS YOUR FAVORITE? Do you picture him as just the kind of lad you'd like to marry? Well, let's see how happy you'd be! Tony was born on April 14, 1932, under the sign of Aries the Ram. That means he's idealistic, adventurous, one of the few Sir Galahads left in the world. In fact, he's so ambitious, high-spirited, generous, and chivalrous that he has a tendency to start things he can't finish. Consistency is not one of his virtues and above all else he dislikes routine. Generally, his disposition is pleasant, his conversation is sparkling, and he has loads of charm which attracts the opposite sex as a flame does moths. From time to time, he's extremely cynical, however.

ON THE WHOLE, like all Aries men, Tony is a shade too impulsive, too enthusiastic about things he hasn't given himself time to appraise. But he has a warm and loving nature; he's fond of gayety and most social amusements. Since Venus, the Goddess of Love, and Mars, the God of War, were both dominant in the heavens when Tony was born, conflicting influences are usually at work in him. On the one hand, he is sensitive to the arts; on the other, he is apt to be overly-aggressive in attaining his goals. But Venus by far is the stronger force, with the result that Tony generally is sweet and gentle. If all this is what you're looking for in a mate, marry an Aries man—like Tony Perkins!

What? There is something touching and odd about this story, printed in the March 1959 issue.

51

SALLY FIELD tells
"THE TRUTH ABOUT THE TEEN KINGS"

PRETTY SALLY FIELD considers herself about the luckiest girl in the world. Not only is her TV series *The Flying Nun* filmed on the same lot where *The Monkees* and Bobby Sherman's new TV show *Here Comes The Brides* are shot, but Sally is often a regular guest on *Happening '68!* Aside from all that, she also frequents the local Hollywood clubs, clothing stores and ice cream parlors where — if you're pert and alert — you can meet some of the MOST *interesting* people!!

Here is a list of the groovy guys Sally has been fortunate enough to get to know well, those whom she doesn't know so well, and even one whom she hasn't met yet — plus Sally's very own personal point of view on each of these tantalizing "Teen Kings"!

DAVY JONES: *"Davy is the most energetic guy I have ever met. He is super friendly, has a fantastic personality and is a beautiful flirt! But his most intriguing quality is his air of mystery. When you look at him, you always wonder what he is really thinking — and you know how batty that can drive a girl!"*

PETER TORK: "Peter is the warmest, most caring, concerned and loving person I have ever known in my life. If the whole world were made up of Peter Torks, it would be like a peaceful and serene heaven."

MICKY DOLENZ: *"He is the total clown. Micky is completely funny and always a joy to be around."*

MIKE NESMITH: "When people first meet Mike, they think he is indifferent. I learned that he is actually a little shy. After you get to know him, and learn how very sincere and honest he is, you gain immense respect and admiration for him."

SAJID KHAN: *"Sajid is another fellow who is somewhat shy. The first thing you notice about him is his great big beautiful brown eyes. They just make you melt. There's no other word to describe the Sajid Khan charisma except 'sexy'!"*

BOBBY SHERMAN: "I've always known that Bobby was a good singer, but it was only lately that I found out what a fine actor he is. Wait'll you see him in Here Comes The Brides on TV this fall. I know you'll flip!"

DINO MARTIN: *"Now, here's a boy I'd like to get to know better (wouldn't you?). When he looks at you with those cool x-ray blue eyes of his — well, you just come unstrung!"*

MARK LINDSAY: "I'd also like to know the 'King' of Happening '68 better! He was very kind and funny when I did the show. Besides being gorgeous, he's tall and manly."

JIM MORRISON: *"I've only met Jim once and seen him on the street twice — and I guess you could say I'm hooked. I've got my fingers crossed, hoping I get to meet him again — and get to know him better!"*

BRENDON BOONE: "I've never met Brendon at all, but you can bet your halo I'd like to! Don't you think a "nun" and a "gorilla" would make a crazy couple?"

You can write to Sally at Screen Gems, 1334 N. Beechwood, Hollywood, Calif. Be sure to put "I'm A *16* Reader" on the outside of your envelope.

Sally Field, then "the Flying Nun," really, really liked the "teen kings" of her era, the late '60s.

RONNY HOWARD plays The Dating Game!

THE RED-HAIRED DARLIN' of ABC's **The Smith Family** decided not to take any chances when he played ABC's smash game show **The Dating Game**. Ronny asked **all** the questions, so he could be **sure** of coming out a winner! Let's join him now for some **Dating Game** fun!!

Ronny fired question after zany question at the three lucky girls playing **The Dating Game** with him. The answers made Ronny laugh a **lot**—while the questions triggered **all** kinds of reactions from (left to right) Debbie, Nola and Cindy!

Nola Greene, a student, must have made Ronny **really** chuckle, cos he chose her as his **Dating Game** dollie! Host Jim Lange looked on as the happy couple got to know each other! Ronny and Nola's **Dating Game** date took them on a fantastic boat trip to Catalina—a beautiful island in California. Don'tya just wish **you** could have been a stowaway?!!

24

Before he went behind the cameras to become one of Hollywood's most important directors, Ronny Howard faced some tough choices!

ADONIS OF THE MONTH

TOM JONES

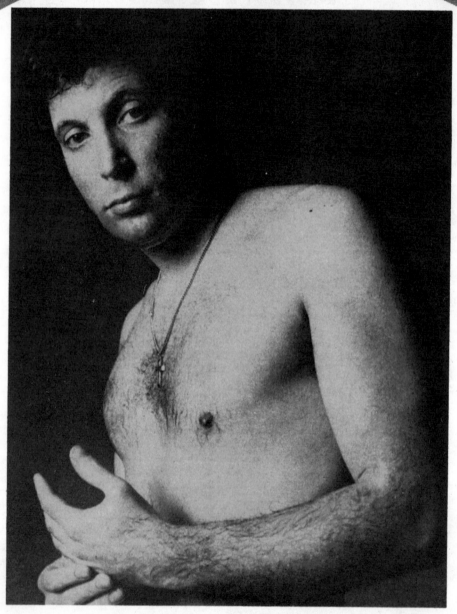

ADONIS was the beautiful youth loved by APHRODITE, goddess of love and beauty in Greek mythology. Now YOU can be APHRODITE — and adore your very own ADONIS!

VITAL STATISTICS ON TOM JONES
Height: Six feet tall.
Weight: 165 pounds.
Hair: Black.
Eyes: Green.
Marital Status: He's married — his wife's name is Linda and they have a son, Mark.
Records: Recent single is *I'll Never Fall In Love Again* and latest LP is *This Is Tom Jones!* Tom is on the Parrot label.
TV: *The Tom Jones Show* can be seen every Thursday on ABC-TV at 9 P.M. (EST).
Address: You can write to Tom Jones at ABC-TV, Hollywood, California. Be sure to put "I'm A *16* Reader" on the outside of your envelope!

Who'da thunk it? Obviously, we did, in the December 1969 issue.

MARK HAMILL
His Hates & Loves!

You Thrilled To Him As "Luke Skywalker" in *Star Wars*, And You Can Hardly Wait Till Next Year When *Star Wars, Part II* Will Be Filmed! And Betcha Can't Believe How Super-Sexy He Looks In His New Movie, *Corvette Summer*—But How Much Do You Know About The **Real Mark Hamill?** Do You Know **Exactly** What Turns Him On—And What Turns Him Off? C'mon And Find Out *All* About Mark And The Things He Really Hates & Really Loves!

What Mark Loves . . .

- Mark *loves* drawing—especially cartoons and he loves painting watercolors too!
- Mark *loves* anything in his favorite colors—orange and blue.
- Mark **loves** watching his favorite actors, Gene Hackman and Harvey Keitel perform in movies.
- Mark *loves* comedies—and he'd like to act in one some day!
- Mark *loves* going to the beach, walking on the beach and living on the beach. In fact, he loves everything about the beach and the ocean too!
- Mark *loves* water sports—like skiing, surfing and sailing!
- Mark **loves** museums and whenever he can, he enjoys going to them—in fact, the things he loves best about New York are the museums there.
- Mark *loves* toys and games and he has one whole room in his apartment where he keeps his collection—including some he recently bought in England.
- Mark *loves* Beatles music—he has all their albums too!
- Mark *loves* being with a girl who has a good sense of humor—he thinks that's lot more important than how she looks.
- Mark really *loves* his family—his mom, Sue—his dad, Bill—his two brothers Will and Patrick—and his four sisters, Terry, Jan, Jeanie and Kim!
- Mark *loves* caring about people—and that means not only his family but his friends and his fans too! Mark really is a guy who knows how to show he cares!
- Mark really, really *loves* getting mail from his fans, and he reads just about every letter he gets! Of course, that may take him the next ten years, but he's not going to stop reading those letters you send him because they really mean so very much to him! You can write to him at the Sackheim Agency, 9301 Wilshire Blvd., Beverly Hills, Cal. 90210 and you **know** he'll really love hearing from you!

What Mark Hates . . .

- Didya know that Mark really **hates** cars? And that's not just because of the terrible accident he was in, he's always hated them. He'd rather walk whenever he possibly can.
- Mark **hates** Los Angeles—and all the smog that's in the air there!
- Mark **hates** New York City in the summertime—it's so hot and dirty then!
- Mark **hates** having to clean up his apartment—he really doesn't mind a messy place at all. Not dirty, just messy.
- Mark **hates** not having enough privacy—although he loves his fans, now that he's famous he feels like he's living in a fishbowl.
- Mark **hates** getting dressed up—he's much happier wearing his old jeans and t-shirts.
- Mark **hates** "plastic" people—like phonies and the kind of people who only like him now that he's so famous.
- Mark **hates** big parties—he prefers intimate gatherings with just a few of his close friends there.
- Mark **hates** feeling cramped and closed in—that's why he loves his new two-bedroom apartment near the beach where it's wide open and free.
- Mark **hates** it when the things he loves don't last—like when his TV series, *The Texas Wheelers* was cancelled.
- Mark **hates** feeling self-conscious and out of place—like when everyone else in a room knows each other and he's the only stranger there.
- Mark **hates** it when a girl plays a game—like pretending she doesn't know things or just acting dumb when she isn't dumb at all!
- Mark **hates** not having enough time for his hobbies and his friends—like when he has to travel a lot and can't get back home for months at a time!

Frenchy's Freakies

Once again 16's official artistic ace, Miss Frenchy Blanch, offers another original set of Monkee ornaments from her overflowing ocean of outstanding observations! Overcoming all obstacles, the oracle of the pen and ink outdoes herself to astound all onlookers. 16 proudly presents Frenchy's latest renditions of Davy, Mike, Peter and Micky.

Artist "Frenchy" was a regular 16 contributor.

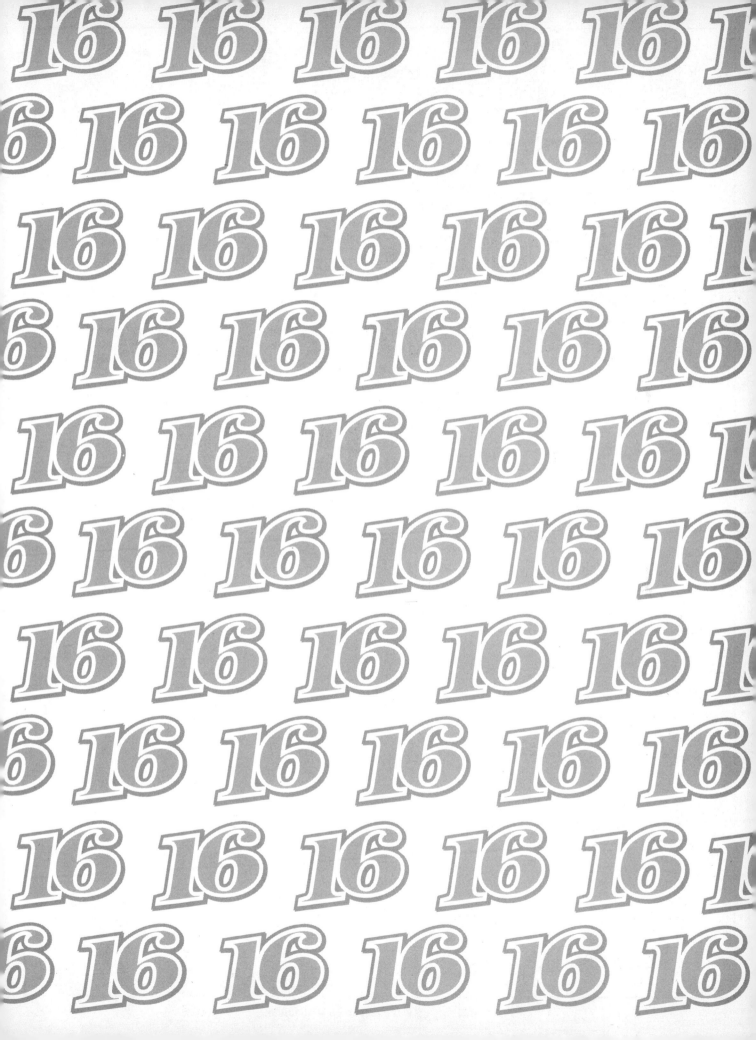

The 70s: TAKE ONE

1970–1974

THE SEVENTIES *16* MAGAZINE 1970–1974

Like the preceding decade, the '70s also, in *16*-land, had a split personality, the early part being a completely different animal from the latter.

Remember the '70s song "We Are Family"? Call it a theme for *16 Magazine* and the idols of the first half of the decade. Aside from the hugely popular Bobby Sherman, the biggest were all, in one way or another, members of a family, i.e., Osmonds, Jacksons, Partridges, Bradys, Williams twins. And no one had yet heard the word *dysfunctional*. Later for all that.

This was the dawn of a new decade, and *16* was flying high. So what, if by 1970 the Brits had long retreated? Even the homegrown Monkees, Raiders, and Cowsills had faded, and Dino, Desi & Billy had grown up and broken up. We ushered in the "holy triumvirate," the three "greatest" teen idols of all time: Bobby Sherman, Donny Osmond, and David Cassidy. These guys didn't just act or sing, they did both. And they worked sales magic: millions of readers flocked to the magazine.

As in the preceding half-decade, girl stars attained cachet by being attached, in one way or another, to boy stars—being someone's (real or TV) sister was best, as Marie Osmond, La Toya Jackson, Susan Dey, and Maureen McCormick could tell you.

But *16* had its non-family pets, too. Or rather, Gloria did. How else to explain the continued coverage of Marc Bolan, a pre–*General Hospital* Rick Springfield, and a mustached Freddie Prinze? None were teen idols (in Rick's case, we were simply premature), but Gloria believed in them all, and insisted on featuring them.

At the home office, there were changes. Gloria was still very much in charge, but there was finally an actual staff, and she gave its members the most important celebrities to be in charge of. She pared down her list, if you will. Gloria personally "handled" the Partridge Family, which included David Cassidy, but covering the Osmonds, the Jacksons, and the Bradys fell to Associate Editor Nola Leone, briefly to Editor Eileen Bradley, and later, to Associate Editor Sandy Newmark. Other editors who arrived on the scene in the early '70s included the authors of this book.

More big changes. For the first time, *16* hired professional studio photographers. Previously Gloria had handled most of the photography chores and trained her staff to do likewise. But there was more money in the early '70s, and the decision to spend it on the publication's lifeblood—better quality photos—made sound business sense. Besides, now that there was competition, you had to look over your shoulder, and the other guys were shepherding Bobby, David, and Donny into the studio. Still, *16* was frugal with the photog dollars; only the biggest acts ever saw the inside of a professional studio for *16*. The rest continued to come up to the New York office—or perhaps Gloria's apartment—and say "cheese" next to the file cabinets, as the editors clicked away.

While we didn't see it as a downside, there were two other changes in the first half of the '70s. We didn't know it yet, but both signaled less than glorious things to come. For one, there was a change in Gloria herself. As she became more involved with her gurus and her spiritual pursuits, she started to phase out—or at least she made noises about wanting to.

Something else. Toward the end of that first half, a chilling trend began to develop: stars who, though age/looks/access-correct, did not *want* to be in the pages of *16*. For whatever reason—they were "artistes," or ac-*tors*, or maybe their peers made fun of them—they did not want to appear next to David/Donny/Bobby. "I don't want to be a teen idol," the phrase no editor of a teen magazine ever wanted to hear, was starting to be whispered…later, that whisper would grow to a growl, then a shout. In fact, the early '70s produced only one such pain in the butt—Randy Mantooth—but the latter half of the decade would produce more. Imperious Gloria, of course, devised a way of working around the situation. In all: it was a wonderful time.

COVER PRICE: 35 cents was the price in 1970; by 1975, it had nearly doubled to 60 cents.

COLOR PINUPS: In May 1971, we introduced "real color pinups," on "thick, shiny paper." In June 1971, we ran our first "pop-out poster." From then on, we flipped back and forth between pin-ups, gatefolds, and posters, but we used them sparingly.

SALES: About 700,000 copies monthly.

Fans were invited to "Share His Pillow Talk" in December 1971. It turned out Bobby often dreamed about you, girl—what else??

SOMETIMES—late at night when you're lying in bed—you really don't feel like sleeping. You're not restless or upset. On the contrary, you just want to rest there, with your head on your pillow, and let all sorts of wonderful, happy thoughts run through your mind. It's like entering a secret dream world and chances are your "special" thoughts are all about that someone who is extra-special to you! Well, sometimes your very favorite guy in the whole wide world — Bobby Sherman — does the very same thing! And if on some moonlit night—you turned and saw Bobby there, lying with his head on his pillow—awake and thoughtful—this is just what he'd say to you, if you could listen in and share Bobby's pillow talk.

BOBBY CONFESSES

I think about you much more than you'll ever know, cos you're on my mind a great deal of the time. When I record, I always try to choose a song I think you will like, and when I'm on stage performing — I'm up there singing just for you! But you're in my thoughts at other times too — times you probably never even imagined! After a long and tiring work session — whether I've come home from the Columbia-Screen Gem Ranch, where I've spent the day filming my new ABC-TV show Getting Together, or other times, when I find myself all alone in a hotel room in some strange city, where I've just returned from one of my "in person" concerts — I feel that I have to unwind and relax a bit before I can manage to fall asleep. And that's when I like to read your letters or sit quietly with my head on my pillow and think about you! It's times like these when I can feel your presence right here with me. It's as though I have pushed a little button that brought us together for a nice, long chat. You see, I know more about you than you may think I do — and it's all the things I've learned from our "visits" together late at night that make me love and understand you the way I do!

WHAT YOU'RE REALLY LIKE

I've told you many times how very much you mean to me, and how much I truly care, but I don't think I've ever really gone into detail and explained just why I think you are so extra-special — and that's what I want to confide to you right now! One of the things I love about you is the fact that you aren't afraid to be you! For instance, look at all the things you do. No matter what it is — there's always a realness that lets me know so much about what you are really and truly like. When you write me a letter, you confess your innermost feelings, and no matter what is on your mind or in your heart — you "tell it like it is"! You're honest, open, and most important of all — you're true to yourself!

I've also noticed that you are enthusiastic in everything you do. In your letters, or during the times I've been lucky enough to meet and talk with you, you've told me all about certain projects you're involved in at school or in your home town — and what you're doing about them. Other times, you've confided your secret dreams and how you want so much for them to come true. With your faith and determination, you can't lose — and I've been lucky enough to see your enthusiasm in action. For instance, there are so many times when I'm on stage singing and I catch a glimpse of you in the audience. Your smiling, happy face is so full of life and love—and it feels great to see that you aren't afraid to express yourself. You don't hold back your feelings. When you want to scream—you do! And because you let out all of your enthusiasm—you help to turn me on and make my show exciting.

I owe so very much to you. You've stuck by me, believing in all of my dreams and my goals. Your loyalty and faith in me has kept me going. That's why it's important for me to let you know that I believe in you too. So, whenever you feel depressed and think, "No one understands me!"—please remember that I, Bobby Sherman, do! You've taught me so much about so many things. But most of all, you've shown me the true meaning of the words "friend" and "love"—and you've shown me that they go together, hand-in-hand. I hope with all my heart that you and I will be friends forever. And once again—thank you for just being you!

21

BOBBY SHERMAN

Years of *16* Popularity: 1969–1971

If you could gather the components of a perfect idol and download them onto the computer, Bobby Sherman would appear on the screen. He is as perfect a specimen as ever applied for, and held, the job.

Between a TV career and a recording career, he was enormously accessible. He really was boyishly cute—not ruggedly handsome. He really was as "deep" as his dimples: there was not a closet rocket scientist behind those twinkly eyes, but a decent, nice, average guy. He actually could sing; and he actually could recite his lines convincingly.

But Bobby's most important quality for the "king of all teen idols" crown is that he really had no other agenda—he knew he wasn't DeNiro and didn't want to be; he knew he wasn't Sinatra and didn't want to be. He didn't want to have a drink or a snort; he surrounded himself with enough security to keep the groupies—and any hint of sexual scandal—away. "There are no skeletons in my closet," he says now, "what my fans expected of me is exactly who I was."

Bobby Sherman was more than content being a teenage idol: not only was it good enough, it was the best. And in many tangible ways, he was the best for a publication such as *16*. Coverage started way back in 1965 (in his host of *Shindig* days) and, in one form or another, extended far into the '70s. His peak years, however, were 1969–71; the top banner of almost every cover in 1970 was devoted to Bobby.

Bobby Sherman respected his audience back then—and felt there was value in being admired by teenage girls. If the fans believed in him—believed he was as sincere and caring as he was portrayed to be—that belief wasn't misplaced, for he believed in them right back. He still does.

BOBBY SHERMAN REMEMBERS

"*16* WAS THE MARRIAGE OF ALL THAT MADE ME POPULAR"

"My first big national exposure was as the 'house singer' on the TV show *Shindig*. I started appearing regularly in *16 Magazine* a little later when I was on *Here Come the Brides*.

"On *Shindig*, I'd sing hit songs from the Top 40 charts of the week—whenever the original artist couldn't be on the show, I'd sing that song, no matter what it was. Of course, 'I Can't Get No Satisfaction' didn't quite work, but we made it happen. It taught me a lot of humility! Because I was known for singing other people's songs, I could not get a recording contract—I couldn't get arrested in those days.

"But then along came intense coverage in *16*, and *Here Come the Brides*, and I could sell anything! That's when I started having hits like 'Hey Little Woman,' 'Easy Come, Easy Go,' 'La La La,' and of course, 'Julie, Do Ya Love Me?' which went platinum.

"For all those years, *16* was constantly running features on me—they were always asking for new material. The whole thing, the TV shows and the records, snowballed into this

Bobby Sherman

phenomenon I did not really understand at the time. But the combination of the TV show, the music, and, as much as anything else, *16 Magazine*, made it happen.

"*16* was the kids' exchange method. It was how they got the info they wanted and got to see what other fans were saying. It was the marriage of all that made me popular for so long. It was part of the 'machinery' that made it all click. And everybody won—especially the audience."

"THE FIRST TIME I TOOK MY SHIRT OFF FOR A PHOTO"

"Gloria Stavers was the editor-in-chief and she was the first person who ever got me to take my shirt off for a photo. I remember it well. I was in New York, and Gloria and her assistant at the time, Nola Leone, asked if they could come up to the hotel where I was staying, ask some questions and take some photos. They were very respectful of the limited time I had to give them, so I certainly said, 'By all means, come up.'

"I knew they'd want me posing in a variety of shirts, so after the first set of photos, I changed my shirt. As I was changing, Gloria said, 'Whoa! You have a nice body—can I get a shot?' It seemed innocent enough—I mean, it wasn't my pants! I knew I could trust Gloria—she was a sweetheart.

"Most of the articles about me in *16* were written in first person. That was fine with me, because it was accurate. I would fill out the questionnaires for them and I did talk a lot with Gloria and with Nola, and they'd elaborate on my thinking. Even if the words weren't exactly as I said them, they *did* know who I was, and kept the articles true to what I would say. They realized that kids and their parents were reading the magazine and they kept it clean. They really knew what they were doing and the questions they asked really came from the readers. *16* did listen to their readers.

"That wasn't the case with all media. In all those years, the only thing that bothered me was when I'd walk over to a magazine rack and I'd see headlines—not in *16*—like 'Bobby's Secret Son.' The article turned out to be about my godson, and I thought, 'What a trick!' I found this very distasteful. I also knew I could count on that never happening in *16*. They never did anything spiteful. I really considered Gloria and Nola like friends and family members. For all those reasons, I steered away from interviews and photo shoots with other magazines that were not as good. *16*—and later, *Tiger Beat*—were those kids' Bibles."

Bobby was a more than willing participant in the hype and the hoopla. He posed any which way he was asked to, with or without shirt. He was cute, he was sexy—but not threatening—he could be "come hither," but the invitation was into his dreams, not his bed. "Bobby Shirtless!" as 16's headlines would trumpet, did sell magazines, lots of 'em.

"I REALLY WAS THIS ROMANTIC GUY"

"In *16*, I was portrayed as this real romantic guy—and I was. I'm into astrology (I'm a Leo, with Cancer rising) and it all fits. As far as, was I as chaste as I was portrayed? That could have been a real problem. But I was surrounded by smart people who were very careful about scandal. I was constantly surrounded by people who kept me away from any possibility of scandal. I also realized that my audience ranged in age from 6 or 7 to 21 years old. And I was clear about being responsible to that audience.

"I've never smoked—I grew up in a house of smokers and I hated it—and the drug scene scared me. I saw what it had done to my friends. If I had a vice in those days, maybe I took a drink or two. In respects to letting my hair down, the rule was: not in the outside world. But when I was home, behind my gates and walls, I could do what I wanted. But I never did anything that would come back to haunt me. Besides, for the most part, I was too tired for romantic entanglements.

Bobby Sherman

"When I met my wife, Patti, she was 17. We waited until she was 18 before we really started dating. She said she wasn't a fan, but it turned out later that she kind of was. She knew who I was—it was hard not to know!—plus, when I picked her up in a Rolls Royce, it kind of gave it away."

"SOME FANS FELT BETRAYED"

"When I got married, we knew the fans would be upset. So, on the advice of Metromedia and my agents, we kept it quiet for a while. Plus, I didn't want to announce it to just one person. I didn't want to slight anyone. In the interim, Patti got pregnant and then had a miscarriage. It was a very nervous time for me. Then when she got pregnant again, she had to have complete bed rest and we didn't want to make an announcement, so that prolonged the whole thing. Although it was never intended to be a lie, it ended up being one year between our actual marriage and the [public] announcement. Some fans felt betrayed, but we had reasons. I felt misunderstood; I didn't realize I was hurting anyone. So I went on a campaign to get my fans back."

"THE FANS ARE DUE RESPECT"

"I always enjoyed meeting the fans. At every concert, radio stations would give away tickets and backstage passes to meet me. There'd be 10 little girls and their parents clutching

their albums. They'd be so tongue-tied and quiet, I actually had to go up to them and ask, 'Would you like me to sign your album?' Then when I was onstage, I'd see these same 10 girls in the front row, screaming and yelling their heads off.

"I've been blessed with good fans. I always respected them, and I still do. A lot of 'teen idols' are afraid of the classification. But my attitude is, the fans make you what you are, period. There is nothing else. It's a responsibility. The fans keep you eating. They're due respect. If you let them down, do something counter to your image, you dig your own grave. They'll grow up—and you won't be able to get arrested. I continue to constantly get fan mail. My fans have stayed loyal. I consider them friends."

"I DIDN'T KNOW WHERE HOME WAS— I COULD'VE WALKED OUT A WINDOW"

"During my 6- or 7-year run as a teen idol, it was a hectic time for me. I didn't know where home was. I was filming *Here Come the Brides* five days a week then flying (all over the U.S.A.) to concerts on weekends. I had to sleep with a nightlight because I didn't know where I was—at home, or in some hotel room somewhere. I could've walked out a window for all I knew. But I never lost sight of the fact that the fans gave me the opportunity to do what I wanted to do."

THE UPSIDE

"My best memories are of the concerts. They were like love-ins. I got as much of a kick out of them as the fans did— and they screamed throughout the whole thing. I could have lip-synched to the Supremes and no one would have known. The fans would throw teddy bears up on the stage, and those old disposable flash cubes—they hurt! They could become lethal, so I'd dodge them. I didn't talk about drugs or sex or anything controversial because the audience was so young. The parents would be there at this proverbial love-in. They had their hands over their ears (because of the noise level) but smiles on their faces. I got letters from the parents saying 'thank you,' and that means the most to me—that the parents respected what their kids were doing."

THE END OF AN ERA

"After *Here Come the Brides*, I tried another TV series, *Getting Together*. It was for ABC, and it did well, but not well enough. It was up against *All in the Family*, and was canceled after 15 weeks. I remember kids storming the station in protest. But for me, the truth was that I needed a break. I was in no hurry to get back in the fast lane. So it was okay. I had no other agenda. And by the time it all started to peter out, I wanted time to myself anyway. I needed to step back.

"The industry perception of me did typecast me. But at the time I felt, 'They can think what they like.' I don't feel I ever got credit for any real acting or singing ability or for being anything deeper than a bubblegum teenage idol. But even if I could, I wouldn't change anything. I was lucky. I had a great business manager and was able to keep all my money, so later on, I was able to pick and choose the things I wanted to do. I'm now a medic with the LAPD. I can contribute back to the community."

"IT WAS A SWEET TIME"

"I don't think this phenomenon could ever be repeated in this computer age. Kids lack a childhood now. They go straight from birth to puberty. The world has shrunk and you get old fast. I'm saddened by that. They can't enjoy a Disneyland life.

"Back then, it was a sweet time in my life."

WHAT YOU ALWAYS WANTED TO KNOW...

- "There never was a Julie. The song was written by someone else who was just looking for a girl's name that hadn't been overused."

- "There never was a feud with David Cassidy. We'd worked together [on the pilot for *The Partridge Family* and later on *Getting Together*]. We'd jammed. It was a manufactured feud. It bothered him as much as it bothered me."

- "If I had to pick one song to be remembered by, it would be 'Easy Come, Easy Go.' It was always one of my favorites and the one I used to open all my concerts."

- Bobby's autobiography, *Still Remembering You*, written with Dena Hill (a former fan and *16 Magazine* reader) came out in 1996. It was published by Contemporary Books.

- Last words: "If I had one wish it would be that everyone learn CPR. It does work; it does save lives."

David Cassidy

Years of *16* Popularity: 1969–1973

David Cassidy was one of the "best" teen idols of them all. He was a born professional (his father was the actor Jack Cassidy), a fine comic actor, an excellent singer, and most cooperative in promoting his image as a fave rave (albeit reluctantly, as he reveals in the following interview). Most of all, he was cute. Very, very cute.

*David posed for several exclusive sessions with a professional Los Angeles studio photographer— he was one of the few stars **16** spent money photographing. And he sure had butt-ability!*

In the late '60s, the fledgling actor began to attract the attention of *16*'s readers and editors with appearances on *Bonanza, Ironside*, and other weekly dramatic shows. In 1970 he got his big break when he was cast as Keith Partridge in the musical series, *The Partridge Family* which costarred his stepmother, Shirley Jones. The role turned him into *16*'s first TV series singing solo star (as opposed to groups like the Monkees or the Osmonds) who was simultaneously a recording artist (the single "I Think I Love You" was a #1 hit) and a concert attraction. He was enormously, incredibly popular. He commanded the top banner of every issue of *16* from January through October of 1971; from then on he and Donny Osmond played tag for the top spot. It must be borne in mind that David's huge following knew and loved him as the slightly goofy Keith Partridge, who lived in a cute house with a cute family that toured as a rock group. The real David Cassidy was very, very unlike the character he played.

He was, and is, immensely famous and adored; you cannot walk down the streets of New York even now with David Cassidy (I have tried it) and get very far.

Most recently, he acted as a host on VH-1, toured with his Partridge Family brother Danny Bonaduce, written his autobiography *C'mon Get Happy*, and acted in the Broadway show *Blood Brothers* (costarring with his own half-brother and former *16* idol, Shaun Cassidy). The following is a recent interview.

How did you first become aware of *16*?

Gloria Stavers contacted me. This was long before *The Partridge Family*. She left a message for me with my agent, and I was told by my manager that it was good business for me to return this call. She was excited when I called her; with her Southern accent, she was businesslike and somehow childlike at the same time. She told me they were getting all this mail on me, and that I was going to be a big star. She said, "I have to know everything about you, because *they* are going to want to know everything."

Your reaction?

I was a little standoffish—that's how I am as a person—and when I heard who Gloria's readers were, I was even more skeptical. But my manager said I should do it. "You're 19," she said, "you're starting out, and if there are fans out there, let them see you." So I did my first interview on the phone, and then when *The Partridge Family* was about to air, Gloria knew

WHO'S YOUR FAVE RAVE?

DAVID INVITES YOU ...

"LOVE ME ALL NIGHT LONG"

Dreamy David—a typical, kissable glossy 16 pinup: this one appeared in the July 1972 issue

David Cassidy

We brought new meaning to up-close and personal!

how big it was going to be, that it was network, the same production people who'd done the Monkees, and she was on top of it, and wanted a lot of pictures, a lot of interview time.

What had you known or heard about her before meeting her?

I'd heard stories that she'd seduced lots of guys that were in the same situation I was in. I never *met* anyone who said it happened to them, but that's what I was expecting. It was not like that at all. She smiled and laughed a lot; she was very open, very friendly. She never, ever was even remotely unprofessional. We were alone in her apartment just after we first met, having a glass of wine, and I was kind of waiting for it to happen. But nothing of the sort was even hinted at, even remotely.

What would you have done if it had?

I'd have said "sure!" At 19, I was dead game for anything, and she was an attractive woman. But it was never an issue.

What do you think all those "seduction" rumors were about?

Well, it's possible that she didn't find me attractive. It's more likely she was being bad-mouthed by men who resented her, men who were then in their 30s and 40s and resented her

independence and power. She was very much a feminist in that respect, and a woman with her own identity, who deserved much more respect than I think she got. Wow! [holding up bound volume of old *16*s] "David's Secret Love Tricks." This is something I should read. "He's got sparkling hazel eyes, and he's certainly got a groovy physique." Really.

What were the consequences to you and your career from being a teen idol?

Well, once you cooperate with them, you're perceived as a lightweight with no talent, and you end up being Fabian Forte, which is the danger when you appeal to children, and you do purely commercial, crass, cutesy stuff.

And you protested that you were a serious actor.

I said that to them, and they all, *16* and all the others, gave me lip service, "Oh, we're going to treat you very seriously," and the next thing you know you're holding a stuffed animal and the flash is going off. I tried to rebel, but the producers let me have it. "We own you, kiddo." And they threatened to twist the knobs, and I'd be hearing from my family, from my manager, the other people on the show, and I'd be accused of letting everyone else on the project down because of my own selfish ambitions. So like it or not, I had to be cutesy.

When in fact…?

I was a wild fucking maniac, banging every girl I could.

You would want your 10-year-old fans to know that?

Then they shouldn't print anything. They shouldn't misrepresent the artist.

How do you tell a pre-pubescent girl that the guy she loves is fucking every starlet in Hollywood?

You might say, "He's somebody who dates a lot of different people."

They never said you didn't. But the point was to make it seem as if you were available to any one of the fans.

Yeah, it's to fulfill a fantasy. I know that. I suppose that's O.K. Look, my problem was, these stories were robbing me of my own identity. They were about Keith Partridge's identity. And Gloria was the master of that. All the others formulated their

On the concert stage,
David got to be somewhat
wilder than Keith Partridge—
but not much.

David personified the perfect teenage fantasy:
every reader imagined herself on the bed
next to him, as he composed a song just for her.

Another—unprintable—side of David,
giving us the finger(s) while goofing off for our
cameras. This shot hung on Gloria Stavers's
office wall.

David Cassidy

DAVID CASSIDY (box on JANUARY 26, 1970) 126 lines
16's ALL STAR FACT SHEET   G-20

FULL REAL NAME: DAVID BRUCE, *20 or after*   STAGE NAME: CASSIDY

NICKNAME (also how you got it):

BIRTHDATE & PLACE: APRIL 12, 1950   Born in N.Y. grew up in New Jersey

PERSONAL DATA (Height, weight and coloring):
5'8"   BROWN
125   HAZEL

FAMILY INFO (names of parents, brothers & sisters):
ONLY CHILD   EVELYN + JACK

HOME INFO (where located and description):
WEST L.A. — MOVING SOON — OWN HOUSE

SCHOOLS ATTENDED: REXFORD H.S. MANY Classmate of Jon + Dino

MARRIAGE INFO: NO, NO, NO.

INSTRUMENTS PLAYED/PART SUNG: acoustic + elec. guitar, drums, sings - doing a demo for Screen Gems

FAVORITES--

SINGING GROUPS: Beatles — anthony Newley

INDIVIDUAL SINGERS: Brando — Bancroft

ACTOR & ACTRESS:

TV SHOWS: Love, american Style — late movies, bored with standard TV shows

COLORS: like em all —

FOODS: Lobster —

HOBBIES: not working, I'm bumming — no surfing — no skiing

SPORTS: plays tennis sometimes — used to basketball game + basketball watch football

WHAT LOOKED FOR IN A GIRL: girls who are bright — can't stand dumb girls — prefer un celebrity — hound — money hunters

WHAT DO YOU LIKE TO DO ON A DATE? anything that's fun — quiet dinners — disco turn him off — dislike plastic people

BUSINESS PLANS & AMBITIONS: act - become director sometime

PERSONAL PLANS & AMBITIONS: stay single till 30 — then find a woman to spend life with

ADDRESS: AGENT   (AUTOGRAPH)

no astrology — one makes his own destiny

David's original handwritten fact sheet.
From his pen to 16's pages

This was television, Hollywood, fantasy, a family show. Let's be real about fantasies.

I know, and I do think it's important for kids to have heroes, and positive role models, as I was. It means a lot to me now. If you had an impact on people when they were very young, you're forever held in a special place, because we're like a blank screen when we're kids, and what's important to us then is so important for the rest of our lives. The first time somebody captures your imagination, the first time you fall in love, you never forget that. Here's "David's Tragic Illness" [looking at an old issue of *16*]. I guess that's when I had my gall-bladder out. It wasn't all that tragic. They were going crazy because of the fans around the hospital.

You seem to have conflicting opinions about that whole time. They got you all wrong, but they created a person who had a good effect, ultimately, on his fans.

I suppose credit has to be given when it comes to creating the image that they did. And certainly to Gloria, who was human and had a soul, and real feelings, and—I believe—respect for me. She was the first one to pick up on me, she had her finger on the pulse, and she had her job to do. Also, she was the perennial teenager; she'd have her camera and her tape recorder, and she'd show up like a fan. Thinking about her, she probably was a Stones fan who had the enthusiasm of an adolescent, and understood her audience, and gave them probably what *she* had wanted. I really resented back then what they were doing to me. But I don't have to live with it now. I only have to live with the fact that I had a positive effect on people, they loved my work, my records, and they loved to read about me and fantasized about me, and all that stuff is important.

magazines after what she did. She was giving children what they wanted, a dream fantasy that was pure sweetness. It wasn't real. It was solely about catering to your audience. If it meant twisting the facts, then so be it. And to me that's wrong.

Honestly, what would have been the alternative?

Print the truth about what I was really like. Reckless, young, wild, out of control.

If you had been portrayed as the randiest guy in Hollywood, it might not have been too good for the show.

Keith Partridge was 16. I was 19. I never did what he did.

Susan Dey

Years of *16* Popularity: 1971–1973

As Laurie Partridge, Keith (David Cassidy) Partridge's one-year-younger sister, Susan Dey was a natural object of interest, verging on envy, for every *16* reader. She had to be the luckiest girl in the world—beautiful, successful, and on the set every working day from dawn to sunset with David. The world knew, correctly, that there was nothing romantic between David and Susan, which would have turned her into a villainous body-snatcher rather than a role model.

Susan's mother had died when she was 8, and she had begun her career as a fashion model in 1968, at the age of 16. Gloria Stavers, in turn, was very fond of her, almost maternally protective, and as she too had been a model at one time, she felt a professional "bonding" with the younger woman.

Still a teenager herself when she made her debut in *The Partridge Family*, Susan was the ideal person for the "older sister confidante" role in the pages of *16*, a position that through the years had been held by Annette Funicello, Cher, and others. Her column, Girl-to-Girl, was dictated by Gloria to an assistant, but Gloria always conferred with Susan about the content of upcoming articles. In brief, efficient, affectionate conversations, the two would settle on the subject matter of a forthcoming column (or two or three), and Gloria would take it from there.

Susan, of course, went on to prominence in several successive TV series, including *L.A. Law*, in which she starred for the first 6 years of the show's run as deputy D.A. Grace Van Owen. She continues to be active in the business.

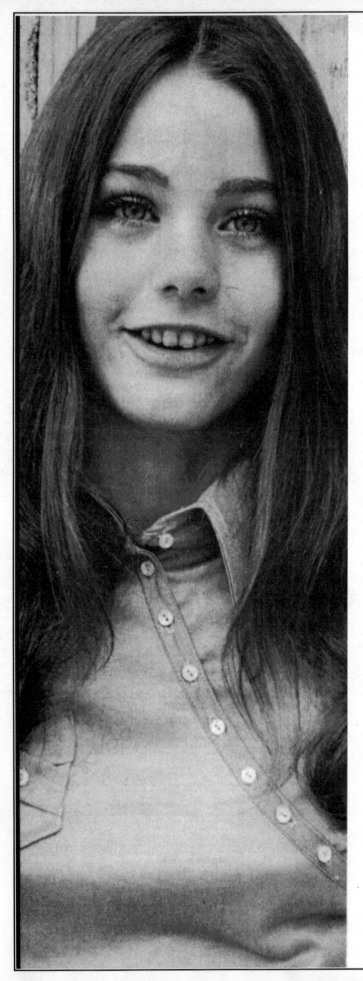

Girl

HELLO AGAIN! This month "we girls" are going to sit down and have a *Girl-to-Girl* talk about some of our greatest problems—"growing pains". When a young girl has a problem (or two or three), adults sometimes laugh her off and say, "It's just growing pains."

For some reason, a lot of folks think "growing pains" are very petty and will pass away very soon. Not so! When I look back and remember some of the things I went through at ages 12, 13 and 14—well, let me tell you, they were *very serious!* But I was quite lucky. My folks (my dad Bob and my stepmother Gail, who married my dad after my own mother passed away when I was about nine) were really "storybook" parents. They were kind and loving and understanding—but, at the same time, they were very strict disciplinarians. That was something that bugged me at the time, but looking back I am sure glad they brought me up "proper"!

Day-Dreaming

When I was about 12 years old, I entered an unbelievable "dream world". It was as if one day all I cared about was horses, puppy dogs and tomboy stuff—and then the next day I was all gooey about real-life guys, teenage idols and romantic poetry. Fortunately, when I went to school, I was able to leave my day-dreaming behind—but, boy, at home I was *something else!* I suddenly *hated* to make up my bed, *hated* to do dishes, *hated* to help out in any way around the house and—most of all—*hated* to be told what to do!

Now, if any of you out there in *16*-land has ever been through this, don't feel strange about it and don't worry about yourself. Every single, normal girl goes through a "day-dreaming" period. Actually day-dreaming isn't a *problem*—the *problem* is that we end up not doing the things we're supposed to do. My stepmom was pretty nice about it. I think she secretly hoped that if she didn't pick on me—maybe I would wise up and start helping out again. You see, we had a rather large family—there was Mom, Dad, my older sister, my younger brother Tommy (boy, is he a "knock out"!—but more about *that* some other time), and my little sister Elizabeth. We were just average, middle-class folks—which means we didn't have a cook or a maid or a butler or a chauffeur. I mean, *who does*?!

Another thing I noticed about my day-dreaming period was that I became "independent". Mom or Dad would say, "Susan, do this," and I would give them a semi-haughty stare and a look as if to say, "I'm *above* all that." But, again—(lucky me!), they didn't push. They gently corrected, occasionally gave strict orders and just decided to wait it out.

After a number of months, I didn't get any better, and finally one day my dad said, "Susan, we're going to have a bit of a talk." He took me into the den, closed the door and

Susan Dey's Girl-to-Girl column from February 1971.

-to-Girl
by SUSAN DEY

sat me down. I got quite nervous. I thought—*Now, this is it! He's really going to let me have it now!* To my surprise, my father was extremely gentle. He talked to me in a slow, patient, painstaking manner.

"Susan," he explained, "there are six people in this household. A household is like a small town or city or community. To make things 'go' properly, everyone has to do their duty. No one person can do everything—and there are lots of tasks we all *have* to do, but we do not want to do. But whether it's a household or real life, Susan," my dad went on, "we each must do our share. It's better if we can do it out of love and understanding. For instance, it's better if you can look around you, see your brother and sisters and—with a heart filled with love for them—want to do your part so that they won't have to do *everything* for you."

With that, Dad got up and left the room. I sat in stunned silence for a long time. How simply, kindly and penetratingly he had made his point. Suddenly, I felt embarrassed and ashamed. I wanted to burst out crying and go beg everyone to forgive me. But as I sat there, just being quiet and letting my emotions subside a bit, it became clear to me that there was *one* thing and *only one* thing to do. That was to get up, put a grin on my face and go out there and do my part—and *do it well!*

All that happened about six years ago, but it's something I'll never forget. Dad's words to me still live in my heart. They have become like a part of my life. I still practice the guidelines he laid down for me that day. Of course, I have learned that he is right — that whether it's your home, or town, or community, we each have to chip in and help. Learning that has not only made life easier for me—it's made life infinitely more beautiful. I found out what the joy of sharing is, and I pass it on to you for what it may be worth.

"Fatty-Poo"

Well, I guess every girl goes through it—or *nearly* every girl. "Overweight" is a super-big problem that simply cannot be passed off as "baby fat" or with a comforting remark like, "Look, you'll grow out of it, don't worry."

Actually, I grew *into* it! I'd been a "skinny-Minnie" until I was about 14 years old. Suddenly, I seemed to gain weight at the drop of a candy bar. I had never been over-indulgent, but I *certainly* never held back—and suddenly there I was, no longer a skinny but a big, fat "fatty-poo"! It was really hard for me to do anything about it. I just loved eating and something in me kept saying, "Oh, it'll go away," or "Wait until tomorrow, *then* you can start dieting."

Once again, my folks quietly waited it out—with a helpful hint here and there. I also noticed that Mom was serving me very small portions of desserts and when I reached for my second helping, she'd say something like, "Oh Susan, din-

ner's over—you don't have time to do that."

After a year of this, Mom took me aside (shades of Dad's "den talk"!) and said, "Susan, we have got to talk about something—your weight."

Well, at least she was direct and to the point! I grinned an embarrassed grin and said, "I guess I have to go on a diet, Mom."

She said, "Right—let's make a list right now of things you can and cannot eat, and I'll do everything I can to help you."

Since I wasn't super-familiar with the *do's* and *don't's* of dieting, I suggested that Mom make the list. "O.K.," she said, "here are the *don't's*—anything chocolate, any kind of candy, ice cream, pizzas, soda pop, bread and butter, potatoes, spaghetti, starchy foods, cakes, and pies. These are all things you *cannot* eat anymore, Susan."

"Gulp," I gulped, but I didn't say anything because I knew she was absolutely right.

"Now, let's see what you *can* eat. You *can eat* all of the following you want—rice, lean meats (chicken, lamb, beef, fish and veal), any vegetable (except potatoes), any salads (but go light on the dressing), fresh fruit, whole milk, skimmed milk, whole wheat bread, No-Cal-type drinks, boiled or poached eggs, and jello."

"Blah," I blah-ed. "I'll do it, Mom," I added, "because I know it's the *only* way I can lose weight."

Every day after that, Mom would hand me a little box or a bag with fresh fruit, some carrots or celery, or something like that in it. She somehow knew that I'd get "snack happy" during the day and I'd have these goodies (?) with me to fall back on. Actually, the hardest part of the whole thing was in the afternoon with my friends! I would go down to the local soda shop. It was the most difficult thing in the world to say *no* to a Coke, ice cream cone or sundae. *But I did it*—using sheer will power and pure determination! If "push came to shove" (in my stomach, that is), I'd whip out my little bag of goodies and start munching on a carrot. At first, everyone laughed at me and I was deeply embarrassed, but somehow I hung in there. Later, though, I noticed that the girls in my crowd were *doing the same thing!* So, ha-ha, I turned out to be a trend-setter in Dietsville!

It took me about six months, but I made it. I lost 15 or 20 pounds, was soon getting back into my old dresses and slacks, and was even thinking very much about a modeling career. But that too is *another* story. So meet me here in the March issue of *16*, which goes on sale January 21! We'll have more *Girl-to-Girl* talk about mutual problems (personal and boy-wise), I'll answer your questions about David, Danny and the *PF* gang, and we'll go over a couple of more "growing pains"—like pimples (ugh!) and wearing braces. See you then!!

29

DONNY OSMOND

Years Of *16* Popularity: 1971–1975

Can Donny Osmond really be pushing 40? And should we still be calling this married father of four by his childhood nickname? Not Donald Osmond? Or Don? It doesn't exactly roll off the tongue that way, does it? Which is the conclusion reached by the performer himself—on more levels than one, and not without a lot of soul searching. For the boyish name, Donny, and his attendant image, forever etched into our collective consciousness, go together like, well…"Sweet 'n' Innocent." Which is certainly how he was portrayed in *16*—and as you'll see, not terribly far from the truth.

In April 1970, *16* printed its first article on the Osmond Family. The five singing brothers, novelty attractions on TV's *The Andy Williams Show*, did not yet have a teenage audience, but they were about to. A similar family singing group, the Jackson 5, had hit big with "I Want You Back" in 1969, and soon the Osmonds, signed by Mike Curb (later, a California politician; now in the country music business) sought to travel that same road. Their first song, "One Bad Apple," came out in 1971. Like the J5, it featured the youngest of the clan singing lead. And it was a huge hit.

There really was perceptible competition between the two groups and their lead singers. But between Donny Osmond and Michael Jackson, there was also a strange and fragile friendship. Both teen idols and their family groups were megastars of their era, and both were aggressively and consistently courted and covered by *16*. Everyone involved—from the record companies to the parent/managers to the boys (and their sisters) themselves—cooperated fully.

Donny Osmond talked to us recently—and candidly—about those days.

Donny Osmond Looks Back

"BEING IN *16* WAS A DOUBLE-EDGED SWORD"

"I was around 12 when I first started appearing in *16* and 13 when 'One Bad Apple' hit the charts. I think I was on the cover more than anyone else. But being in the magazine was almost embarrassing in a way. It was a love-hate relationship. Of course, [the magazine] created my stardom, but it was also the very thing that was giving me that teenybopper image. It's rewarding in one sense, but boy, it's emotionally taxing in another.

"It was embarrassing because I was just one member of a group—and I was singled out and soloed out. That became most apparent when we'd go out on tour, during our individual introductions. Alan would introduce himself, then we'd go to Wayne, then Merrill, then Jay. Whenever they'd hit Donny, the place would really go wild—it was embarrassing! Here was this little 13-year-old boy, who'd been working with his brothers since he was 5, as part of a group, and now I was being singled out. I was always pushed to the front when we were having our pictures taken, and I was always the one soloed out for quotes. Although there wasn't as much

The Osmond Brothers—or, as 16 sometimes referred to them, "the Os Bros"—did the Dreamsville thing in 1971. (l. to r.) Wayne, Merrill, Jay, Donny. (front) Alan.

DONNY:
"Help ME—I'm Shy!"

IF the phone rings at our house—or if we are on the road, in our hotel suite—I am the first Osmond to answer it. If I get a letter—and I'm happy to say that I do get quite a few—I really dig sitting down and writing an answer. After shows, if a bunch of girls come by and see us in the dressing room or near the stage door, I love talking and chatting with them. But if you get me alone with a girl—well, I must admit I'm very shy.

I KNOW YOU CARE

You may find this hard to believe, but even though I'm in show business and I've been performing on stage in front of thousands of people for as long as I can remember—I'm *really* a very shy guy. There's something about being in front of an audience. No matter how nervous I may be before stepping out on that stage—the moment I'm up there in front of you, I feel absolutely fine! I guess the reason I feel so at ease on stage is because *you* are there and I know you care. You give me confidence, and my main concern is to entertain you and make sure that you have a good time. While I'm on stage, I'm not nervous and I probably don't look at all shy. But the truth is, I *am* shy— and I'd like you to help me overcome this feeling.

WHERE ARE YOU?

I love to read your letters and I can't help but wonder what you're really like. My biggest wish is that someday I will meet each and every person who has been nice enough to write to me. I kind of think it would be fun to really get to know my special pen pals—and that's why I need *your* help.

It isn't always possible for me to find you. You could be anywhere—at an airport, walking down the main street of your home town, or standing in the middle of a group of girls outside a stage door. There are literally hundreds of possible places where our paths could cross, and yet—I may not

know it's *you*! You see, I do read your letters and we have shared many secrets with each other—but I've never seen your face! That's why I want to ask you a big favor. My brothers and I do a lot of traveling and we'll probably be visiting your home town one of these days—or you may be somewhere else at the same time we are. When that day comes—and you see me—please remember that I *do* want to meet you. And if you'd like to talk to me half as much as I'd like to get to know you—please come over to me and say, "Hello!".

YOU & ME

If you're the least bit shy yourself, I'll understand—so don't let that stop you from approaching me. I'd really be disappointed if we came so close and then didn't get to meet. And I'm sure that once we are face-to-face, we'll both forget our shyness and become good friends.

There's just one thing I want you to remember: I want to meet *YOU*! In other words, I want you to just be yourself—not someone you think I'd like. The truth of the matter is I love girls and there's very little you could do that would turn me off. In fact, there's only one thing I don't like—and that's a girl (or anyone for that matter) who's a phony, someone who pretends to be something she isn't. So always remember when you're meeting *anyone*—give them a chance to know and like the *real* you. And if you meet me, please try to be *understanding* about my shyness!

Thanks for listening to me, and don't forget—I'll be looking for you—*soon*!

FOR MORE PIX AND FAX ON DONNY AND THE OSMONDS—PLUS A PEEK INTO THEIR PAST AND A LOOK AT THEIR PRIVATE SCRAPBOOK—BE SURE TO PICK UP A COPY OF THE MARCH ISSUE OF 16 MAGAZINE—ON SALE JANUARY 21!!

He's So Shy—and he needs you, girl: from the February 1971 issue.

Donny Osmond

jealousy as you might think, I imagine it was in the hearts of some of the brothers. Like, 'What's the deal with Donny? Why is everyone interested in him?' There was this little bit of antagonizing embarrassment because of all that publicity about me.

"When I look at the emotional challenges my own [teenage] sons have now, and I think, 'Man, everything I did, everything I said was in print!' I wonder how I got through it all. That's why, probably, in many ways, I was such a recluse and loved my privacy so much during my teen years."

"I HAD NO FRIENDS AND NO ONE TO TALK TO…"

"A lot of teenagers aren't close with their parents, so when they have problems, or issues, they go to their friends. During my teen years, I had no one I could go to. I had no friends. And I really couldn't talk to my parents or my siblings about real personal problems, because they were my professional partners. They had their own stress and I related to them on a professional basis.

"When Marie and I were young kids, we were very, very, close. We'd play together all the time. We remained close when she first joined the group, but less so as we began *The Donny and Marie Show*. That was when we started working together every waking hour—and it happens, you're bound to rub each other the wrong way. So the relationship between myself and Marie became a professional one and we stopped relating to each other just on sibling level."

"…EXCEPT MICHAEL JACKSON"

"The only person I could relate to in those days was Michael Jackson, and he to me, not only because we went through a lot of the same experiences at the same time, but also because there were other, uncanny parallels. We had similar upbringings, we were both the 7th child in the family…our mothers had the same birthday. And at one time, both our middle brothers, Jermaine and Merrill, were the lead singers of the group. When our younger brothers, Randy and Jimmy, joined later, they both played congas.

"I first met Michael at the CNE [Canadian National Exposition] in Toronto.

The Osmond Brothers and the J5 were both booked to perform. We were onstage first. I remember being in the middle of our act, and looking over to the wings and seeing Michael there, peering out from backstage, watching me perform. I laugh at this memory now, but the truth is, as I danced and sang, I thought, 'I'll show *you* how it's done, buddy!'

"After the performances, we all met back at the hotel and that's how we first got to know each other. Later, Michael would invite me over to his house in Encino and we just had the greatest time talking. We talked about all those experiences of being raised in the business, and not really having a childhood. Both our fathers were strict, but mine wasn't as bad as Joe. Whenever I'd go over to Michael's house, Joe gave me the coldest shoulder anyone could ever have.

"We didn't hang out that much, because we were so busy, but we were friends. In 1971, we were in England together. The Osmonds and the J5 were booked into the Churchill Hotel—we were on one floor and they were on the other. Michael and I would play games with the lights in our rooms in the middle of the night. I'd turn my light on and all the fans outside would scream, 'Donny! Donny! Donny!' Then I'd shut mine off and he'd turn his on and they'd scream, 'Michael! Michael! Michael!'

"One of the most cathartic moments of my life was going to see Michael when we were both in our 20s. That's when we could really reminisce, look back on all we'd been

Worlds apart in every way, Donny and Michael did have a tenuous friendship: this is one of the few shots ever taken of them together.

Donny Osmond

through. It saddens me every time I hear another scurrilous rumor about what's going on in his life."

"I WAS A VERY NORMAL TEENAGER"

"Was I like the image in *16 Magazine*? In a lot of ways, yes. This image of being a nice, clean-cut guy that everybody liked was not concocted. It was actually really me. We came from a good, strong Mormon background. We did not smoke, drink, or any of that stuff. I won't tell you I was an angel—I was a normal teenager—but I *will* tell you that I never, ever, had sexual experiences before my marriage. To me, that's sacred.

"But to the public, the image was, 'Donny Osmond's *so* sweet,' it was sick, y'know? Now put yourself in my shoes for a second. Here I am trying to be a good kid, very moral and just do what's right. There's lots of people like that. But I got raked over the coals for it. It makes a person want to rebel, just for the sake of changing it all. But I wasn't the rebellious type.

"I kept being criticized quite a bit for it. And I kept thinking, 'Why do I need to be criticized for my lifestyle?' But a lot of it had to do with the fact that I was publicized so much and criticism comes with the turf to a certain degree. Looking back, I had terrible emotional times because of being scrutinized and criticized. I used to feel, 'Why can't I just live my life?' And I had no one to say that to.

"But *16* did portray me accurately. I really was an electronics whiz—in fact, electronics was my only outlet—and I did install a lot of electronic equipment in our house. And yes, my favorite color really was purple."

WHAT THE GIRLS NEVER KNEW

"Although I couldn't date till I was 16, I really was as interested in girls as *16* made me out to be. There were girls all over the United States who wrote to me and they probably never knew that I carried their pictures around with me. I mean, in those letters, there were certain girls who just got my heart goin'. I can't remember any names now, and I remained a good Mormon boy, but I had pictures of lots of girls.

"After our concerts, our stage manager would go out and bring certain girls backstage to meet me. Without wanting to have sex with them, I just hoped that they would like me and want to get to know me beyond the image. Even though I kinda liked the image 'cause it made me bigger than life. That was a great part."

"I MARRIED A FAN"

"Remember those stories in *16* about Donny finding his one 'n' only among the ranks of his fans? My wife, Debbie, went to Provo High in Utah. Although she played it down, she used to read *16 Magazine*—only she really liked David Cassidy! But she would see in *16* 'Win a Date with Donny' and she entered it. No, she didn't win back then, but ultimately, she won.

"In spite of the fact that she knew who I was, she didn't fawn all over me; she was so grounded with her religious views, and busy with her cheerleading. But while I liked that, it also gave me a reality check. I'll never forget the first time she said no to a date. My reaction was, 'Do you *know* who you're talking to here? You can't say no!'

"So I'd come up with all these clever dates. I'd get a limo, drive her up on the fairway where a catered dinner would be waiting, and had violins serenading her. I guess I was very 'romantique'! That's what 'Donny' would have done."

"I MISSED OUT ON SCHOOL"

"But there were some places where the image and reality clashed. Education is one place.

"I really put myself through school. I used to say that I got my education through correspondence courses, but between me, you, and the world, I really didn't do that much work, especially as far as tests were concerned. I excelled in areas that I enjoyed, but I let the others dwindle. So I have certain holes as far as my education is concerned. In hindsight, it bothers me.

"We didn't really have tutors that much, except when I worked in TV in Los Angeles on *The Donny and Marie Show*. There, by law, I had to have a tutor. But on the road, I was so busy, going from show to show, to show to show…my parents did the best they could in trying to maintain some kind of schedule, but unless you live that lifestyle, you can't really understand how impossible that was."

"A LOT OF THE SUCCESS WAS HANDED TO ME BY *16 MAGAZINE*"

"I didn't select the music, others chose what I recorded, from 'Puppy Love,' to 'Go Away, Little Girl.' I didn't do any of that stuff. I just did a good job of doing what I was told. And we were very successful. Back in the '70s, every time we'd get another gold or platinum record, I'd just think, 'Oh, that's

In September 1972, according to 16, Donny Luvs You—in fact, he really did!

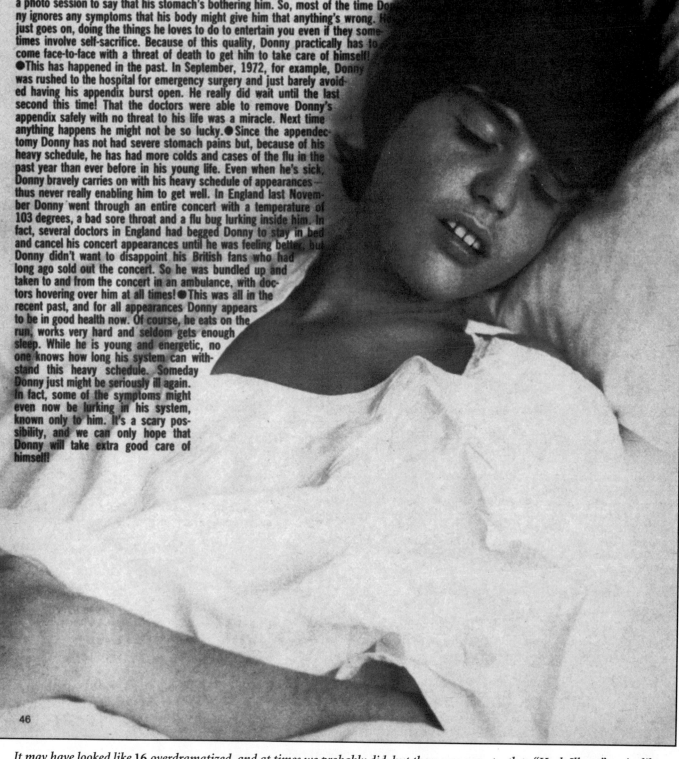

DONNY'S HUSH ILLNESS!

●It is an unfortunate fact of life that illness tends to strike at the most unexpected and generally least opportune moment in a person's life. Donny Osmond, for a 15-year-old strong young man, has seemed to have more than his share of sickness—especially during the course of the past few years. ●Could it be that he's working too hard? Does he feel pushed beyond his capacity? It's no secret that Donny could keep busy for 28 hours a day if there were an extra four hours to be added. Only Donny knows how he really feels, and this is knowledge that he generally doesn't share with others. Because he's not the type to complain, he'll never interrupt a recording session to say he has a headache or stop a photo session to say that his stomach's bothering him. So, most of the time Donny ignores any symptoms that his body might give him that anything's wrong. He just goes on, doing the things he loves to do to entertain you even if they sometimes involve self-sacrifice. Because of this quality, Donny practically has to come face-to-face with a threat of death to get him to take care of himself!
●This has happened in the past. In September, 1972, for example, Donny was rushed to the hospital for emergency surgery and just barely avoided having his appendix burst open. He really did wait until the last second this time! That the doctors were able to remove Donny's appendix safely with no threat to his life was a miracle. Next time anything happens he might not be so lucky. ●Since the appendectomy Donny has not had severe stomach pains but, because of his heavy schedule, he has had more colds and cases of the flu in the past year than ever before in his young life. Even when he's sick, Donny bravely carries on with his heavy schedule of appearances— thus never really enabling him to get well. In England last November Donny went through an entire concert with a temperature of 103 degrees, a bad sore throat and a flu bug lurking inside him. In fact, several doctors in England had begged Donny to stay in bed and cancel his concert appearances until he was feeling better, but Donny didn't want to disappoint his British fans who had long ago sold out the concert. So he was bundled up and taken to and from the concert in an ambulance, with doctors hovering over him at all times! ●This was all in the recent past, and for all appearances Donny appears to be in good health now. Of course, he eats on the run, works very hard and seldom gets enough sleep. While he is young and energetic, no one knows how long his system can withstand this heavy schedule. Someday Donny just might be seriously ill again. In fact, some of the symptoms might even now be lurking in his system, known only to him. It's a scary possibility, and we can only hope that Donny will take extra good care of himself!

46

*It may have looked like **16** overdramatized, and at times we probably did, but there was some truth to "Hush Illness"stories like these: Donny was frequently exhausted and hospitalized more than once. This is from the May 1973 issue.*

Donny Osmond

comment to an engineer. And Donny was destroyed. I reminded him that a boy's voice changing is a normal part of growing up, nothing to be ashamed of. But that didn't make him feel any better. Then I said, 'Well, you grew 3 inches last year—are you upset about that, too?' That's when he smiled and said, 'Absolutely not!'

"The other instance was more frightening. I was taking pictures of Donny for the magazine, and I noticed that he looked really tired and pale. I asked him if something was wrong, and he admitted he wasn't feeling very well. I suggested we stop and do the photo session another day. But Donny insisted we go on, saying, 'No, do your job. You have to get these pictures. I don't want to let the family down.'

"A few hours later, Donny collapsed and had to be rushed to the hospital. He had a burst appendix. A few more hours and he would have died. Remember that story in **16** with the sensationalist headline, 'The Night Donny Almost Died'? It was real."

Marie Osmond

Years of *16* Popularity: 1973–1976

To fans of Donny and the Osmond Brothers in the '70s, Marie Osmond had the best job in the world. She was neither beautiful, brilliant, nor prodigiously talented: she was in most ways, especially in her pre–*Donny and Marie* days, as average as any *16* reader. But she seemed to have the perfect family life, as the adored youngest—and only girl—in a large and ostensibly close clan. Even better, of course, Marie got to do the one thing fans coveted most: spend every waking day sharing breathing space with America's most famous teen idol, Donny Osmond. Best of all, via her Secret Sister Marie column, she was more than open to "sharing" the inside scoop about her life with Donny and her famous family with *16*'s hungry readers.

She still is. Only now, she's willing to talk about not only the perks of being Marie Osmond—the travel, the close encounters with everyone from Lucille Ball to Paul McCartney—but also the reality of a "work ethic" that denied her a childhood, and the pain of terrible insecurity as the spotlight glared ever so blindingly on an average kid from Utah.

In a recent interview conducted for this book, Marie got real.

Marie Osmond Remembers

"I WASN'T SO MUCH PUSHED INTO IT"

"The '70s was an incredible era. *16 Magazine* was like the kids' Bible. They carried it around, they lived it. That's how they found out everything about the stars they loved.

"My first memory of *16 Magazine* was going up to their offices with my brothers. They were just becoming popular.

I really didn't—at that time—want to do what they did. And I wasn't so much pushed into it, but my father did put us all to work in one way or another.

"At first, I had really resigned myself to getting into the back end of things. I studied secretarial skills, I took shorthand when I was 11. I would go to the box office with my mother and watch them do the statements, the receipts. My job would be to count the 'dead wood,' the extra tickets that for one reason or another weren't paid for. I was good at it too. They called me, 'the little terror,' in the box office, because I could find mistakes. I would find $600, $700 mistakes. I loved that side of it.

"I would also steam my brothers' stage clothes, and pack, and do all those kinds of things. I was more of an assistant. But that doesn't mean I had no stage experience at all. I had performed at 6 or 7 in Sweden with the family, and I'd done commercials in Japan, so I was used somewhat in the act. By the time I was 11½, they decided to add me to the

"I never really understood what the girls saw in him," Marie admits she thought of her famous sib then. Back in the days these shots were done for 16, brother and sister were close. Later, in their Donny and Marie Show days, not so much.

Marie Osmond

[stage] show. I did 'Where Is the Love?' at Caesar's Palace in Las Vegas, and that kicked off my career. After that, at 12½, I did 'Paper Roses,' which became a #1 country song. I actually still hold the record for the youngest female country artist to have a #1 record. I actually hold quite a few records—youngest to host a TV show is one of them, too. So why did I go the country route? I never had the desire to sing what my brothers were singing. And I always loved country music. The whole scene was very different from rock 'n' roll in the '70s. Especially at the radio stations, it was friendly and warm and felt like a family. But the other reason was that I didn't want to be successful because of my brothers. I wanted to earn it myself."

"THE MONKEY ON MY BACK"

"Because of the press we got, especially in *16 Magazine*, it looked as if I led a charmed life. And there were lots of parts of my life that I really loved. But there were lots of parts that were just…*hard*. I don't remember a lot of my Donny & Marie times, because I was so busy working. It was all I could do to memorize 350 pages of script in 2½ days. It was all I could do to get that stuff learned. And I was going to school at the same time. To this day, I'm not a good speller, and my grammar isn't always perfect either.

"There was so much 'monkey on my back,' so much to learn, and putting in 18-hour days was absolutely *common*. Were there child labor laws? Of course there were—but after being at the studio for the allotted time, I'd go home and work more. I knew that if I didn't cram, go into my room and memorize and memorize and work on my lip-synch and get my timing down and work on my dance routines in front of the mirror by myself—there's no way I'd be able to tape the show. On top of that, I always had homework. I had no time for anything else."

"I REGRET THAT I WAS NEVER A KID"

"I worked 24 hours a day, '8' days a week (is what it felt like). I felt there was never a break. Now, looking back, I realized I never would have achieved so much in my life without that. I developed a strong work ethic. Now I'm not afraid of hard work. Throw it in my face—I'm not afraid of a good challenge.

"I never went to public school. But I'd see friends who did, and I'd think, 'What are you doing with your life? How can you just sit and walk and talk and laugh and do silly things and not *do* anything?' I'd just feel, 'what about time? How can you waste so much time?' when I had so much to cram in. I look at my life now and think I probably would have relaxed more. I'm still a big achiever, I still do many things at once. But I think it's an abnormal work ethic. I play hard too, I just pack a lot in—I consider myself a 'life-a-holic.'"

"I REMEMBER GOING TO MY DRESSING ROOM AND JUST SOBBING"

"Was I insecure? Oh yes, absolutely! I mean, *you* try being a 14-year-old girl and they put you in an outfit—and, y'know, my mouth was too big for my face, my body was too small for my head—and then they throw you next to Raquel Welch! And the next week they stand you next to Farrah Fawcett and Cheryl Ladd and Jaclyn Smith: every week (on *The Donny and Marie Show*) it was another *babe*. And they were beautiful women. And I remember going into my dressing room and just *sobbing*. It was very hard to be always compared—because I knew people were comparing me—that was really difficult. And it bred insecurity.

"A lot of kids go through this, but they go through it in school, with their friends. I did it in front of millions of people every week."

"MY ONLY SHOWBIZ CRUSH— DAVID CASSIDY!"

"I didn't have a lot of crushes on famous people, 'cause I got to meet most everybody. I mean, Sly Stone once asked me out! It's one of those things where you're with people, you admire them, you work with them, you get to know them, then you're friends. But that said, I was kind of excited to meet David Cassidy. I was pretty young at the time, and he was at a recording studio where my brothers were. I remember I heard his clogs first. David wore them all the time and that's what I heard, those clogs coming around the corner of the studio.

"Then I met him and I thought, 'Gosh, he's not much taller than my brothers!'"

SECRET SISTER MARIE

"My *16 Magazine* column, Secret Sister Marie, wasn't just a front. There was a woman who traveled with me, Marge Burton—she drove me back and forth to places. And that's when we'd do the column, in the car. I'd tell Marge what I wanted to say and she'd write it. My mother would proof it.

Secret Sister Marie
16 Magazine
745 Fifth Avenue
New York, N.Y. 10022

Secret Sister Marie

This Month, Sweet Sis Marie Catches You Up On All The Latest Osmond Goings-On *And* Sets The Record Straight On Some High-Flyin' Rumors!

Hi!—and welcome to my very first column of the New Year! Because we've been so unbelievably busy lately, I'm afraid I skipped writing my **Secret Sister Marie** column for last month—and I didn't get the chance to wish you **all** the very happiest of holidays! Anyway, I **hope** your Christmas was a joyous one—I know that **your** love certainly made our Christmas the best ever! We were lucky enough to be home in Utah for the holidays (we'd just finished a big concert tour of Europe and the United States—I even got the chance to sing **Paper Roses** on stage with my brothers during a couple of their concerts—it was **so** thrilling!). In Utah we spent the weeks just before Christmas resting up and getting ready for the holidays. I knitted Christmas stockings for everyone—they were one foot wide by three feet tall!—and we stuffed 'em with all sorts of fabulous goodies! All-in-all, it was a very "homey" Christmas—of course, our "newlyweds" Merrill and Mary were busy-as-bees setting up housekeeping and buying furniture for their new digs.

In January, *Donny* and I had a semi-vacation—we spent one week in Hawaii where we filmed a commercial for a local product. Mother—who's taken up photography as her latest hobby—came along with us and took loads of pix! Hope to have some of them to show you in next month's column. Hawaii is just so beautiful—it sure was a great way to start off the New Year!

And, because a new year calls for a fresh start—I'd like to start by setting the record straight on a few things that I've been getting lots of letters about. (Mostly they're rumors—so here goes!)

Rumor Number One: I Appeared At **The Grand Ole Opry** In Nashville, Tennessee On December 15, 1973. This is untrue—I did go to Nashville, but not until the 27th of December and **that** was to cut my brand-new album, and not to perform anywhere! It was **such** a wonderful experience—Sonny James (who produced my *Paper Roses* LP) worked on my new album along with family friend Mike Curb. It should be out any day now—I sure hope you like it.

Rumor Number Two: Jay Is Doing A Solo Album Called **Meet My Drums.**

No—again, this is not true. (I wonder how this one got started—probably one of *Jay's* jokes!) *Jay is,* however, working on an LP now—but it's not a solo effort—it's a new *Osmond* LP, which is due to be released in the spring.

Rumor Number Three: The *Osmonds* Are Making A Movie. Well—this isn't exactly true—but it's not exactly false either! What I mean is—we've been looking at movie scripts to find one we all like. So far, no decisions have been made—but there *is* one script that mother likes a lot and we're all having turns reading it. Soon as we've O.K.'d it—I'll be sure and let *you* know all the details!

Well—I'm just about out of room for now. Please keep writing cos I sure appreciate hearing from you! Bye for now! Love, Marie.

Here's a shot of me just going on stage at Madison Square Garden in New York City (November 23)—I sang **Paper Roses,** it was an exhilarating experience!

23

Marie took 16 *readers into the Osmond circle with her monthly column; this one was printed in April 1974.*

Marie Osmond

I'm pretty sure a lot of it came from my mother, and a lot of it *16* elaborated on and 'gooey-ed' up. They tended to make us very gooey."

LOVE, FAMILY, APPLE PIE?

"I learned at a young age to believe things, not just because my family did. I'm a very strong individual and I was a strong kid. I'm not a parrot. *16 Magazine* made us out to be naïve goody-goodies. And my image was that Marie was kind of an airhead. In print, it was always, 'love, family, piece of cake, apple pie.' And we do have a close family. But families aren't close unless they work at it. And families don't get along unless they work at it. And very strong-thinking individuals don't always get along. We had to learn to respect each other and get along. But we weren't the Brady Bunch without working at it. With all the time we spent together, I'm amazed we're still friends.

"People felt I was naïve, but I think *they* were naïve to think that—because you cannot grow up in the world of showbiz and be naïve. Everything and anything was presented to me—I made choices. In the '70s I was not hip because I didn't smoke, drink, or do drugs. The only reason I chose not to do it was because I saw what was happening to some of my friends. So I chose to be 'squeaky clean.' Nowadays, you're stupid if you do it because it ruins your brains and your talent and you aren't able to cope with things. It's interesting how things are cyclical."

THE PERKS: *"THIS IS PAUL McCARTNEY"*

"All in all, it was a fun era of my life and I'm grateful for it. There were definite perks, besides the ease of meeting boys and famous people. I always had the best wardrobe and makeup artists, and fantastic designers always did my outfits for me.

"One of the most fun things that ever happened to me was when I was in London. I got a phone call and the voice on the other end said, 'This is Paul McCartney and my daughter would really love to meet Donny. Is there any way possible...?' I thought that was pretty cool, 'cause I was a huge Paul McCartney fan.

"See, there *were* a lot of perks being Donny's sister—although (back then) I never could see what the girls saw in him. Of course, now we love each other to pieces. He's an incredibly talented guy and deserves everything he has."

THE JACKSON 5

Where they went, we went: Japan.
(l. to r.) Marlon, Tito, Jermaine, Mike, Randy, and Jackie.

Years of *16* Popularity: 1970–1975

Although *16 Magazine* had basically remained "untainted" by the sexual/political/recreational-drug revolution of the '60s, Gloria Stavers was well aware of the risk in continuing to ignore the tenor of the times. It was time to make *16* hip again—or, in a word used with abandon during the next few years, "soulful." However, detailing the sexual conquests of the stars, their drug use, or even their expletive-filled colloquialisms wasn't the route. Instead, she decreed that the road to cutting-edge hipness, teen idol–style, wove through the Sunset Boulevard offices of Motown Records—via Gary, Indiana, that is.

"Mike" takes a dip in his backyard pool.

Throughout the '60s, the amount of play celebrities got in *16* was largely determined by tallying the "unsolicited" mail from the readers. In 1970 Gloria broke with tradition, deciding to heavily cover a group completely unknown to her readers. She also chose, for the first time ever, to present *as teen idols*, a black pop act. Rhythm 'n' blues stars had frequently appeared in the magazine before, but only to promote their music—and keep *16*'s contacts with record company execs tight. Black artists had never been portrayed in the magazine as sex symbols. Since *16*'s readers were overwhelmingly white and provincial, doing so introduced the fantasy of inter-racial dating. Though never quite spelled out, the intimation was crystal clear: it's okay, safe, for *you, girl*, to explore the possibility of having a black, "superbad" boyfriend. Of course, the articles were mostly about a Dream Date with someone, not "Spend the Night with…" articles. (*16*'s most daring J5 cover line called the group "Afro-Disiacs.") Still, all-in-all, pretty heavy stuff for *16 Magazine* in the early '70s.

While the Jackson 5 had been promoted by Motown—and by 1970 had already racked up three hit singles—they had yet to reach a widespread white audience, and *16* had no reader mail on them. Yet Gloria had a feeling about the group and went with it. "Get them in the magazine" was the order given to Associate Editor Sandy Newmark—for, by this time, Gloria had a staff to do much of the grunt work—and starting with the April 1970 issue, we did. Back in those early issues, oldest brother Jackie was still going by his given name, Sigmund, as was Toriano—Tito.

Covering the Jackson 5 was really not as daring as it may have seemed back then. The way Gloria looked at it, and presented it, the Jacksons were really just an extension of

The Jackson Five

that "one big happy family" thing that was happening on television at the time, with *The Brady Bunch* and *The Partridge Family*. In the teen music world, the Osmonds were just starting to break big, especially Donny. *16* saw the Jacksons as a black, and somewhat hipper, Osmonds. But the focus wasn't on Michael as the teen idol; he was merely cutesy. Instead, the concentration was on making 15-year-old Jermaine the love object. Gloria simply decided he was better looking than the others.

That the middle Jackson brother (or *bro,* as Gloria would edit it) wanted no part of this, that he was, in fact, intensely shy and retiring, had little charisma, and didn't even want to be in showbiz at this time—let alone appear shirtless in a national teen magazine—was of little consequence. "It's the fantasy they're buying," Gloria would constantly remind her staff. That Jermaine, or anyone else, might not live up to that in real life was irrelevant. "Tellin' it like it is," in *16*–land, still meant tellin' it Gloria's way.

It was a philosophy that Motown Records' executives (who were in complete control of the Jackson 5 at the time) had no objection to. They gladly gave *16* complete access.

Michael and his brothers posed for many a studio session with 16's professional photographer; muscle men they weren't! This was as close to shirtless as we got Mike…
…Jermaine on the other hand, was "the hunk."

Berry Gordy knew that Gloria could get the group out to a white teen audience better and faster than anyone. (Indeed, in the beginning, there were no magazines specifically catering to black teens; *Right On!* started up later on.)

And it was a philosophy that, once put into action, worked very well for all concerned. Throughout the early '70s, the Jacksons, or J5, were neck in neck in popularity with the Osmonds, David Cassidy & the Partridge Family, and the perennial Bobby Sherman.

The complete access meant exclusive photo sessions, interviews, updates on everything the boys were doing, and visits to the family's home in Encino, California. It also meant road trips with the group.

In 1973, *16* got a call from Joe Jackson asking, "Would you like to come to Japan with us?" Motown was sending the group on a promotional tour and allowing them to take only two journalists along; *16*'s Sandy Newmark was one of the two. "It was the chance of a lifetime; I had to go," Sandy says now of her response. "Here I could be with them 24 hours a day, discover what they were like, and have enough real information for a year's worth of issues." Gloria, however, wasn't so easily convinced. For one thing, although Motown was footing the bill, *16* would have to incur some expense, and the company was notoriously cheap. For another, Gloria didn't care all that much about the boys' "real" personalities; what went on behind the scenes was immaterial to her. She was in the business of image-molding, not reporting.

As it played out, the stories that were written in *16* detailing the Japan trip had Gloria's stamp all over them. She titled the first one, "Jump On Their Soul Jet"—nowhere on the magazine's cover was the word *Japan* used. The follow-up piece did mention that they were in a foreign land, but Gloria refused to ditch the fantasy: she called it, "J5 Make Love In Japan."

In the photo-intense stories the boys were presented as loving every minute of it; thrilled to be meeting their fans, soaking up the culture, reveling in the attention and adoration.

Nothing could have been further from the truth. As Sandy remembers it, they had *no* interest in meeting their fans. They wanted to be left alone. They wanted to get back to the hotel, get back on the buses—get back home. They didn't want to sightsee, had no interest in Japanese culture, could not master the use of chopsticks, and were completely turned off by Japanese food. If not for fast food restaurants, they would have starved. This was a family who kept stacks of McDonald's burgers frozen in the fridge at home.

The Jackson Five

Of course, like most teenage boys, they wanted to go out and fool around. "The older ones were rambunctious, normal kids," Newmark recalls, "but Joe would have none of it. He was determined that they were going to tow the line and not wander off, but adhere strictly to the schedule: be on the bus, do a rehearsal, stay at the hotel until performance time; then wake up the next morning, get back on the bus, and go to another city. In between were public appearances, and that was it. They were in Japan for two weeks—and in that time, they did five concerts in several cities. But there was never any down time."

Throughout *16*'s coverage of the Jacksons, each boy was presented as available and virginal. As Sandy learned in Japan, that wasn't quite the story either. "The three older boys, Jackie, Tito, and Jermaine, were very much sexually active, and involved in relationships at the time. Jackie was seeing Enid (they eventually married and subsequently divorced); Tito and Deedee (they also married and divorced; several years later, she was mysteriously drowned) were hot and heavy, and Jermaine had already begun a relationship with Hazel Gordy. You get the point. All the boys ever talked about was how much they missed their girlfriends and how much they wanted to get back home."

And though no improprieties occurred with Sandy herself (who was married with a young child at home), there were some *moments*: "Jackie was very sexy—that was the first time I really noticed. And Joe was very flirty. It wasn't terribly overt—after all, his wife was on the trip—but it was there, nevertheless."

In spite of the less-than-accurate way they were covered in *16*, the older boys never complained or asked to be handled in a more adult way. For one thing, in those days, they did whatever Motown, or their father Joe—who really cracked the whip—wanted them to. For another, they were glad just to receive any coverage at all.

By this time, it was clear that Michael was the star. (In Japan, it was all about Michael, who was mobbed; the others were virtually ignored.) Most other U.S. publications could barely distinguish one brother from the other, let alone write about them as individual personalities. *16* did, mainly because Gloria insisted on it. Gloria had seen to it that *her* readers did know a Jackie from a Marlon, and each boy had his coterie of fans. It wasn't about fair play or massaging egos; it was about selling magazines. Gloria wanted each of those fans to *have* to pick up the magazine. The individual stories on each Jackson bro invested each with an identity unique to him. Jackie ("the oldest, wisest"), Tito ("the most musical"), and Marlon ("the shy one") were grateful for that.

They might, however, have had a quarrel with the language Gloria used in their stories. She would edit the copy to make it sound as if the boys were very "street"—or her idea of street, using phrases like "soul brother," "getting it on," "boss," "bubblegum soul," "jive," "right on," and "superbad."

In reality they *never* spoke that way. They'd been groomed by Berry Gordy and Suzanne DePasse (who is now a successful movie and television producer), and were constantly surrounded by white lawyers, tutors, road managers. While *16* insisted on portraying them as "black and proud," Michael proudly showed Sandy a picture of his idol—it was Fred Astaire, not James Brown.

No matter, the magic formula for success was working. American teenagers did get to know the J5—on their own level. *16* may not have covered the music, or the behind-the-scenes realities, but it was the only magazine that told the readers what the boys ate, how they dressed, what their favorite colors were, whether they slept on their stomachs or backs. Where else were the fans going to find that out? Accurate or not, *16* presented the boys on a level the readers could relate to. And that bred success: for the band and for the magazine.

MICHAEL JACKSON

Before the lawsuits and the space suits; before the hints and allegations; before the cosmetic surgery that made him look like the brother from another planet; before the crotch-grabbing; before he was "wacko Jacko" there was a sweet, soft-spoken boy with an engaging, outgoing personality and the purest voice on any planet. *16*'s readers knew him as Mike. We liked Mike.

Within the pages of *16*, Mike quickly advanced from merely cutesy, to soulful (that word again), to an accessible, nonthreatening teen idol. (Though, like his brothers, he was pressed into posing near-shirtless, he never could quite cut it as a hunk.) *16* portrayed "marvelous Mike" (frequently interspersed with "musical Mike") as chatty, witty, mischievous and very much interested in what *you, girl*, had to say. The funny thing is, in the very early stages of J5-mania, that wasn't far off. Between the ages of 11 and 13—and with several hit records to his credit—Michael really *was* talkative, inquisitive, and precocious.

The Secret LIFE of MICHAEL JACKSON!

IF YOU'RE *the kind of girl who digs mystery and craves excitement, you'd better hold on to your stack of Jackson 5 LPs—cos you're about to get the low-down on that super-talented J5-er Michael Jackson and the life he leads off-stage and away from the TV cameras and recording studios!! In other words, you're about to get an inside look at the oh-so-hush-hush secret life of Michael Jackson!!*

MICHAEL MEETS THE BRADYS

You might say that Michael's secret life began one day last summer, when Michael and his talented brothers—Jackie, Tito, Jermaine and Marlon—were at ABC-TV's Hollywood studios taping part of their Goin' Back To Indiana special, which was aired last September 19th. Those lovable kids—Maureen McCormick, Barry Williams, Chris Knight, Eve Plumb, Susan Olsen and Mike Lookinland—who make up ABC-TV's The Brady Bunch, were also shooting that day. Well, maybe it was fate that the two groups met— being on the same lot on the very same day—for during the afternoon the Jackson 5 and the Brady Bunch came face-to-face— and a happier bunch of faces you couldn't find in all of California!

Especially thrilled about the meeting was Michael Jackson, for The Brady Bunch is one of his favorite TV shows. In the short time they got to chat that day, Michael was immediately drawn to Chris Knight and Maureen McCormick. He really dug Eve, Susan, Mike and Barry too, but somehow Chris and Maureen seemed to be on the exact same wavelength as Michael. Because of the heavy work scheduled that day for the J5 in connection with their TV special, the Bradys and the J5 didn't get nearly enough time together—but in the short span they did spend talking, Michael managed to exchange phone numbers with Chris and Maureen!

Maybe because the Brady gang were so busy filming their TV series and doing personal appearances—and because the Jackson 5 are constantly on the go with recording dates and concert tours

In May 1972, **16** *revealed "The Secret Life of Michael Jackson." In fact, it was about Michael getting Brady Bunch-er Maureen McCormick's phone number, and what their conversations were like.*

—months passed by without Michael calling or seeing Maureen or Chris. But a couple of weeks before Christmas, Michael was cleaning out one of his chest drawers at home and found the slip of paper on which he had written Maureen and Chris' phone numbers. As you've probably guessed already, before you can say the name of the J5's latest hit record—Michael was dialing the phone and asking for Maureen!

When Maureen answered and heard Michael's voice, she was very pleased, cos during the many months that had passed she had planned to call Michael and say hello—but things had come up which compelled her to put off her call.

That first time they talked, the telephone wires at the Jackson and McCormick homes were busy for at least two hours! There were just so many things to be said—experiences and incidents that had to be told, and just plain old gossip about what was happening! When Michael and Maureen finally realized that they had been talking for two hours, they couldn't understand where the time had gone!

One of the many things they shared was their mutual admiration for each other. Maureen, who has just embarked upon a singing career, was very interested in Michael's views on singing—and Michael, who has always had a secret desire to act, found himself asking "Mo" (as Maureen is called by her friends) the many questions about acting he had stored up—one of which was, "How do you cry when they want you to?" When Michael and Maureen said goodbye to each other that night, they promised each other to speak again soon—and Michael checked Chris Knight's home phone number with Maureen.

BOY TALK

The next evening, at just about the same time he had phoned Maureen, Michael rang up Chris Knight. When Chris got on the phone, Michael greeted him by saying, "Hi, dude, it's M.J.! How ya' doin'?" Chris and Michael also found that they had very much to say to each other and, when the time came to hang up—cos Chris had an early call at the studio the next morning—both boys didn't want to! It seemed as though they talked about every subject under the sun, but like any other two friends, they always had more to say to each other—and they didn't want to save it until the next time they spoke!

The phone calls between the McCormick, Knight and Jackson households continued for weeks. When the J5 left on a concert tour, the phone calls stopped for a week or so, but after Michael returned home to California—once again the friendly threesome picked up where they had left off and resumed their groovy phone conversations!

It was really great, for soon all three found themselves looking forward to calling each other every night! In fact, Michael, Maureen and Chris joked about putting in a private three-way line—so that all three could talk and listen to one another at the same time! During many of their conversations they tried to make plans to get together, but one of them was always going someplace or had to do something. Finally, there came a day when all three would be free—Sunday January 9th. So all three made plans to go ice skating at a nearby skating rink!

Since Chris and Maureen live pretty close to each other—and Michael's home was nearby too—the rink was a perfect idea. Michael suggested inviting the other kids from The Brady Bunch to come along—and Maureen and Chris readily agreed. But after checking it out, Maureen learned that Barry Williams would be away and that Mike Lookinland wouldn't be able to make it. However, Eve Plumb and Susan Olsen would be there, along with Maureen and Chris—or so they all thought at the time. But at the last minute Chris had to bow out because he came down with the flu! Michael was disappointed that all of the Bradys couldn't make it, for he had hoped to get to know Mike Lookinland and Barry Williams a little better. And poor Chris—coming down with the flu! Well, Michael decided, he would just have to draw a personal "get well" card for Chris and send him a special note along with it!

●●●●●●●●●●●●●●●●●●●●●●●●●●

JERMAINE SPEAKS!

Hey, wait a minute, folks! This is that *other* Jackson 5 *lover*-boy-dude—namely *me*, Jermaine—and I'm cutting in on the line to have a few words with *you*! After all, "little brother" Michael can't hog the phone *all day*, you know! But it looks like he's done a pretty good job—huh?! In fact, he's used up all our space this month! Never mind that, though, little soul sister—cos your main man Jermaine will be *right here* in the June ish of sweet *16*—which goes on sale April 20—not only to whisper sweet nothings in your shell-like ear when we have *our* private phone-in, but to also tip you off to the *whole truth* and nothing but 'bout that super-sexy skating party Michael had with his *three* "girl friends," Maureen, Susan and Eve! So meet me 'n Michael —and the *rest* of the Jackson 5 —*right here* in the next issue of *16*!!

17

The Jackson Five

Outside the compound with parents Joe and Katherine.

He also felt entirely comfortable with *16*'s editior Eileen Bradley, whom he used to phone up at all hours with special requests. "Can you get me Jodie Foster's phone number?" he'd want to know, "or Tatum O'Neal's?" Michael had a crush on Maureen McCormick of the *Brady Bunch*—hers was tops on his most-wanted phone numbers list. More often than not Michael got what he wanted. Eileen, after checking with the parents of the girls, did facilitate those juvenile showbiz friendships. He also felt comfortable enough to tell the magazine—though it was never printed—that he'd named his dog Hitler.

Michael's openness would only last a few years. By the age of 14 he'd clammed up, become secretive, solitary, guarded, and suspicious. The reasons—a growing cynicism about the music business, his family, the money, abuse—have been speculated on through the years. Back then, certainly, we could not account for it, but simply rolled with it.

By 1973 Michael, whom *16*'s Sandy and Eileen had come to know during countless plane rides and bus trips through Japan, wore a long woolen scarf around his neck in the hottest weather ("to protect my voice," he'd whisper). He was reclusive and sheltered, and had become very much a clinging Mama's boy. Sandy remembers, "It was like the family was divided down the middle into two camps: Jackie, Tito, Jermaine, and even Marlon to an extent, sided with Joe—they were the macho men—while Michael, La Toya, and Janet clung to Katherine. Those three were very religious and painfully shy.

"Michael and I did develop a friendship of sorts. Mainly, I felt sorry for him. He seemed so overwhelmed, it was all too much for him to handle. He was very guarded at a very young age. In some ways he was very mature—you could have intimate conversations—yet in so many others he was just a little boy. I remember passing a note to him—many of our conversations were held that way—that said, 'We'll always be friends. You can count on me.'

"Off the plane, Michael would wander by himself around the hotel grounds. Never buddying up to one of his brothers or sisters, he was always alone. I remember at one hotel, there was a pond stocked with fish; Michael would sit and stare at it for hours. I tried to join him once, strolling the hotel grounds, but suddenly it was hard to get him to chat. In spite of whatever 'intimacy' we'd achieved on a plane or bus, Michael would pull back. He didn't really trust me—or anyone, it seemed."

Michael came out of his shell only when he was allowed to roam around a toy store (his favorite souvenir was a clock that told time in different parts of the world) and, of course, when he was onstage performing. Michael Jackson, by 14 years old, came to life only onstage.

THE GIRLS: LA TOYA & JANET

Before the tabloid tell-alls; the faux marriage; the Playboy spread; the weird snakes; the psychic hotlines; and the Howard Stern interviews; there was La Toya Jackson, shy, unassuming middle sister of the J5.

And before the monster hits; the TV series and movies; the $80 million recording contract; the *Rolling Stone* cover, there was the youngest Jackson, Janet. During much of the J5 heyday, she was a toddler.

Back in the early '70s, Joe Jackson was very chauvinistic. As hard as he pushed the boys into the spotlight, the girls were practically hidden. He did not want them to be involved in showbiz and so they were not groomed for it. Mostly, the women stayed home and were shielded from public view. Few even knew of their existence.

At the time, that was fine with La Toya and Janet. They made it very clear they wanted no part of that world. The

J5 MAKE LOVE IN JAPAN!

Whether Posing At A Tokyo Shopping Arcade Or Trying On Kimonos Or Being Welcomed At The Airport, Those Jiving J5'ers Were Loved In Japan As They're Universally Adored In This Country!

In September 1973 they "Made Love" in Japan. There was little about the trip they loved.

J5 AFRO-DISIACS!!

You Know That They Turn You On—But What Turns Them On And Off? It Takes More Than "Love Potion #9" To Turn Them On Cos These Are Mighty Special Boys. And You May Be Surprised At What Turns Them Off, Too!

MICHAEL

ON
* A happy smile
* Understanding his feelings
* Doing things on impulse
* Gifts of jewelry, novelties

OFF
* Rude, nosy questions
* Eating eggs
* Any sign of phoniness
* Sitting still for more than five minutes

MARLON

ON
* Taking pictures
* Buying clothes
* Dancing
* Anything French

OFF
* Losing a game
* Sloppiness
* Someone who hates teasing
* An invasion of his privacy

JERMAINE

ON
* Shiny, bright cars (expensive!)
* Sweet-smelling perfume
* Food—especially hamburgers
* Soft romantic music

OFF
* Restrictions on his life-style
* Any "exotic" foreign foods
* Unfeminine girls
* Being late for anything

TITO

ON
* His wife DeeDee
* Anything electrical or mechanical
* Crazy hats
* Photography

OFF
* Snobbish people
* Large parties
* Lies
* Anyone who doesn't like jazz

JACKIE

ON
* Fast cars custom-made
* Gold jewelry
* Women—of all types
* Lobster and steak

OFF
* Bad manners in anyone
* Aggressiveness in girls
* Anyone who doesn't like sports
* Curfews

28

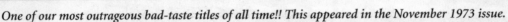

One of our most outrageous bad-taste titles of all time!! This appeared in the November 1973 issue.

Tell It To Toya!

This Month, La Toya Jackson Answers Your Questions About Her Brother Michael!!

Hello, again! Wow, so many of you have been writing to me and asking me questions about my brother Michael that I've decided to devote my column this month to answering some of those questions. I know I'll *never* get around to *all* the questions *all* of you have ever asked about Michael, but let me try to answer the ones that appear most frequently in your letters! O.K., here goes—

1. *What is Michael's birthday?*
Michael was born on August 29, 1958.

2. *What sign of the zodiac is Michael?*
Michael is a Virgo.

3. *What's his whole name?*
Michael was christened Michael Joe Jackson. The Joe is for our father, whose name is Joe as well.

4. *What kind of girl does Michael like?*
Boy, I sure get asked this one a lot! Well, Michael likes girls who are cute and who have a good sense of humor. It also helps if they are into music. But as far as looks go, it's much more important to Michael how she acts and what kind of personality she has than how good-looking she is.

5. *How tall is he?*
Last I looked he was about 5' 7" and still growing!

6. *How much does he weigh?*
Michael's kind of skinny—I think he weighs about 125 pounds.

7. *When is Michael most happy?*
That's easy—when he's making music!

11. *Does Michael smoke cigarettes?*
No!—and he says he never will. It's terrible for anyone to do, and particularly terrible for anyone who sings.

12. *Which are Michael's favorite groups?*
Sometimes I think his favorite is whatever group he happens to be listening to at the moment, but I know he digs Sly and the Family Stone, the Staple Singers, and Led Zeppelin.

13. *Who is his favorite singer?*
Michael likes lots of singers, but his all time favorite singer is probably the great Joe Tex.

14. *What hobbies does Michael have?*
He loves to go horseback riding, and he's also a terrific artist. He's great at drawing cartoons, and I remember once he said that if he couldn't be in show business for any reason, he'd have been a cartoonist.

8. *What is his favorite color?*
I'd say it was a toss-up between red and blue, but lately he likes green also!

9. *What is Michael's favorite TV show?*
He's liked *Sanford & Son* from the beginning, and it's still his favorite.

10. *What kind of food does he like?*
Lots of kinds, but he especially loves Mexican food and pineapples.

15. *Does Michael go to the movies?*
Are you kidding? Michael is a movie-nut from the word go! His favorite kind is horror movies, full of creatures and monsters and ghosts and alien beings from outer space and all that stuff.

16. *Is Michael ever nervous about performing?*
Not Michael! He's got fear conquered. He once said, "When you know you're good at what you do, then you don't worry." And it's not conceited when he says that—it's just that he's confident that he's always doing his best.

17. *What does he think of his fans?*
Why, I guess he loves them more than anything else in the world!

18. *Does he plan on getting married?*
Someday, I guess he will. But it's not something that's big on his mind right now.

19. *Does he read books?*
Yes, and very heavy ones. He loves Ernest Hemmingway, William Faulkner and James Joyce!

20. *Where can I write to Michael?*
You can write to him at Suite 1023, 6255 Sunset Blvd., Los Angeles, Cal. 90028.

22

In her March 1975 column, "Toya" told all about Michael!

The Jackson Five

La Toya and baby sister Janet—who knew she'd be among the world's most successful performers one day?

La Toya *16* knew was excruciatingly shy. She'd run and hide in her room when people came over. Asked by *16*'s editors if she'd ever like to perform, she was appalled at the notion. "I'm gonna do nails, or some sort of trade," La Toya replied in all seriousness.

When Gloria Stavers learned of La Toya's existence, she pounced upon a plan. Even though La Toya herself was not a performer, she was certainly close enough to some very famous ones. Why not have La Toya write a column in *16 Magazine*? After all, Marie Osmond was doing one (Secret Sister Marie) and wouldn't this be the perfect complement?

The monthly column was immediately dubbed, in *16*'s inimitable alliterative manner, "Tell It to Toya." The idea was that La Toya would report on her brothers' exciting lives, draw the readers into the "real, intimate, family-centered world" of the Jackson family. Except, as it turned out, Toya didn't have much to tell. The middle Jackson

sister *had* no "insider scoops" on her brothers: she was as much an outsider as any *16* reader. Moreover, "La Toya couldn't talk—she was completely nonverbal, noncommunicative. She lived a very sheltered life. So I had to write the column myself," Sandy Newmark revealed.

The deception wasn't a problem. The group, Motown, even Joe was happy with the result. La Toya eventually grew to love the exposure, though she often balked at having her picture taken—"I'm so fat," she'd complain. Of course, by the time her first columns came out, she'd completely shed her baby fat and was quite thin.

Janet Jackson was a preschooler in those days. There was no clue that she'd one day pose on the cover of *Rolling Stone* with only her boyfriend's hands covering her breasts. Janet was the complete antithesis of what she is now. She was just a shy, clingy little kid who hid behind her mother's apron. Who knew?

The Brady Bunch

Years of *16* Popularity: 1970–1973

A beloved TV family, who first appeared on network television in 1969, the Brady Bunch should have been custom-made for *16* success. The appeal of the story was the happy household of Mom and her three daughters from a previous marriage, Dad and his three sons ditto, and the wise and wonderful housekeeper, Alice. Kids in America wanted to be part of the idealized Brady family. As Florence Henderson (who played Mom) said of the show, "Our series was more or less written through the eyes of a child, a child who hoped that they had a family like we had."

The Brady Bunch featured six good-looking potential faves in your living room every week. Additionally, the show generated several offshoots: before the original series ended its run in August 1974, there were an animated cartoon series, a *Brady Bunch Variety Hour*, a touring show starring the six Brady kids, and several record albums.

The clan reappeared on TV in a string of shows from 1979 to 1981 called *The Brady Brides*. As a testament to the show's enduring popularity, 1988's *A Very Brady Christmas* was the highest-rated TV movie of the year. Another series went on the air in 1990, and there have been two Hollywood movies in this decade. Like it or not, the Bradys are America's longest-running fictional family. The cast members remain close to this day.

In spite of being part of the American cultural landscape, and also in spite of its appealing cast, the Brady Bunch never was a true *16 Magazine* sensation. There was no (with the possible exception of Chris Knight) real teen idol in the series, and the Brady boys were in competition with David Cassidy, Donny Osmond, and Bobby Sherman, three of the biggest idols ever. There were cover lines about the Bradys, but they never had the banner. In an unusual switch, it wasn't any of the boys, but Maureen McCormick (Marsha) who emerged as the most popular Brady. Her Dear Maureen advice column, a *16* staple for several years, generated incredible amounts of mail, though it was of course the work of *16*'s editors.

Chris Knight (Peter), now no longer active in show business, and Barry Williams (Greg), who still performs, shared their very different perspectives with the authors of this book. Maureen McCormick was also approached, but declined our request for an interview.

Chris Knight

"I HATED IT; I WANTED TO BE NORMAL"

"Most kids do need idols and people to feel close to and follow. I never did, and I always wondered 'Why are they doing it, why am I that person now? God, it's strange.' I hated it, I hated it. I just wanted to be normal. And it wasn't that I felt abnormal, it's just that I felt I was being treated as such. I really didn't like the attention. I liked the work. But I did what I was told, and I tried to do it pleasingly. And I did it patiently,

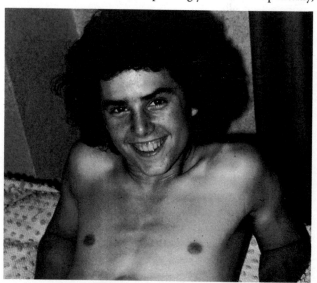

Chris Knight on a chenille bedspread in his Atlantic City hotel; this picture was used in 16's Adonis Kit, a collection of photos of topless boys that was sold separately via direct mail.

The Brady Bunch

the cute and cuddly stuff, because I knew that one day it would be over. Yeah, I hated it. One of the outgrowths of the show being canceled was that I wasn't going to have to deal with *16 Magazine* anymore. I didn't want to do any more interviews, and I felt gleeful inside.

"I rejected the basic sentimentality that characterized the Brady Bunch. When I went through my 'young buck, young artist' thing at 17, the Brady thing was something to be scorned. It wasn't respected for the one thing that mattered to me during that period of time, which was artistic purity. It was successful, it made money, but what was it? It was completely not respected by the creative community that gave it breath, but it was loved by the public. So I actually developed a contempt for the very public that supported me on television. 'Contempt' is too strong a word; 'detachment' is better, a decided detachment, because although they were supporting me, I was decidedly not one of them. My 'art' was above them.

"I knew that this was not a show that I as a kid would watch. Now I see it's that I was living in Los Angeles, being supported by towns in Wisconsin and a whole different mentality. On balance, I'm completely at ease with it now, because I understand why it's been a success: the issues themselves are universal, mostly how to get along with your sister or brother, and very basic, moral little plays. And also, it showed a functional family that was well centered, and for the many children whose families weren't working so well, the Bradys became a surrogate family.

"My own family was completely dysfunctional, so I know what the appeal was. And when kids get older, in college, for example, and they realize that all their friends watched it, and you all have something in common. You can make fun of it, or say 'God that was great!' because it was so stupid and silly. Like the *Batman* series. But it's a known quantity, and you can gather around it. It becomes flypaper.

"Would I want my kids to watch the show, or to have watched it if I had been a father back then? My own mother told me that parents in dysfunctional families would not have wanted to face the question, 'Why isn't our family like that?' But my own mother had given up on our family. I don't buy that it was wrong to watch *The Brady Bunch* because it was a fantasy. It can't do any kid any harm to watch it. Yeah, I'd let my kids watch it, and have a very difficult time figuring out what else they should watch."

Barry Williams

"WHO I REALLY WAS NEVER HAD A CHANCE"

"I was between 16 and 18 during the height of the *16 Magazine* popularity. I was aware of the magazine before I was in it, because girls used to bring it to school. I thought some of the pictures were cheesy, beef-cakey, and I decided early on that if I was ever in the magazine, I wouldn't want to pose like that. Of course, you could probably find some shirtless pictures of me if you tried.

"In general, I never thought about becoming a teen idol. The acting I'd done before *The Brady Bunch* was serious, and I thought of *16* as being the celebrity side of it all, especially with all the *wows* and *gees* in the articles. Having said that, I was never embarrassed to be in it. I loved being an actor and all the perks that went with it, the attention we got. Our lives were built totally around the show. I didn't realize what a hit we were until we started doing concerts—then, going into a 12,000-seat arena with kids screaming, it was amazing, I was thrilled. We did an album, which did well; it's not musically very good, but it's funny. The music, in combination with the live show and the TV series, really spurred our popularity with the teens.

"Was that really me in the pages of *16*? It was the part that readers would be interested in, but it didn't come close to representing who I really was. As far as Maureen's column went, I'm *sure* she didn't sit down and write the column. But she could have; the six of us kids spent more time with each other than with our own families. Yes, Maureen and I did date, we did make out, but we never gave an interview about it; how that got into *16* as something we talked about, I'll never know.

"We'd do an interview, in person or on the phone, and from that, 32 articles would spring. But I never had any negative repercussions from anything printed about me in that magazine. Elsewhere, yes, but not in *16*. I was never teased by my peers about being in *16*, because I went to private schools in Los Angeles, where, if anything, I was envied. Susan Olsen told me that kids at her school thought she *was* actually Cindy Brady, and when she portrayed a tattletale on one episode, her classmates were reluctant to speak to her! Chris has always been such a *real* guy. He always took the business with a grain of salt.

Barry Williams' SECRET DATE BOOK!

Everyone has kept a diary at one time or another. Where else but in a diary could you keep a record of your secret thoughts and feelings? A diary is written *by* yourself — *about* yourself — and *to* yourself. It's a book you write for your *eyes* alone to read. A diary is a *personal* and *private* thing!

YOU KNOW you shouldn't open the brown leather diary in front of you. It's not *yours!* It belongs to someone else! But how *else* can you find out who might have lost it? You turn to the first page and read: *THIS DIARY IS THE PERSONAL PROPERTY OF BARRY WILLIAMS.* Barry Williams? Not Barry Williams of *The Brady Bunch* on TV? The handwriting looks like Barry's, though. You've seen his autographed pin-ups in *16* — and maybe it really *is* the same Barry Williams you've been watching every week. Stranger things than that have happened!

You can't resist taking a look at just *one* of the pages. You know you shouldn't, but you feel that just *one* page couldn't hurt anything. You pick a page at random and begin to read:

SATURDAY (5:30 P.M.): Well, tonight's the night! I wonder what she'll think when she opens her front door and finds me standing there? She'll be surprised — that's for sure! She doesn't suspect a thing! I hope she likes those flowers. I've always had a knack for choosing the right flowers for my dates. I hope it doesn't fail me now! I want this date to be perfect. I want it to be a date she'll never forget!

I hope she likes seafood! I've already reserved a quiet table for two at the restaurant overlooking the beach. All they serve there is seafood! Oh, well, there's no sense in worrying about it. It's too late to change my plans now! I've got a lot to do before 8:30. I've still got to get dressed

too — so I'd better get cracking!

(7:30): One more hour to go — and I'm restless! I hope I look sharp tonight. This new blue jacket fits me like a glove — and it's comfortable too! My sportscar is washed and polished — and full of gas! I'm a little nervous, though! I think I'll just go out for a walk. I'm going to take you along with me, diary — just in case I want to write in you again!

(7:45): Here I am. Just sitting at the bus stop — killing some time. It's a great night. The moon is shining — and it's full too! The sky is filled with stars — and I'm not so nervous anymore. I want this night to be a special one. I'm not going to risk ruining it by being nervous. I'm going to be myself. Not Barry Williams of TV — just plain Barry Williams. I hope she'll be natural too. She lives around here — just a block away from where I'm sitting. I'd better run back and get my car. I don't want to be late — not on our first date together. I've planned quite an evening — and later we'll take a ride along the coast. Maybe we'll even park — and listen to the waves. I'm sure we have a lot in common.

We'll visit a disco or two. Just to take a look — or listen to the music — or dance a little. We'll play it by ear — and follow no plan. It's going to be a fantastic evening! I can feel it in my bones!

That's all that is written in Barry's diary — and it's the very *last* entry you've turned to! *Wow*, you wonder who the lucky girl could be! Imagine! A surprise date with Barry Williams! That girl was really in for the date of her life! Wonder if she's anyone you know. If she is, you'll hear about it! (Who could keep a date with Barry Williams a secret!)

Then you begin to wonder if it just might be *you* Barry was writing about! It *could* be! Why not? The doorbell is ringing, isn't it? It's 8:30, isn't it? *Go on!* Open the door!!

For **JOHN COWSILL'S SECRET DATE BOOK** — turn to page 44!

An early attempt to make Barry Williams into a guy you'd want to have a date with, from the June 1970 issue.

BRADY BUNCH BUST-UP

"Have you heard that Chris is leaving the Bradys?"

"No, I haven't, but is it true?"

"Well, I don't know, but it seems possible. How about Barry? Now that he's got a Paramount solo single, *Cheyenne*, I suppose that means he'll split too."

"Well, I don't know, but if Chris and Barry go, I'm sure that Maureen will go make movies."

"Oh, my gosh! What are we going to do on Friday nights with no *BB*s to watch? Do you think it's *really true*?"

16 states unequivocally that the *Brady Bunch* is not busting up! But, kids, that's how rumors get started!

That smashing sextet of boisterous Bradys are definitely, but *definitely*, back on your goggle box. And if you're a Doubting Thomas, just tune your telly in to ABC at eight o'clock every Friday night and have a ball watching the *BB*s in action. And if *that* ain't enough for you, watch the *BB*s Saturday morning in animation with their real live voices on ABC at 10:30 AM.

Sure it's true that each of these adorable kids is branching out and doing other things besides telly. Barry and Eve, of course, are singing stars. Chris hasn't yet made up his mind what else he wants to do, but the offers are sure pouring in. Maureen is thinking of following in Susan Dey's footsteps and making a movie. Naughty-but-nice Mike Lookinland has a lot of irons in the fire. And don'tcha dare fret! Smashingly-sassy Susan Olsen has things up her sleeve *too*!

These unusually wonderful kids who really dig each other on camera have decided to broaden their musical careers collectively. That is, they're making records together, and they made personal appearances at fairs last summer throughout the country. For those of you who weren't lucky enough to see them in person, Dick Clark's *American Bandstand* had them on as guests last spring and they were spiffy! In fact, these kids are not only close with each other, but they're close with their TV mom and dad, Florence Henderson and Robert Reed, too!

So remember, no matter what you read anywhere else, the *Brady* Bunch as a team is going far.

So, Sally Snoops and Gladys Gossips, put your waggling tongues to sleep. Hang up your phone and stop spreading those nasty rumors about the "Brady Bunch bust-up"!

Watch these kids harmonize! Each Brady adds his own special ingredient to give all of their songs that distinct-

A rumor created to be refuted: in November 1972, the Brady Bunch was far from breaking up.

"Dear Maureen—"

HI THERE, _16_-ers! And welcome back to my column _Dear Maureen!_ I look forward to helping you with your particular problems every month in _16_. If you have a problem you'd like me to help you solve, just write me a letter at the address shown at the bottom of this page and—sooner or later—my answer to you will show up right here in _16_!!

That Brady Beauty Tells You How To Get A Boy To Notice You & What To Do When Your Best Friend Is A Runaway

HOW TO GET _HIM!_
Dear Maureen,
Last year when I was in the fourth grade I fell in love with a boy in my class named Hector. Now I am in the fifth grade and I still love him. He doesn't pay any attention to me, so I don't know if he likes me. I just can't tell. I know that you think I'm too young to be in love, but it's true. Can you help me, Maureen?
Margret Meater
Jackson Heights, N.Y.

• _Dear Margret,_
Of course you're not too young to be in love! Love can come to anyone at any time, and nobody can tell you you're not in love when you know you are!

Now, what about Hector? He probably doesn't know how you feel about him—and he could be as shy as you in expressing his feelings. And, you know, people usually are inclined to like people who like them. It's very flattering to be liked, and when a boy learns that someone likes him—even if he hasn't thought very much about her before—his first reaction is to feel favorably disposed towards her (at the least he'll think she has excellent taste!) and that's certainly a good beginning.

But first, make sure you are as "likeable" as you can possibly be. Pay attention to your grooming, your speech, your manners, your poise and your personality. Become interested in things, and be an interesting person. Developing your natural assets will give you confidence in yourself, and once you are somewhat confident of your own attractiveness, you can subtly let Hector know that you like him. (He doesn't have to know that you've been suffering in silence for years because of him—but simply that you like him.) Perhaps a mutual friend can drop a hint, or maybe you can simply break the ice with a basic question about something that concerns you both—like schoolwork or that old standby, the weather. Just show by your manner, your voice, your eyes, that you think he's an interesting person, worth knowing and listening to. Then it's up to Hector, and you'll know—by his _manner,_ his _voice,_ his _eyes_—something of what he thinks of you. If he shows any kind of interest, you'll know that you've made a start. But, if worse comes to worse and you strike out completely—well, by then you'll have so much going for you that there's sure to be someone else _real soon,_ and this time it won't take you two years to get things off the ground!

RUNAWAY

Dear Maureen,
Recently, my best friend told me she was planning to run away from home because her parents—especially her mother—were so mean to her. Then she ran away. She's written to me, so I know where she is, and she says she's a little scared, but that she's OK. Also, she asked me **never** to tell her parents where she is. Well, her parents are frantic and since they know we're best friends, they ask me _every day_ if I've heard anything from her. I feel sorry for them, especially her dad (I also feel sorry for him for having to be married to her mother!), but I can't betray my friend. Maureen, I really feel caught in the middle of this and it's making me crazy. I can't discuss it with anyone around here. _Please_ tell me what to do.
Sally D.
Shaker Heights, Ohio

• _Dear Sally,_
In running away as she did, your friend—besides causing her parents to suffer—has been very unfair in putting such a heavy burden on you. You should write your friend and try to persuade her to call her parents and let them know how—_if not where—she is. Maybe they can work things out, maybe not. But at least her parents will know she is alive and will probably stop asking you questions which you can now answer only by being dishonest, on the one hand, or betraying your friend, on the other. Your responsibilities to your friend include neither lying nor "going crazy," but her responsibility to you certainly does include getting you out of this intolerable situation!_

That's all for this month. Meet me here in the March issue of _16_—on sale January 23—and we'll carry on with our conversation. In the meantime, if _you've_ got a problem you'd like me to help you with, write to me at _Dear Maureen, 16 Magazine, 745 Fifth Avenue, New York, N.Y. 10022._

This Dear Maureen column, from February 1973, was in fact written by Danny Fields;
no matter who wrote these advice columns, the editors always urged readers to develop "inner qualities" as a path to popularity.

The Brady Bunch

"It was essentially a nurturing environment. It was the most professional bunch of kids on any set, anywhere. It's different today; there are more pitfalls, because of the enormous amount of money being thrown at kids in the biz. But we never complained, ever, about someone having more lines or being featured more than someone else.

"I dated a fan once. I think she wrote me a letter, through an address in *16*. I was curious—what is a fan? It seemed harmless enough. We went ice-skating in Santa Monica, and the whole time she was looking over her shoulder. I couldn't figure out why. It turned out she'd brought a whole group of friends and she wanted to make sure they knew she was with me. She cared about what I did, not who I was. Who I really was, in fact, never had a chance.

"If there was a downside to those years, it was not getting to hang out with friends my own age. I was so happy to be working, I didn't realize what I was missing. I didn't sleep a lot. I was always working. The best part was doing something you enjoy, every day, and I loved the work.

Barry—in a typical 16 pose.

Maureen "writing" her column.

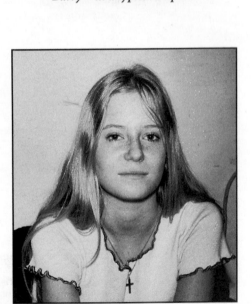

Eve Plumb played Jan.

Susan Olsen was Cindy, the baby Brady.

WHO'S YOUR FAVE RAVE?

RANDY MANTOOTH

Years of *16* Popularity: 1972–1975

"I'm Lonely!" "Nobody Loves Me!" "I've Been Lied About!" Such were the angst-ridden headlines routinely blared in **16** about a young actor who achieved instant, and unsettling, fame in a ground-breaking NBC series about heroic paramedics called *Emergency!* In an era of toothsome, "come on, get happy" teen idols like David Cassidy, Donny Osmond, and the J5, Randolph Mantooth was a breed apart; he sowed discontent every unsmiling step of the way. Stage-trained and all of 21 at the time, Randy rarely broke from his persona: intense, moody, mysterious and, if one were to believe **16 Magazine**, often tortured.

Of course, the angst only served to make him all the more appealing. Fans were wild for him. "At one point in the '70s," a still awestruck Randy Mantooth remembers, "*TV Guide* took a fan mail poll. I came in second—Hank Aaron was first, and the President was third."

What those frenzied, letter-writing fans never knew, because **16** took great pains to hide it, was that Randy remained "mysterious and tortured" for the simple reason that he adamantly, absolutely, and from the beginning, refused to do any and all interviews with us.

Up until that point in the magazine's history, no one important—that is, no one the readers voted (with their mail) their top star month after month, for 3 years in this case—had been this obstinate. It was our first such dilemma, but it would not prove insurmountable. Led by the indomitable Gloria Stavers, **16** determined to give its readers what they wanted, whether the object of their desire wanted it or not. We simply, and ardently, worked around Randy.

The *modus operandi* was simple. The network, NBC, cooperated fully, supplying whatever biographical information

In July 1973 we assumed Randy was "Lonely for Love." We were lonely—for an interview!

they had, plus photo after photo from the TV show. We used it all, over and over again, every which way imaginable: and we got very imaginative at times. Mantooth-mania reigned supreme for a period of 2½ years.

What did we find to write about? From the NBC-supplied bio, we learned that Randy's birthday was in September. From that tidbit, we devised the article "Randy's Love-O-Scope," using basic astrological information. The fact that he was single made him "Lonely." You get the idea. Fans got their monthly dose, while Randy remained elusive and resentful; he never got over hating every second of it. What he did get over was resenting the fans, however. Big time.

After *Emergency!*'s run, Randy starred in two short-lived series, worked in theater, did TV movies and episodic guest appearances. He has portrayed the character Alex Masters on the now-canceled ABC soap *The City*. An older, wiser, mellower, articulate, funny (who knew??), and absolutely charming Randy Mantooth willingly agreed to be interviewed and "set the record straight."

Randy Mantooth

"THE LAST THING I WANTED WAS TO BE A HUNK"

"I remember *16* well. I was very difficult. You're basically dealing with a 20-year-old kid, who went to the American Academy of Dramatic Arts, did theater in New York, and felt that he was probably more important than he really was.

"The last thing in the world that he wanted in his life was to be a hunk. He wanted to be an actor, to be known as an actor, to be as good an actor as he possibly could be.

"So here I am, 21, and all of a sudden I find out that show business isn't run that way. They don't give a damn whether you're a good actor or not, they only care whether little girls fantasize over you. That was so offensive to me. And it was a big shock, a big wake-up call for me—only I really never woke up. I felt that I could fight it. At first, I refused to do certain interviews; later, I refused to do all of them—including *TV Guide*—mainly because it was a constant reminder that I was being given this hunk status, which at that time, I resented."

"WE'RE GONNA MAKE IT UP"

"Still, that wasn't the most compelling reason that I didn't cooperate specifically with *16 Magazine*. *16* was persona non grata with me because somebody—I don't know who it was, just a voice on the phone—called me with a message. After I made it clear that I wasn't going to do an interview, this person said, 'Look, Randy, we think it's best that you do the article, because if you don't, we're just gonna make it up!'

"I now know this person was speaking out of sheer frustration. But at the time, I took those words literally. I was infuriated. Because, basically, they did make it up. They patched in past interviews I had done here and there and put it all in a 'new' interview and made it sound like I had said it. And I didn't say any of that—not to *16*, anyway.

"I'd read it, and it was as if somebody else was talking and using my picture. It was so far from me, I couldn't believe it. They would have lists of 'What Randy Loves,' and while some of it was true, some of it was sheer fantasy, just absolute made-up baloney and, again, *none* of it was ever said to *16*. So I resented that, and I never really got over it."

"I WAS YOUNG AND STUPID"

"But I now know, first off, how the business is run. And I now know also that this magazine had to make a living, had to stay afloat, and at that particular point in time I was a key figure. At the time, again, I was young and stupid—that's all I can say; 21 and incredibly stupid. And probably filled up with myself more than I should have been. Couldn't help it; it wasn't malicious. But I look back on it now and I kind of cringe. I could have handled that a lot better. And I was pretty headstrong. My agents, the network, would all try to talk to me. But I just absolutely had this vision of who I was—however false that was—and nobody was going to rob me of it."

"THE ARTICLES FED MY FURY"

"I must be honest. While I never cooperated, I did see most of the articles. I would see the magazine in grocery stores, places like that. I never would have bought one, but if it was there, I would look at it. And it would feed my fury when I would read it.

"But, that said, I also have to be honest with you: most of the articles that I have now, have all been mailed to me over the years by longtime fans, who are constantly sending me this stuff. I don't think I realized just how much of an impact I did have, until much, much later. Ninety-five percent of my mail *now* is almost all *Emergency!* fan mail. It blows my mind."

"I REALLY WASN'T AN ASSHOLE"

"In spite of my not cooperating, and their threat to 'make it all up,' *16* probably got a lot of (facts) right. Mind you, it was a war I started and felt justified in. Now, in hindsight, I probably regret it. I probably made a lot of people think I was an asshole, when I knew I wasn't. I was just kind of a willful boy who needed to be yanked up short by somebody who had some power over me. Only no one did.

"I started to resent my own popularity after a while. We're all raised in obscurity, so we know how to deal with obscurity very well. We don't know any other way. Then, all of a sudden, notoriety hits. For me, it was all in a matter of 9 months. One day, I'd be walking down the street, nobody knew who I was, I didn't turn heads—and I was fightin' like hell just to get a date. Just like everybody else, I was insecure. And then nine months later, I'm God?? I don't think so!"

"I HAVE NO ONE TO BLAME BUT MYSELF"

"One of the turning points in my life, with regard to

RANDY'S SECRET LAMENT—
"NOBODY LOVES ME!"

Who Would Believe That Handsome Randy Mantooth Feels Unloved And Unwanted? But It's **True**....

It is a damp, chilly night in the Topanga Canyon wilderness, northwest of Los Angeles. Rain has been falling on and off for several days, and the hills and roads of the canyon are covered with mud. In a small, isolated house, nestled against the side of a towering hill, a thin, intense young man sits in an armchair in front of a roaring fire. He sips a cup of tea and stares morosely into the flames. From two large speakers on the floor behind him, the melancholy strains of a Mahler symphony pour forth, filling the small room with the tragic and mournful music of the great German composer.

The young man goes into the kitchen, pours himself another cup of tea, and returns to the fireplace. The flaming logs have now turned into glowing red coals. Should he put another piece of wood in the fire, or should he let it die out? **Oh well,** he thinks, **might as well keep it going a bit longer—there's nothing else to do.** He tosses a new log into the hearth, and watches as it starts to crackle and burn. Another lonely night in the life of Randy Mantooth drags slowly on . . .

Rejects Love

As every reader of **16** knows, Randy is a self-proclaimed "loner"—avoiding parties, crowds and the general trappings of the Hollywood social scene. Of course, this is by his own choice. Anyone as attractive, popular and talented as Randy is could go to dozens of parties a month, and date as many girls as he wanted to. But Randy seems not to want to—he would rather be alone. Or would he?

"It's funny about Randy," says a close associate of his, who asked that his name not be printed. "He claims that he's not interested in going out to parties, or dating lots of girls. But sometimes I get the feeling that Randy is really still afraid of being rejected. So he rejects everyone else first! That way, he doesn't give anyone a chance to turn him down. He's protected, and he's safe—he takes no risks. As a result, he very rarely gets an opportunity to make contacts with people, and to establish deep relationships. And I think, deep down, it's because he's afraid to. I bet he wants to be loved, just like everybody else does."

Another friend, someone who's known Randy since he was a teenager in Santa Barbara, had these very revealing comments to make: "When it comes

to emotional commitments, Randy has always taken the initiative—but in a **negative** way! He's always had this 'Who-could-ever-want-to-love-**me**?' attitude. Then, he closes off any possibility of that happening, and **then** he says, 'See, I was right! Nobody loves me—why should they?' Well, love is a two-way thing—you've got to open yourself up to receive it, and you've got to demonstrate that you've got love in you to give. Randy does neither, and he ends up defeating himself. Nobody **is** going to love you unless you let them, and he won't let them!"

Continued On Page 46

3

Randy Mantooth

fame, was a *TV Guide* article I did. It was very negative, said things like I loathed being a teen idol and, in fact, just dumped my fan mail in the corner of my dressing room and didn't deal with it.

"It didn't upset me because I did say it. I had no one to blame but myself. I have no bitterness toward that writer at all. In fact that writer gave me every chance to change what I was saying—he called me after the interview was over to be sure I didn't want to change anything. He threw me a life preserver, but as a stubborn and willful boy, I was waiting for a helicopter.

"And I wasn't upset that I had said it, but that I really did feel and act that way. That was really an epiphany to me to a certain degree. That was when all of a sudden I went, 'Randy, you gotta take a break, or you gotta get out of this business, because not only did you do something that was not right, you said you did it and you even sounded boastful that you did it.' And that was when I really questioned whether I was suited for this business. I stayed in it as an actor, and from that moment on, I always avoided fame.

"Now that I get to set the record straight: I overstated what I really did with my fan mail. I didn't dump it. Even though it was so overwhelming to me and I couldn't read it all, I did read a lot of it. They used to deliver it in huge boxes, and I would put it in the corner of my dressing room. Every time I would have a few moments, I would reach over and grab a fistful, and read it. Since there was no physical way I could get through all of it, I hired somebody to deal with it, to send some sort of response, a picture, to everyone who wrote. That worked for a while, but it got too expensive. I was only making about $1,400, $1,500 a week. Now, it was the '70s, but still, I was under contract at the studio, so I couldn't negotiate with them as a free agent—they had all the cards. So that was a mitigating circumstance. It got to a point where I couldn't afford the fan mail service, so I let that drop.

"Now, there's not one piece of mail that I don't answer, no matter how mundane. Sometimes my mail is the written equivalent of grunts. It's like, 'Like you, send picture.' I write 'em back, 'Here picture.' I'm being a bit of a smart-ass, but I do answer them all."

"TO EVERYONE I REJECTED— I APOLOGIZE PROFUSELY"

"I didn't deal with fans as well as I might have. I would hide, and wear hats and glasses. And then finally one day it hit me, out of the blue, I'm spending more energy hiding than I am by simply turning around and going, 'Thanks, I appreciate that,' which is how I do it now. Because that's all they really want.

"And it's not that I'm trying to make up for the past; what I'm trying to say is that I have learned a lot. I now know how people feel. It takes so much courage for them to walk up to somebody—sometimes, literally they're shaking! I get starstruck, too, and I can't do that. I want to approach an actor or a ball star, football, baseball, or whatever. I don't have the courage, to get up and do what they obviously have the courage to do. To get up and maybe get rejected by that person.

"So to all those people who got rejected by that jerk who played Johnny Gage, I apologize profusely. There's nothing I can do about it; all I can say is as you get older, you begin to realize that these are real people and you made such an impact on their lives, that when they see the real person, and this real person turns out to be a jerk, it's devastating. And it's happened in my business with me, working with actors that I so admired, to find out that they're jerks. When people like Charles Barkley say, 'I'm no role model,' I say, dude, wake up, because you are. You may not want to be—I didn't—but you are. You have a hell of a responsibility that comes along with the fame, which I don't like—but it comes along with the money, which I do like.

"I appreciate the chance to set the record straight. This is the way I feel now…check with me in 40 years, though, I might feel differently. Call me again when I'm 80 and on my deathbed, and all those old *Emergency!* fans, they'll probably be the paramedics, trying to keep me alive!"

Andy & David Williams

Years of *16* Popularity: 1973–1975

Andy and David Williams were a bonanza for *16*. Identical twins, born in Las Vegas on February 22, 1959, they're the nephews of crooning TV star Andy Williams, raised in a show business environment, adorable, and eager (or it seemed at the time) to set the hearts of teenaged girls a-thumping.

They were the first and only twins ever featured big-time in *16*, and of course much fuss was made about how to tell them apart, and which one was for *you*. Readers learned that David was an inch taller than his brother, tended to be the more aggressive of the two, and liked cookies; Andy kicked off his shoes as soon as he got home, was the more musical of the two (of course they made records), and snacked on potato chips and dips. True connoisseurs could tell them apart by the way they wore their thick blond bangs.

The Williams twins were always a pleasure to work with, well-behaved, professional, and eager to be cute. It turns out that all the cuddliness started to turn sour when Andy and David reached their midteens. The twins grew resentful of the image they were being forced to present, underwent analysis, and emerged as a serious songwriting and singing team, performing acoustically and making albums.

We spoke to David and Andrew (as he now prefers to be called) while working on this book. David was visiting Andrew's house in Los Angeles when we talked.

David

"I ENDED UP FEELING LIKE AN ALIEN"

"Those years are all kind of a blur. We were given the opportunity to do it, starting at twelve years old, and we didn't really know what we were getting into. We had always sung together, and a picture of us got into a teen magazine, and a lot of fan mail came in, and that led to getting a record deal. It happened really fast. It was like a fantasy, unreal, like I wasn't really experiencing it. I knew I had wanted to be in show business; it just happened sooner than it should have.

"At the time, I felt really lucky not to be going to school, because I didn't like school. I didn't feel deprived of anything when it was happening. Years after that, I wished that I would have had more of a childhood, experienced more time being around other kids. But it was, in its way, a great experience, and we got to meet a lot of interesting people, traveled around the world, things that would not happen to kids growing up in what you would call a normal way.

Andy (left) and David Williams in the pool.

Posing for the accompanying Kiss Blitz are David (top) and Andy.

ANDY & DAVID—

Kissing Girls Is Unabashedly One Of Andy & David's All-Time *Favorite* Activities! They Enjoy This "Sport" Indoors, Outdoors—And Even In Between Revolving Doors! Matter Of Fact, They've Become Such Experts On This Tasty Subject, They've Made Up This Little "Kiss-Blitz-Board"—To Show *You* What Kinda Kissers They Really Are And When, Where, How & Why They Kiss!

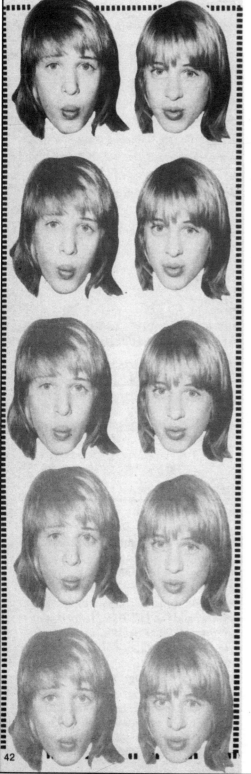

ANDY's KISSES

Kind Number One:
KUTE 'N KWIK KISSES!

When: on the spur-of-the-moment, **very** impulsively!
Where: on your cheek, mostly.
How: with his lips pursed just **very** slightly!
Why: cos he feels like it!

Kind Number Two:
KOOL KISSES

When: at a restaurant, at a party—whenever he thinks it would surprise **you** most!
Where: just brushing your neck, shoulders—**maybe** your lips.
How: with cool, calculated precision!
Why: cos he wants to show you he likes you—as more than just a friend—but he wants to play it super-cool.

Kind Number Three:
KUDDLY KISSES

When: you're out on a date, or he's walked you home from school.
Where: on your eyelids, earlobes or cheeks.
How: with his arms lightly around your waist, eyes slightly open and lips pursed.
Why: cos he finds you too kissable 'n kuddly to resist!

Kind Number Four:
QUIET & CARING KISSES

When: you're alone and have known each other for a **long** time!
Where: on your lips!
How: with his arms around you, pressing your body very gently close to his—his eyes closed and lips slightly parted.
Why: cos the boy's in **love** (with **you**!)

DAVID'S KISSES

Kind Number One:
KUTE 'N KWIK KISSES

When: mostly outdoors, in the presence of others—or if he's got to rush off somewhere.
Where: a peck on your nose, corner of your eye or forehead—anywhere **but** your cheek!
How: with his lips pursed just slightly, eyes open.
Why: cos something you did made you look so irresistable to him at that moment, he just couldn't help himself!

Kind Number Two:
KOOL KISSES

When: instead of saying "hello" when he comes to your house to pick you up for a date, or when you visit him at a recording session.
Where: your hand, your eyes and your hair.
How: with his eyes downcast, lips very slightly open.
Why: cos he wants you to know you're special, but he doesn't want to be conspicuous.

Kind Number Three:
KUDDLY KISSES

When: you're going for a walk in the park, or a swim at the beach.
Where: your neck, shoulders, ears.
How: with your face cupped in his hands, his eyes open, his lips forming a half-smile.
Why: cos he really finds you fun, cute, bright and **very** special!

Kind Number Four:
QUIET & CARING KISSES

When: you're alone after a **fabulous** date!
Where: definitely on your lips!
How: with his arms softly caressing your back, his eyes **almost** closed, his lips apart.
Why: he **cares** for you **very** much—he may not be in **love** just yet, but he's gettin' there!

42

The joys of osculation, with the Williams twins, from May 1974.

Andy & David Williams

"Still, if I had kids, I would never let them do that. It's hard enough as it is to be a kid without being thrust into such an adult world, having to function like an adult, taking the criticism that an adult would be expected to put up with. So I ended up feeling pretty much like an alien, not a kid, not a grown-up.

"I'm writing songs on my own now, and living in New York, where I moved six months ago. I'm putting them all down, not really thinking about where they're going to go. It could be another project for the Williams Brothers, or something else. We decided to take some time apart."

"KIND OF A FLUKE"

[Andrew, joining the conversation, is asked if the two of them felt like the "princes in the tower," the two kids against a hostile world.]

"We were definitely hanging onto each other; I don't know if I would put it *that* dramatically. We were thirteen when we started, that's a pretty early age to become a performer. It was exciting and confusing at the same time. There wasn't much grounding for us.

"I think we would have become what we became, songwriters and performers, in any case; that's what we had always wanted to be. If we hadn't had the teen idol thing, we would still have been musicians. It was kind of a fluke, the teen thing. As it was, we got to learn a tremendous amount about the different sides of show business, not just because of that part, but because of my father being a manager and my uncle a singer in our earlier years.

"We stopped the teen-fan thing when we were 16. We pretty much called the shots on everything, there was no direction from anyone, no master vision. One day we just said, 'It's time to stop doing this now'; we both felt it at the same time. But it would have been so difficult to just jump over and say, 'Look, we're serious now!' so we took time off, started writing music, studying music, going to music school, and we reemerged in the L.A. club scene.

"When you're facing the world as musicians trying to be accepted as musicians, and you've been through all that hysteria stuff, you realize that the *real* thing is a completely different experience. Because what I call the real thing, we built that from the ground up, and it happened in a much more organic way than the teen thing, which just sort of exploded, I guess because of the magazine exposure.

"Do I remember all the stuff they wrote about us? It was all kind of eerie. 'Devilish David and Angelic Andy,' I remember that one because of the headline, but to jump back into my frame of mind back then is really difficult for me to do right now.

"I'm producing records now, a new artist named Scott Thomas, and I'm working on Victoria Williams' [no relation] next album."

Asked if they had a message for their fans, David and Andrew responded simultaneously.

"We still love you!"

Rick Springfield

Years of *16* Popularity:
1973–1974 and 1981–1982

Rick Springfield was Gloria Stavers's last attempt at "creating" a teen idol. The ingredients for success were there. A tall, studly, shaggy-haired rocker with an exotic—okay, Australian—accent, Rick was handsome, young, and at the outset, quite malleable. He wasn't without rock-cred, either: as the leader of the Australian teen rock band Zoot he came equipped with a repertoire and a #1 single, "Speak to the Sky."

What he didn't have, as yet, was success here and the interest of American teenage girls—exactly what *16* could deliver, should Gloria Stavers deem him worthy. Rick Springfield landed on American soil in 1972; that very day, guitar in tow, he landed at *16*'s offices for his first "look-see." It went well. Rick charmed Gloria and her staff; interviews and photo shoots were ordered up posthaste. By early 1973, Rick began appearing regularly in *16*'s pages, offered up as the ideal Dream Date: a new boy in town who knew no one, a lonely-luscious lad, lookin' for love, who needed *you, girl.* But Rick was never portrayed as some wimpy goody-two-shoes: his rocker edge was always alluded to, via such articles as "Rick—Red Hot 'n' X-Rated!" In case readers didn't get the message, most stories came illustrated with bare-chested photos, many of which were taken in Gloria's apartment.

Astonishingly, the formula did not work, at least not as it should have. While Rick did end up on the music charts—a reworked American version of "Speak to the Sky" became a Top 20 hit—he failed to capture hearts. What happened? Had the great Glo lost her touch? Why were readers not responding?

While there was no readily apparent answer, without reader support Rick faded from the pages of *16*. When he did reemerge, several years later, it was as an actor in the soap *General Hospital* and with a #1 song, "Jessie's Girl." Finally, *16*'s readers were interested, but it was too late; Rick was not, and was quite vehement about his opposition. He would not do interviews and certainly not pose, seductively or any other way, exclusively for *16*. Bowing to reader demand, we ended up buying photos and picking through what info we could amass from other sources.

Now a successful actor who starred on the syndicated TV series *High Tide*, Rick graciously agreed to participate in this book. Via fax, he painstakingly typed out his answers and advised, "I just told the truth here, so feel free to use or delete whatever you think is appropriate or otherwise." We deleted for space considerations only.

The shaggy and fringed Rick we first met in 1973.

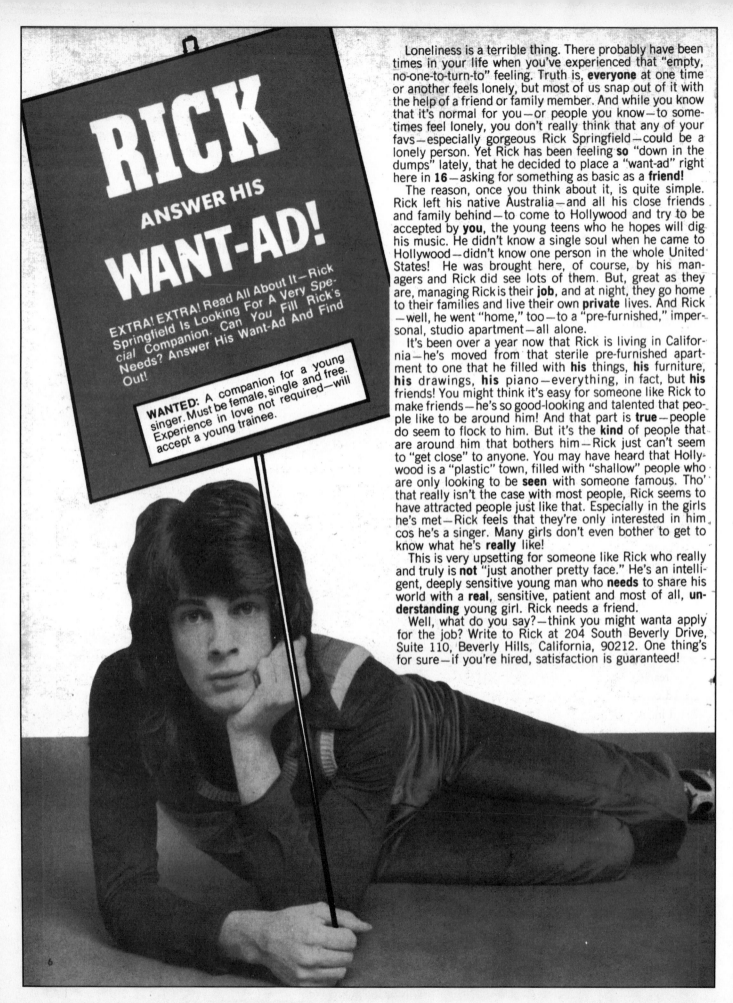

RICK

ANSWER HIS

WANT-AD!

EXTRA! EXTRA! Read All About It—Rick Springfield Is Looking For A Very Special Companion. Can You Fill Rick's Needs? Answer His Want-Ad And Find Out!

WANTED: A companion for a young singer. Must be female, single and free. Experience in love not required—will accept a young trainee.

Loneliness is a terrible thing. There probably have been times in your life when you've experienced that "empty, no-one-to-turn-to" feeling. Truth is, **everyone** at one time or another feels lonely, but most of us snap out of it with the help of a friend or family member. And while you know that it's normal for you—or people you know—to sometimes feel lonely, you don't really think that any of your favs—especially gorgeous Rick Springfield—could be a lonely person. Yet Rick has been feeling **so** "down in the dumps" lately, that he decided to place a "want-ad" right here in 16—asking for something as basic as a **friend!**

The reason, once you think about it, is quite simple. Rick left his native Australia—and all his close friends and family behind—to come to Hollywood and try to be accepted by **you,** the young teens who he hopes will dig his music. He didn't know a single soul when he came to Hollywood—didn't know one person in the whole United States! He was brought here, of course, by his managers and Rick did see lots of them. But, great as they are, managing Rick is their **job,** and at night, they go home to their families and live their own **private** lives. And Rick —well, he went "home," too—to a "pre-furnished," impersonal, studio apartment—all alone.

It's been over a year now that Rick is living in California—he's moved from that sterile pre-furnished apartment to one that he filled with **his** things, **his** furniture, **his** drawings, **his** piano—everything, in fact, but **his** friends! You might think it's easy for someone like Rick to make friends—he's so good-looking and talented that people like to be around him! And that part is **true**—people do seem to flock to him. But it's the **kind** of people that are around him that bothers him—Rick just can't seem to "get close" to anyone. You may have heard that Hollywood is a "plastic" town, filled with "shallow" people who are only looking to be **seen** with someone famous. Tho' that really isn't the case with most people, Rick seems to have attracted people just like that. Especially in the girls he's met—Rick feels that they're only interested in him cos he's a singer. Many girls don't even bother to get to know what he's **really** like!

This is very upsetting for someone like Rick who really and truly is **not** "just another pretty face." He's an intelligent, deeply sensitive young man who **needs** to share his world with a **real,** sensitive, patient and most of all, **understanding** young girl. Rick needs a friend.

Well, what do you say?—think you might wanta apply for the job? Write to Rick at 204 South Beverly Drive, Suite 110, Beverly Hills, California, 90212. One thing's for sure—if you're hired, satisfaction is guaranteed!

In the September 1973 issue, Rick "advertised" for a "very special companion."

RICK SPRINGFIELD ANSWERS THE REAL QUESTIONS!

What are your first memories of 16?

I remember walking down a New York street by myself on my way to **16 Mag** headquarters for the first time (certain I was going to be mugged at any moment) having just arrived in the U.S. from Australia (24 hours and no sleep, I was so excited) and *eager* to please. I had a brief photo session and interview and heard the words, "He looks like a teeny-bopper Rolling Stone." I think they were referring to my slightly dissipated appearance. I was already 22 and had spent the last six years on the road with bands. I didn't know what a "teen"magazine was at the time and hadn't heard of **16**. I figured that this must be the start of the Big Time. I thought all "press" was just a bunch of journalists who loved my music and who felt, like me, that it was only a matter of time. It wasn't till I started to *read* some of the "interviews" (like "Rick Tells You His Dream Date") that I started seeing what was going on. I was torn between the instant acceptance, the ease of getting press, versus the fear of repercussions on any musical integrity I aspired to.

What did you want at the time? Was rock 'n' roll your dream? Or acting? Just being famous?

At that time, I wanted America to hear my music. That was my dream. I trusted my manager, Steve Binder, and the record company to know what was right for me, to get me heard in the U.S. On the other hand, I loved writing to my mom and dad in Australia, telling them how many girls had recognized me at Disneyland (even though at the time, none of them had heard any of my music). Acting hadn't even entered my head at this point.

What were the dynamics between you and Gloria? Did she persuade you to pose suggestively?

I think if I'd been older, I would have appreciated Gloria a lot more. We started off in a business relationship—"I'll do this for you, you'll sell lots of magazines for me." But as time went on, I began to get the feeling there was more going on. There

began to be a distinct sexual thing happening whenever we'd get together that was somewhat confusing to me. I really couldn't understand how this "older woman" could be turned on to me. The photos we began to take for the magazine began to change. I think she was also seeing how far she could push the sexuality in her magazine. I remember doing a session in her New York apartment where I was lying on her bed with no shirt on and the zipper of my pants pulled halfway down. The photo made it to the magazine, too. I was very into it, listening to her Jim Morrison stories and her belief that the "girls" were ready for this pushing of the teen envelope. She is one of my strongest memories from that period of my life.

Did you ever feel demeaned by the stuff you did in *16*? Embarrassed?

No, I felt Gloria was trying something new with me and I was into it at the time. Also, the attention was new and very persuasive then. My wife, Barbara, actually remembers putting a photo of me on her wall when she was 11 (though she was more into David Cassidy at the time, she did think I was cute). When [the attention] started to reappear in the '80s was when it became a little embarrassing. I was trying my best to distance myself from the teen press then and get whatever credibility I could garner at the time.

When you were first in *16*, nothing was really happening professionally— the music hadn't taken off yet, you weren't acting yet. Basically, you received publicity just for being cute and "the hot new thing." How did that make you feel?

At first, the attention was great. Landing in America and getting instant press. But I began to feel the pressure of not having any sizable hit "anything" to back it up. The songs I was writing then were about suicide, divorce, dead soldiers from World War II, Greta Garbo, pregnant girls…basically nothing a 10-year-old girl would relate to. And yet I was still being photographed, still telling "The 10 Things That Make Me Blush." It finally hit me when I was sitting in my crappy Hollywood apartment, two months behind in the rent, being sued for $250,000 by a former manager, raiding my loose change jar to buy a frozen TV dinner at Ralph's, and reading a fan letter from a **16** reader telling me how she wanted to visit Hollywood and see the mansion I lived in.

Rick Springfield

Were you the guy *16* said you were?

HA HA HA!!! Of course not. Who was? It was a 37-year-old magazine editor's concept of how to sell a 24-year-old singer to a 12-year-old magazine buyer.

What's the biggest misconception fans had about you in those days?

That I actually *had* money and that I *didn't* want to have sex with their mothers or older sisters.

You had it all— looks, talent, willingness to cooperate: why do you think you weren't successful?

It wasn't the right time. The ingredients weren't there yet. I was a fairly dark fellow and as I said, I was writing songs that had nothing to do with, "I think I love you." It was more like, "I want to fuck you, then kill myself."

You redirected your energies toward acting and, without any help from *16*, became a teen idol after all. Do you have a sense of irony about that?

Not really, I do believe that nothing can be forced. I "knew"at some point in my life "something" would happen and I was not surprised when it finally did. At the time of "Jessie's Girl"and *General Hospital*, I was 32, so the idea of being in a teen magazine was almost funny to me then. As much as I had courted it in the '70s, I ran from it in the '80s, knowing what it was and what it would do to the musical credibility I had desired for so long. In the end it was a moot point.

Did you read your fan mail?

I never got my *16 Mag* fan mail. I think my managers looked at it as a "data base," and kept it to ponder over. As I said, the only one I remember was the girl who wanted to see my "mansion."

Have your fans from the *16* days followed you?

Most fans have the connection from the '80s. Though some drag out the *Beginnings* album (1972) and the occasional *16 Mag* photo of me in all my 23-year-old "prepubescent" glory.

Looking over the trajectory of your career— is there a moral to the story?

I felt I had hit a wall after the collapse of the '70s teen period. Up until then my musical career had been one high after another (mainly in Australia). In the early '70s I felt I had taken on America and failed. I got very depressed and thought about suicide often. Getting involved in my first acting class was probably what saved me. It got me back with people again. Once I reconnected with my vision (which I have had to do several times in my life so far) things started moving again. There is no moral yet. It's too soon. But if I had to tell my sons a lesson I learned so far, it would be: Never give up.

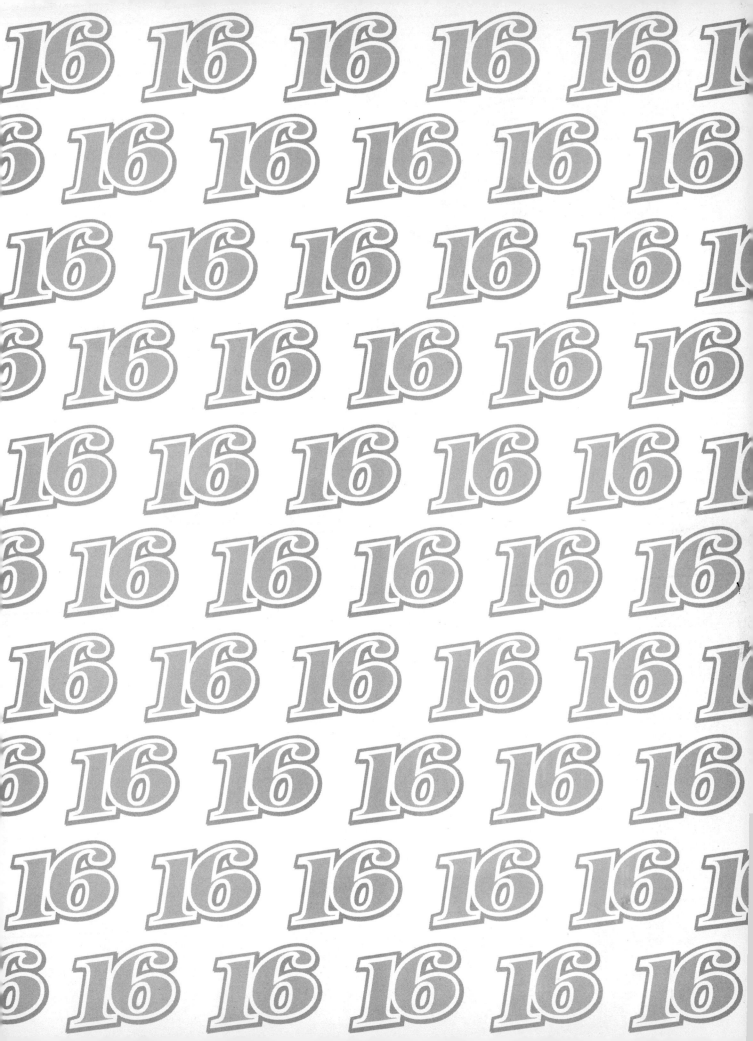

The 70s:

TAKE TWO

1975–1979

THE SEVENTIES *16* MAGAZINE 1975–1979

The second half of the '70s ushered in an eclectic mix of celebrities, sensibilities, and staff, all of which was reflected in the pages of *16*. It wasn't always a smooth blend and for a while, it seemed as if perhaps the magazine had lost its way, or forgotten its fantasy mantra. How else to explain the proliferation of such nonromantic figures as the chubby, balding Elton John and the hirsute, scary Alice Cooper? Neither of them exactly springs to mind when enumerating famous teen idols, yet both were huge in *16*'s pages and on the cover.

For the most part, the family scene was passé. The Bradys and the Partridges had fallen from TV ratings favor; the Osmonds had splintered into *The Donny and Marie Show,* and the J5, well, Michael just splintered altogether. The only blood relations prominent in *16* were Brett, Mark & Bill: the Hudson Brothers. Of course, there was David's half-brother Shaun Cassidy and a baby Bee Gee, but that was it for kin.

In a fairly huge departure from any previous era, TV stars took over from rockers in the popularity polls. Scott Baio, Leif Garrett, the Johns (Schneider and Travolta), Frank Poncherello and Arthur Fonzarelli (*CHiPs's* Ponch and *Happy Days's* Fonzie) all had weekly series, and while some of them, er, sang, none did it *on* his TV series. And then there was *16*'s first real movie star in a long time, Matt Dillon.

Thank God for the Bay City Rollers. In the latter half of the '70's, they alone upheld the *16* pop star tradition—and a good thing, sales-wise, they came 'round when they did. For as appealing as actors are, they never sold as many magazines as musicians did. The tartan-clad Rollers weren't the Beatles, but they did have accents (Scottish); they weren't the Monkees, but they did have pop hits ("Suh-suh-suh-Saturday Ni-ight!"); and there were five to love. You could pick your fave rave Roller.

Arguably, the biggest change in *16* in this half of the decade had less to do with the stars covered, less even than with the changing, more permissive climate vis-à-vis sex, and everything to do with Gloria Stavers leaving. She threatened, then took it back; Chambrun (her boss) threatened, then took her back. The end came for real in 1975. She wasn't so much pushed, and she didn't so much jump, as she left via some tangled combination of the two.

The staff that was in place that year had been trained by Gloria and fought valiantly to live up to her legacy, but in the end, they weren't her. Perhaps they had her eye, and enough of her style, but times had changed, and they did not have her power, persuasiveness, perseverance. None of them made the magazine their lives, as Gloria had done.

There was a shift in the demographic, too. There were simply fewer teenagers around to buy the magazine and fewer stars those potential readers really had a passion for. And most chillingly of all, many of those stars just did not *want* to be in *16* and made it clear. It was a struggle to get some of the interviews and photo shoots needed. Still, except for Elton John, who never did an actual one-on-one *16* interview, all the stars of the late '70s did participate to one degree or another. Some did so reluctantly; while others really did value their fans and look back on the era with a great deal of fondness, as the next section exemplifies.

COVER PRICE: In 1975, it had been 60 cents; by 1979, it had risen to $1.

COLOR PAGES: While the expensive "pop-out" posters were for the most part lost, due to lower sales, *16* did offer its readers gatefolds and centerfolds and more individual pinups.

SALES: Down to about half a million circulation per month.

The Bay City Rollers

Years of *16* Popularity: 1976–1978.

The Bay City Rollers had 13 cover banners (the top line above the logo) in a row, more than any other idols in the history of the magazine up to that point.

A massive, international "teenybopper" phenomenon from Scotland, the Bay City Rollers originated as a "legitimate" rock band, but were soon manipulated by the British press and by their manager, Tam Paton, into a group that played nearly exclusively for young girls. Fans could wear "Roller gear" (inexpensive to recreate, and certainly distinctive) and the scorn visited on the group by (most) males and older, "serious" rock fans only made the true believers love them all the more. They were huge in the U.K. and Europe by the time they broke in America with the #1 hit, "Saturday Night," late in 1975.

We had watched the rising popularity of the Rollers in the U.K., but *16*'s publisher, the crusty Jacques Chambrun, was skeptical about their American potential. Arista, their record company, partly to raise *16*'s enthusiasm for the group and partly to get our opinion of their chances of success in America, flew me (Danny Fields) and journalist Lisa Robinson to Glasgow, where the group was doing a special concert at the small Apollo Theater. The publisher was annoyed that I was taking a long weekend for such frivolities; he certainly never would have paid for the trip.

I had never seen anything like it. Here was one of Europe's largest urban centers virtually paralyzed because the Bay City Rollers were in town. Main streets were shut off, police barricades were everywhere. There was a rumor that the group was staying at the same hotel where they put us journalists, and the streets and plazas around the building were a sea of near-hysterical fans. I had only to pull a curtain aside a few inches to raise a roar from the crowd—I could have been a Bay City Roller checking out the fans. Actually, the group was staying outside the city, at the request of the Glasgow police force. During the night, some girls actually tried to scale the walls of the hotel and had to be brought down by the fire department.

Later that weekend I got to meet the group, and their manager, Tam Paton, with whom I became close friends. I said I would do my best in the pages of *16*, but that the band really did need a hit in America to get things going. When I returned, I started putting 2-page stories in *16* introducing the Rollers. Within months, they had their hit, and instantly became #1 in our mail tallies. Chambrun of course was pleased, but never once acknowledged that I had spotted them early on. He was a real bastard.

My access to the group was virtually unlimited. I toured the country with them, stayed next-door to them in hotels (where the floors they were occupying were sealed off), and visited and photographed them at home in Scotland. Once, on a trip from Detroit into Canada, I was alone in the car with their passports and discovered, not to my surprise, that they were all, except for Les, a bit older than they were letting on. I kept their secret, of course. Another rumor was that there were some gay doings within the group. I can say now that there were indeed *some*; Tam was openly gay, and was actually sent to jail in Scotland on some trumped-up charges of corrupting the morals of a minor. It was an entrapment situation. Although I can assure you that the BCR were a joy to work

The original lineup, left to right: Eric Faulkner, Alan Longmuir, Les McKeown, Derek Longmuir, and Woody Wood.

16 MAGAZINE

VOL. 18 NO. 12   JUNE 1977

IAN *ISN'T* MARRYING!
Page 5

ARE YOU IN HIS STARS?
Page 60

FABULOUS COLOR PIN-UP
Page 67

HE ANSWERS YOUR QUESTIONS
Page 10

HOW TO MAKE HIM LOVE YOU
Page 18

EXCLUSIVE INTERVIEW
Page 30

MOST DARING PHOTO
Page 34

ALL YOU WANT TO KNOW
Page 56

SECRETS REVEALED
Page 58

WHO'S COOLER?
Page 26

DANNY FIELDS—Editor
RANDI REISFELD—Editor
CHRIS DI NAPOLI—Art Director
HEDY END—Associate Editor
NANCY LA REINE—Consulting Editor
PAT WADSLEY—Contributing Editor
GEORGIA WINTERS—Editor Emeritus
JEAN LEWIS—West Coast Editor
KATHERINE HALL—Publisher-President
Business Office
16 Magazine, Inc.
745 Fifth Avenue, New York, N.Y. 10022

A contents page dominated by the Rollers.

Eric and Woody, backstage.

Ian Mitchell, who replaced Alan, lasted in the band for 7 months, and left "to keep my sanity" (said the press release), reads about himself.

16 took you up close and personal, in this case to a sweaty soundcheck.

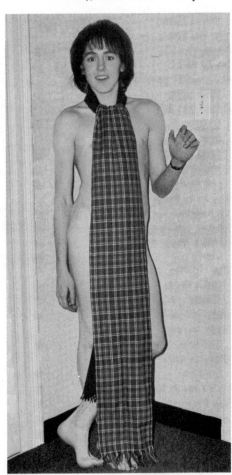

An overwrought fan being escorted from the stage.

Ian was replaced in December 1976 by Pat McGlynn, seen here in traditional and very versatile Roller gear. This photo became a 16 centerfold, with the headline "Pat—Most Daring Photo Ever!"

with, and as my last big project as co-editor of *16*, a great note upon which to exit, life within the group apparently was not so much fun. A press release actually boasted, "No group in history has had a greater number of nervous breakdowns…. All the Rollers have been on Valium at one time or another for their nerves….Eric Faulkner was treated for a nervous breakdown and sleeping pill overdose….Also affected is Tam Paton, who himself suffered a nervous breakdown after their last tour and is on daily tranquilizers." And that's what they revealed officially!

We contacted lead singer Les McKeown via E-mail, and the result was sort of a questionnaire that Les filled out in London and sent to us in New York. We've shortened the questions, but left the answers entire and intact.

Les McKeown:
"[It was] an obscene violation of our talents."

Did the group time, plan, anticipate, or worry about its ultimate acceptance in the U.S.?

The BCR were on a roller coaster ride that was not under any business control. It was too massive. It was obvious that we would overcome the U.S.A., mainly due to the fans wanting it to happen, and we were so cute, sexy, and talented.

How were you treated in the teen fan press?

The teen magazines all over the world produced mags in the same way—lots of pictures, made-up stories. We were familiar with the format, and were constantly fascinated with the bollocks printed under our name.

Do you feel you were treated fairly? There is a perception among musicians that teen magazines tend to compromise one's "artistic integrity."

No one in our capacity gets fair treatment. We were a gift to all involved, the press and the industry. I recall at the end it being an obscene violation of our talents, a wasted opportunity. We were not well-suited for the U.S.A.'s way of ingestion. Artistic integrity is similar to personal integrity, either you got it or you ain't. No one can give it or take it away except yourself.

Was it a blast, hard work, or both? Did you ever date a fan?

It was very formidable toil, but also enjoyable, like any other feat of endurance. It had its ups and downs. Yes, we met fans officially, and informally.

Your manager was openly gay, and there were rumors about others within the group, except about you, who was famously "straight." Any comments?

I can only say that if the manager had thought with his cerebrum instead of his…, we would have been in a better situation when it broke up. Maybe what people said [about us] was "easy meat…but not the singer." Intercourse without the element of love is for the sophomoric.

What are your thoughts about the whole trip?

Great years, I could recommend it to anyone, it will be part of me *ad infinitum*.

How are you?

I'm wonderfully steady, calm, wild, creative, responsible, loving, and gorgeous.

What have you been doing?

Music, life, music.

Where can your fans write to you?

Rollermaniaks World Headquarters
P.O. Box 142
Staines, TW18 2EW
U.K.

A message for your fans who will always love you?

Keep in touch; what goes around comes around. I'm still in love with you.

[*Editor's note: E-mail is not one's favorite way of doing an interview. Obviously, there were answers of Les's that we would have liked to have followed up on. Wouldn't you? Also, there are now serious legal battles being fought over the group's name; Les is only allowed to perform (with four new members) as "Les McKeown's Bay City Rollers."*]

HENRY "Fonzie" WINKLER

Years of *16* Popularity: 1976–1977

The "Fonz" is an American icon. Just about every teenager in America in the mid-'70s could, and did, imitate his thumbs-up signature greeting, "Aaayyh." We met him on ABC-TV's *Happy Days*, a sitcom about '50s teenagers, which ran from 1974–1983. It starred TV veteran Ron Howard as clean-teen Richie Cunningham, Marion Ross as his apple-pie mom, and Tom Bosley as "Mr.C," the wise and loving dad. Richie's best friend Potsie, played by Anson Williams, was designed to be Richie's counterpart, the show's nominal know-it-all. In fact, the Arthur Fonzarelli character was fifth-billed when the show debuted in January 1974. But like *77 Sunset Strip*'s "Kookie" before him, and *Family Matters*' Urkel after him, it wasn't long before the popular "fifth wheel" roared into center stage, did a wheelie, and flipped up to near-the-top billing. The audience demanded it and rewarded the show with an upswing in the ratings.

It wasn't only the elevation of the motorcyle-riding, leather-jacketed teenage tough that made *Happy Days* the most-watched show on television during the '76-'77 season, it was the actor who breathed life into him. Henry Winkler took what could have been a cardboard greaser and made him vulnerable, human, yet ever hip. And was Fonzie ever the epitome of hip: too cool for school, yet the last word on everything. Girls wanted to be with him; boys wanted to be him.

And *16* needed to include him, even if, at 27 years old, Henry Winkler was a bit long in the tooth for most readers' fantasies. However, as is always the case with actors, it's the character, stupid: like all the other girls in America, *16*'s innocent teenyboppers had it bad for the Fonz. And through-

out 1976, certainly his banner year as a teen idol, it was the Fonz they got. *16* made little attempt, on the cover, anyway, to identify the actor by his real name—even if the stories inside were always Henry-centric.

His fame was enormous: some weeks he got over 50,000 pieces of fan mail. His fame was ubiquitous: *Happy Days* continues to air all over the world. His fame endures: thanks to Nickelodeon's Nick at Night reruns, today's 6-year-olds can do the thumbs-up "aaayyh" as well as their parents ever did. And his fame is immortalized: Fonzie's leather jacket is enshrined in the Smithsonian Museum.

Yet even at the height of hoopla, Henry Winkler never let it go to his head. Intelligent, well-mannered, and good-humored, Henry always went along with the program, making himself available for *16*'s interviews. And, sidebar: he is the only star of that magnitude, in this author's experience, who remained humble, gracious, just human: someone who under other circumstances, you'd call a friend.

After *Happy Days*, Henry—married and the father of three—became a Hollywood hyphenate: actor-producer-director. His film credits include *Night Shift*; he produced the long-running hit series *MacGyver* and, through his Fair Dinkum Productions, a slew of after-school specials and TV movies. Today, he co-executive produces *Sightings*, a hit series about all things paranormal, which is in its sixth season and has spawned books, videos, and a Website. Last year he acted in Wes Craven's *Scream*, "my first horror film."

The man himself hasn't changed. He remains intelligent, gracious, and friendly. He reminisced with us in a recent interview.

WHO'S YOUR FAVE RAVE?

AN INTIMATE INTERVIEW WITH HENRY WINKLER

Do you remember being in *16*?

Of course I do. At the time, *16* was one of the major, major magazines of its kind. It was all over the newsstands—that *I* should be in it was shocking, a real rush.

Yet *16* furthered the Fonzie image, which at some point you must have wanted to get away from…?

Ultimately, no, because I think I realized early on that it was always going to be a part of me. It still happens today. I never felt limited by it, if that's what you mean.

You were part of an ensemble cast, yet clearly the standout, and the one who got all the press. Certainly, *16* focused on you, with only an odd article on Ronny or Anson—did that cause friction among the cast members?

There was never any friction. In the beginning of the fourth season, I had one chat with Ronny Howard about the enormity of what was going on with my character, as opposed to him being the star of the show. I'll never forget it; we were driving home from a location shoot, he was at the wheel. And he was very open with me, he just said everything he wanted to say that one time. Ultimately, Ron's overriding feeling was that Fonzie's popularity was good for the show. And that was the most important piece of it. And I never shoved it in anyone's face; I didn't abuse it. Our friendship was bigger than that and remained that way. If the other cast members felt any resentment, they never showed it to me.

Your teen idol years coincided with "Johnny" Travolta's when he was playing another cool TV tough teen, Barbarino on *Welcome Back, Kotter*. In one *16* article, we pitted you against each other for the "king of cool" title. Did you see that piece? Did it bother you?

Probably, but *16* wasn't the only one who did that. Several publications went with that angle. It bothered both of us, sure, because it was totally made up—I always had a nice relationship with John.

Looking back now, are you surprised at John's career track?

Not at all. Look how wonderful he is. John's been up and he's been down. But he's a lovely, wonderful guy who's great at what he does. That warmth and gentleness always comes through, in all his work.

Did you have a clue that Ron Howard would be so successful as a director in later years?

Absolutely. When you were in the presence of Ron, even when he was 17 years old, you knew you were in the presence of greatness. He's one powerful dude. And Ronny always knew what he wanted to do—although I laugh when I think back on the times he'd ask me, "What do you think? Do you think I'd be a good director?"

What didn't *16*'s readers know about you at the time that you wished they could have?

Probably that my self-image was nowhere close to the Fonz's. I was dyslexic, school was always hard for me. But I think in my interviews, I was pretty open about all that. Now if I could say something to kids, I'd try to instill in them that the most important thing is a sense of self—and it has to come from inside, not from other people telling you how great you are: that's like cotton candy, it'll just fall apart. A sense of self-worth and a sense of future is what it's all about.

Did you read your fan mail?

I was overwhelmed by it, but in the beginning I had it delivered to my apartment, where I spent a lot of time reading it. I'd answer as much as I could. I'd use the backs of old scripts—I'd take a page where Fonzie had some dialogue, write a note, and mail it back. To this day I meet people who remember getting a letter back from me. Then it got to the point where I was getting 50,000 letters a week and I had to hire a fan mail service to handle it. People would send gifts, jewelry, hooked rugs, puppets of the Fonz—I got a lot of those long chains of bubblegum wrappers. The outpouring of warmth is something I'll never forget.

AN INTIMATE INTERVIEW WITH FONZIE!

You know him as 'The Fonz'—the smart-talking, wise-cracking lovable hipster who stars on TV's *Happy Days*. He rides a motorcycle, knows everything there is to know about cars, engines and especially about being cool. 'The Fonz' is irresistable to girls—even tho he doesn't have a whole lot to say and doesn't seem to be the world's deepest thinker.

But Henry Winkler, the handsome actor who brings Fonzie to life each week is a dude of a different color. Contrary to Fonzie, Henry has *lots* of say—on a variety of subjects—and now, in this intimate interview, he'd like to share some thoughts with you!

● **First of all, tell us about your childhood—what kind of kid were you?**

Well, I grew up in New York City so I was kind of a "street kid." Not that I got into trouble, but I was never bored! My parents, Harry and Ilse, emigrated here from Europe and worked very hard to make a living. By the time I was 10, my dad's lumber business was doing very well, so we always had enough money. But I was very sheltered—not allowed to see what my parents thought was bad for me, or go places they didn't approve of. I was sent to private school right after elementary school—so I could get a really good education. That was very important to my parents. I hope this doesn't sound like I didn't get along with my mom and dad—cause I really did. Most of the time I was not rebellious—I did what they told me and liked it! I was very close with my sister, Beatrice, who's a few years older than me. I guess I had a pretty normal childhood all-in-all—I went to school, played with my friends and did a lot of daydreaming.

● **What did you daydream about?**

Oh, the usual things—girls, and how the future was going to be.

● **You mean, about what you wanted to be when you grew up?**

Sure—about how famous I would be. I always wanted to be an actor and had visions of academy awards and stuff. I

once even wrote an acceptance speech for my imaginary award! If I ever get a real one, maybe I'll use it!

"I was very sheltered—not allowed to see what my parents thought was bad for me, or go places they didn't approve of."

● **What did your parents think about your plans?**

They didn't know about them. At least—not for a long while. I think my dad assumed that I was going to join his business, especially since I never said anything to the contrary. Of course, they finally found out—and when they did, they were very encouraging. If my dad was disappointed at my choice not to follow in his footsteps, he didn't show it.

● **So much has been written about Fonzie—what do you think of him?**

I like him. I mean, obviously I'm very different than he is, but I can't help admiring a lot about him—I mean, who doesn't want to be super-cool? And who wouldn't want to have all those girls after him? I'm not saying I'd really want to live his life, but I'd like him as a friend.

● **You played a character similar to Fonzie in the movie, *The Lords Of Flatbush*. Are you afraid of being typecast?**

Not really. I was also in the TV movie *Katherine* and played a very different role. I think people know I can be a versatile actor.

● **If you could be anyone else in the whole world, who would you pick?**

I really can't think of one specific person I'd like to be, but if I weren't an actor I'd wish to be a child

22

"Fans—especially 16 readers—write to me and tell me they like what I'm doing ... from the bottom of my heart, I really appreciate that."

psychologist—and a rock star on the side! I really dig children—and I love finding out what makes them tick. But I'd also love to be a rock star!

● Where do you live now?
I have an apartment in West Hollywood. It's got one bedroom and lots of plants and stereo equipment—the essentials of my life!

● Have you furnished it?
No—I'm not really into that.

● You have a lot of fans—what do you think about them?
They're the greatest—and I'm not just saying that to be nice. I've travelled all around the country and gotten to meet a lot of fans and it's really been the greatest experience of my life. It's an indescribable feeling when you go somewhere and 2000 kids come to meet you. I'm a really lucky guy.

● A lot of people want to know about your love life—first of all, what kind of girls are you attracted to?
I'm attracted by a lot of different girls. I like a girl to have what I call "deep down dirt"—you know, earthy and not superficial. I mean, a pretty girl is O.K., but what is "pretty" if you don't have anything to back it up? I like wit in a girl and most of all, the ability to transcend herself. I'm turned on by a girl who isn't so wrapped up in herself and how she appears to others. I like a generous girl.

● What three tips would you give a girl who wanted you to like her?
Be honest—with tenderness beneath it. Be able to show your feelings with affection. And most of all, be your own woman!

● When you give presents to a girl, what do you usually pick?
Something that relates to the atmosphere of the girl.

● What?
Well, I mean, not something obvious or ordinary. I would have to get some vibes about the girl, and then pick something I instinctively know she'd like—even if it's something she never knew she wanted!

● Do you have a special girlfriend?
No. So far I've struck out in that department.

● Would you like to get married someday?
Yes. Absolutely—some day *soon*. I'm definitely looking forward to finding one woman to settle down with. I want a woman with her own life—and I want kids and I want to travel with my family. I think that's the best education you can give to kids—travelling around the world, seeing different people, tasting different cultures.

● Where have you been, outside of the United States?
All over! I've studied in Germany and Switzerland and travelled in England, Scotland, France and Italy.

● Which country did you like best?
I liked them all, for each one is unique and beautiful in its own way. But if I had to choose just one, I'd say Switzerland. It's *so* beautiful there.

" ... a pretty girl is O.K., but what is 'pretty' if you don't have anything to back it up?"

"I'm definitely looking forward to finding one woman to settle down with ... and I want kids ..."

● Could you describe your own personality?
I'm moody—although I know when my bad moods are coming and I try not to foist them on others. My moods can change in a minute, so the bad ones don't usually last too long. I'm pretty sensitive, and concerned about other people's feelings—I'm also more of a "thinker" than a "doer". All-in-all, I'm pretty happy, but I'm always looking for something better. I guess I'll never be completely satisfied.

● What are your plans for the future?
To obtain peace of mind. I want to live my life so I never have to defend it, in any way. I want to be who I am and not who others think I should be.

● That's a pretty tall order!
Yes—and I'm working towards it.

● Do you have a message—anything you'd like to say—to 16's readers?
Acting is a two-way street. I create a character and hopefully, the audience likes it. Fans—especially **16** readers—write to me and tell me that they like what I'm doing and from the bottom of my heart, *I really appreciate that*. I love my fans and if I could give them one piece of advice I'd say—just realize that it's everybody's responsibility to get it together with themselves. Don't let anyone intimidate you—don't let anyone stop you from reaching your goal—not your friends, not big companies, not even the government. You're really terrific—believe in yourself. Even Fonzie would have to agree with that!

You can write to Henry "Fonzie" Winkler at Paramount Studios, Happy Days Set, 5451 Marathon, Los Angeles, Cal.

ALICE COOPER

Years of *16* Popularity: 1973–1976

There was a vacancy in the "edgy" niche of *16*'s stable of faves in the early '70s, and Alice Cooper was perfect for the spot. He had *big* youth-oriented hit singles ("Eighteen," "School's Out"), a girl's name, a unique look, rock and roll credibility, a reputation in the music business for professionalism and a sweet personality (and unquestioned heterosexuality), a great stage act, a home in New York City, lots of the same friends Gloria Stavers had, and an unbelievable amount of press that depicted him as the Devil of Depravity itself, the Thing above all others from which America's youth must be saved.

Marc Bolan of T. Rex, Gloria's first choice for alternative fave, was not making it commercially in America; David Bowie was godlike (so it was perceived), aloof, and faintly exotic (i.e., not a lot of fun) for the purpose; and Iggy Pop was impossibly scary. Alice was just right; his act and persona were pure Grand Guignol/Hammer Films, very much in the tradition of *Dark Shadows*, which had been such a hit with *16*'s readers in the late '60s. His records sold in the millions, and Alice and his management were very easy to deal with; they lived and had offices in Greenwich Village and Greenwich, Connecticut, and hung out at Max's Kansas City, where many of Gloria's friends had regular tables every night as well.

What was established between *16* and its readers vis-à-vis Alice Cooper was that yes, he was a bit scary and mysterious, but mainly that he was totally misunderstood and wrongfully hated by the adult establishment. Since Alice was "one of us," we had to be wary of all attempts to suppress him or even keep him from playing in "your hometown." *We*, the editors and readers, knew he was basically a sweet person and he would *never* really murder a chicken onstage, but we could just as surely count on our parents and other such authoritarian types not to get it, and to disapprove. They had to be fought at every turn. The editors, Alice, and the readers (we like to believe) had great fun with our coverage of this most entertaining star.

A One-on-One with Alice

Danny Fields was assigned by Gloria to be responsible for the Alice stories in *16*, and Danny and Alice had the following phone conversation, about the preparation of this book, on October 27, 1996. Both were excited that the Yankees had won the World Series the night before, so we pick up the chat after the obligatory baseball babble:

AC: A book about *16*, the magazine I never belonged in!

DF: You had a great run, about three years.

AC: It was weird that Gloria decided I would be in the ranks of the David Cassidys. Maybe I was anti–David Cassidy.

DF: I think you were in the ranks of *Dark Shadows*, the Stones, the Doors. Why do you think *16* came after you?

AC: There was so much press on Alice, so much photography, so much news, I was the joke on Johnny Carson, I was in the sights of all the comedians. I guess I was the alternate to all the squeaky clean guys.

DF: What did Gloria say to you?

AC: You belong in this magazine, is what she said. Very matter of fact. I guess I had a lower opinion of my teenage sex appeal than she did.

DF: Did you worry that exposure in *16* would compromise you as a valid rock group?

AC: We realized that our original fans probably did not read *16*. It was a plus for us, a piece of cake, not our normal fans or target audience, but great to pick them up. It didn't occur to us that being in *16* would be a negative with our older, male fans, and it never was.

DF: We had more fun with you than with anyone. Do you remember anything in particular?

AC: Alice against Donny, things like that. I thought it should be Alice against Bowie, or Alice against T. Rex, but here it was Alice against Donny. I thought what a perspective this must be for middle America! I would imagine that I was scarier in *16* than I was in the other magazines.

ALICE

"I'M NOT DIRTY!"

Alice Cooper Takes Up His Own Defense—Point By Point!

Hello out there! It's me, Alice Cooper. I've been reading your mail, and tho most of it by far is really positive and encouraging, I still get occasional hostile vibes from some of you. Now, I don't mind being put down for what I am and for what I **do** do (them's the chances you take!)—but I get a little confused when I'm hated for the **wrong** reasons!

Anyhow, here are some quotes from a few less-than-loving (to put it mildly!) letters I've read, and I'll try as best I can to answer these criticisms. Here goes!

"I think you're dirty!"
  E.E., Albany, N.Y.
Dear E.E.,
  I'm not dirty! I take two showers a day and wash my hair four times a week. And I have a very exciting shower that shpritzes from all directions—I'd love to show it to you!

"You encourage violence and cruelty!"
  R.B., Macon, Ga.
Dear R.B.,
  We don't encourage violence and cruelty—we just depict them, and make fun of them besides. We think our audiences get rid of their hostilities by seeing our show. There is no documented instance of anyone doing anything violent right after leaving one of our concerts—they always wait a few days.

"You're a queer!"
  D.N., Santa Barbara, Cal.
Dear D.N.,
  Who, me?! How can you say that? I like girls so much that I've even taken a girl's name! But some of my best friends are—each to his or her own, I always say. (Editors Note: For a fuller discussion of this delicate subject, see *Is Alice A Fag?* in the August issue of SPEC, on sale June 18.)

"You're a filthy sadist!"
  S.P., Duluth, Minn.
Dear S.P.,
  As I told E.E., I am scrupulously clean!

"You can't sing and your band stinks! Give me the Osmonds anytime!"
  O.O., Provo, Utah
Dear O.O.,
  This is hitting below the belt! I can defend myself on personal issues, but I won't stick up for my music—you can take it or leave it. And I like the Osmonds, too! (Editors Note: We think Alice's music is fabulous—and so do millions of concert goers and record-buyers. So there!)

"You don't **really** believe in all that stuff you do—it's just a gimmick!"
  J.A., Framingham, Mass.
Dear J.A.,
  Everyone needs a gimmick. Let's see how far you get without one!

"You're an alcoholic!"
  L.R., West Orange, N.J.
Dear L.R.,
  Not quite!

"You used to kill chickens in your stage act—how could you do anything so awful?"
  T.T., Boca Raton, Fla.
Dear T.T.,
  I couldn't—and never have. It's just one of those rumors (like the one that I used to be on Leave It To Beaver) that just gets started and keeps making the rounds, with no factual basis at all. I love animals, birds and reptiles, and I'd never hurt them. I hope this settles that question once and forever.

Whew! Well, that's it for now. Wasn't it fun? Just keep that hate mail coming (to P.O. Box 320, Old Chelsea Station, New York, N.Y. 10011)! It's always good to know what's on your dear little minds! **Lots** of love, and see you later.

Alice ×××

36

Alice took on the "hostile vibes" from readers, defending himself in the July '74 issue.

Alice Cooper

DF: That was the point—make the reader shiver and then throw herself into the protective arms of her fantasy boyfriend.

AC: I liked it, though; my mom liked it, too, because they painted me in a different way. You know, I always had a hard time with those questionnaires, because my first reaction was to get really gross with them, but then I realized who was reading it, and I figured I might as well give some nice, sweet answers every once in a while, because this was for younger kids. I could play that game.

DF: We set up a generation-gap thing with you, that you were really likable, not threatening, but that the parents would hate you, and that's what we were going for. We did a lot of stories like, "Will Alice Be Banned in Your Hometown?"

AC: Oh, that was perfect. Did they ever do stories on Iggy?

DF: Not really—maybe in the Sing Along column—otherwise, he *was* too dangerous.

AC: Yeah, he truly was. Iggy lived it.

DF: Plus you had hits.

AC: That's it, those Top 10 hits bring you into all levels, even today. To this day I go in and see the people at our shows, and they're from 11 to 50. The older fans have albums I don't even remember recording, and they know every song.

DF: When you looked out into the audience back in the '70s, did you see the older male fans plus the kids who read *16*?

AC: Well, you didn't really see the kids who would have been reading *16* down right in front of the stage. The kids in front wanted to be covered with blood, to be hit with something. It was the prototype of the mosh pit, not for young girls. A lot of people tell me they went to the concerts with their parents: "They would sit there and they hated it, but they knew I wanted to go, and then after they saw you, they didn't think it was so bad."

DF: Were there any misperceptions about you that you ever saw in *16*, that made you say, "They got this wrong. It doesn't really apply to me"?

AC: People always believed what they wanted to believe about me. My whole career was based on very little reality. Most of the rumors about Alice were invented by us. We just let the audience run with their imagination, and the press was even worse. They loved to invent all kinds of things; it was terrific stuff. We'd get to a city and pick up the papers and say, "Wow, that's a good one! Oh, we like that one!" I'm still living down the "passing around of the bowl that everyone spits in, and I drink it"—it's like the good old American legend about the guy who gives his girlfriend Spanish fly at the drive-in, and then finds her impaled on the gearshift. I've heard that one a billion times, people really believe it happened, sometime, somewhere. Or that one about someone taking a crap and me eating it—and it's always been me, Iggy, or Frank Zappa, or Ozzie, and I've heard 25 different versions of each of these stories. They asked me about the spit thing the other day, and I said, "Well, first of all, it wasn't a bowl." [Laughs.] Those kind of rumors, I don't know if they got to *16*.

DF: No, nothing repulsive. Just daring, but not gross.

AC: Alice as a little mysterious, yeah. I loved it. Every time there was something in *16*, I would go, "Well, this is weird, man, to be in *16*, but it's great." Because it was something I never expected. I expected to be in *Rolling Stone* and *Crawdaddy* and *Circus*, but *16* was one of those plusses, this was a perk of the business, being in *16*.

DF: And you had no competition.

AC: I was for the girl who was going to become an alternative chick. I filled in the cracks pretty good. I do have pretty eyes though, so I fit in that way.

DF: Do you remember the story we did, "Alice Teaches You How to Put On Makeup"? Did you think you were bending any sexual stereotypes with that kind of thing?

AC: I always hoped they knew that this was kidding. And actually, I did have some pretty good eye makeup ideas. So it wasn't all bull. My real fans didn't know how to put on makeup, so it did help them, I'm sure of that.

DF: Any message for your fans?

AC: I'm 48 years old and better looking now than I ever was. It's incredible. And in better shape. And all those little girls are in their 30s, at the height of their sexual powers. It's just a shame that every time I walk down the street I get mistaken for Brad Pitt, it's a pity. I look so good, they don't know it's me.

One of 16's more historic covers featured two of our boldest stretches: "Donny—I Want to Be Like Alice," and "J5 Afro-Disiacs."

Elton John

Years of *16* Popularity: 1975–1977

An unstoppable hit-maker in the early '70s, Elton John became one of those unlikely teen idols whose oddness helps define the category. Unlovely, asexual (so it was thought), flamboyant, yet a remarkably talented singer, performer, and musician, he was for teenage girls what Liberace was to their grandmothers. His persona was harmless, goofy, and garish. His songs were so good, so singable, so recognizable, they appealed to audiences of all ages. Elton, alas, appealed to the readers of *16* very strongly as well.

Elton John was an act we were less than eager to cover, because from the beginning, he and his management were decidedly unwilling to cooperate with the teen fan press. With such enormous mainstream acceptance, why should they participate in "low level" publicity outlets?

But because his popularity demanded it, by 1975 we had to cover him as a major idol. We either bought every picture of Elton from photo agencies, or went to press conferences and took our own. At one such event, at the Troubadour in Los Angeles, Connie Papas of his management company stopped *16*'s Danny Fields on the way out and demanded that he hand over to her the roles of film he had shot, knowing they would appear in *16*, which was *infra dig* for her client. Danny was the spy from *16*, and Elton was an *artiste*. Danny refused Connie's request.

Much to our chagrin, Elton became the #1 most requested star by our readers; he got the most fan mail. Elton was so big that we did a one-shot special on him (unauthorized, of course), titled "Elton." Getting anything on Elton was a challenge; he simply would not cooperate, and we bought stories and pictures galore. Reporting on Elton became very expensive and frustrating.

Suddenly, the bubble burst when Elton told *Rolling Stone* magazine that he was "bisexual." There was an incredible amount of mail at *16*'s offices, which went something like this: "My older brother says he read that Elton John is a bisexual. He is making fun of me for loving someone he says is a fag. I know this could not be true. I am relying on *16* to print the truth about this terrible rumor. I love Elton so much, and I know this is a lie by people who are jealous of him. Please say it isn't so."

Well, the editors of *16* could usually tell readers to pay no attention to the vicious slanders so often hurled at their faves, but when it comes from the mouth of the fave himself, there was little denying to be done. We printed one of the many thousands of letters asking us to "say it isn't so," and then quoted Elton's very own confession right from *Rolling Stone*. Our response to the letter was to the effect that Elton's bisexuality apparently could not be denied, but that there was no reason for anyone who loved him for his talent, his adorableness, his music, his wonderful shows, his fantastic costumes, etc., etc., to stop loving him. In fact, we stressed that this was indeed a time for all fans to rally around Elton, and to show their support for him, in what must be (and indeed was) a very difficult time for him. We never did a major story on this delicate subject; and we left it as a letter to the editor and an editorial response.

Our begging the readers not to give up on Elton just because he was an admitted bisexual did no good at all. We thought it ironic that we had to plead with our readers to continue to idolize the one act that was our biggest pain in the ass to get material on; in any case, Elton's fickle teenage fans dropped him like the hot potato he had made of himself. Within two months of the *Rolling Stone* article, the mail for Elton John had virtually ceased, and so did *16*'s coverage of him.

From an editorial perspective, we were glad to be relieved of having to give Elton John major coverage with a minor amount of pictorial and verbal resources, not to mention the negative vibes from his team. But we certainly admired him for being one of the first superstars to come out of the closet, were appalled by the amount of flack he took because of it, and are glad to see that his career, talent, and reputation have weathered that historical storm with gloriously flying colors.

ELTON
The Girl He Chooses—
SHE COULD BE YOU!

This article "The Girl He Chooses," was clearly done as a 16 standard, with the assumption that every guy we wrote about was available to you: even when the editors knew otherwise. This is from the July 1975 issue.

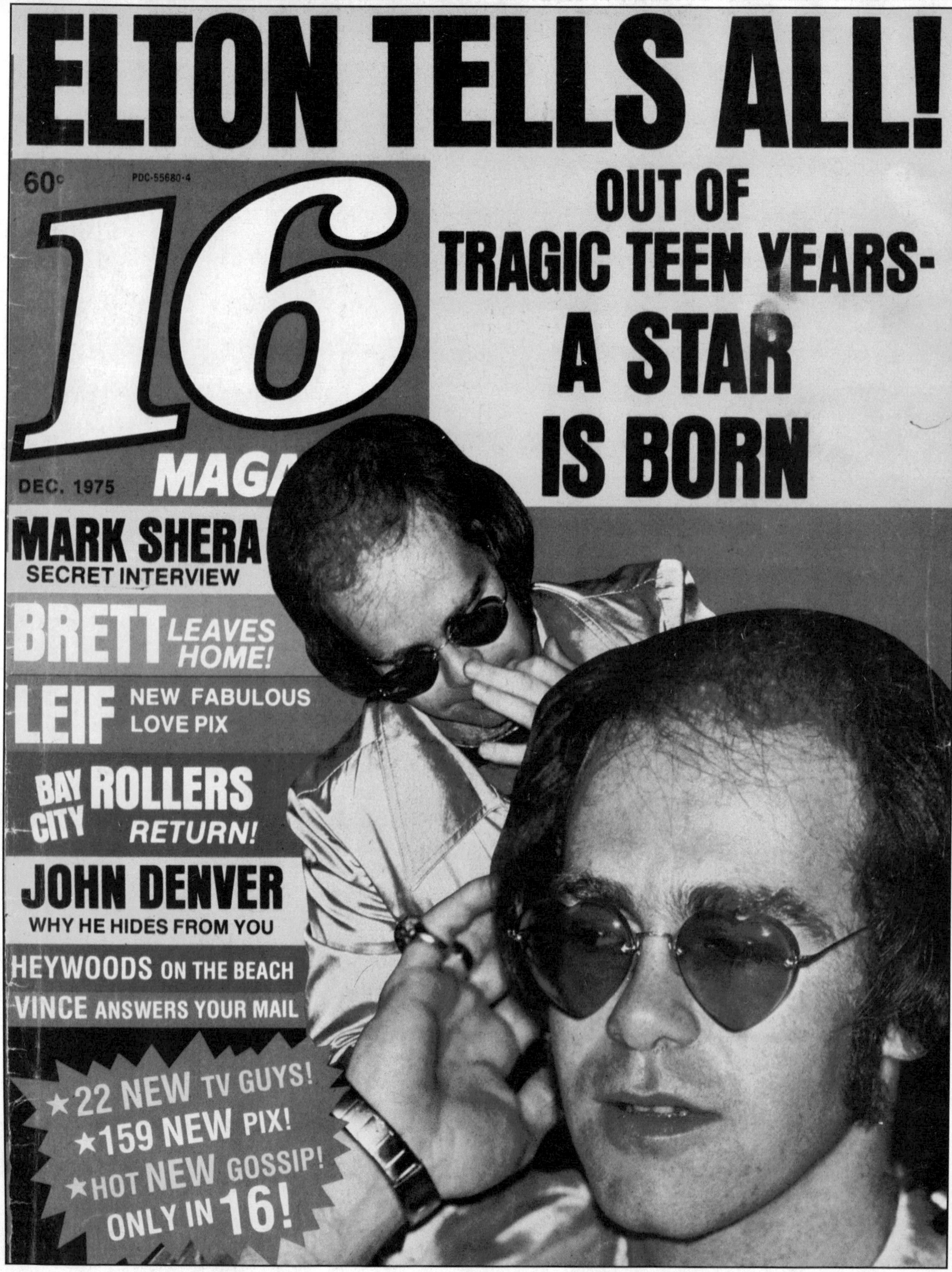

ELTON TELLS ALL!

60¢

PDC-55680-4

16

DEC. 1975

MAGA

OUT OF TRAGIC TEEN YEARS- A STAR IS BORN

MARK SHERA SECRET INTERVIEW

BRETT *LEAVES HOME!*

LEIF NEW FABULOUS LOVE PIX

BAY CITY ROLLERS *RETURN!*

JOHN DENVER WHY HE HIDES FROM YOU

HEYWOODS ON THE BEACH

VINCE ANSWERS YOUR MAIL

★ 22 NEW TV GUYS!
★ 159 NEW PIX!
★ HOT NEW GOSSIP!
ONLY IN **16**!

Some people may think that Elton John doesn't seem to be a very likely candidate for wedded bliss—but Reggie Dwight is almost ready to settle down near home and hearth!

Reginald Dwight was born on March 25, 1947, in Pinner, Middlesex, grew up, and became the fantastically world famous super-star Elton Hercules John.

But as wild as Elton seems today, as far-out as his clothes and actions seem to make him—there's still a lot of the small town boy named Reggie shining through! And that part of Elton is looking forward to the day when he can sit back and share his remarkable life with a very special lady!

Elton has no idea of who exactly that lady will be, but he can give you a good idea of the qualities she'll possess!

HE'S NOT EASY!

Elton will admit to not being the easiest person to live with! He's pretty set in his ways and the girl he finally marries will do a little bit more adapting to his sort of life than he will to hers.

Such as the matter of his house! Elton is an antiques freak. His split level mansion in Surrey, England, is cluttered with costly antiques and lovely French art deco objects. As Elton says, "It's so cluttered that it would look like the British museum if it weren't for the gold records on my ceiling." Obviously, the girl that Elton makes his mate would have to share his love of fine antiques or else live in a separate house—and that wouldn't be very much fun, would it?

She'd also have to get used to Elton's generosity! Elton's known far and wide for the lavish gifts he presents to his

If you're the kind of person who worries about the future, Elton's not the man for you!

friends! Elton feels that "you can't take it with you, so why not spend it while you have it." So, if you're the kind of person who worries about the future, Elton's not the man for you! You'll have to get used to him spending thousands of dollars on the latest fashions for you. Elton's such a clothes addict that it's a safe bet he'll want his wife to be one, too. Then there are glamourous trips all over the world, those fabulous antiques he so loves and any number of things that strike his fancy! Not such a bad life when you think of it!

Another passion of Elton's you'd learn to share is his love of sports! In fact, the only woman Elton has publicly professed love for is Billie Jean King, the tennis pro. That mini-romance is in the past, though, and Elton's better half would have to share his fondness for football, tennis and horseracing.

Just think, if you really begin to like horseracing Elton might buy you your own thoroughbred racehorse like he did for his manager, John Reid. Or if your favorite sport turns out to be football—he'll buy you your own football team! Never a dull moment with Elton!

But, where does the simple country boy from Pinner come into the scene?

Well, Elton does like the simple pleasures, too! He takes great joy in good solid home-cooked meals and looks

The only woman Elton has publicly professed love for is Billie Jean King, the tennis pro.

forward to the day when he can hang up his frying pan and let the lady of the house take over the kitchen!

He's also quite a family man! He was an only child and has always sworn that he wants a huge family to make up for it! He dreams of a large house (even bigger than the one he lives in today) full of children and animals and friends dropping in to listen to music and talk!

But, there will be many nights when Elton and his lady-love are home alone, just the two of them, sitting by the fire, listening to quiet music and getting to know each other all over again! Underneath Elton's glittery facade, he's one of the most romantic, affectionate and deepest human beings you'll ever know.

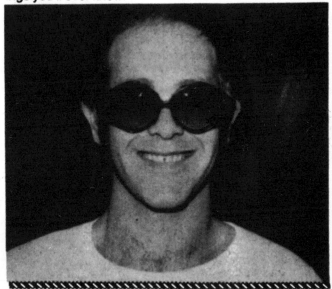

Underneath Elton's glittery facade, he's one of the most romantic, affectionate and deepest human beings you'll ever know.

So, this is how life with Elton would be! Could you match up to what Elton John needs and expects his wife to be? If so, maybe *you* could be the girl Elton chooses.

You can write to Elton at Box 3568, Hollywood, Ca. 90028. ∎

The Hudson Brothers

Years of *16* Popularity: 1974–1976

Originally the core of a rock group from Portland, Oregon, with high musical aspirations, Bill, Mark, and Brett Hudson leapt into front-cover status in *16* when they did a series of 5 one-hour variety shows on CBS in the late summer of 1974. There was also a Saturday morning show, and a few years later a syndicated comedy called *Bonkers*. Huge with young audiences, and close friends with such stars as Elton John, Cher, and John Lennon, the trio never got the recognition they felt was due to them as musicians or performers from audiences their own age. This was a pity, for they were most deserving, but in any case today they all have very successful careers in TV and music.

Zany, lovable, and quick-witted is what the Hudson Brothers were on TV, and in the pages of *16*. The cutest of the group was youngest brother Brett, but Mark and Bill were adored as well by *16*'s readers, though perhaps not as "boyfriend" material. Gloria Stavers had been quite aware of the group as recording artists and potential teen idols before their TV break, and assigned Randi Reisfeld and Danny Fields to do most of the Hudsons' coverage. Both editors will verify that there was no group of performers they'd worked with of whom they'd ever been fonder.

We interviewed Bill and Brett separately for this book in the autumn of 1996.

Bill Hudson Confides

You were in *16* before you were TV stars.
We were a band called the New Yorkers, and then Everyday Hudson, and we met Gloria three or four years before we became the Hudson Brothers and turned up on TV. She would run little blurbs on us from time to time. She listened to our music.

What was your impression of Gloria Stavers?
I always thought Gloria was totally fantastic. Completely, totally cool, totally smart, she was a very hot female to me. I found her extremely attractive in every way, shape, and form.

Did you ever hear anyone say that she became involved with the guys she put in the magazine? Or that it helped you get in the magazine if you did?
No, and let me say you did not have to. If you did, it was completely by choice. And I'll leave the rest to your imagination. I'm here to tell you, because I loved her, first-hand, that she never made it a *quid pro quo*. It was never that way. But when it was put out there, it was your choice. That's how I'll leave it. The rest of them are full of shit, and I speak from experience. She was very sexy, and completely professional, and I'll always love her.

What did you think of *16* Magazine then?
Back then, from 1965 through 1970, *16* was more in keeping with the spirit of the

The huggable Hudsons cuddle with 16's own Randi Reisfeld after breakfast at the Brasserie. (l. to r.) Brett, Mark, and Bill.

The Hudson Brothers

times than any of the magazines. *16* was there for the infancy of rock and roll, it was exactly the pulse of rock and roll. There was no stigma for musicians to be in *16*…then.

But there was by the mid-'70s; did you resent that you sacrificed musical credibility to be TV stars—and in consequence stars of *16*?

No, I don't, it certainly wasn't the fault of the magazine. If you were on TV, you didn't get your albums taken seriously. Our *Hollywood Situation* album was reviewed in one of the big FM radio tip sheets, and the guy loved it, but he warned radio programmers that the Hudson Brothers were TV stars. I want to make the point that *16* had no play in that, because *16* did exactly what it should have done, which was to embrace the Hudson Brothers. It was TV that put us on the map, and we made our own bed, so at that point, *16* was really our place. And we loved you guys.

Any derision from your musical cronies?

Not at all. Cher had suffered the same thing. John Lennon, who was very close to us, jokingly called us "the Kings of Saturday Morning," knowing full well what the implications were. No, performers in the industry knew the way things happened; it was the guys in suits who did the packaging and the pigeonholing.

How do you think your image came across in *16*? David Cassidy said he was screwing every girl in Hollywood, and he resented being portrayed as the innocent teenager that he played on his series.

I have no resentments whatsoever. I was sleeping with everyone too, and marrying most of the actresses. I kind of liked it, and what I liked is that no one knew the real me. What happens is, it's just a degree of illusion. Who's the real Neil Young? He's portraying as much of an image as I am portraying Bill Hudson. He wears an engineer hat and collects vintage train sets and plays with them in his basement. It's an illusion. My reality was that I was doing TV, I had a morning show, I'd replaced Sonny and Cher on network, and we were the Apple Pie Heroes, according to *TV Guide*. That's what we were, and we knew that. We couldn't play against our image, it was too powerful. The power of TV is so great. There was no way our fans would believe we were fucking everything that moved and smoking pot and hanging with Aerosmith,

Lennon, McCartney, Harry Nilsson—unless we told them, and why should we do that? There was nothing to be gained at that time from smashing the image.

Did you feel that you couldn't be photographed smoking a cigarette? Unclean stuff?

I never felt that. Anyhow, most everything we did that people would know about could always be written off as wacky: Oh, they're wacky. We could put cigarettes in our mouths and drop our pants, and we were like little kids. We felt very free with you guys, you know, because you knew us and we were all working on the same project. There was something great about that. We were much less free with *Rolling Stone* or *Hit Parader*, because they would love to find something that they could turn ugly. But you saw what it was for real. So we posed for a picture as if we were peeing in a fountain, but we knew you wouldn't print it. In *Rolling Stone*, that'd be all they'd print, and they'd highlight where my hand was.

You used to tour with the Osmonds— what was that like?

They were always trying to convert us to Mormonism. We sublet their apartment in Hollywood, and John Lennon was staying in the basement part of the apartment, because he was all fucked-up emotionally, he was going through that thing with Yoko. And Alan used to call me every morning at

The fountain "peeing" pic that didn't get printed then.

The Hudson Brothers

5 fucking o'clock, and say, "Bill, can we come over? We're with one of the Elders, and he would like to talk to you about our philosophies." I said, "Alan, it's 5 A.M. Fuck off."

Any more thoughts about *16*?
We couldn't have asked for more support from any organization or group of people. You know what? The most negative conversation I ever had about *16* is the one we're having right now. Even to question its validity is negative.

Did you expect, when you started on TV, that you'd be getting all this attention from the fan magazines?
No, we didn't expect exactly that. But I knew what I was getting into, and that's what I did for a living. I never said, "Hey, I'm going to be a teen idol!" It just started happening, and you went with the flow. That's where my market was. I looked at it in a very businesslike way. My brothers and I were nothing like the image portrayed in the magazine.

What do you mean?
Well, we weren't any goody-two-shoes. We did screw around a lot, and the magazine portrayed this fantasy life. We were pretty wild boys.

You mean you had a normal Hollywood sex life?
I would have to say a little abnormal. It was pretty wild. It was a wide open time. There was no fear of death, we had sexual freedom, and we took full advantage of that.

Did being teen idols hold you back musically?
It totally negated us musically. But my brothers and I had a problem from birth, and the problem was that we were funny. And that killed us anywhere. If we could have held back the goofing around, we would have had a shot musically. We were presented to CBS as three musicians, but they changed it into identical suits, capped our teeth, and made us a package. I'm in TV now, and I've learned from the mistakes that were made on me. If I find a piece of talent I like, I'm not going to change him. I think once we were seen wearing the same suit, with *H*'s on our chest, musically we were dead.

What model were they trying to reinvent with you?
We replaced Sonny and Cher in the summer, and they just plugged us in that format. I think they were trying to plug us into the Osmond thing, too.

You were the sex god of the group, so did that mean you got laid more? If so, were your brothers envious?
My brothers were very supportive of my hunk success. Yeah, although we didn't keep score. The truth is, we had our own individual fans. Yes, I had the bulk of them because I was…whatever the hell I was, oh, the hunk, thank you. But as far as bottom line getting laid, I think my brothers did pretty well. There were women all over the place.

Any misconceptions you'd like to correct now?
I just wish people could have listened to the music and forget the *H*'s on the sweaters. We were proud of the music then, and we're proud of it now. But I wouldn't give up that run for all the tea in China. It was a blast. Yeah, there were problems, like in any business, but the bottom line is, we had a blast.

Any message for the fans who loved you in *16*?
I loved our fans. The Hudson Brothers had real hard-core fans, and they were great. They were into what we did. Do I wish people would have taken our music more seriously? Absolutely. Would I change anything? Nah, probably not. You know, my kids—I have a 13-year-old daughter, Tess, and a 9-year-old son, Jonathan—they talk about the Hudson Brothers not as if they were talking about their dad and uncles, but like they're other people, and that's very cool.

SHAUN CASSIDY

Years of *16* Popularity: 1977–1979

Shaun Cassidy defined late '70s teen idols in the same way Leif Garrett did. He captured the double-edged/Jekyll & Hyde feel of the moment—clean-cut and wholesome as a *Hardy Boy*; defiant, frenzied, and sexy as a rock star who toured the U.S.A. and Europe in skintight stage outfits and released "six or seven" (he can't remember) albums.

The combination of acting and rock 'n' roll has always been the most potent in terms of teen idolatry; it was also, of course, the path taken by David Cassidy only a few years earlier. But Shaun was never simply following in the footsteps of his older brother—he did what he wanted to do, pretty much the way he wanted to do it. And the lessons learned the hard way by David were never lost on Shaun Cassidy. Nor were the ones he learned at the knees of his legendary performer parents, Shirley Jones and Jack Cassidy.

Shaun Cassidy was able to rise far beyond any sort of "former teen idol" prejudice, in large part because he went into it all with his eyes open and never allowed himself to get carried away with it. Today, Shaun is one of Hollywood's most respected television producers and writers. Although his TV series, *American Gothic*, lasted one short season, the critical respect it garnered has only helped Shaun: he recently signed a multimillion-dollar production deal with Universal TV and has many other projects in the pipeline.

As Shaun Cassidy, now a father of two, looks back on his teen idol years, it is with a mix of pragmatism and pride. Positive memories dominate.

SHAUN CASSIDY

"I WAS NEVER ALLOWED TO BE ANONYMOUS"

"I was aware of *16* because my brother David had been in it. I'd also seen my mom in it because of *The Partridge Family*. I'd grown up understanding the concept that my parents were in show business, so it wasn't surprising to see them in any kind of publication. But to see David in there was amusing, because I just knew him as my brother. And then I obviously got used to that. But then to see myself in the magazine was kind of mind-boggling because I didn't feel I'd done anything to deserve that kind of publicity.

"I was also aware of David's feelings about it all—he pretty much hated it, because he felt very pigeonholed by all the press. I didn't have that kind of experience though.

"Before I started with rock 'n' roll, I was 16, 17 years old, and the press, if there was any press, was based on my relationship with David—not about anything I had accomplished on my own. Then I got into a punk rock band called Longfellow. I'd play high school rock gigs, and little clubs on Sunset Boulevard in Hollywood. And there was this big press

Before The Hardy Boys, *Shaun was a punk rocker.*

Shaun allowed us into his home during his Hardy Boys *days, and we in turn took the readers "behind closed doors."*

being this incredibly dull interview, and I'm sure I was, because I was so cautious about everything I said.

"Because [in reality] I was...I don't know what an average 17-year-old is...but I guess I was one, and that included all kinds of things that you couldn't say in *16 Magazine*. Which was...sex, drugs, and rock 'n' roll. That's what I was into at that time...oh, yeah. And I don't know anyone coming of age at that time [in the late '70s who wasn't].

"The perception, the image...this is what I find: the press finds something they can hang their hat on, and that's what they promote. And the side of me *16* promoted—as very available to the fans, very tender, caring, wholesome, romantic but nonsexual, family-oriented—is part of who I was, but it's edited, parts are excluded. It was not an inaccurate side of me (except I was hardly nonsexual), but it was only a specific part of the picture."

"I WAS SANTA CLAUS—AND THESE KIDS WERE NOT MINE TO CORRUPT"

"And it worked—in *16*'s interests, certainly, and from my point of view, too. I felt that portrayal was being responsible toward what I perceived as children—who were in fact my audience. I felt like, I'm Santa Claus and I don't want to blow anybody's perception of Santa Claus, so I will put on my best face and be as good an example to a 10-year-old, or an eleven-year-old, as I can be. And I didn't view the audience out there as mine to corrupt. I viewed them as mine to try and set a positive example for.

"Now I choose not to be any more specific about exactly what I was really doing in those days, because I have children of my own. I'm equally protective of what I say now, as I may have been then."

"PERSONALLY, IT WAS ISOLATING"

"All that said, the magazines were to me—not to discount their power to their audience—just a very small part of the experience I was going through, which was a very isolating experience. It immediately set me apart from everybody my age. I literally couldn't go out of the house for a few years—which isn't unique, it's every pop star's experience in history: the Elvis syndrome. If you take it seriously and you buy into it and you surround yourself with people who will play into that, it's going to be tough to recover.

"My mother and father both, in different ways, handled it pretty well; my mother more so. She always viewed it as her

turnout. I found it astounding and scary because I was never allowed to be anonymous, and I certainly wasn't ready to make my debut; but there I was, and photographers were all over the place. The pictures ended up all over the world and I ended up in all kinds of magazines—but it was still purely because of David.

"And so, by the time I was actually doing something on my own, whether it was *The Hardy Boys* or my own records, and the press started to cover it—not just pop press, but legit press—I already had a lot of experience seeing David go through it as well as going through it on my own, undeservedly."

THE IMAGE VS. THE REALITY: "I KNEW ENOUGH TO BE GUARDED"

"I think *16* and the press in general gave me a pretty fair shake. But again, I knew enough to be very wary and very guarded around them. There's an early interview I did with Andy Warhol in *Interview* magazine where he talks about me

The Excitement Of A Shaun Cassidy Concert—In Your Very Own Home Town *And* Right Here In **16!** Be There With Shaun On Stage—*And* Backstage!!

SHAUN ON STAGE!

What a glorious spring it's been—made even more terrif by the fact that teen dream Shaun Cassidy virtually hop-scotched the country to give live concerts each 'n every weekend! Did Shaun hit *your* town? If he did—and you were lucky enough to catch him—you know how unbelievably exciting it all was! If you missed him, or if *he* missed *your* corner of the world—don't despair! You know there'll always be a next time—in fact, a brand-new concert tour is in the planning stages right now and for sure, if Shaun skipped over you *this* time, he'll try not to the next time! Meantime, have a look at Shaun *now*—as *he* looked during his concerts in Salt Lake City, Utah and Denver, Colorado and find out what Shaun's hectic on-the-road, on stage and backstage life is like up close!

THE TRIP

The date was February 4—a Saturday. Shaun left Los Angeles Friday night, February 3 after a full day of filming *The Hardy Boys* and took a 7:30 PM flight to Salt Lake City. Shaun and the band—plus the entourage of people that always go with him, including sound and lighting crews, publicists, record company

More SHAUN! Turn The Page

Shaun opens the show with *That's Rock 'N Roll*—"C'mon everybody—get down and get with it!"

He swings into *Da Doo Ron Ron!*

Arms raised, Shaun finishes off *Hey Deanie*.

He uses his scarf in his act—in all sorts of different ways!

"What am I bid for one, slightly used, white scarf?" Shaun wants to know. At each concert, he tosses it out into the audience—wouldn't *you* like to catch it??

Shaun gets down on his knees for more dramatic impact on slow songs like *Teen Dream*.

Shaun's stage costumes are always made of shiny satin—this time, he's wearing a top with glittery gold eyelets.

23

The sexy side of Shaun—in his tight pants rocker guise—swept into "your" town via this June 1978 article.

SHAUN
In Your Town!

Shaun Cassidy

business, and that was taught to us, that this is a job, and you go to work and then, as if you were a dentist, you leave it at the office and you go home and have a life. And if other people around the world viewed show business people as different, we didn't believe that—or I didn't believe that. But the isolating part is that other people think of you as something you're not.

"Of course, I'd had the experience of people wanting to be around me because of what I did and not who I was, since I was a little kid—I came from a famous family. I grew up with that [sense of guardedness] in me."

"*16* HELPED MY CAREER— BUT I HELPED THEIR SALES"

"Yes, being in the magazine helped *The Hardy Boys* ratings and my record sales, but I think they all fed each other. I've heard that if there is a real hot show with young people on it, the magazine sales increase, and when there aren't, the magazines hurt. So I do think one helps the other.

"One thing I do remember about *16* in particular was that it struck me as an edgier teen magazine than the others, which may seem strange. But it had more of a New York sensibility. I mean, you didn't see the New York Dolls in the other teen magazines, and I think Danny Fields had a lot to do with that. The Ramones were in it. *16* covered who was at CBGB—it was an interesting dynamic at work. It had a wider variety of celebs—and had people in there that might alienate the audience that I was being so protective of!"

"I WROTE YOU A LETTER IN 1977"

"I don't know how much fan mail I got; I didn't see much of it. I get letters to this day, saying 'I sent you a thing in 1977 and I never heard back,' and 'I was a member of your fan club.' Actually, adults come up to me all the time and say that.

"I don't remember why I didn't see it. I may have hired someone else…the whole period was like a blur for me, and that's not because of drugs. I was sober through the whole thing. It just went so fast and so furious and so beyond any kind of reality. My reality was the hotel room I was in that day and the five or six close friends that I managed to hang on to through the experience.

"The idea of being a pop star really appealed to me, at 13. And when I got into it I found it wasn't as enthralling as I thought it might be. And I also wasn't making records I was particularly proud of, so I didn't have a lot of passion for it. The concerts are like a blur to me—it's like it was all one concert, I

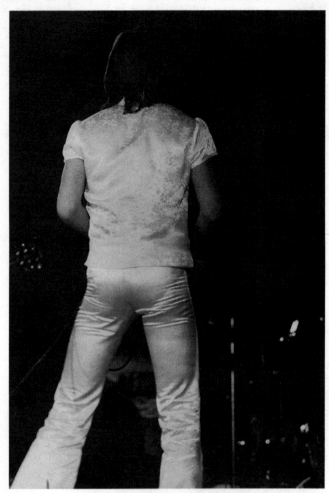

We also went onstage with him— and could not resist taking, and printing, this one.

kind of remember one. And I was doing this TV show at the same time. I was flying out on weekends to do the concerts."

AN EARLY MARRIAGE: "I NEEDED MY OWN HOME"

"I got married at 21 [to Ann Pennington] but the articles in *16*, right up until the time of the marriage, basically denied that Ann and I were an item. That was not my doing. I was basically free and open about the whole relationship. Someone else may have tried to put some spin control on it behind my back. I was surprised at the time, to see some of the press was suppressing it. It certainly wasn't coming from me.

"Part of the reason I got married so young is because I wanted some kind of grounding, and I wanted to move into my own home with my own family and lock the door and not come out. And I did for a few years. I didn't come out at all. But I was happy at home, and I had a good reason to be."

Shaun Cassidy

"SUCCESS AND FAILURE ARE BOTH IMPOSTERS"

"Being able to stay home and self-educate was a luxury afforded to me because of my early success. Which in the end was a good thing for me, but for others it's been a really destructive thing.

"In my case, being a teen idol was all positive because it didn't have a real adverse affect on me. And I don't think the magazines ever do unless you believe them, but that's not just *16*, that's any press—if you believe your own press, you're going to be in trouble—the good and the bad press.

"Jose Ferrer said, 'Success and failure are both imposters,' and that's true. You can't believe either one of them. You just have to be true to yourself. But if you're surrounded by people who believe everything that's being said about you in magazines, and they say, wow, you're on the cover of *People* magazine and that means you're a big deal and we're gonna treat you differently from now on, then you're never gonna have anyone you can go to—and that includes your parents, because a lot of times the parents believe, 'hey, my kid is Elvis.' Then where is your ground? Where do you turn to? It's gone, and that's where the tragedies come.

"I was lucky. That never happened to me. My early success and all those subsequent years of learning is the reason I'm able to do what I'm doing now—writing, producing. This just didn't happen like yesterday, it's really been all that experience leading up to this. And for that, I'm grateful."

Leif Garrett

Leif Garrett

Answers 16 Intimate (& Grown-Up) Questions!

How did you feel about being in *16*?

You know, before I was in the magazine, I had no real awareness of it. But once *16* started running stuff, it was like, this is cool. I had absolutely no problem with it. The only thing was, after a while, I was like, "I don't want to do any more photo shoots!" But you know, having somebody write about you in the beginning is very flattering. I felt that then.

Years of *16* Popularity: 1975–1980

That Leif Garrett is destined to be remembered more as a teen idol pinup than for any body of work he ever produced says nothing about any talent he may or may not have had—and everything about his youth, inexperience, and vulnerability. Leif's androgynously pretty face lent itself to coverboy status; the naïveté of the adults around him lent itself to the exploitation of those looks. Because that strategy was wildly successful, it completely superceded any training he might have received.

Leif lived in the public eye, and in the pages of *16 Magazine*, from the age of 13 until his 20th birthday. The coverage began with the short-lived series *Three for the Road* and took him through six rock 'n' roll albums, his own TV special, and several world concert tours. Through it all, he collected gold records, awards, accolades, and the hearts of millions of young fans.

To those devotees, Leif was the perfect boyfriend. He was presented as kind and caring but just cutting edge enough to be interesting. *16*'s Leif Garrett was hard-working, somewhat mischievous, always fun-loving, and, most importantly, available and looking for the right girl. What was really going on with Leif during those hectic, halcyon days was quite another story. As you're about to find out.

Oh, and by the way—once and for all—you pronounce it *Layf*. "Rhymes with safe," he always used to say.

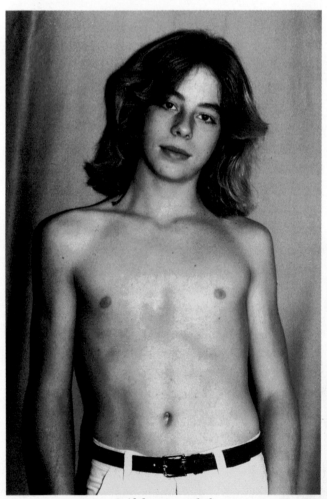

Leif the sex symbol.

Leif Garrett

Did *16* portray you accurately, Leif?

Probably not—well, in one sense, yeah, because photos don't lie. But I think I was made out to be a little more innocent than I was, in the sense that, when you're in the business, and you deal with it daily, you mature. You deal with adults and your perspectives change a little bit. For the most part it was fairly accurate—but believe me, you guys weren't writing about the mischief I was getting into!

You can tell us now— what kind of mischief *were* you getting into?

Well, you know. I mean like anybody at that age who's thrown into an arena of adults. Naturally some of those adults were, if you will, bad influences. There was a little dabbling in the darker side of things.

Like drugs and sex and booze?

I don't think of sex as being dark! But yeah, like trying pot, drinking. I remember being 16 in New Orleans and doing a promo for a record, and the heads of my record label, in their oblivious, callous way, left me with people I shouldn't have been with. People that were like, "Hey man, you want a line?" And "Hey, man, you want to smoke?" "Hey man, let's drink." I mean, basically adults in the rock 'n' roll world doing things I'd never been exposed to at that time. I got thrown into a world I was too young for—it was really baptism by fire.

Did it ever scare you?

It embarrassed me more. There was this record company guy traveling with me who was literally manhandling the deejays at the radio stations we'd visit. And I was like, "I don't want to know about this." I was embarrassed—I would apologize to the deejays. I was like, "If you want to play it, man, play it, but if it's not your standard of music, then fuck it."

During this time, did *16* continue to portray you as being "squeaky clean"?

I think out of all of us, like Andy Gibb and Shaun Cassidy and myself, who are all from the same era, I was probably the most on the cutting edge—as far as the way I was dressing and things, my attitude. In the beginning, *16* portrayed me exactly as I was—a nice, clean young man. But as I got older and more cutting edge, *16* was also aware of it—certainly more than any other magazine.

Looking back, how do you feel about posing shirtless for pinups?

It's funny because after a year or two of being on the road promoting the record, I really adopted this rock 'n' roll attitude, so it didn't seem funny to me at the time. But looking back in retro, I now kind of go, *"Wow—what was I thinking?"* It's so weird, this sort of semi-developed young man. Plus it makes me think how weird it might have been for those pedophiles out there! Which is something we never thought about back then. There was a certain amount of innocence that we've sort of lost in the '90s.

You started out as a child actor— how did you become a rocker?

My getting into music was simply the record company literally coming to me and saying, "Do you want to make a record?" And that was a direct result of *16* and the other magazines. Because they saw how popular I was getting, how much fan mail I was getting. I had become the #1 mail-getting teen idol of the time. They were delivering huge duffel bags—like, five, six a day to my house—packed, full. It was ridiculous.

So because of your popularity in *16*, the record company came to you out of the blue and said, "Do you want to make a record?" Had you any musical experience before?

I had no vocal training whatsoever and no experience with an instrument. My sole musical experience before that consisted of an audition when I was 8 years old—I auditioned for a singing part in *Mame*, with Lucille Ball. I tested with her and sang a song to her. But that was it—so my involvement with music was really kind of strange and scary. But I quickly adapted very well. I wish I'd been forced to get more training, because again, it was baptism by fire. There was no time—the mistakes were made in public, in front of people, rather than at home, rehearsing. There were times when I was scared to death. There was a photograph taken of me at my very first concert at Magic Mountain [theme park] in L.A. at the amphitheater. And all I was scheduled to do was go out and lip-synch "Surfin' USA," which was my first single. And this photograph of me—I was crazy nervous—you can see it in my face and my hands and my body language. But the minute I went out onstage—I'm not going to say I lost the nervousness, but it was more like excitement. I really kind of tuned in and turned on to it right away. Like, whoa! Look how powerful

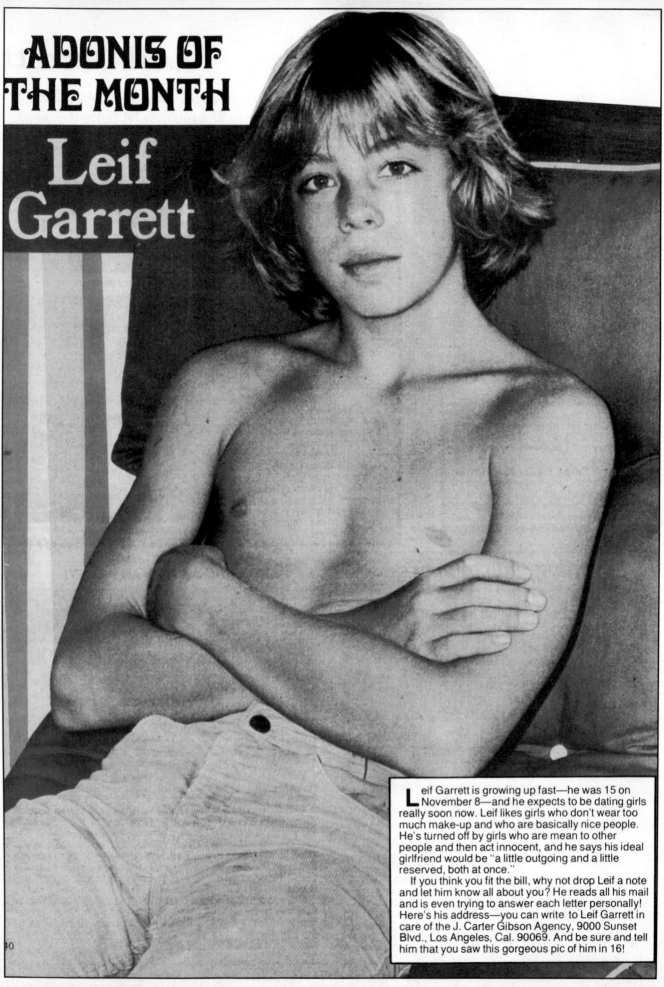

ADONIS OF THE MONTH

Leif Garrett

Leif Garrett is growing up fast—he was 15 on November 8—and he expects to be dating girls really soon now. Leif likes girls who don't wear too much make-up and who are basically nice people. He's turned off by girls who are mean to other people and then act innocent, and he says his ideal girlfriend would be ''a little outgoing and a little reserved, both at once.''

If you think you fit the bill, why not drop Leif a note and let him know all about you? He reads all his mail and is even trying to answer each letter personally! Here's his address—you can write to Leif Garrett in care of the J. Carter Gibson Agency, 9000 Sunset Blvd., Los Angeles, Cal. 90069. And be sure and tell him that you saw this gorgeous pic of him in 16!

"What was I thinking?" Leif says now about those pre-adolescent sexy poses. This appeared in the January 1977 issue.

Leif Garrett

this can be, to…I don't want to say manipulate…but to be able to get the immediate feedback reaction. Plus, listen, at that age too, I'm thinking about girls. So to have, all of a sudden, 10,000 to 15,000 girls going, "Leif! Leif!"… This was my wildest, wettest dream and I loved it. I really got off on the adreneline and never looked back.

What was the worst part of being a teen idol?
Being ripped off by my record company—they ripped me off so badly. [Clearly, this is Leif's opinion—we're sure his record company disagrees!] I don't want to say I harbor bad feelings, but I certainly have no desire to shake their hands, nor would I if I met them in public. I bought them a building here in

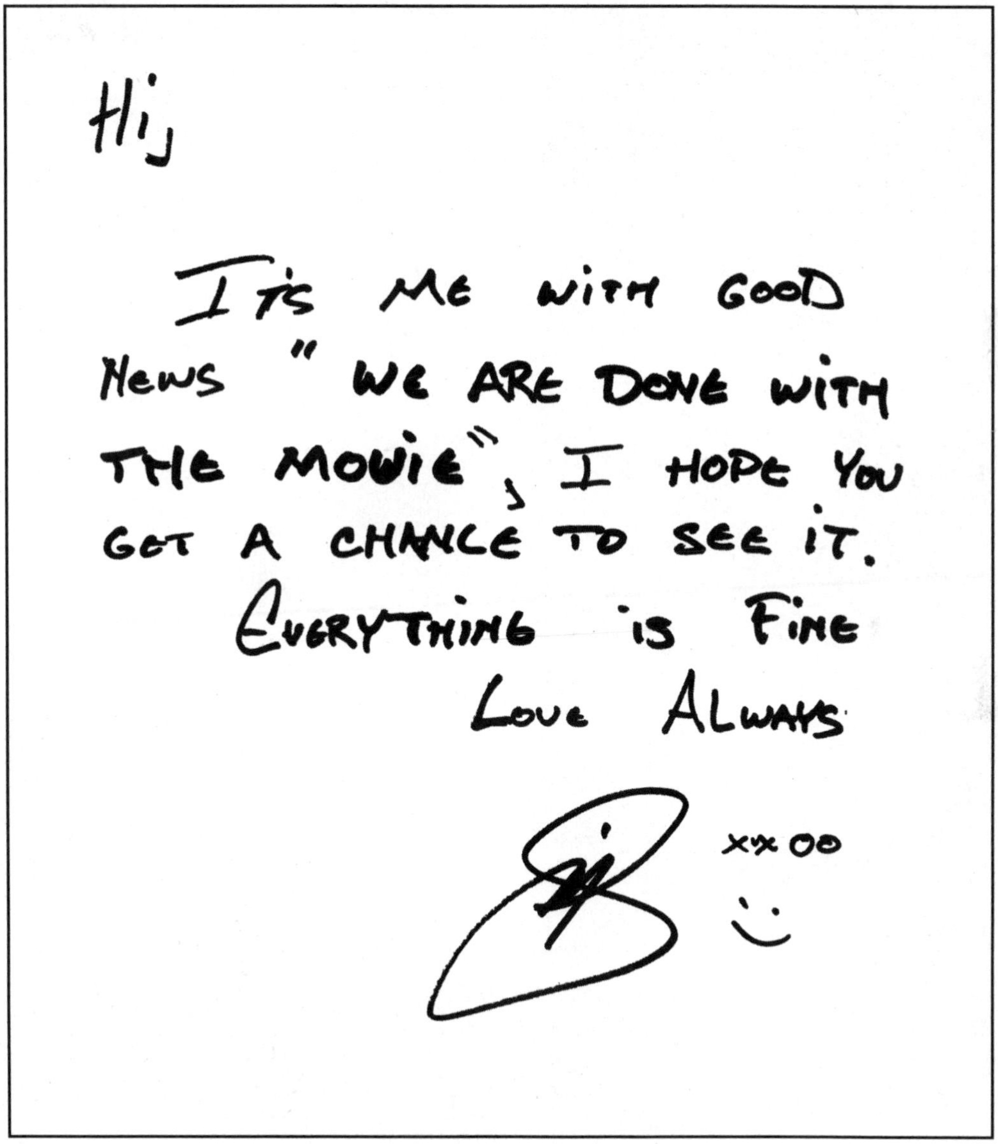

Hi,

It's me with good news "we are done with the movie", I hope you get a chance to see it. Everything is fine
Love Always

xx oo
:)

A handwritten letter, with love from Leif to you, girl!

Visit LEIF At Home!

Join Hunky Leif Garrett As He Takes You On A *Very* Personal And Private Tour Of His Spacious Garden Apartment High In The Hollywood Hills!

Hi! Welcome to my Hollywood Hills home—I've been waiting for you!

Here, why don't you join me in a game of backgammon—with all these dice, how can you lose?

Or would you rather join me at the baby grand piano in the living room? Know how to play "Chopsticks"?!

This is *my* chair—can you tell?

I'll just sit here—I kind of like this corner of the couch!

16

Behind closed doors with Leif—into the kitchen, the bedroom, and beyond. This is from the February 1979 issue.

Mind if I get comfortable? It's been a very busy morning. I think I'll just take a minute to check for any early phone messages on my answering machine. This thing's a lifesaver!

This is our dining area—my mom, sister, and I eat here together every chance we get—and we do a lot of talking and catching up on each other's activities! Sit down—let's have something!

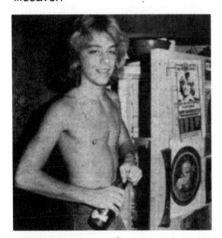

I'll get some Perrier mineral water. How do you like all these antique posters—my mom loves them, and antique oak furniture too—the place is full of it. 'Course she didn't forget to put me up on the refrigerator too! Look!

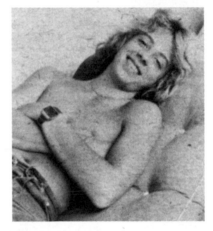

This is the terrace. It's small, but I love to come out here and relax. Sometimes I put on Crosby, Stills & Nash or the Rolling Stones' albums—real loud—and then I listen from here!

Oh, here's a pillow that one of my fans sent me—isn't it nice!

And how about this poster—I'm really proud of this! It was used by my record company to introduce my very first album! Oops, there goes the phone—come on!

Hi, Stan! It's my manager—excuse me for just one second?

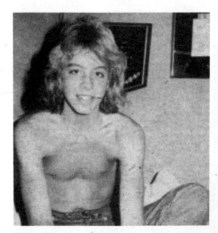

Well, this is it—this is *my* room! I keep the awards I've gotten right here over my bed. They mean a lot to me and I like having them there when I wake up!

(Please Turn The Page)

17

Leif Garrett

Santa Monica with all the money I made for them—and then they took me for another few million.

Why wasn't there anyone to protect you from that?

That's a good question. That's the one thing, the only thing that really sticks with me. Where was the logic of my mother, just to go, "Hey, where's the money?" But I don't hold this against my mother—although if there is someone to hold it against, it's her. It's that she herself was caught up in it more than I was. All the hype and the hoopla and "how great it's going to be" and "how much money we're going to make." She was just trusting. Because of the way she was raised, being a trusting person. But I know from experience and common logic that this would not have happened, no matter what, if roles were reversed, if I was the parent. I'm just someone who asks too many questions and questions authority more than my mom ever did.

What was the best part of all this?

It was a crazy ride. My fondest memories of the whole thing, besides all the lovely young ladies, is all the travel I've done. I've probably been around the world three or four times. I've been to places I'll never go to again.

Speaking of lovely young ladies…the Leif Garrett 16's readers knew didn't have a girlfriend, was always looking for the right girl…

Which is true!

Did you ever stop being the guy 16 said you were?

I never stopped being me. And I still think I have that innocence in me—although it's not real big. But I still feel that I'm that kid. But after the age of 17 or so, I always had a girlfriend. All those articles saying, "Leif's Looking…"—really, I was always going out with Nicolette Sheridan. We went out for five or six years. So in terms of *16 Magazine*, that was probably the biggest misportrayal.

Did it bother you to be portrayed as eligible when in fact you weren't?

It used to bother me. And I used to tell editors that I do have a girlfriend. And they'd be like, "It doesn't matter." They still chose not to print that. Of course in my early teenage years, it was true—I really didn't have a girlfriend then.

What's your message to all the fans who idolized you back then?

To anyone who bought a poster or a record or watched my TV show—thank you. Thank you for a really incredible time in my life, and for allowing me the opportunity to do all that stuff. Because if it weren't for the fans, buying the records and posters, I wouldn't have been able to do everything I did. So everyone indirectly has had an influence in my life and it's all been an incredible journey.

SCOTT BAIO

Years of *16* Popularity: 1977–1983

That a scrawny Italian kid from Brooklyn, New York, should end up being one of the longest-running *16* teen idols isn't all that surprising—after all, skinny kids like Frankie Avalon, Fabian, Dion, even John Travolta, had working-class backgrounds and teen idol pedigrees. But unlike those predecessors, Scott Baio was neither a crooner (though he did, uh, record) nor a movie star. An immensely appealing doe-eyed kid, the secret to his longevity was that he had the right look; and perhaps because of his constant teen mag coverage, he just kept working.

With each new project, the fan base grew. In fact, Scott Baio actually was more popular in his later teen idol years than at the beginning. Although he appeared in almost every single issue, starting in July 1977 until the end of 1983, he was usually more of a mainstay than the main course. His picture was hardly ever on the cover. Instead he was constantly overshadowed by other late '70s icons like the Bay City Rollers, Leif Garrett, Andy Gibb and even KISS. It wasn't until 1982 that his photo took coverboy prominence, and even then, he only held it for a few issues.

16's first coverage of Scott predated *Happy Days*. It was prodded by the unsolicited fan mail that came in after his 1976 kiddie gangster flick (with Jodie Foster) *Bugsy Malone*. That, plus the fact that he was about to start work in a TV series, *Blansky's Beauties*, was what led *16* to his modest home in Brooklyn, camera in tow, to get the Scott scoop. After that first interview, we did more, chronicling his starring roles in *Happy Days, Joanie Loves Chachi, Charles in Charge,* and in several teen-themed movies.

Now a showbiz hyphenate—actor-director—Scott talked to us about those years from his Los Angeles home.

Scott Baio Looks Back

"I GOT REALLY LUCKY"

"I started out in this business really young. I had no conception of fan magazines. I had done some commercials, then I got *Bugsy Malone*. My older brother and sister were acting, too. But no one had ever gotten fan mail, or any kind of attention. So when *16 Magazine* came to interview me, I had no idea what it meant. I just remember thinking it was cool that anybody wanted to interview me.

"When I was 14 or so, my parents picked up and moved the entire family to L.A. so I could pursue an acting career. I got right into *Happy Days* and then, *Joanie Loves Chachi*. It was great for me, but I'm sure it was very stressful and traumatic for my entire family.

"But my parents never made me feel pressure. They were always incredibly supportive and sacrificed a great deal for me and my brother and sister. I was lucky; I had a lot of adults looking out for me—especially my father—and people that I worked with. Gary Marshall, who created *Happy Days,* was like a second father to me. There are guys my age now who were on hit TV series when they were kids, and went in a total opposite direction. They got all screwed up, because they didn't have anyone to look out for them."

MY IMAGE: GENERIC— BUT NOT INACCURATE . . .

"I think I was portrayed pretty much the same as everyone else in *16*. It was all pretty generic, wasn't it? But I didn't have a problem with it. It was sort of the same structure for each. I never said, 'I didn't say that', or 'I wasn't there.' I think *16* was pretty accurate at a surface level. I don't think you got into deep issues, how you felt about the rain forests, what's your relationship with your parents and how did it affect your childhood. But I think on a not-that-esoteric of a level, it was pretty accurate."

. . .EXCEPT FOR THE GIRLS

"I guess the one area where my real life completely differed from the way I was portrayed had to do with girls. You always presented me as being completely available, as not

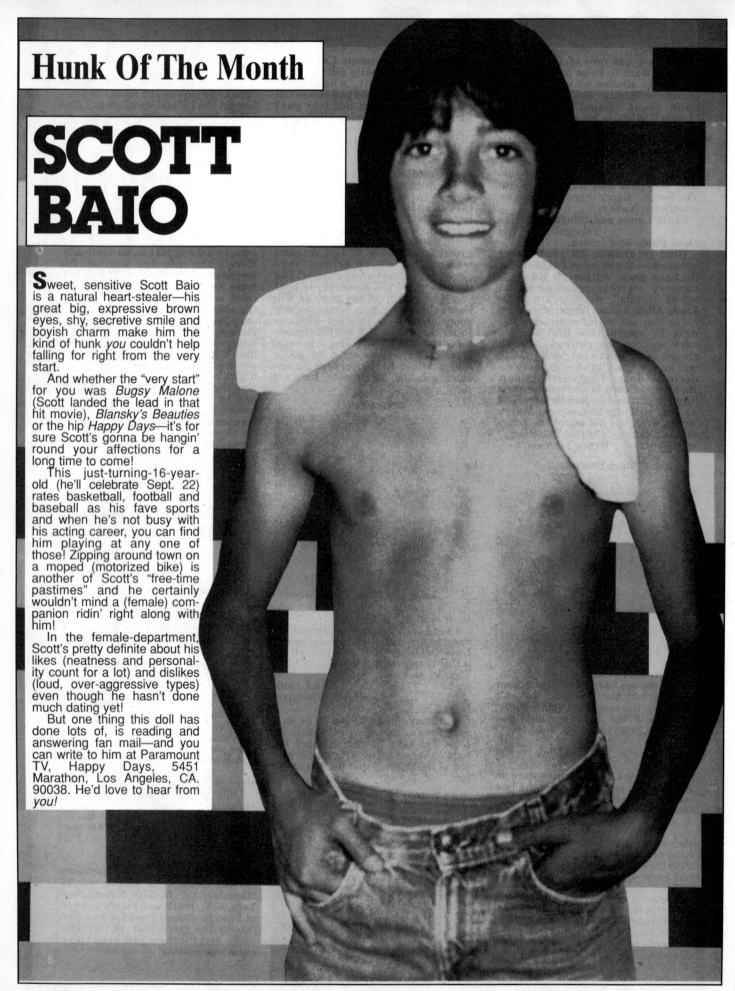

Hunk Of The Month

SCOTT BAIO

Sweet, sensitive Scott Baio is a natural heart-stealer—his great big, expressive brown eyes, shy, secretive smile and boyish charm make him the kind of hunk *you* couldn't help falling for right from the very start.

And whether the "very start" for you was *Bugsy Malone* (Scott landed the lead in that hit movie), *Blansky's Beauties* or the hip *Happy Days*—it's for sure Scott's gonna be hangin' round your affections for a long time to come!

This just-turning-16-year-old (he'll celebrate Sept. 22) rates basketball, football and baseball as his fave sports and when he's not busy with his acting career, you can find him playing at any one of those! Zipping around town on a moped (motorized bike) is another of Scott's "free-time pastimes" and he certainly wouldn't mind a (female) companion ridin' right along with him!

In the female-department, Scott's pretty definite about his likes (neatness and personality count for a lot) and dislikes (loud, over-aggressive types) even though he hasn't done much dating yet!

But one thing this doll has done lots of, is reading and answering fan mail—and you can write to him at Paramount TV, Happy Days, 5451 Marathon, Los Angeles, CA. 90038. He'd love to hear from *you!*

In November 1977, skinny 16-year-old Scott was Hunk of the Month.

$1.50   JUNE 1982   14308

16
MAGAZINE

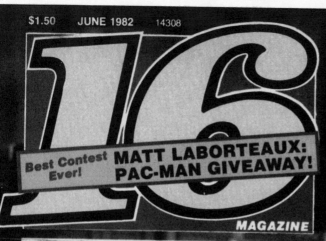

SCOTT BAIO
Happy Days Gone Forever?

Best Contest Ever! **MATT LABORTEAUX: PAC-MAN GIVEAWAY!**

STEVE PERRY
Journey—Man On The Spot!

RICK SPRINGFIELD
Peek Into His Private World, Part 2!

- **DOOBIES:** Come Along As *16's* Winner Meets Her Favorites!
- **TIM HUTTON:** The Pain That Won't Go Away
- **THE POLICE:** Every Little Thing They Do Is Magic
- **JOHN SCHNEIDER:** Win The *Dukes Of Hazzard* LP!
- **KISS IN CONCERT:** On Fridays!
- **HALL & OATES:** Top-To-Toe!
- **OLIVIA NEWTON-JOHN:** Gettin' Physical!
- **16's** Fourth Annual Look-A-Like Contest! Win Prizes!

STYX
How To Meet Them: Sure Fire Tips!

Plus: CHRIS ATKINS, LOVERBOY, TOM WOPAT, VAN HALEN, CLARK BRANDON, RALPH MACCHIO, TIMMY GIBBS, *Solid Gold's* TONY & ALEX, JOE CALI, *TAPS* BOYS, ANDREW STEVENS And More!

Color Centerfolds! MATT DILLON AC/DC

June 1982: Scott's first major cover!

Scott Baio

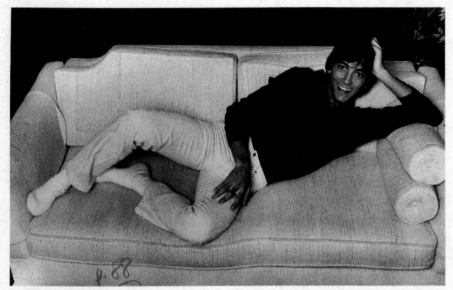

Bed, Baio & beyond: this shot was taken by **16** *in his L.A. home*

however, I realized this is not how I make my living. I never had a problem with things I couldn't do. If I couldn't do it, I'd just say no. Somebody wanted me to dance—I can't do it. Thank you! I never had an ego—I know what I can do and I know what I can't, and I always knew. "

BEING STIGMATIZED

"'Does being a teen idol stigmatize you?' That was the question—are you afraid no one will let you grow? I got that question every year till I was 27 years old. And I said 'Hey, I'm 27. I'm on a series. At what point do you guys let it go—when I'm 50?' I don't have a problem with it, and I never had a problem with it.

"That said, however, as I got older, I went through a phase where I didn't want to be associated with teen magazines because, yes, I was afraid of being pigeonholed into this teen idol thing.

"But in retrospect, I think [being a teen idol is] a great thing because that's a huge audience, and when you're younger you don't think in terms of audience. You think in terms of work. But I think the magazines at the time were incredibly helpful."

WHY HE WAS SO POPULAR

"Why'd I last so long? I gotta tell you, I think this business is 80% luck and 20% talent. Because there are people who are more talented than me. There are people who are more talented than Al Pacino. But they haven't had the lucky break. I was lucky enough to have someone see me in a movie, and it brought me to L.A. I think it's the right place, right time, who's looking out for you. All that stuff. And of course talent helps.

"I also worked very hard, took most of the jobs that were offered to me. I just recently learned to enjoy my time off. Cause I never could. And thankfully I never had any, because if I did, I would have lost my mind. You sort of get into that trap of, 'if I'm not working, I'm nothing.' And my whole life was work. I had no other life.

"Maybe another reason for my popularity was a reflection of the times. It was a lot more innocent back then. It was cool to be a straight, clean kid. If you were straight—I don't mean sexually, I mean in terms of no drugs—you were a good boy,

having a girlfriend. Which was probably what I told you because, in those days, the thing was [for a teen idol] to never have a girlfriend, so that the readers would believe they had a chance with me. And even though it wasn't true, I had no problem with that. If the girls I really *was* dating had a problem with it—and some of them did—I was like, tough shit. It's my job honey, what can I tell you?

"Who did I really date in those days? Lots of girls. They weren't all actresses, but in terms of the ones who were: Kristy McNichol and I met when we did an episode of *The Love Boat* together, and we did have a little thing going. And it was true that Erin Moran—who played Joanie Cunningham on *Happy Days* and J*oanie Loves Chachi*—and I really were going out. Then there was Melissa Gilbert (*Little House on the Prairie*), only even *I* was never sure what that was. We went out a couple of times, that was it. We were never like boyfriend or girlfriend; we never made out or anything. By the time I dated Heather Locklear, Nicolette Sheridan, and Pamela Anderson, I was older already, and there was no point in trying to hide it."

MY SHORT MUSICAL CAREER

"I made two albums. The whole music thing was just an offshoot of my popularity. I never thought I could sing. I was asked to sing on *Happy Days* and I was like, 'no, no! That's something I don't do.' And [the producers] said, 'will you give it a shot?' I sort of liked it. And then somebody approached me to do a record and I enjoyed the record making process. I didn't think I was all that talented. After the two albums,

Scott Baio

Did we miss an opportunity to promote 16? Not often.

and you were the All-American thing, that's what *16* was looking for, the All-American boy. And it was cool to be nice. And I think now, it's almost cool to be a gangbanger—it's a different mentality now.

"There were fewer teen idols in those days. I remember it was me, Shaun Cassidy, Leif, Andy Gibb came a little later, John Schneider. But I was never friendly with the other kids who were acting in those days. There's always a sense of com-petition with anybody in your age group, with anything you do. Whether you're playing ball, or checkers, or it's on the level of, who's got more mail, or who's got more pictures taken, who's on more covers—you do think about that. But then you can't keep up and it's like, who gives a shit? But I never hung out with anybody in the business. I still don't; I think it's real boring. Who gives a shit—[all the talk about] 'I'm doing this, I'm doing this,' who cares?"

Scott Baio

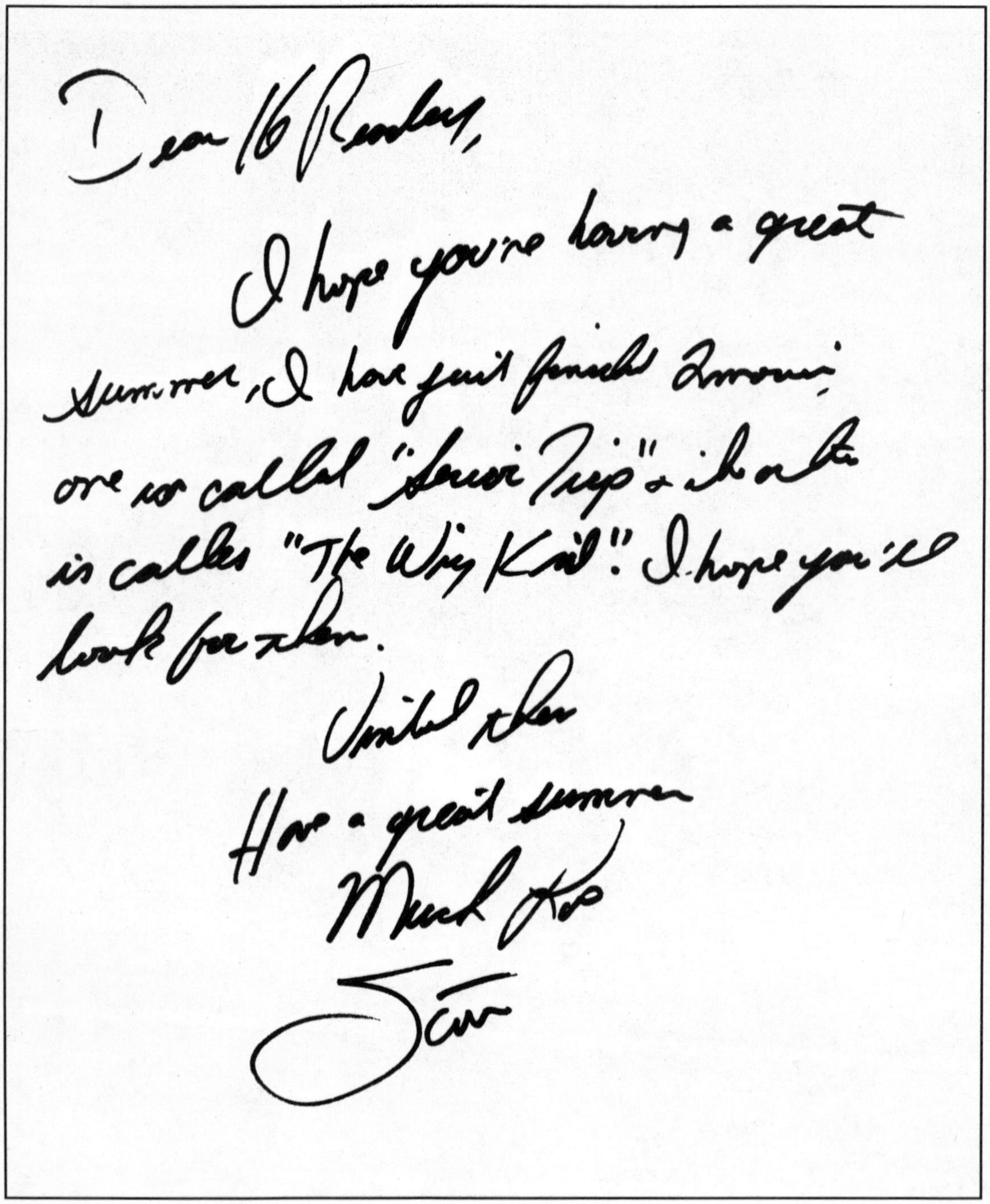

Dear 16 Readers,

I hope you're having a great summer. I have just finished a movie, one is so called "Senior Trip" & it's also is called "The Wig Kid"! I hope you'll look for them.

Untill then
Have a great summer
Much Love
Scott

A BIZARRE LIFE FOR A KID

"As a director, I've had the chance to work with the 'teen idols' of today. I gotta tell ya, these kids talk like CPAs. I don't envy these kids, I think it was easier for me. TV networks weren't so quick to cancel shows back then, so there was more of a security blanket that you had. And to tell you the truth, I don't know if I'd want my kid to be an actor. As great a time as I had, and I wouldn't trade it for anything in the world, there are certain things that I missed, that I'll never be able to do. Going to a prom, being a member of a fraternity, being a guy who's 15–16 years old, you're becoming a man, that's a great time of life, which as a working actor, I missed out on. To be 15 years old and to be isolated on a studio and not have any real contact with the world is sort of a bizarre kind of life for a kid.

Kristy McNichol

Years of *16* Popularity: 1977–1980

Kristy McNichol grew up on screen, and in the pages of *16*. Through her years on the tender TV drama *Family*, and later in movies like *Little Darlings*, Kristy became one of the top girl teen idols of the decade. In the late '70s she was the only female teen idol written about regularly in *16*'s pages. Although the raw talent was there—she won an Emmy Award for her portrayal of *Family*'s Buddy—Kristy also had all the right ingredients for teen idol stardom: she wasn't an intimidating glamour babe (see: Brooke Shields), which meant she wasn't out to "steal" the boy heartthrobs of the day (see: Brooke Shields). She seemed, instead, every inch the "Buddy" next door, the girl with the perfect "Family," someone you could dish with and confide in.

"That is very much who I was," Kristy allows today. "It wasn't a manufactured image. It was cutesy, but honest."

Speaking of honesty, now it can be told: she kind of was, in fact, "stealing" the heart of at least one teen idol peer. "Scott Baio and I were a serious little couple at 13 years old," Kristy admits.

Today, after taking a much-publicized break from acting (she bailed out during the last season of *Empty Nest* due to emotional problems), Kristy is poised to return to the business. She is also a familiar face on the charity tennis circuit and an active fund-raiser for ChildHelp USA because, she says (echoing a very Buddy-like sentiment), "Giving back is really important."

Kristy McNichol On The Spot!

"On the Spot" was a *16* stock story—a way of answering actual letters from fans, while dispensing "the fax" about the star. Just as Kristy was a willing correspondent back then, the now 34-year-old good sport allowed us to put her "On the Spot" once again.

Did you think it was cool to be in *16*?

I thought *16* was cool! I actually bought it every month—I remember so clearly running down to our local market, the Universal Star Market, every month to grab the latest copy and paste David and Donny pinups on the inside of my notebook, in that clear-plastic protective wrapping. I was a big David Cassidy fan and later a Donny Osmond fan. When I was in it myself, it was fun, but I never took it that seriously. It wasn't a big deal. I just wasn't into myself as a kid, or later as a teen.

Did you ever get to meet David or Donny?

I did [meet Donny], and it was a dream come true. In fact, before I met him, I was a bigger David Cassidy fan. But I visited the set of the *Here's Lucy* show, which my mom, Carolyn was acting on, and Donny must have been a guest star or something. He was so great, so cute, a little prince. Later, I met the whole family, when my brother Jimmy and I guested on *The Donny and Marie Show*. Everyone was so wonderful, I wanted the Osmond family to adopt me.

In *16* you were always "the girl next door," not sexy or glamorous. How did you feel about that?

I felt very comfortable with it. That's who I was—kind of a fun, outdoorsy, active, sports-loving, girl-next-door type, that's exactly what I was. The thing about *16,* and this is how it was different from other magazines back then—and certainly now—is that it gave the public the idea who these stars really were. It wasn't fluff, and it wasn't "let's point out the negative." Yes, it was cutesy and it was simple, but it was honest. With *16,* you really got who the person was. I wish we could go back to those days.

What about you in real life— was it reflected accurately in *16*?

If people had misconceptions about me, it wasn't because of *16*. It was just the natural tendency of people to confuse actors with their characters. And the one I played on *Family*, little Buddy, was smart, together, nothing was ever wrong, she had all the answers, she was the best friend everyone wanted.

Kristy On The Spot!

Family's Own Kristy McNichol Tackles Your Letters & Questions!

SCHOOLDAYS?

Dear Kristy,
I'm curious about how you go to school—where do you find the time when you're busy acting on TV?
Ginger McCauley
Stanhope, Ia.

Dear Ginger,
Actually, I go to school right in the middle of filming *Family*. I have a tutor right on the set and I spend at least three hours of every day studying with her. I kind of like that arrangement, though sometimes it's lonely. But whenever there's a guest star on the show who's under 18 she or he gets to "go to school" with me for that week!

WORST HABIT?

Dear Kristy,
I read so much about you all the time and everything seems so perfect. Is it true, or do you have any bad habits?
Tara Kingston
Norman, Ok.

Dear Tara,
Sure, I have bad habits, just like anyone else! Sometimes I get moody, you know, everyone has their moments—but I guess my worst habit would be a toss-up between biting my nails (they're really bad!) or my constant "cleaning up." People don't seem to appreciate my whisking away a glass or something before they were finished with it!

FAVE ACTORS & SINGERS

Dear Kristy,
You are my fave actress, but I was wondering—who are your favorites? Also, who's your favorite singer?
Janie Horowitz
Atlanta, Ga.

Dear Janie,
I have lots of favorites—let's see, I guess my all-time best actors would be Kris Kristofferson, Barbra Streisand and Lucille Ball. As for singers, my favorite group is Chicago. And thanks for the compliment!

DATES?

Dear Kristy,
I'm confused—I read in a magazine that you're not allowed to date until you're 16, but then I saw pictures of you with different guys, like Scott Baio and Jeb Adams. What's the story, do you date or not?
Matt Bryanson
Tallahassee, Fl.

Dear Matt,
I didn't actually start single dating until just recently (I turned 16 on Sept. 11). Those pix that you saw of me were mainly going to parties and my mom was always close behind—so was my brother, Jimmy! I like to go out and have a good time with a lot of people, I'm definitely not serious about any one guy!

VITAL STATISTICS

Dear Kristy,
I've seen a lot of articles about you, but I still don't know how tall you are, how much you weigh and what color your eyes and hair are!
Kim Volare
Columbus, Montana

Dear Kim,
I think I can help you out on that one! I'm 5'2½" tall, weigh about 95 lbs. and I have brown hair and dark brown—almost black, really—eyes!

HOW DID SHE GET STARTED?

Dear Kristy,
I just became a fan of yours so I don't know a lot of stuff. Could you tell me how you first got started in show business?
Laura Sommers
Pittsburgh, Pa.

Dear Laura,
I kind of fell into it in a way. See, my mom did some acting when we were very small and she used to take us with her whenever she got a part. Pretty soon Jimmy and I got interested and mom agreed to let us try. We started off in commercials—I got my first job when I was eight.

PARENTAL RULES

Dear Kristy,
Do you ever have fights with your mom? I do sometimes and I was wondering about you. I mean, you seem to get along so well—is she very strict or not?
Stefanie Schenker
Wausaukee, Wi.

Dear Stefanie,
Let's say we have some disagreements sometimes. I can't really call them fights. And yes, my mom is what I'd call strict—like there are only certain movies she lets me see and she insists I go to bed by 11:30 on weeknights. She also doesn't want me wearing too much make-up. Basically, I listen to her, even though I don't always want to. But she is my mom, after all!

FAVE COLORS

Dear Kristy,
I'm one of your biggest fans and I know a lot of stuff about you, but I don't remember reading if you have any special favorite colors. Do you?
Tommy Goodson
Longville, La.

Dear Tommy,
I sure do! Red, blue and purple are my faves and even though I used to have a crush on Donny Osmond, that is not the reason I love purple. I just do!

SPORTS

Dear Kristy,
I know you're very athletic and are good at all kinds of sports, but what's your favorite?
Lynette Wathens
Oaklawn, Ill.

Dear Lynette,
Let's see—I like baseball (I'm a Dodgers and Steve Garvey fan), basketball and football. Also, skiing, speedboating and my latest fave is skateboarding.

FAN MAIL

Dear Kristy,
I know you get a lot of fan mail—do you ever read any of it? And do you ever answer anyone's letter? Where can I write to you and be sure you'll get it?
Erica Dunsberry
London, Ontario, Canada

Dear Erica,
'Course I read my mail—that is, as much as I can. It's fun and some of it gets answered. But even if I don't get to answer all of them, I want you to know that I appreciate getting 'em! You can write to me at ABC-TV, 4151 Prospect Ave., Hollywood, Cal., 90027 or c/o Don Schwartz Assoc., 8721 W. Sunset Blvd., Los Angeles, Cal., 90069.

Well, that's about all I have room for now—thanks for writing! Love, Kristy.

Kristy on the spot, in November 1978.

Kristy McNichol

Well, in real life, of course, I wasn't all that. Buddy was an exceptional character, I was human! I didn't have all the answers, I wasn't perfect. I'm still not. Living up to the pressure of being perceived as someone more perfect than you actually are was sometimes hard.

I sent you a letter in 1977… did you ever see any of that mail?

I read a lot of it, before it got overwhelming. When that happened, when they started delivering it in sacks, I hired a professional service to deal with it and at least make sure everyone got a response. I tried to read as much as I could; I felt that was important.

You were more famous than a lot of the guys *16* wrote about, but you never got your photo on the cover—did that used to bother you?

No, because being a fan, too, I understood better than anyone that boys were who the girl readers wanted. Besides, I just wasn't that vain.

Do you feel you missed out by not going to regular school?

I actually spent a lot of time in a regular classroom, but for the most part, I was tutored on the set of whatever TV show or movie I was working on. I really did like both situations. I liked mixing with kids, but when I was tutored it was only three hours, as opposed to eight in a classroom, and in those days, that was appealing. I don't think I missed out per se, but my education *was* probably compromised because of it. I've heard other working kids complain about being in a regular classroom because they get teased, but I didn't encounter a lot of that. When I was in *Apple's Way*, some kids taunted me, "There's that little Apple girl." There was one boy who was a bully, but I'd just punch him out after school!

What effect did being a *16* teen idol have on your career?

I didn't encounter negative industry perceptions, so it never hurt me in terms of my career. If anything, it helped, certainly in terms of a fan base. They get to know who it is they're watching—then, they grow up and they grow with you. Once you hook into being a fan, you're always a fan. I know that from being on both sides of it. Someone I idolized way back then, I still want to see today—I jumped at the chance to see Donny Osmond on *The Rosie O'Donnell Show*.

Was there ever anything between you and your *Little Darlings* co-star, Matt Dillon?

We were friends. What I remember most about Matt was the night the entire cast went bowling and he taught me how to smoke cigarettes— "the cool way."

What about the rumor that you were dating Scott Baio?

That one was true. We were a serious little couple when we were 14 years old! We met on a *Love Boat* episode and we really hit it off. The ship really was sailing on the sea, and we'd constantly have to ditch my little brother Tommy so we could kiss behind the curtains of the big ship. I run into Scott all the time now, at coffee shops…he's after all the sexy blondes now; we don't hang out.

Did you feel pressured to keep up a certain image?

No, because the image portrayed really was me. I did at times feel pressure to keep working, though. I felt, "You know what, everyone's looking at me, going, 'Come on, get another role.'" That was hard sometimes.

Did *16* ever write anything about you that embarrassed you?

No, but I didn't like how I looked in some of the pictures. I thought I had a tendency to look goofy.

Do you have any message for your now grown-up fans?

Just this: If I had kids, I'd rather they read *16* over any other celebrity-oriented magazine. *16* captured a real honest, nice truth and made it fun. I wish more publications were like it.

*With Little Darlings's co-star Matt Dillon: they both autographed a **16** Magazine article, to be given away to a lucky reader.*

Andy Gibb

Years of *16* Popularity: 1977–1980

From our pile of dopey hats came this winning chapeau for our Mystery Pic department; would you have guessed the identity of this glamorous guy?

The youngest brother of Barry, Robin, and Maurice Gibb, aka the Bee Gees, Andy was born in 1958, and experienced idolatry first in Australia—where in 1975 he had a hit single called "Words and Music" and got to tour the continent of his birth as opening act for the Bay City Rollers. He became an international heartthrob in the wake of three #1 hits, "I Just Want to Be Your Everything," "(Love Is) Thicker than Water" (which replaced "Stayin' Alive" by his older brothers at the top of the charts), "Shadow Dancing," and five more Top 20s.

Managed by the immensely powerful (and even more immensely publicity-conscious) Stigwood Organization, Andy was put through his paces by his handlers; this regimen included dutiful visits to *16*'s offices. He is remembered by the staff as pleasant and cooperative (e.g., posing for an idiotic Mystery Pic), but kind of dull. His image was that of a full-blown romantic dreamboat, and many stories were fantasies;

he probably came across in *16* as far more interesting and compelling than we knew him to be. He was always "the boy who might like you," when actually his girlfriends were very much in the Victoria Principal (his main squeeze, so to speak) mode.

Drug problems plagued Andy's career, though of course they were not alluded to in *16*: he was fired as the host of the TV show *Solid Gold* for not showing up for tapings and then was tossed out of Broadway's *Joseph and the Amazing Technicolor Dreamcoat* later that same year, 1982. A hitch at the Betty Ford clinic attracted lots of publicity, as did Andy's bankruptcy petition in Florida. He died just days after his 30th birthday, in England; the official cause of death was given as an "inflammatory heart virus," which struck many as a euphemism for something the family was unwilling to reveal, perhaps an OD, as was widely rumored in the entertainment industry at the time.

Andy Gibb Love Is...

A play on the title of his hit single gave us the perfect headline for this story from the September 1978 issue.

In His Hit Song, Andy Told You That "Love Is . . . Thicker Than Water"—But Did You Ever Wonder What Love *Really* Is To That Freckled Fox, Andrew Roy Gibb? Here Are Just *Some* Of The Ways Andy Spells L-O-V-E!

Love Is...

MY FAMILY! That's a pretty basic one, I guess, but we're lots closer than most families, I think. Even though there are so many of us (or maybe *because* of that) we have really special feelings for each other. I know that not only my brothers—but my sisters and parents, too—helped me a lot in getting my career together. Without their encouragement and love, don't know where I'd be! I really *enjoy* being in the company of my family—guess that's why I'll always live as close to them as possible! They're a nice, warm feeling—like love!

MUSIC! It's such a part of me—writing it, playing it, singing it and just listening to it, I can't ever seem to get enough of it. Maybe it's something I was born with—my parents were professional music people (my dad played with a big band and my mom sang in one) and of course my brothers started out quite young, so it was always all around me. But no matter if I succeed or fail as a musician, I'll always love it!

DANCING! I have to admit, that's a pretty recent love. I was always kinda shy on the dance floor and so didn't do much of it—but now that I've started, you can't tear me away from the disco. It's really part of loving music, I suppose, and letting it carry my body away, without worrying about how I look to other people as I whirl around. It's fun—yeah, just like love!

MIAMI BEACH! That's where I'm living right now, in a waterfront home in Miami Shores and boy, is it super! You know, I've lived in a lot of places, so I can compare it to living in England, the Isle of Man, Australia, Ibiza, and California, too. But Miami has perfect weather, it's nice and quiet—away from all the hustle-bustle phoniness of Hollywood and it's got the water right there! If I could pick a place I really love to live, it would be Miami—and here I am!

TAKING RISKS! Now this one may seem strange, but if you really want to know me—and know what love really *is* to me—you can't skip by this part of my personality. Yep, I'll admit it, I love taking risks, especially dangerous ones. There's nothing quite like the feeling of parachuting behind a speedboat, or racing motorcycles (once I fractured my ankle doing this), skin diving, hang gliding or flying planes. I've gotten into nearly all of these sports on a dare—but I can't say I've ever regretted doing any of them!

AUSTRALIA! Now I know I just said I love Miami Beach, but I *do* get sentimental about Australia sometimes, too—and what's love if not a sweet sentiment? You see, I was brought up there and I used to love going to the outback, it's so outrageous. You can ride on a highway from Sydney to Adelaide (two big cities) and kangaroos will jump right in front of your car! It's a good way of life out there, especially living in the countryside—it's magnificent.

GIRLS! Well, it would be hard to leave this one out, right? You know I've gotten a kind of reputation lately, for being a bit of a run around—but believe me, it's not true. I *do* love girls—especially sincere, considerate ones—but I'd rather spend my time with *one* special lady than run around with many different ones. Sure, I'm attracted to all sorts of ladies, I can't say I have one type—and it takes me a while to get to know people—but I'll know *my* girl when I find her! Again, it's like love—you know when it's real.

CURLING UP WITH A GOOD BOOK—and a cup of tea! Is that hard to imagine? Well, it's true. My idea of paradise—after a day on the water—is going home by myself and settling in for the night with a good novel and a cup of tea at my side. It's so relaxing—that's right, like love!

BEING ROMANTIC! Do you know what I mean? Being romantic is enjoying the beauty of the simple, natural things in life, sending roses to a girl, going out to a quiet, candlelit dinner in an out-of-the-way restaurant. I like to talk—and to listen. I like to remember special dates and do something special to commemorate them. Maybe it's not very "macho" or whatever you want to call it, but I'm an admitted romantic!

DOGS! Yes, I really do love the little pups—and the big ones, too. I've always grown up with them and I know what special care and attention they need—that's why I don't have one right now. But I will some day—my favorite breed is the Staffordshire bull terrier.

BEING & FEELING HEALTHY! There's no feeling like it! That's why I don't smoke or drink and don't like to stay up late partying too much—it wears me out! Instead, I like to get "worn out" in other ways—like swimming, diving, and skiing. I like the feeling of the ocean breeze in my hair and the sun beating down on me. It's so refreshing—like being in love!

YOU! Yes, I've saved the best for last. What can I tell you about the incomparable feeling of knowing *you* are in my corner, rooting for me? It's a feeling of love that can't be matched and I wish I could run up 'n hug you real tight! And maybe someday I will—until we meet, though, remember, I *am* thinking of you and it's *your* love that keeps me happy and fulfilled.

John Schneider

Years of *16* Popularity: 1979–1983

An authentic TV icon, lanky, blond John Schneider had an "aw, shucks" appeal, transmitted chiefly through his role as rambunctious country boy Bo Duke on CBS's hillbilly-hit series, *The Dukes of Hazzard*. Because John was younger and cuter than his co-star Tom Wopat, *16*'s readers chose him as the teen idol of the show. John remembers the entire era with great fondness.

Although John insists that *16* presented him as exactly who he was, during all those years of coverage there was one major misconception: one detail neither the fans nor the magazine ever knew. John Schneider was actually six years *younger* than he said he was.

"They held auditions for *The Dukes of Hazzard* down in Atlanta," John explains, "and they were looking for authentic country folks between 24 and 30 years old. And there I was—18 and from New York. I really wanted that part. So my agent simply told them I was 24, that I was born in 1954, instead of 1960. After I got the role, I stuck with that story for a long time. It didn't bother me at the time—after all, when you're 18, you want to be older. And if I hadn't done that, I wouldn't have gotten the job."

In spite of that one fib, the combination of John's earnest, Dudley Do-right persona and strapping country boy sex appeal was real. Now 37, John is a born-again Christian, and a leading force in the Children's Miracle Network, along with Marie Osmond. He is still active on the showbiz scene, and turns up in the occasional TV movie (his most recent was the Family Channel's *Night of the Twisters*). He will participate in a *Dukes of Hazzard* TV reunion movie. But his main business these days is FaithWorks, a company that produces and distributes family-fare videos. He lives in San Antonio with his second wife, Elly, and their three children. It was from his Texas office that he spoke with us.

John Schneider Looks Back

"*Dukes of Hazzard* was my big break, but I'd been acting since I was 8 years old, mainly in children's theater. So when *Dukes* happened, it was the first time any more people than could fit into one room had ever seen me do anything. So with that came tremendous…I don't want to call it notoriety and I don't want to call it intrusion—but it's somewhere in between. Some of that, of course, was because of *16 Magazine*.

"I was aware of *16* because I'd been a *Partridge Family* fan. And I liked bubblegum music. The Archies' 'Sugar, Sugar' was the first 45 I ever bought—for 49 cents at Caldor. So I knew about that whole scene. I knew about Leif Garrett—I was very much into music, as was he at that point. I was also aware of *16* because there were people around me who always had it. And even though I was only 18 at the time, I knew the value of being in the program—which sounds like AA—but what I mean is, I knew the value of having your name and your likeness out there in the magazines. So when *The Dukes* happened, I really looked forward to it. Which isn't to say that its success didn't take me by surprise, because it did. And the sheer volume of letters that came in through *16* of course really surprised me."

We caught up with big John backstage on the Dukes *set…*

John Schneider

GETTING COCKY

"I understood right away that I was suddenly thrust into being a role model, and that was okay with me. I knew I had to take that seriously and not abuse it. If you are given a position where people are going to look up to you, you need to fill it. And if you say you're going to do something, you need to do it.

"Which isn't to say that there weren't times when all the hype and hoopla didn't go to my head. When you work as an actor, there are people around you combing your hair, doing your makeup, providing your wardrobe—and bringing you fan mail. Was I obnoxious in those days? Certainly I never thought of it that way. But I look back at interviews I did in those days and I do come off as kind of cocky. I thought I was being self-assured, but when I reread them, it looked pretty darn cocky. I look back now and just go, 'Ouch.'

"Of course, I'm looking back from the perspective of someone who's had a fairly good-sized dose of reality, going straight from *The Dukes* to…where was my next job coming from? So none of the pampering and adulation goes to my head anymore. 'Cause if I'm by the coffee machine, I'll get everyone else coffee too."

FACTUAL FAVES

"The fans didn't confuse me with Bo Duke because of the magazine. *16* reflected who John Schneider was, down to the most minute details. Everything you printed was absolutely true. We did not fabricate anything. I mean, it felt weird reading about 'John's Favorite Foods'—who cares? But [the fans] did. I was sent cookies through the mail because I think I said in one article that I loved chocolate chip cookies. Well, I was inundated with chocolate chip cookies. And I did love them.

"As for the other stuff that was written about me, yes, I really was messy in those days, and I still bite my nails. Yes, I loved ice cream, gum, and being recognized. Of course, that last one sounds a little cocky now, but it was true and still is.

"Many articles dealt with what kind of girls I liked, and again, *16* was accurate in saying I went for optimistic, outgoing types who cared about their appearance and other people. And the best kind of date really was a quiet evening at home, candlelight dinner—no movies or rock concerts. I liked to talk to people, have real conversations; I still do.

"Then there were the articles covering my relationship with Melinda Naud. They were all true. We all make mistakes. It was an interesting, interesting time in my life. She was my first girlfriend in L.A. and the relationship lasted a whole lot longer than it should have.

"And when I went out with Marie Osmond, *16* didn't sensationalize it, which was nice. You wrote that I was more of an escort than a date, and that was true. Marie and I met at the People's Choice Awards and we became friends. We've maintained a friendship all these years because of the Children's Miracle Network.

"Not everything *16* printed about me was positive. I was a workaholic. I said that back then, and it was true. In those days, I thought it was the most important thing, but now I realize the error of that. I know now that God didn't put us here to do great work. He put us here to raise great children, be a good husband, be a good wife. I'm supposed to provide for my family and change the world I live in by providing quality, and I do that through my company, FaithWorks."

THE NEW DUKES

"Another thing that I'll always remember is *16* being there accurately for us during the whole big mess when Tom and I quit and they hired two actors to take our place. The studio tried to paint us as greedy, and just wanting more money, but *16* stood behind us. You printed that we left

John Schneider & You...

A Personal Rap & Handwritten Note!

*I*f you know anything about big beautiful "Bo Duke"— that's John Schneider, of course—you know that he's one of the busiest people in all of show business. But one thing John is never too busy for is sayin' "hi" and letting you share in every part of his life! 16 caught up with John backstage at the March Of Dimes telethon in Atlantic City, New Jersey—and sat him down for a private rap.

16'S readers know you've been incredibly busy, John—can you fill everyone in on what you've been up to?

John: Be glad to! The main thing of course is *The Dukes Of Hazzard*. I've been working on that since the actor's strike ended last year and we don't get a break until the end of June '81!

16: Do you still enjoy playing "Bo Duke?"

John: You know it! I think *The Dukes* is great entertainment and it's the kind of show where no one ever gets hurt and everyone's happy in the end.

16: Is it important to you that there's no violence in *The Dukes Of Hazzard*?

John: Yes, it is. Being in the public eye is a great responsibility and I treat it with care. I know that lots of kids copy "Bo" and "Luke" and that's why it's important that the show be wholesome, honest and that people in it have respect for one another. Anyway, I think entertainment should be just that—*entertaining!* I don't go for those heavy, depressing all-too realistic dramas.

16: What kind of entertainment do you like?

John: I love those old-fashioned, romantic love stories that the movies used to be full of. The best picture I've seen recently is *Altered States*—despite what you see in those television ads, it's really a beautiful love story.

16: Speaking of love stories, will you be starring in any movies soon?

John: I've got lots of plans for feature films up my sleeve, but none that I can talk about right now! Soon as I *can* tell you, though, I *will!*

16: How about TV specials—will you have another one?

John: For sure! I was real happy about the first one, *Back Home* and from what other people have told me, it was fairly popular. Right now, in fact, I'm starting to write the script for my second special.

16: You're involved in the writing, too?

John: I'm involved in every part of it—I want it to be *really* special!

16: What's happening with your album?

John: It's happening! I had hoped it would be out the first week of this month, but it looks like it'll take an extra few weeks of what's called "sweetening" to get it just right.

16: Can you tell us what to expect?

John: I can tell you *not* to expect a country album—or a straight rock LP, either. It's kind of a middle-of-the road record that I hope will have something for everyone on it.

16: Are there any original tunes on it?

John: To be honest, I've only written four songs in my life—and while I thought I'd have at least two of them on the album, I've since thought better of the idea.

16: Will you do a concert tour to promote the album?

John: I'll introduce people to it in every way I can. Expect to see me at record store autograph parties, singing on talk shows and hopefully, a concert tour, too. I certainly don't know when, though!

16: Between *The Dukes*, movie plans, television specials and record albums—how do you have time for a private life?

John: I don't really—but that's okay. All I've ever wanted was a show business career and I don't mind working every second towards that. And if I can help bring joy to even one person, I'm happy.

To all of my friends who write, watch, and read 16. Thank you for your support. I couldn't do it without you. Be good, stay happy + healthy, your friend always

John Schneider

A *Dukes* Giveaway! Turn To Page 30!

9

John rapped and penned a note in the June 1981 issue.

John Schneider

because of creativity issues, which was true, but it was more than that. There were bookkeeping issues. It was a legal point, not a greed point. I'm not at liberty, nor will I ever be, to discuss exactly what happened—that's part of our agreement. But it was not because we wanted more money. And *16* stood by Tom and me and treated us with the utmost respect."

"BEING A *16* TEEN IDOL HELPED ME SAVE A LIFE"

"Looking back, the best part of being a *16 Magazine* teen idol was how it put me in the position of being able to help people. I did an interview with *16* and I talked about how when I was kid, I was fat, and then I lost 50 pounds. In it, I said that if I could do it, anyone could do it. And I got letters from people who were motivated to lose weight because of that.

"But the biggest thing that came out of the magazine for me was being able to help save a life. There was a young lady who was going through a particularly rough time, and was contemplating suicide. She was a fan of mine through *The Dukes*, and she got an address for my fan club in *16 Magazine*. She wrote to me about what was happening to her. And my mother, who was running the fan club, wrote her a very encouraging letter. And that helped her turn a corner. I still keep in touch with this woman, and she attributes having lived through that summer to having read about me in *16*, and getting the letter back from my mother.

"So if you talk to people who say *16 Magazine* is fluff, I can say firsthand that *16* saved at least one life. And if that happened once, I know there are many people out there— maybe they got a letter from Davy Jones or someone—who were also helped by finding a way to reach out to whoever they idolized. I've seen it work."

"I WAS THE DUMB BLOND FOR A WHILE"

"Was there a downside to being in *16*? Well, sometimes there was a little too much red in the 4-color separations!

"Of course, the more exposure you get in a magazine that the industry regards as fluff could hurt you. It could

...and backstage at Busch Gardens, even as he caught a few winks.

make you the dumb blond, and I was the dumb blond for a while. But you know, that's okay, that's really their problem. It's not mine. Because the good overrides the bad. My fans have followed me, especially people that have gotten nostalgic. When the Nashville Network aired *Dukes* reruns in 1996, it did incredible numbers. And the TV movie I did, *Night of the Twisters,* gave the Family Channel its highest ratings ever. I'm sure that when parents watched that with their kids, some of the moms might've said, 'Son, your mom had that guy's poster on her wall.'"

THE END OF THE INNOCENCE

"I wouldn't go so far as to say it was a more innocent time, but it had the appearance of a more innocent time. As angelic and All-American as I may have looked in those days, I knew that being a celebrity might bring the possibility of being chased by women and that was something I wanted. It was another value of being in the magazine that I understood. So whether it was really more innocent deep down—probably not. But it was certainly more polite and more responsible. We seem to have lost that—politeness and responsibility.

"I'm 37 and have a couple of kids now. People like me who look back on the days of *The Dukes of Hazzard* and *16 Magazine* and John and Tom and Cathy and all that stuff and say, 'I miss those times. I'd like to taste, feel, and smell them again'—I'm one of those people. And hopefully, with my company, that's exactly what I'm providing now."

MATT DILLON

Years of *16* Popularity: 1979–1983

Tom Cruise did it; Kurt Russell did it; John Travolta did it in spades: so why hasn't Matt Dillon joined the ranks of million-dollar movie superstars? He was the most likely suspect. Matt had drop-dead hauntingly gorgeous looks, a depth of talent couched in a well of mystery, and, more than anything, the personal magnetism that spells *star*. He always had it. Take it from us—we were there.

Among his "brat-pack" colleagues, Matt was the one all eyes turned to when he entered a room—even when that room held the young, handsome, and buff-bodied Patrick Swayze, Rob Lowe, and even Tom Cruise. To be around him was to be affected by him. Tales of Matt snuck into every conversation; there wasn't a costar or colleague who didn't feel impelled to imitate Matt's walk, his New Yawk talk, his cooler-than-thou attitude. Matt just always had "it," the indefinable *x*-factor that makes a star. Yet he never really became one—not in the mass-market way many of his peers did. Instead of vaulting from teen angst flicks like *The Outsiders* into big-bucks blockbusters, Matt has carved a career out of small, independent, and quirky films.

Don't think for a moment that it hasn't been about choice. *Independent* and *quirky* are two words that best describe the actor himself. And the more people pressuring him to go with the flow, the less likely he'd ever be to do so.

Matt Dillon, discovered in a junior high school hallway, was always acting: acting tough, acting cool, acting anything but the middle-class, Irish Catholic, suburban kid he really was. At 15 he made his first movie, *Over the Edge*, and that's when *16* discovered him. He first appeared in the July 1979 issue, not in a feature story, but in a small photo accompanied

If Matt wasn't 16's most enthusiastic teen idol, he still looked straight into the camera: he was always cool.

by an item. That Matt was neither rocker nor TV star worked against him in the pages of *16*; up until that time (this is pre-VCR, after all) few exclusive-to-the-movies stars were covered extensively. It wasn't really worth our while; "out of sight, out of mind" was a teen magazine truism, and with a film actor, who knew when or if he'd ever be back in fans' faces again?

But Matt was a big draw from the get-go. Overwhelming response to that one small item came in, and editors had no choice but to follow up. Good move: it turned out that the bewitching newcomer indeed had more movies lined up, and just the kind teens were inclined to see. They included

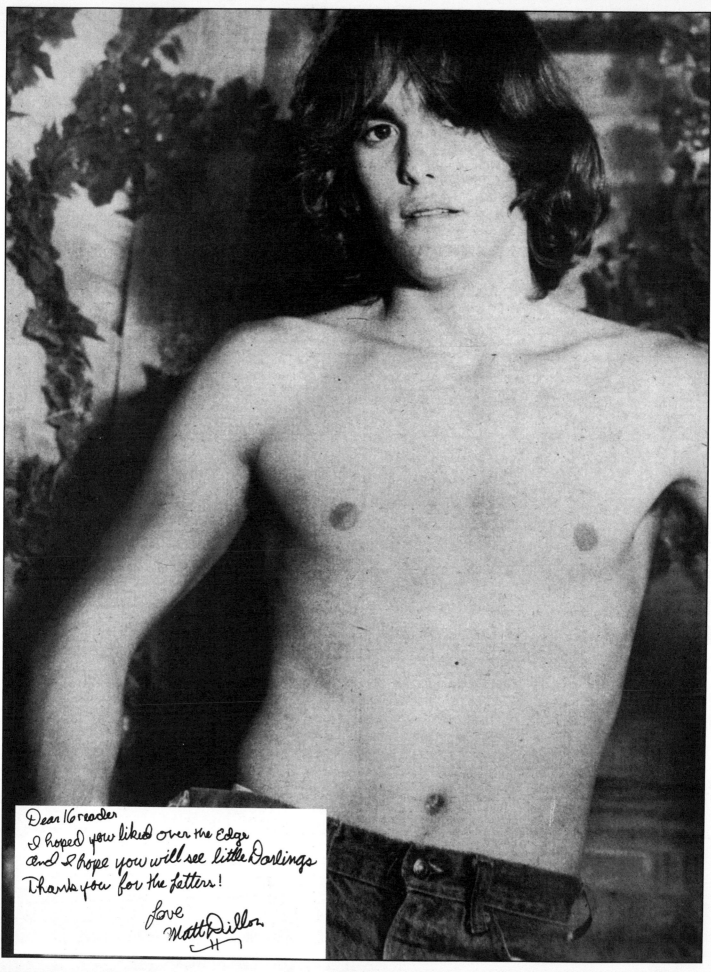

Dear 16 reader
I hoped you liked Over the Edge
and I hope you will see little Darlings
Thank you for the Letters!
Love
Matt Dillon

*He'd only done one movie, Over the Edge, but already warranted a 2-page shirtless spread:
this is from the November 1979 issue. And yes, he really did write the love note.*

♥Darlin'♥ Matt Dillon!

What made you stop and stare at the gorgeous new face in the July issue of **16**? Was it Matt's sexy, soulful eyes or his oh-so-touchable brown hair? One thing for sure—you fell for this 15 year-old hot number the instant you saw him, and the flood of letters to **16**'s Nancy La Reine is proof! "Tell me more about Matt Dillon!" you wrote—and your mag-with-all-the-answers is pleased to oblige!

As you may know by now, Matt has one movie out already called *Over The Edge* and he's finished another with Kristy McNichol and Tatum O'Neal called *Little Darlings*—Matt plays Kristy's summer camp love "Randy" and there are gonna be fireworks when their explosive romance hits the screen in 1980! Meanwhile, Matt's busy working on the movie *My Bodyguard*, and he plans to take acting classes soon—he's very serious about his career! He loves sinking his pearly whites into juicy dramatic parts, and he goes to the movies all the time—*Rocky*, and *The Lords Of Flatbush* are two of his favorites! As for TV, Matt digs watching old movies and *Saturday Night Live*—he doesn't really remember the series *Gunsmoke* very well, though he's always being reminded about that show since "Matt Dillon" was the sheriff's name on it! People ask him where his badge is and don't quite believe him when he tells them his name—he actually was born Matthew Dillon but he's been called Matt all his life! The teasing doesn't bother him, though—easy-going Matt is used to nicknames and currently has two! He answers to "Flick" (that's from being a movie star) and "Bounce"—that's from the lively way he walks! Active Matt isn't the type to sit still for long—when he's not acting or in school he loves going to parties where rock music is playing (he digs The Who, Eric Clapton, and Jethro Tull) and keeps his 5'9", 145 lb. frame in shape with karate, swimming, and football. Matt takes the train from home town New Rochelle, New York to Manhattan to take in concerts 'n movies, see *Over The Edge* buddy Vinnie Spano, and of course take girls out for dates—he can't wait till February 18 when he'll turn 16 and be able to drive! Are you a friendly, fun-loving girl who loves rock music, lively households (he's got two cats and a dog at home besides a sister and four brothers!), and knows how to cook? Then you just might be the girl Matt wants beside him in the sportscar he hopes to get—he definitely would date a fan! He'd love to take you out for pizza or cheesecake and he'd love it if you offered to make him dinner—Matt's kitchen specialty is toast!

Matt gets a terrific kick out of reading your letters and hopes you'll keep sending them ℅ Frank Tobin, Paramount Pictures, 1 Gulf & Western Plaza, New York, N.Y. 10023—he promises to answer as many as he can!

My Bodyguard and *Little Darlings* with teen princess Kristy McNichol. Matt was going to be around for a while.

How did "I dare you to knock the chip off my shoulder" Matt feel about being in the gushy pages of *16*? Not as hostile as might be imagined. He was rather ambivalent about it all, leaning more toward coactive than contemptuous. Matt's manager, Vic Ramos, the man who discovered him, was also ambivalent. But Paramount, the movie company behind *Little Darlings*, urged cooperation to help the movie.

And so Matt Dillon, at ages 15 to 18, pretty much played the game, albeit his way. The rebel 'tude was always there— we never felt he was a friend—but the dude never played rude. In fact, he was actually a pleasure to work with. And work with him we did. We covered Matt on movie sets, traipsing all the way to Tulsa, Oklahoma, for *The Outsiders*. Closer to home, we photographed him in our offices, even took him to Central Park for a shoot. Heads turned everywhere we went, and they weren't lookin' at us.

Over the years, we got to know him ever so slightly better. If Matt has a rep for being a partier, guess what, he always was. There were girls; there was music; there was a whole lot of shakin' goin' on. Two A.M. in the lobby of the Excelsior Hotel in Tulsa: there's a huge indoor fountain and it's just too tempting. Matt and his cohorts (Tom Cruise, Emilio Estevez, Rob Lowe—get the picture??) shove each other in for a dunking. They're loud, they're raucous, they're about to be booted from the hotel. Editor Randi Reisfeld happens to come down to the lobby. Sopping wet, Matt stops dead in his tracks, looks her straight in the eye, and tosses a dare her way: "You came for a story; you got one now."

We printed it, too, only distilled into *16* language, which made it seem more like a bunch of mischievous but lovable boys just fooling around. We left out anything more ominous that might have been fueling that romp in the night.

Eventually, Matt's bent for offbeat projects took him out of the pages of *16*. While readers could be counted to gobble up his S. E. Hinton trilogy (in addition to *The Outsiders*, he starred in *Tex* and *Rumble Fish*) not many would follow him into *Drugstore Cowboy*.

And so Matt Dillon did make the leap from teen idol to adult actor. He did it, pardon the cliché, his way, and we have every expectation he'll continue to do just that.

JOHN TRAVOLTA

Years of *16* Popularity: 1976–1978

John Travolta tops the (short) list of former '70s teen idols who made a Hall of Fame leap into the majors. There were peaks and valleys in his career, to be sure, but today he is an international movie star, revered as much for his talent (two Oscar nominations for Best Actor) as for his box office clout. Movie stars don't come much bigger. Or with fatter paychecks. Since *Pulp Fiction, Get Shorty,* and *Michael,* J.T.'s reported salary for one among several upcoming movies is in the $20 million range, the ballpark where Schwarzenegger plays. Welcome back, indeed.

We, of course, remember Johnny Travolta when he played in the minor leagues. His banner year as a *16* pinup was 1976. But it wasn't his shiny white suit and disco moves in *Saturday Night Fever* that spiked fevers among our readers—it was his tight jeans, electric blue eyes, and soft shaggy hair. It was always Barbarino, the sweetest sweathog to ever fumble his way into American living rooms. A grammatically challenged TV "tough," *Welcome Back, Kotter*'s Vinnie Barbarino exuded a puppyish sex appeal coupled with a sweet vulnerability. How could you not love him? America's teenage girls went (sweat)hog-wild.

And he sang, too. In 1976, John had yet to don his dancing shoes, but he did release a pop album, remembered (?) best for the single, "Let Her In," which actually made the charts.

Fascinating but true: Johnny, we knew ye…pretty darn well, as it turns out. John Travolta, in his teen idol days, cooperated fully with *16 Magazine*. No diva he. At 22 years old, he posed for the pix, answered each 'n' every no-matter-how-dumb question, held up the campy Dreamsville prizes, actually penned the handwritten letters. And he did it all good-naturedly and with a candor that in retrospect is truly

amazing. And it just "shows to go ya'" he hasn't really changed very much.

Today, John Travolta is known for his opulent lifestyle. Two decades ago, Johnny Travolta took *16*'s readers into his gleaming new high-rise apartment in Beverly Hills. He was single, the bedroom was a mess, but it was the most opulently furnished bachelor pad we'd ever seen, with white carpet, antique chairs and tables, a rolltop desk, and (lest we forget it was the '70s) hanging Tiffany lamps.

He has a fleet of 'em now, but even back then he owned his own airplane. "I just got my pilot's license," John explained to the readers, "and I bought a two-seat Ercoupe." Further, he even explained the correlation between his two passions. "My older sister Ellen was in showbiz and I'd always gone to the airport to see her off, so in my mind, there was always a connection between acting and flying. Kids' minds work in funny ways," he added.

Most astonishingly perhaps, John talked openly about Scientology. In the May 1976 issue of *16*, in response to the question, "What are your other interests [besides acting]?" he said, "I'm deeply into Scientology." Perhaps naïvely, we asked him to expand on that. "First of all, it's not really a religion or anything like that," he answered. "It's more of a way of life. It's knowing how to know…it's a science of the mind to help you understand your own mind as well as the minds of others. It's really helped me to be a happier person."

At the time, Scientology had not become as controversial as it would later on; *16*'s editors simply thought John's personal beliefs sent a positive message out there. That the editors really understood what he was talking about—or expected readers to—is unlikely. We quickly beat a path to familiar ground with the follow-up question, "Are you into any special kind of music?"

Personal beliefs and opulence may not have phased us; the girlfriend issue was something else again. All through his TV time at the top, John was, according to *16*, pretty much available. "I don't have a steady girlfriend," he was quoted as saying time and again. That simply wasn't true. For John did have someone very special in his life, and she wasn't just a girlfriend. She was a woman two decades his senior, and he was passionately in love with her. John and actress Diana Hyland were a very committed pair, and her untimely death, at the age of 41, by all accounts devastated him.

Later in the decade and into the early '80s, John Travolta would become ubiquitous. *Kotter* ran until 1979; by then

John Travolta
Sweathog-To-Superstar!

John Caught Your Eye On Kotter, *Gave You* Saturday Night Fever, *Then Drove You* Grease-*Crazy During Those Hot "Summer Nights"—And He's Making* More *Movies Just For* You!

What do *you* want for Christmas? How about John Travolta in a great new flick! Gorgeous John will be coming your way in *Moment By Moment*, a beautiful love story about a young delivery boy and a lonely lady (played by Lily Tomlin)—what a dreamy present! After that, the next Travolta-flick will be *American Gigolo*—John will play a very unselfish fella who loves women so much that his only care in life is making his girlfriends happy, even if he gets hurt doing it! And looking to the future, John is set to star in *Godfather III*—he'll play Al ("Michael Corleone") Pacino's son all grown up and ready to head the powerful clan! John's going to star in two more pictures after these, and one just might be *Prince of the City*, a movie about a crusading New York City detective. The other has no title yet, but whatever it is, it'll be fantastic with John as the star!

This 24-year-old, blue-eyed fox has come a long way from local amateur theater in Englewood, New Jersey (his home town) and second-banana parts on Broadway—John was "Doody" in the stage version of *Grease*—and he never dreamed he'd be playing "Danny Zuko" in the movies a few years later! He's thrilled that two of his closest friends from those Broadway days are hitting it big in Hollywood—Jeff

"Kenickie" Conaway and old flame Marilu Henner are both in the new hit TV series *Taxi!* John's own series is back, natch—*Kotter's* kid "Barbarino" hasn't graduated, and this season he's going to be driving nurses, doctors and patients crazy—he's got a part time job as a hospital orderly!

Busy John hasn't had much time to himself lately, but he tries to save some of those precious off-camera hours for his family. He flies back East to see his parents, brothers, and sisters whenever he can—and having two private airplanes makes the trip a lot easier! John owns a DC-3 jet and brand new Rockwell Commander 114—he loves to fly them for business and pleasure! Closer to home (a new house in Studio City, Cal.), John drives from set to set in his shiny new Mercedes 450 SL, but he keeps his '55 T-bird in top shape for special occasions—it's the perfect car for *Grease's* star!

Right now, John's career comes first, but this romantic hunk would love to get married and have a family some day so meeting girls is still priority business! No matter how busy John is, he always tries to read as many of *your* letters as he can—it makes him happy to know you care! Write to him c/o CMC, 8899 Beverly Blvd., Suite 906, Los Angeles, Ca. 90048.

You Can Win John Travolta's Grease Scrapbook!

If you loved this fab fifties flick and have seen it more times than you can count, if you've memorized the words to every song on the fantastic soundtrack LP, and if you can't stop thinking about John and the rest of the terrific cast, then you've got *Grease*mania, and we've got a super-special surprise for *you!*

John picked out a beautiful bunch of 8x10 glossy pix of some of his best scenes in the movie, and **16** has preserved 'em forever in **two** gorgeous scrapbooks! There are great close-up shots of John as "Danny Zuko", and

action-packed pix of him singing with his "T-Bird" pals, hand-jivin' at the dance contest, and makin' time with his ever-lovin' "Sandy"—lovely Olivia Newton-John! There are 10 fantastic pix in each scrapbook—and every one will bring those great *Grease* moments to life for **two** very lucky fans. Wouldn't *you* love to win this terrific gift from John? All you have to do is print your name and address clearly on the coupon and mail it to **16**—the winners will be selected at random. Be sure to check the March issue of **16** to see if you've won!

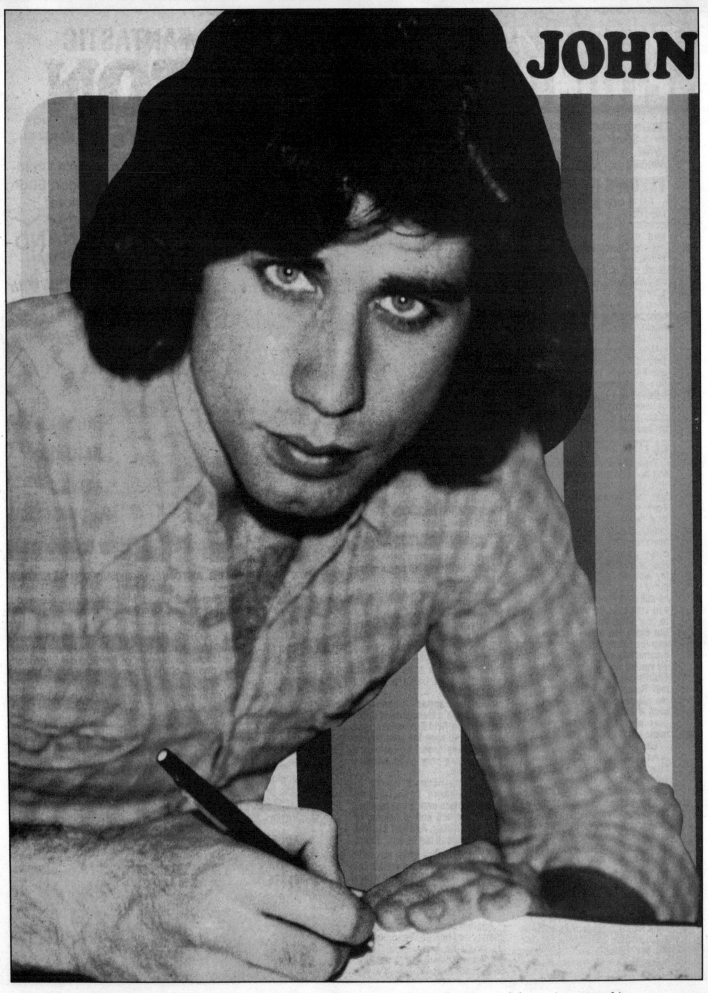

JOHN

In the August 1976 issue, John wrote to 16's readers: no scam; the handwriting and the sentiments are his.

"VINNIE BARBARINO" TRAVOLTA
Writes You A PERSONAL Letter!

Isn't it great to get personal letters?—especially when they're filled with warm and wonderful wishes from someone you really dig! Well, tall 'n temptin' TV star John Travolta knows how super it is to get those kinds of letters—he gets them every day from *you*! And now, through **16**, John wants to send you his very own personal message—in his very own handwriting! So have a gander at John's note—naturally, it came straight from his heart!

Dear 16 Readers,

I've wanted to drop you a line for sometime now and I'm glad to finally have the chance. I can't believe the great letters you've been sending these past few months... It's so nice to know there's someone out there who cares!

I've been keeping quite busy between the show and moving into a new apartment, and as soon as I have the place together you'll hear about it in "16." In the meantime keep in touch because I love to hear from you!

Love,
John.

P.S. If you'd like to write back to John, his address is ABC-TV, 4151 Prospect Avenue, Los Angeles, Cal. 90027.

"My Favorite Things" By JOHN TRAVOLTA

Hi, I'm John Travolta—better known as 'Vinnie Barbarino', I guess! I'm really glad that **16** gave me this chance to say 'hi' to everyone and to thank you all for the terrific letters you've been sending me. I read them all, you know—and since I get so many asking what I'm really like, I thought I'd clue you in by showing you some of the things I like best! What better way to get to know someone than by the things he digs the most, right? Well, I thought so, anyway. So I gathered together some of my very favorite things—and here they are!

I guess you know by now that I'm an airplane-freak. I'm really nuts over just about anything that flies! So when I got this American Airlines' cardboard cutout—it's over three feet long!—I hung it up right in my dining room, so I could see it every day. It's originally from Paramount Studios—it was used as a prop in one of their old movies.

More books! See, I told you I loved reading—but these books are about something entirely different. I'm into Scientology. It means a lot to me and that's why I picked out these two books—'Diametrics 551' and 'Scientology, A New Slant On Life'—as two of my favorite things.

Here's something you'd never suspect of 'Barbarino'—I'm a bookworm! Yup, whenever I have time, I love to read—in fact, I've got shelves of books all over my apartment! Here's one of my all-time favorites—it's simply called *Aviation* and it's got just about all there is to know about my number-one hobby.

Here's something a fan sent me—'John's Place' is a cute little plaque that adorns my kitchen wall. I think it's super!

John Travolta

J.T. was already a movie star and a singing star. *Saturday Night Fever* earned him superstardom and an Oscar nomination; *Grease* (1978) electrified audiences and earned him, via his take of the soundtrack, enormous royalties.

By then he was already out of our orbit and no longer wanted to be a teen idol. But it didn't really matter; just as he'd moved on, so had *16*'s readers. Still, a place in the hearts of every Barbarino fan is reserved for John Travolta. Former *16* readers are no doubt among those who flock to his movies now and help pay that humongo salary. Did we know he'd be such a huge star twenty years later? We can't claim that much prescience, but surely some of the qualities that endeared him to teenagers back then account for his overwhelming appeal now.

> **C'mon Over To John Travolta's Place And Find Out What Makes Him Tick By Sharing Some Of His Very Favorite Things!**

If I gave you a million guesses, you'd *never* guess who drew this incredible painting of me—so I won't keep you in suspense! It was done by 'Horshak' himself—**Ron Palillo!** All the *'Kotter'* cast are great friends and Ron's a professional artist! He drew up one of these for each member of the cast—isn't it dynomite?!

Here's another gift from a cast member—a framed black & white plaque that say 'John Travolta as Barbarino'—that's in case I forget who I am! Only kidding, it's sure a great way of remembering my first big part. It was done by Helaine Lembeck, who plays 'Judy' on *Welcome Back, Kotter.*

As you can see, I like putting my favorite things on the wall! These are some framed mementos that are very special to me—first big interviews in magazines like People. I'm real proud of these. And next to them is my one and only plant. I'm a plant person, but I have trouble keeping them alive! This one is my pride and joy—the only one that ever lived! It's hanging in my bedroom, so I can talk to it before I fall asleep!

Well, that's about it for now. I hope you liked some of my things and maybe even got to know me a little better. Now, you've got to respond by telling me about your fave things! Here's where you can write to me: John Travolta, ABC-TV, 4151 Prospect Ave., Los Angeles, Cal., 90027. I'm waiting to hear from you!

Author Randi Reisfeld took these shots of John in his apartment on Doheny Drive in Beverly Hills. The only clue that a 22-year-old single guy lived there was the bedroom—the floor was piled high with messy clothes. During the photo shoot/interview John was cooperative, if not particularly friendly. He smiled for the camera, but only broke into a real belly laugh once. Reisfeld leaned back on an outdoor table to get a better shot, unaware that the surface was wet. When she got up, a huge water stain covered her butt. John erupted in peals of laughter. Reisfeld checked her humiliation at the door and left with what she'd come for: a great interview, exclusive photos, and a John Travolta story.

237

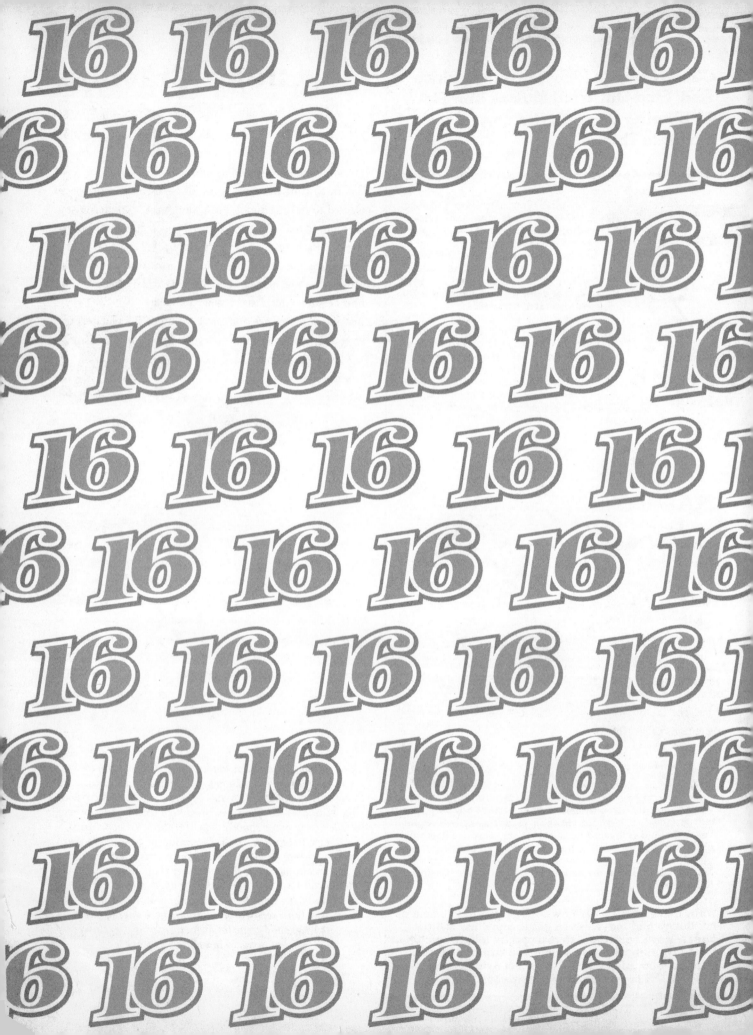

About the Authors

You're Telling Us!

Hi! We're **16**'s editors, Randi Reisfeld and Danny Fields, and we're going to be doing this column from now on. So we hope you'll send your letters and comments to us—we promise to read *each and every one*—and let us know what you like and don't about **16**! We sure welcome any comments you have—and we'll be glad to get your questions answered, too! Thanks for believin' in **16**—we love you! Our address is: Randi & Danny, **16** Magazine, 745 Fifth Avenue, New York, N.Y. 10022.

Only two people could have written this book. Both have been involved with the celebrity scene and *16 Magazine* for over two decades; both are considered experts in their fields and have had much related success in publishing. Perhaps most significantly, Randi Reisfeld and Danny Fields for a time co-edited *16 Magazine*.

RANDI REISFELD, fresh out of the City College of New York, interviewed for the position of secretary to Gloria Stavers. She wasn't really qualified for the job (steno was not her strong suit) and didn't get it—not exactly. But because Gloria's eminently qualified secretary was leaving, and no one else who'd come in for the position met with Gloria's approval, Reisfeld was a last resort. She was offered a temporary position assisting Gloria. Reisfeld's job was supposed to last six weeks: 25 years later, she was still there. No longer a secretary chasing down errant paper clips, however, Reisfeld rose through the **16** ranks, as it were, and became the publication's editorial director. Stavers was her mentor, as was Nola Leone.

In addition to helming **16**, Ms. Reisfeld is also the author of several successful celebrity biographies, including such '80s-into-'90s icons as New Kids on the Block and the stars of *Beverly Hills, 90210*.

Currently, she writes young adult fiction, including several novels based on the movie and TV series *Clueless* and *Moesha*.

Ms. Reisfeld lives in the New York area with her family.

DANNY FIELDS, a native of New York City, drifted into the music business in 1966 after attending Penn, Harvard Law School, and NYU. His first job was at *Datebook* magazine, and he met **16**'s Gloria Stavers in the spring of that year. They became friends soon afterwards.

In his 30 years in the music business, Fields has been editor of *Hullabaloo* magazine; publicist at Elektra and Atlantic Records; a deejay on WFMU, personal manager of Iggy and the Stooges, Lou Reed, the MC5, the Ramones, Steve Forbert and Paleface; columnist for *Spin* magazine and a writer for *Details;* and interviewed by many authors for many books, most notably by Jean Stein for "Edie," where his "voice" is a major part of the book, and by Legs McNeil and Gillian McCain for the oral history of punk rock, *Please Kill Me,* which is dedicated to him. He is the co-author, with Cyrinda Foxe-Tyler, of the recently published *Dream On,* her life story. Fields has been a member of the prestigious Nominating Committee of the Rock and Roll Hall of Fame for the past eight years, for six years was the producer of "Rock Today," a weekly syndicated radio show with a large national audience; and was the weekly New York columnist for *Hits* magazine, a music business trade publication.

Danny worked with Gloria at **16** as her assistant from 1972–1974, and became Co-Editor-in-Chief with Randi Reisfeld when Gloria left **16**.